Subjective Consciousness

Some mental events are conscious, some are unconscious. What is
the difference between the two? Uriah Kriegel offers the following
answer: whatever else they may represent, conscious states always
also represent themselves (where unconscious ones do not, at least
not in the right way). The book develops this 'self-representational'
approach to consciousness along several dimensions—including
phenomenological, ontological, and scientific—and defends it from
common and uncommon criticisms.

Uriah Kriegel is Professor of Philosophy and Cognitive Science and
Associate Director of the Center for Consciousness Studies at the
University of Arizona.

Subjective Consciousness

A Self-Representational Theory

Uriah Kriegel

OXFORD
UNIVERSITY PRESS

OXFORD
UNIVERSITY PRESS

Great Clarendon Street, Oxford OX2 6DP

Oxford University Press is a department of the University of Oxford.
It furthers the University's objective of excellence in research, scholarship,
and education by publishing worldwide in

Oxford New York

Auckland Cape Town Dar es Salaam Hong Kong Karachi
Kuala Lumpur Madrid Melbourne Mexico City Nairobi
New Delhi Shanghai Taipei Toronto

With offices in

Argentina Austria Brazil Chile Czech Republic France Greece
Guatemala Hungary Italy Japan Poland Portugal Singapore
South Korea Switzerland Thailand Turkey Ukraine Vietnam

Oxford is a registered trade mark of Oxford University Press
in the UK and in certain other countries

Published in the United States
by Oxford University Press Inc., New York

British Library Cataloguing in Publication Data

Data available

Library of Congress Cataloging in Publication Data

Subjective consciousness : a self-representational theory / edited by Uriah Kriegel.
    p. cm.
  Includes bibliographical references and index.
  ISBN 978–0–19–957035–5
  1. Consciousness. 2. Mental representation. I. Kriegel, Uriah.
  B808.9.S83 2009
  126—dc22   2009009575

Typeset by Laserwords Private Limited, Chennai, India
Printed in the United Kingdom by
Lightning Source UK Ltd., Milton Keynes

ISBN 978–0–19–957035–5 (Hbk.)
ISBN 978–0–19–969470–9 (Pbk.)

Contents

1

The Self-Representational Theory of Consciousness

1. A Theory of Consciousness at First Pass

This book presents a theory of consciousness. This very first section offers a first pass at the theory, the rest of this opening chapter a second pass, and the remainder of the book the third pass.

When I have a conscious experience of the blue sky, there is something it is like for me to have the experience. In particular, there is a bluish way it is like for me to have it. This "bluish way it is like for me" constitutes the phenomenal character of my experience. Phenomenal character is the property that makes a phenomenally conscious state (i) the phenomenally conscious state it is and (ii) a phenomenally conscious state at all.

The bluish way it is like for me has two distinguishable components: (i) the *bluish* component and (ii) the *for-me* component. I call the former *qualitative character* and the latter *subjective character*. To a first approximation, phenomenal character is just the compresence of qualitative character and subjective character. To a second approximation, there is a more specific division of conceptual labor between qualitative and subjective character: a phenomenally conscious state's qualitative character is what makes it the phenomenally conscious state it is, while its subjective character is what makes it a phenomenally conscious state at all. Thus, my conscious experience of the blue sky is the conscious experience it is in virtue of its bluishness, but it is a conscious experience at all in virtue of its for-me-ness.

A full theory of phenomenal consciousness would include accounts of both qualitative and subjective character. But the account of subjective character is of greater philosophical significance. For subjective character is what makes something a phenomenally conscious state *at all*, and the mystery of consciousness is in the first instance the problem of understanding why there is phenomenal consciousness *at all*.

The theory of consciousness to be presented here revolves around the idea that phenomenally conscious states have qualitative character in virtue of representing environmental features and subjective character in virtue of representing *themselves*. More specifically, the qualitative character of a conscious state consists in its representing certain response-dependent properties of external objects; its subjective character consists in its representing itself in a suitable way. Thus, my experience of the blue sky represents both the sky and itself. It has its qualitative character (bluishness) in virtue of representing the sky's property of being disposed to elicit a certain appropriate response in appropriate respondents; it has its subjective character (for-me-ness) in virtue of representing itself in an appropriate way.

It follows that what makes something a phenomenally conscious state (at all) is suitable self-representation. The reasoning is this: a phenomenally conscious state's subjective character is what makes it a phenomenally conscious state (at all); such a state has subjective character in virtue of suitably representing itself; therefore, it is a phenomenally conscious state (at all) in virtue of suitably representing itself. What accounts for there being phenomenal consciousness at all, then, is the fact that some mental states self-represent in the right way. I call this *the self-representational theory of consciousness*, or *self-representationalism* for short.

2. The Concept of Phenomenal Consciousness

It is often felt that different theories of consciousness have tended to target different phenomena under the heading of "phenomenal consciousness." To some, this suggests that many disputes among theories of consciousness are purely verbal, resting on different senses of the terms in play. On this "pluralist" view of things, genuine progress would require, in the first instance, careful distinguishing and systematic labeling of the plurality of phenomena that go by the name "consciousness."[1]

---

[1] The term pluralism is used by Block (1995) to refer to his own distinction between four different phenomena that are sometimes targeted by the theory of consciousness, and that he calls "phenomenal consciousness," "access consciousness," "monitoring consciousness," and "self-consciousness."

I want to agree that different theories of consciousness have targeted different phenomena, yet insist that the pluralist attitude is somewhat misleading. Thus, it is natural to hold that so-called representationalists about consciousness have effectively offered a theory of something like what I have called qualitative character, while higher-order theorists have targeted something like what I have called subjective character.[2] At the same time, although at one level philosophers may have chased different phenomena, at another there is only one phenomenon that preoccupies them—namely, whatever property generates in them the sense of mystery as they contemplate the nature of consciousness and its place in the world. The term "phenomenal consciousness" has come into wide usage as a tag for that property.

With this in mind, I propose the following terminological regime. The term "consciousness" is, of course, an ordinary, everyday term to be understood intuitively. We can then use this intuitive understanding in fixing the reference of the technical term "*phenomenal* consciousness" with the following rigidified definite description: "the property F, such that, in the actual world, F is responsible for the mystery of consciousness." This description can be precisified in a number of ways. For example, suppose we read "responsible" causally, and construed "mystery" in terms of the sense that the facts of consciousness are not deducible from the physical facts. Then we could offer the following precisification: "phenomenal consciousness is the property F, such that, in the actual world, F causally produces (in the suitably reflective subject, say) the sense that the facts of

---

[2] Representational theories hold that a conscious state's phenomenal character is constituted by (an aspect of) its representational content. For representational theories, see mainly Dretske 1995 and Tye 1992, 1995, 2000, and 2002. A more complex version is developed in Shoemaker 1994a, 1994c, and 2002. All modern versions are inspired to some extent by the so-called transparency of experience: the only introspectively accessible properties of conscious experiences are their representational properties (see Harman 1990). Higher-order theories hold that a conscious state's phenomenal character is constituted by its figuring in the representational content of a numerically distinct higher-order state. The most worked-out version of higher-order theory is no doubt David Rosenthal's (1986, 1990, 1993, 2002a, 2005). For other versions, see mainly Armstrong 1968, Lycan 1996 and 2004, Carruthers 1998 and 2000, and Van Gulick 2001, 2004, and 2006. Most or all of these views are inspired by the so-called transitivity principle: conscious states are states we are conscious (or aware) of (see Rosenthal 1986). Interestingly, the work of some fierce critics of representational and higher-order theories betrays a commendation (implicit or explicit) of these theories for at least targeting the right phenomenon. This can be seen, for instance, in Block's criticism (1990a, 1996) of representational theories and Levine's criticism (2001) of higher-order theories. In the present terminology, Block seems to hold that the phenomenon that needs to be targeted is qualitative character, whereas Levine believes it is subjective character.

consciousness cannot be deduced from physical facts." Other precisifications will attend different understandings of some of the elements in the rigidified definite description we have started with. But all will construe *phenomenal* consciousness as whatever property is the source of the mystery surrounding consciousness.

My contention is that this is the most accurate and most profitable way to fix our ideas with respect to the notion of *phenomenal* consciousness. It is the most accurate, because it captures the reason the notion has come into wide usage in philosophical circles, and it is the most profitable, because it allows us to extract the substantive core in many debates on consciousness that seem to be an unclear mix of the substantive and the verbal.

For example, when representationalists about consciousness debate higher-order theorists, there is a feeling that at one level they are concerned with different properties but also that at another level there is a genuine disagreement between them. This feeling is vindicated and explicated by the characterization of phenomenal consciousness proposed here. Although representationalists and higher-order theorists may offer accounts of different properties, in that the former target qualitative character and the latter subjective character, there is also a substantive disagreement between them — namely, over which of these properties is responsible for the mystery of consciousness. Representationalists seem wedded to the idea that qualitative character is the property that, in the actual world, is the source of mystery. Higher-order theorists hold that subjective character is that property.

The notion of phenomenal consciousness is sometimes introduced by reference to the "what-it-is-like" locution. While there is something about that locution that resonates, it is probably unlikely to be of much help to the uninitiated, and does not illuminate the function served by the term "*phenomenal* consciousness" in the relevant discourse. Most importantly, it is of no help in extracting the substantive core of partially confused disputes, since typically disputants disagree on what kinds of state have something it is like to be in. Thus, higher-order theorists typically maintain that there is nothing it is like to be in a mental state with a qualitative character but no subjective character, whereas representationalists hold that there is. Intuitions regarding the appropriate applicability of what-it-is-like talk seem to lie downstream of philosophical theorizing at this level of nuance. My contention is that the notion of phenomenal consciousness is best introduced in terms of the aforementioned rigidified definite description, or more generally in terms of whatever property is responsible for the sense of mystery that surrounds consciousness.

Note well: the term "mystery" in the definite description should be taken to denote *prima facie* mystery rather than *ultima facie* mystery. In speaking of the mystery of consciousness, I do not mean to imply that consciousness is an *ultimate* mystery—that is, one that will not succumb to eventual demystification.[3] I *do* mean to suggest, however, that it is a *genuine* mystery—that is, that our sense of mystery upon contemplating the nature of consciousness is rational and appropriate and is not based on sheer confusion.

The existence of this genuine *prima facie* mystery can be appreciated by dualists and physicalists alike. David Chalmers, a dualist, uses what he calls the "hard problem" of consciousness, in contrast with the "easy problems" (Chalmers 1995a, 1995b, and 1996), to bring it out. Joseph Levine, a physicalist, uses the label "explanatory gap" to denote an associated problem (Levine 1983). I will discuss the nature of the mystery, and the relationship between these labels for it, in Chapter 8. For now, I only wish to stress that, regardless of wider motivation, many philosophers have a sense that consciousness involves a certain mystery not found in other aspects of nature, and use the term "phenomenal consciousness" to refer to whatever produces this mystery.

The kernel of truth in the pluralist attitude is that, in the theory of consciousness more than elsewhere, different explanatory edifices are often matched with different conceptions of the phenomenon in need of explanation. But it does not follow, and is a mistake to suppose, that all conceptions of the phenomenon in need of explanation are equally good. On the contrary, some misidentify the source of the mystery of consciousness, while others identify it correctly. Thus the theory of consciousness is essentially a package deal comprising an account of the explanans alongside an account of the explanandum.[4] Both accounts are supposed to *get things right*. The account of the explanandum is supposed to get things right by identifying correctly the source of the *prima facie* mystery surrounding consciousness; the account of the explanans is supposed to

---

[3] The view that it *is* an ultimate mystery *has* been defended, most notably by Colin McGinn (1989a, 1995, 1999, 2004).

[4] To be sure, the explanandum of all theories of consciousness is, by definition, phenomenal character, the property that makes a conscious experience (i) the conscious experience it is and (ii) a conscious experience at all. But already at the next level of description, accounts differ on the nature of this property.

get right what ultimately demystifies that source. On this view of things, unlike on the pluralist approach, homing in on the explanandum is not just a matter of judicious stipulation, but involves substantive claims. Correlatively, debates over the nature of consciousness are rarely if ever purely verbal. When we are tempted to claim they are, it is because we forget that non-verbal disputes in the theory of consciousness can concern not only the nature of the explanans but also the nature of the explanandum—that is, can concern which property is responsible for the mystery of consciousness.

If we adopt the characterization of phenomenal consciousness in terms of the aforementioned rigidified definite description, it will probably fall out that there is only one property denoted by "phenomenal consciousness." This is to be distinguished from (*a*) the view that there is *more* than one such property and (*b*) the view that there is *less* than one (that is, no) such property.

For there to be *less* than one property denoted by "phenomenal consciousness," there would have to be no single property systematically responsible for our sense of mystery. The sense of mystery would have to be elicited on different occasions by unrelated properties or be altogether grounded in a web of confusions. While this is a coherent position, it is not antecedently plausible: a very compelling argument would have to be adduced if we are to take it seriously. And in one sense, even that scenario would not show that there is less than one property denoted by "phenomenal consciousness," only that the one property is *disjunctive*.

For there to be *more* than one property denoted by "phenomenal consciousness," there would have to be multiple properties, each of which is independently responsible for the sense of mystery that descends upon us when we contemplate the way consciousness fits into the natural world. This, again, is antecedently implausible. It is perhaps plausible that multiple properties *conspire* to generate this sense of mystery. But this would not mean that "phenomenal consciousness" has several denotata, only that it has a *conjunctive* denotatum. If, for instance, qualitative character and subjective character have to conspire to mystify us, then the denotatum of "phenomenal consciousness" is the conjunctive property of being both qualitative and subjective. What is required for "phenomenal consciousness" to have several denotata (for example, to be ambiguous as between qualitative character and subjective character) is that several distinct properties suffice individually to generate the mystery in an overdetermining fashion (for example, that qualitative and subjective character mystify us severally and independently).[5] This is not altogether impossible, but nor is it *prima facie* plausible. And it is only under those conditions that the pluralist attitude portrayed at the opening would be well founded.

The main point is that statements about what needs to be explained in the theory of consciousness are better thought of as substantive claims about what generates the mystery of consciousness than as bare stipulations. Taking them to be stipulations only fudges over the source of the philosophic anxiety surrounding consciousness. There could be endless accounts of different stipulated notions of consciousness, but the only ones that would speak to that philosophic anxiety would be those that target whatever it is that generates the mystery of consciousness in the first place.

3. The Structure of Phenomenal Character

Turning, then, to the nature of the explanandum, consider my conscious experience as I look out of my window at the blue sky. My experience has many properties. The great majority are completely uninteresting: it is happening on a Tuesday, it is occurring 648 years after the death of the tallest man of the fourteenth century, and so on. My experience *has* those properties, but we are uninterested in them, partly because we already understand them perfectly well.

Some of my experience's properties are more interesting. Thus, the experience has a strong impact on working memory; it implicates neural activation in V4; it carries information about the sky.[6] These broadly psychological properties are more interesting, partly because our understanding of them is presently imperfect. At the same time, we have a good sense of how a comprehensive explanation of these properties would—will—go. We do not stand mystified by them.

---

[5] Even under these conditions, it could be argued that phenomenal consciousness ought to be identified with a single property—namely, the *disjunctive* property such that each of its disjuncts is one of those overdetermining sources of mystery. Arguably, this view is mandated by the use of the definite article in the rigidified description.

[6] Of course, some philosophers may deny any of these claims, but it is premature at this point to address particular philosophical doctrines of the sort that would have to be involved. I list these as reasonable properties we can expect, at least in a pre-philosophical mood, conscious states to have.

Getting closer to something that may genuinely mystify us, there is the fact that there is something it is like for me to have my experience.[7] In particular, there is a bluish way it is like for me to have it. As I said at the opening, we can distinguish two *aspects*, or *components*, of this "bluish way it is like for me." There is, on the one hand, the *bluish* component, which I call the experience's qualitative character, and, on the other hand, the *for-me* component, which I call the experience's subjective character.[8]

When a colorblind person looks at the same sky under the same conditions, there is a psychologically real difference between her experience and mine. The psychologically real dimension along which our experiences differ is what I call qualitative character. We need not commit at this stage to any particular view of qualitative character. Without pretending that this provides an analysis, let us say only the following: qualitative properties "correspond" to sensible features in the environment.[9] There is a potential qualitative property of a given creature's conscious experience for every property in the creature's environment that is sensible by that creature. An experience's qualitative character at a time may be thought of as the set, or sum, of all qualitative properties the experience instantiates at that time.

As for subjective character, to say that my experience has subjective character is to point to a certain *awareness* I have of my experience. Conscious experiences are not states that we may *host*, as it were, unawares. Freudian suppressed states, sub-personal states, and a variety of other unconscious states may occur within us completely unbeknownst to us, but the intuition is that conscious experiences are different. A mental state of which one is completely unaware is not a conscious experience. In this sense, my conscious experience is not only *in me*, it is also *for me*.[10]

---

[7] The locution, in its present usage, is due to Farrell (1950), but was brought into wide usage through Nagel (1974). As I said in the previous section, the expression may not be of much use in introducing the notion of phenomenal consciousness to the uninitiated. But I am here addressing myself to the initiated, and anyway am not (yet) claiming that what-it-is-like-for-me is the same as phenomenal consciousness.

[8] There is a question as to whether the qualitative and the subjective are really separable. Even if they are not separable in reality, however, they are certainly separable "in thought." That is, there is a *conceptual* distinction to draw here even if no *property* distinction corresponds. I will say more on this in Chapter 2.

[9] We may construe the environment here to include the subject's body.

[10] There is much more to be said about the nature of subjective character, or for that matter qualitative character. And more *will* be said in Chapter 2. On the other hand, I find that anything one says in this area is contestable, and to that extent amounts to a substantive claim. For this reason, I do

One reason it is useful to draw the distinction between qualitative and subjective character is that, as already noted, philosophical theories of consciousness have tended to fall into two groups, one targeting qualitative character, the other targeting subjective character.[11]

There are several possible views about the interrelations among phenomenal, qualitative, and subjective character. This matter will be discussed in greater detail in Chapter 2. For now, we can just say that four central positions stand out. One view is that phenomenal character is identical with qualitative character; this seems to be the view, for example, of typical representationalists. Another view is that it is identical with subjective character; this seems to be the view, for example, of higher-order theorists. Yet another view is that phenomenal character is identical with something like the compresence, or conjunction, of qualitative and subjective character. Finally, there is the view that phenomenal consciousness bears no constitutive relations to either qualitative or subjective character.

There are two views I am attracted to. The first is less plausible but very clear—that phenomenal character is identical to subjective character (that is, that subjective character is the source of the mystery of consciousness). The second is more plausible but also more complicated—that phenomenal character is some kind of complex property involving both subjective and qualitative character. It is hard to argue about such matters, though I will discuss them in more detail in Chapter 2 and the Appendix. For now, and merely by way of gesturing at the sensibility behind the views I am attracted to, consider the following.

Regarding the first view, arguably, the (genuine) puzzlement over the fact that a bunch of neurons vibrating inside the skull is associated with a yellowish qualitative character is no different from that surrounding the fact that a bunch of atoms lurching in the void is associated with a yellow color. It is no more surprising that neurons can underlie yellowishness than that atoms can underlie yellowness.[12] And yet the latter is not deeply

not wish to expand on the nature of subjective and qualitative character in the context of introducing them. I say just enough to get the reader a sense of what I am talking about.

[11] Thus, representational theories seem to target qualitative character, while higher-order theories seem to target subjective character. As I argued in the previous section, this chasm should be thought of not as a mere verbal dispute, but as a substantive dispute about the source of the mystery of consciousness.

[12] This observation is due to Shoemaker (1994a). It should be noted, however, that some philosophers have made this observation in the service of the converse claim: that the explanatory gap between

mystifying. By contrast, the mystery surrounding the fact that a bunch of neurons vibrating inside the skull is associated with a for-me-ness has no parallel in the non-mental realm. It is surprising that neurons can underlie for-me-ness, and there is no analogous surprise regarding what atoms can underlie. This phenomenon is thus more suitable to capture the distinctive mystery presented by consciousness.[13]

As for the second view, I am attracted to it by considering that, when we say that a mental state is phenomenally conscious, there must be (*a*) something that makes it the phenomenally conscious state *it is* and (*b*) something that makes it a phenomenally conscious state *at all*. For the reason adduced in the previous paragraph and other reasons, I hold that subjective character is what makes a mental state phenomenally conscious *at all*. But this leaves somewhat unclear what makes it the phenomenally conscious state *it is*, once it is phenomenally conscious at all. One natural thought is that it is the state's qualitative character that makes it the phenomenally conscious state it is. The upshot is the view that qualitative character provides the identity conditions of phenomenality while subjective character provides its existence conditions: what makes a mental state phenomenally conscious at all (rather than a non-phenomenal state) is its subjective character; what makes it the phenomenally conscious state it is (rather than another) is its qualitative character.

According to this Division of Conceptual Labor thesis, my experience's qualitative character (its bluishness) determines *what* phenomenally con- scious state it is, whereas its subjective character (its for-me-ness) determines *that* it is a phenomenally conscious state. Thus, for a mental state to *become* phenomenally conscious, it must acquire a subjective character; once it *has*, so to speak, become phenomenally conscious, it is its qualitative character that makes it the specific type of phenomenally conscious state it is.[14]

---

consciousness and neural matter is nothing but the explanatory gap between the manifest image of external objects and their scientific image (Byrne 2006).

[13] This consideration is quick and dirty and I do not intend to lean on it heavily at this stage. It is merely a characterization of my tendencies in this area. A more systematic approach to the issues that arise here will come to the fore at the end of Chapter 2.

[14] I am using here the language of process purely metaphorically. There is no real process in which a mental state first becomes a conscious experience at all and later—after a time lag—becomes a particular type of conscious experience. Obviously, the two occur simultaneously. In fact, under most reasonable understandings of "occur," they are the one and the same occurrence.

One odd feature of this position, as stated, is the complete divorce of identity and existence conditions. Typically, what makes something the F it is and what makes it an F at all are not completely unrelated, but are rather related as determinate to determinable. What makes something a car at all is that it is an automobile machine (plus bells and whistles), whereas what makes it the car it is is its being an automobile machine *of a certain make*. Being an automobile machine of a certain make is a determinate of being an automobile machine. Likewise, if the bluish qualitative character of my experience is what makes it the phenomenally conscious state it is, then we should expect that what makes it a phenomenally conscious state at all is that it is has *some* qualitative character. Here subjective character falls out of the picture altogether—implausibly.

The solution is to think of the key feature of my conscious experience as *bluish-for-me-ness* (rather than as a feature factorizable into two components, bluishness and for-me-ness). In a way, this is to hold that subjective character and qualitative character are not separate properties, but in some (admittedly problematic) sense are aspects of a single property.[15] Attractively, bluish-for-me-ness is a determinate of for-me-ness (or "something-for-me-ness," if you will). This generates the desired result that the existence and identity conditions of phenomenality are related as determinable to determinate.

This is the position I favor on the structure of phenomenal consciousness, and I will develop it more in Chapter 2. It casts phenomenal character as a matter of a complex compresence of qualitative character and subjective character, which are not entirely separable. Accordingly, a theory of phenomenal consciousness must address each. Chapter 3 develops an account of qualitative character and Chapter 4 one of subjective character. The following chapters focus on aspects of subjective character. The reason is that, in the picture we ended up with, there is still a more central place for subjective character, since it constitutes the existence condition of phenomenality. This is important because, although the deep mystery of consciousness does have to do with why and how conscious episodes differ from each other, it is much more concerned with why and how there are conscious episodes *to begin with*—that is, why there exists such a thing as consciousness *at all*.[16]

---

[15] After all, even though my experience of the sky is *for me*, not every aspect of it is for me in the relevant sense. Plausibly, the only aspect of it that is for me in the relevant sense is its bluishness.

[16] The mystifying fact is primarily that there are some events in this world that seem categorically different from the brute, blind, inanimate proceedings of the unconscious realm. Thus the mystery

4. A Narrow Representational Account of Qualitative Character

The purpose of a reductive theory of phenomenal consciousness is to account for phenomenal character in non-phenomenal terms. If the non-phenomenal terms employed in the account are purely physical, the result is a *physicalist* theory of consciousness. But it is not definitional of a reductive theory that it is physicalist. What is definitional is that it accounts for the phenomenal in non-phenomenal terms.

The primary goal of this book is to provide a reductive and hopefully physicalist account of phenomenal character. A reductive account of phenomenal character would comprise two parts: a reductive account of what makes a phenomenally conscious state the phenomenally conscious state it is, and an account of what makes a phenomenally conscious state a phenomenally conscious state at all. Given the Division of Conceptual Labor thesis from the previous section, the first part would be constituted by a reductive account of qualitative character, the second by a reductive account of subjective character.

In Chapter 3 I defend a representationalist account of qualitative character: a conscious experience's qualitative character is constituted by (an aspect of) its representational content. On such a view, whatever else my experience of the blue sky represents, it also represents features of the sky. Naturally, the sky has many different features, and accordingly my experience instantiates many different representational properties in relation to it. On the account I will defend, only a very specific subset of these representational properties is constitutive of its qualitative character. In particular, only the representation of certain response-dependent properties of the sky can be constitutive of my experience's qualitative character.

How are we to understand the relevant response-dependent properties? Answering this question is one way of fleshing out one's specific version of *response-dependent representationalism* (as I will call the view).

concerns in the first instance what makes something a conscious state *in the first place* and only derivatively what makes it the conscious state it is *given that it is one*. This suggests that subjective character ought to be the central target of the theory of consciousness, in that the demystification of consciousness would require most centrally the demystification of subjective character.

Much of Chapter 3 will be dedicated to homing in on the relevant response-dependent properties. In any event, one result of this kind of response-dependent representationalism is that it casts the representational content constitutive of qualitative character as *narrow content*.[17] Conscious experiences may well have wide representational properties, but those are not constitutive of their qualitative character.

My main concern in the book, however, will be the reductive account of subjective character. There are two kinds of reason for this focus. The insubstantial reasons are (*a*) that the literature strikes me as much more advanced when it comes to qualitative character than to subjective character, (*b*) that a representationalist view very similar to the one I will defend has already been defended in the literature (for example, in Shoemaker 1994a), and (*c*) that the newer ideas I have to offer pertain mostly to subjective character. The substantial reasons have to do with the fact that subjective character is, on the view presented here, what makes a phenomenally conscious state such a state at all, and that this is the deeper nexus of the philosophical mystery surrounding consciousness. That is, the existence (as opposed to identity) condition of phenomenality is the more pressing aspect of consciousness to account for, and subjective character is what needs to be understood in order to do so.

5. A Self-Representational Account of Subjective Character

The central thesis of the book is that what makes something a phenomenally conscious state at all, what constitutes its subjective character, is a certain kind of *self-representation*: a mental state has phenomenal character at all when, and only when, it represents itself in the right way. All and only phenomenally conscious states are suitably self-representing. Thus, whatever else a conscious state represents, it always also represents itself,

---

[17] I am appealing here to the distinction, originally drawn by Putnam (1975), between *narrow* and *wide* content. Narrow content is content that is fully determined by the non-relational properties of the subject of the state whose content it is. Wide content is content that is *not* so determined. At least this is one way to draw the distinction. Narrow representationalism about qualitative character, then, is the view that the qualitative character of a conscious experience is constituted by aspects of the experience's content that are fully determined by the non-relational properties of the subject. I first defended a version of this view (under the name "internalist representationalism") in Kriegel 2002a.

and it is in virtue of representing itself that it *is* a conscious state. This is self-representationalism.

Although out of the limelight in modern discussions of consciousness, self-representationalism has quite a venerable history behind it. One of its early clear and explicit endorsements is by Franz Brentano, who, in his *Psychology from an Empirical Standpoint*, wrote this (1874: 153–4):

> [Every conscious act] includes within it a consciousness of itself. Therefore, every [conscious] act, no matter how simple, has a double object, a primary and a secondary object. The simplest act, for example the act of hearing, has as its primary object the sound, and for its secondary object, itself, the mental phenomenon in which the sound is heard.[18]

Thus, the auditory conscious experience of a bagpipe sound is intentionally directed both at the bagpipe and at itself. Against the background of a representational conception of intentionality, this would commit one to the thesis that all conscious states are self-representing.[19] Brentano may have adopted this view from Aristotle. Although Aristotle is not nearly as explicit as Brentano, he does write in the *Metaphysics* that conscious "knowing, perceiving, believing, and thinking are always of something else, but of themselves on the side."[20]

But what does it mean for a mental state to represent itself? Answering this question is one way of fleshing out self-representationalism. Different answers will result in different versions of the view. I will offer my own take in Chapters 4 and 6. In any event, pending a compelling argument to

---

[18] I am quoting from the 1973 English translation. The view is first introduced by Brentano in Section 7 of chapter II ("Inner Consciousness") in Book 2, which is entitled "A Presentation and the Presentation of that Presentation are Given in One and the Same Act." In this section, Brentano canvasses his conception of conscious experiences as self-representational.

[19] One could consider a representational conception of intentionality either as a tautological thesis or as a substantive but true thesis, depending on one's understanding of these terms. I have seen both in the literature. In recent philosophy of mind it is more common to treat such a conception as a tautology, but there are exceptions (e.g., Cummins 1989).

[20] 201074^{b}35–6. I am using here Caston's translation (2002). At least one scholar has suggested to me that "on the side" is not the best translation, and "as a byproduct" would be more appropriate. It is not clear that this makes a substantial difference for our present purposes. There are also passages in *De Anima* that can be read as endorsing self-representationalism. For a sustained self-representationalist interpretation of Aristotle, see Caston 2002. Caston notes that an interpretation of Aristotle along these lines is also to be found in a dissertation on the unity of mental life in Aristotelian philosophy, written under Brentano's supervision by one J. Herman Schell.

the contrary, there is no reason to suspect that there is something deeply unintelligible about the notion of a self-representing state.

Familiar forms of self-representation occur in linguistic expressions.[21] The token sentence "This very sentence is written in Garamond" is self-representing. As it happens, it is a true sentence, and it itself is a constituent of its truthmaker.[22] On the plausible suppositions that, in order to be true, a sentence must make semantic contact with its truthmaker, and that semantic contact is achieved through, perhaps even constituted by, representation of the truthmaker's constituents, this true sentence must represent its truthmaker's constituents, which include it itself.[23, 24] I am not citing this form of sentential self-reference as an accurate model of conscious-making self-representation. I am adducing it merely by way of addressing a potential worry to the effect that the very notion of self-representation is somehow deeply unintelligible.

It is useful to see self-representationalism as the upshot of two claims. The first is that all phenomenally conscious states are conscious in virtue of being *represented* (in the right way). The second is that no phenomenally conscious state is conscious in virtue of being represented by a *numerically distinct* state—that is, a state other than itself. It follows from these two claims that all phenomenally conscious states are phenomenally conscious in virtue of being represented (in the right way) by a mental state that is not numerically distinct from themselves—that is, in virtue of self-representing (in the right way).

More formally, we might state the master argument as follows. For any phenomenally conscious state C,

1. C is conscious in virtue of being suitably represented;
2. it is not the case that C is conscious in virtue of being represented by a numerically distinct state; therefore,

---

[21] There are also more rigorous mathematical models of self-representation, especially in nonwell-founded set theory (see Williford 2006 and Landini MS).

[22] If one prefers to think of truthmakers as states of affairs, one could say that this sentence's truthmaker is the state of affairs consisting in its instantiation of the property of being written in Times New Roman.

[23] Somewhat unmelodiously, I am using the phrase "it itself" as an indirect reflexive. I will say much more about the semantic peculiarities of indirect reflexives in Chapter 4. For seminal work on this, see Castañeda 1966 and 1969.

[24] Let me emphasize that.

3. C is conscious in virtue of being suitably represented by itself; that is,

4. C is conscious in virtue of suitably representing itself.[25]

The argument is   clearly valid, so the two premises do entail self-representationalism. The question is whether they are true. In the next two sections, I sketch the main motivation for each.

6. Phenomenal Consciousness and Inner Awareness

The first premise in the master argument for self-representationalism is the claim that a conscious state is conscious in virtue of being suitably represented. Impressionistically put, the general motivation for this premise is the thought that it is somehow essential to a conscious state that its subject be aware of it. Conscious states are not states that just happen to take place *in* us, whether or not we are aware of their taking place; they are also *for* us, precisely in the sense that there is something it is like *for* us to have those states. Mental states that merely occur *in* us, but of which we are completely unaware, are not conscious experiences.[26]

Let us call awareness of external features and objects in one's environment or body *outer awareness*, and awareness of internal events and states in one's own mental life *inner awareness*. The thought under consideration is that inner awareness is somehow essential to phenomenal consciousness. For starters, a mental state is phenomenally conscious only if its subject has inner awareness of it. But, more strongly, the *right kind* of inner awareness is not only a necessary condition but also a sufficient condition for phenomenality. It is this inner awareness that ultimately makes the mental

---

[25] Here and in what follows, I am leaving the quantifier outside the indented presentation of the argument for stylistic reasons, but it should be clear that the presentation in the text is equivalent to the following:

1. for any conscious state C, C is conscious in virtue of being suitably represented;
2. for any conscious state C, it is not the case that C is conscious in virtue of being represented by a numerically distinct state; therefore,
3. for any conscious state C, C is conscious in virtue of being suitably represented by itself; that is,
4. for any conscious state C, C is conscious in virtue of suitably representing itself.

[26] There are a number of issues and potential objections that arise quite immediately for this line of thought. But I am offering it here not as an official argument but as a gesture toward the kind of thought that motivates the idea that conscious states are necessarily represented. The "official" argumentation will be offered in Chapter 4.

state phenomenally conscious at all. For it is when the subject has this inner awareness of it that the state acquires subjective character, and subjective character is what makes a state phenomenally conscious at all.

It may be thought doubtful that one is always aware of one's concurrent conscious experiences. As I have my conscious experience of the blue sky, I am not attending to myself and my experience in the least. The focus of my awareness is on the blue sky, not my experience of it. However, it does not follow from the fact that my experience is not in the focus of my awareness that it is not in my awareness at all. While the focus of our awareness is most manifest to us, there are a host of objects and features that routinely lie in the *periphery* of awareness. Thus, as I stare at the laptop before me, the laptop occupies the focus of my visual awareness. But at the periphery of my visual awareness are a number of objects lying on the far edge of my desk: a pen, a coffee mug, a copy of the *Tractatus*.[27] As I will argue in Chapter 5, the focus/periphery distinction applies not only to visual awareness, but to all awareness, including inner awareness. My claim is that in the case of my experience of the sky, although I am not focally aware of the experience itself, but rather of the sky, I am nonetheless peripherally aware of the experience itself. That is, the experience combines focal outer awareness of the sky with peripheral inner awareness of itself.

Plausibly, being aware of something is just representing it in the right way. For a subject to be aware of a rainbow *just is* for her to harbor the right sort of mental representation of the rainbow. This representational treatment of awareness extends to inner awareness as well. Thus to be aware of, say, a growing anxiety *just is* to harbor a mental representation of one's anxiety. From the representational treatment of awareness and the thesis that inner awareness is essential to phenomenal consciousness, it follows that conscious states are essentially states of which their subject has a mental representation.

In summary, the motivation behind the claim that conscious states are conscious in virtue of being represented in the right way derives from the

---

[27] These objects are presented rather vaguely and inaccurately in my experience, but they are presented nonetheless. Thus, I would never be able to make out, on the basis of my experience alone, that the book is the *Tractatus*. But it would be obviously erroneous to infer that I am therefore altogether unaware of the book. Rather, we should say that I am aware of it, not *focally*, however, but *peripherally*. These issues will be discussed more fully in Chapter 5.

thought that conscious states are states we are aware of, albeit peripherally, and that such awareness is a form of representation. We may thus present the following sub-argument for the first premise of the master argument. For any conscious state C of a subject S,

1. C is conscious in virtue of S's being suitably aware of C;
2. for S to be suitably aware of C is for C to be suitably represented by S; therefore,
3. C is conscious in virtue of being suitably represented by S; therefore,
4. C is conscious in virtue of being suitably represented.

The next phase of the master argument is the move from being represented to being self-represented.

7. Inner Awareness and Self-Representation

When a conscious state is represented, either it is represented by itself, or it is represented by a state other than itself, a numerically distinct state. To the extent that conscious states are conscious precisely in virtue of being represented in the right way, there are three possibilities: (a) all conscious states are conscious in virtue of being represented by themselves; (b) all conscious states are conscious in virtue of being represented by numerically distinct states; (c) some conscious states are conscious in virtue of being represented by themselves and some in virtue of being represented by numerically distinct states. Self-representationalism holds that (a) is true. The argument will be pursued in Chapter 4. Here let me offer only a preliminary sketch of a central part of that chapter's argumentative strategy.

One way to argue for (a) above is by elimination—that is, by arguing against (b) and (c). It is rather implausible, on the face of it, that some conscious states are conscious in virtue of being represented one way while others are conscious in virtue of being represented another way. One would expect a certain underlying unity, at a reasonable degree of abstraction, among conscious states. Indeed, if conscious states form a natural kind, as they probably do, they should boast a relatively concrete "underlying nature" common to all of them. These considerations militate against (c).

The argument against (b) proceeds by destructive dilemma. When a mental state is represented by a numerically distinct state, the numerically distinct state must be either *conscious* or *unconscious*. Let us consider the following dilemma: are all conscious states conscious in virtue of being represented by numerically distinct conscious state, or not? If they are not, then (*b*1) some or all conscious states are conscious in virtue of being represented by numerically distinct *unconscious* states. (This is effectively the view of higher-order theories.[28]) If they are, then (*b*2) all conscious states are conscious in virtue of being represented by numerically distinct conscious states. The argument against (*b*) consists in showing that neither (*b*1) nor (*b*2) is plausible.

The case against (*b*2) is straightforward: (*b*2) leads to infinite regress. If every conscious state was necessarily represented by a numerically distinct conscious state, then the occurrence of a single conscious state would implicate an infinity of mental states. But this is doubly implausible: it fails to offer an explanatory account of what makes a conscious state conscious, and it is empirically implausible (perhaps impossible).[29]

As for (*b*1), the main argument against it is somewhat more delicate, and will be only outlined here.[30] In the previous section I said that conscious states are states we are aware of. But how do we know that we are aware of our conscious states? That is, on what basis do we come to subscribe to the thesis that conscious states are states we are aware of? It seems incorrect to say that we subscribe to the thesis purely on the strength of third-person evidence. It is not as though we have consulted experimental data that pointed to the existence of such awareness. Rather, we subscribe on the strength of some kind of first-hand, first-person knowledge of our awareness of our conscious states. However, we would not have such knowledge of awareness if the awareness were grounded in unconscious representations. For our knowledge of unconscious states is always third-person knowledge. So, if our awareness of our conscious states was grounded in unconscious

---

[28] More specifically, contemporary higher-order theories hold that *most* conscious states are conscious in virtue of being suitably represented by unconscious states, but *some* are conscious in virtue of being suitably represented by conscious states. The latter are conscious states that are being explicitly introspected. The former are all other conscious states, and obviously constitute the great majority of conscious states.

[29] As Leibniz says, if this were the case, we would never get past the first thought. He writes: "It is impossible that we should always reflect explicitly on all our thoughts; [otherwise] the mind would reflect on each reflection *ad infinitum* . . . It must be that . . . eventually some thought is allowed to occur without being thought about; otherwise I would dwell forever on the same thing" (quoted in Gennaro 1999: 355–6).

[30] I will develop it more fully in Chapter 4 below. I first floated this argument in Kriegel 2003a.

states, our knowledge of it would be the sort of third-person knowledge it does not in fact seem to be.

To repeat, this is only a sketch of a line of argument against (*b1*) that will be fleshed out and defended in much greater detail in Chapter 4. Note, however, that, since (*b1*) is in fact the view of higher-order theories, many of the arguments in the literature against higher-order theories apply. Those too will be rehearsed and/or developed in Chapter 4. Perhaps the best known of those arguments is the argument from "targetless" higher-order representations. According to (*b1*), what makes a conscious state conscious is that it is targeted by a numerically distinct, hence higher-order, representation. But what happens when a subject has a higher-order representation that misrepresents not only the *properties*, but also the very *existence*, of a lower-order target? Higher-order theory seems committed to saying that the subject is having no conscious experience, even though what she is going through is subjectively indistinguishable from the having of a conscious experience. This means, quite absurdly, that there is no conscious state the subject is in, but there is something it is like for her to be in the conscious state she is not in.[31]

If the above considerations are correct, then neither (*b2*) nor (*b1*) can be made to work, which, given the non-viability of (*c*), entails that (*a*) is the only viable position: all conscious states are conscious in virtue of being represented by themselves. To recapitulate, the presented argument for this turns on two basic ideas. First, it is implausible that a conscious state is conscious in virtue of being represented by an *unconscious state*. But if it is conscious in virtue of being represented by a conscious state, the representing conscious state cannot be numerically distinct from the represented conscious state, on pain of vicious regress or disunity. It follows that the representing and represented conscious states are one and the same—that is, that conscious states are self-representing. We may thus present the following sub-argument for the second premise of the master argument. For any conscious state C,

1. it is not the case that C is conscious in virtue of being unconsciously represented; and,
2. it is not the case that C is conscious in virtue of being consciously represented by a numerically distinct state; therefore,

---

[31] Again, I will elaborate on this, and other problems for higher-order theories, in Chapter 4.

3. it is not the case that C is conscious in virtue of being represented by a numerically distinct state.

If we connect the argument of this section with the argument of the previous section, we obtain the following partial fleshing-out of the master argument. For any conscious state C of a subject S,

1. C is conscious in virtue of S's being suitably aware of C;
2. for S to be suitably aware of C is for C to be suitably represented by S; therefore,
3. C is conscious in virtue of being suitably represented by S; therefore,
4. C is conscious in virtue of being suitably represented;
5. it is not the case that C is conscious in virtue of being unconsciously represented; and,
6. it is not the case that C is conscious in virtue of being consciously represented by a numerically distinct state; therefore,
7. it is not the case that C is conscious in virtue of being represented by a numerically distinct state; therefore,
8. C is conscious in virtue of being suitably represented by itself; that is,
9. C is conscious in virtue of suitably representing itself.

The master argument can be further fleshed out, of course. The present formulation is intended mainly to give a sense of the basic pull of the self-representational approach to phenomenal consciousness.

8. Plan of the Book

The combination of response-dependent representationalism about qualitative character and self-representationalism about subjective character delivers a fully representational account of phenomenal character. It is an unusual representational account in many ways, but nonetheless it is true, on this account, that what makes a conscious experience the conscious experience it is, and a conscious experience at all, is the nature of its representational content. The experience's non-representational properties play no constitutive role (though they may play a causal role) in making it a conscious experience.

The book divides broadly into two parts. The first consists of Chapters 2–4, which develop and defend the account of phenomenal character sketched here. Chapter 2 develops and defends my conception of the explanandum of the theory of consciousness, Chapter 3 my specific version of a representational account of qualitative character, and Chapter 4 the self-representational account of subjective character. The second part of the book consists of Chapters 5–8, which zoom in on central aspects of subjective character—and develop the self-representational approach to them. Chapter 5 discusses the phenomenological nature of consciousness, Chapter 6 offers an ontological assay of consciousness, Chapter 7 hypothesizes on the scientific nature of consciousness, and Chapter 8 considers the prospects for a physicalist reduction of consciousness.

The express goal of the book as a whole is to make the case for the self-representational theory of consciousness. But in the end, what I can reasonably hope is to convince the reader that the theory should be taken seriously, at least on a par with extant philosophical theories of consciousness. The idea that phenomenal consciousness is injected into the world when subjects' internal states acquire the capacity to represent themselves has more initial appeal to it, it seems to me, than what we have become accustomed to in contemporary discussions of consciousness. The burden of this book is to show that this initial appeal does not dissipate, but on the contrary deepens, upon closer examination. In other words, the goal is to show that the self-representational theory of consciousness is not only antecedently attractive, but can be fleshed out in a theoretically compelling way—no less compelling, at any rate, than the known alternatives.[32]

---

[32] For comments on a previous draft of this chapter I would like to thank David Bourget, Jordi Fernández, Terry Horgan, Bill Lycan, Robert Lurz, Galen Strawson, Ken Williford, Dan Zahavi, and an anonymous referee for OUP. I have also benefited from relevant conversations on it with David Chalmers, Chris Hill, Brendan Jackson, Derk Pereboom, and Daniel Stoljar.

2

Conceptual Preliminaries

The purpose of the present chapter is to draw some conceptual and terminological distinctions that ought to facilitate discussion in forthcoming chapters. The distinctions I will draw are by and large familiar and unoriginal. There are four main ones: creature consciousness versus state consciousness, transitive consciousness versus intransitive consciousness, phenomenal consciousness versus access consciousness, and qualitative character versus subjective character. Only this fourth is to some degree unfamiliar.[1] There are only two additional "novelties" in the chapter. The first is the claim, in Section 1, that transitive consciousness implies intransitive consciousness and cannot occur in its absence. The second is the claim, in Section 2, that phenomenal consciousness is the categorical basis of access consciousness.[2]

1. "Is Conscious"

A theory of phenomenal consciousness is concerned with the property responsible for generating the mystery of consciousness. There is no guarantee that that property is the same as the property (or one of the proper*ties*) picked out by the everyday term "consciousness" and its cognates. Nonetheless, firming our grasp on the grammatical behavior of the ordinary-language predicate "is conscious" will be useful, if only

[1] It is relatively unfamiliar as a *terminological* distinction, though a very close distinction is drawn by Levine (2001). Arguably, the distinction is not so unfamiliar as a *conceptual* distinction, since it is operative in the views of most higher-order theorists.
[2] However, I have argued for the two claims before and will not have anything new to say here. The claim about transitive and intransitive consciousness is made in Kriegel 2004a, the one about phenomenal and access consciousness in Kriegel 2006b.

by way of clarifying the relation between the property (or properties) it denotes and phenomenal consciousness.

For this reason, the present section engages in *conceptual analysis* of "consciousness." Most of the common wisdom in this area we owe to David Rosenthal (see Rosenthal 1986, 1990), though his treatment closely parallels one already to be found in Tugendhat 1979. It is somewhat unclear whether Rosenthal means his various distinctions between senses of "is conscious" to be theoretically illuminating distinctions that go to some natural joints or simply to reflect grammatical distinctions that bring out the contours of the folk concept of consciousness. Only the latter endeavor is correctly describable as conceptual analysis. So it is unclear whether Rosenthal took himself to be doing conceptual analysis. It is very clear, however, that Tugendhat was drawing essentially the same distinctions as an exercise in conceptual analysis, and I will follow in his footsteps.

Some philosophers take conceptual analysis to be bankrupt, others to be inconsequential or just plain boring. This is not the platform to launch a defense of conceptual analysis as a philosophical method, so let me just state that I happen to find conceptual analysis both viable and fruitful. That said, very little of what I will say in this section will make a difference for the rest of the book, so the reader with distaste for conceptual analysis can safely skip it. What follows is merely an attempt at illuminating some of the ordinary usages of "conscious" and its cognates in everyday life, and if it is unhelpful it can be ignored.[3]

In examining the linguistic behavior of a predicate, we are not interested (as linguists would be) in *every* grammatical distinction. We are interested only in those grammatical distinctions that reflect putative metaphysical differences—for example, differences in the property picked out by the predicate. In Rosenthal's analysis, there are two axes along which grammatical differences in the ordinary usage of "is conscious" reflect differences in property picked out, resulting in a small matrix

---

[3] A critic may also grant that conceptual analysis is useful in some areas, but maintain that the term "consciousness" simply does not have the kind of well-behaved core usage in everyday life that would lend it to conceptual analysis. I disagree, but, again, if it turned out that this is true, then what follows in this section can be safely forgotten.

separating four different consciousness properties. Consider the following three reports:

1. "Jane is conscious."
2. "Jane is conscious of the chocolate."
3. "Jane's desire to eat the chocolate is conscious."

In each of these, the predicate "is conscious" is used to denote a property. But, at least on the face of it, the property denoted is different in each case. (1) attributes to Jane an ostensibly monadic or intrinsic property, the property of being a conscious creature, as opposed to being a zombie or brain-dead. (2) attributes to Jane an ostensibly relational property, the property of standing in the conscious-of relation to a piece of chocolate. (3) attributes an ostensibly monadic or intrinsic property, not to Jane, however, but to her desire. Given the fundamental differences in the grammatical forms of the reports, we ought to treat the properties denoted in them as at least conceptually distinct.[4,5]

In choosing a terminology by which to label the properties denoted in (1)–(3), we should take note of the reports' similarities and dissimilarities. (1) is similar to (2) and dissimilar to (3) in ascribing a property to Jane rather than to one of Jane's particular mental states. But (1) is also similar to (3) and dissimilar to (2) in ascribing an ostensibly intrinsic, rather than relational, property. To reflect these (dis)similarities, Rosenthal (1986) introduces a pair of terminological distinctions.

---

[4] To say that two properties are *conceptually* distinct is to say that there is a conceptually possible world in which one is instantiated but the other is not. This is to be distinguished from a claim of metaphysical distinctness between properties. To say that two properties are *metaphysically* distinct is to say that there is a metaphysically possible world in which one is instantiated but the other is not. Thus, whenever two different concepts are used to pick out the same property, we can trivially say that the concepts pick out conceptually distinct properties.

[5] Under certain assumptions, these grammatical distinctions would *entail* differences in the property picked out. Three assumptions stand out. The first and most problematic is that, when the property picked out is *ostensibly* thus-and-so, then it is *actually* thus-and-so. (In this relatively unrestricted form, the assumption is most certainly false.) The second is that an intrinsic or monadic property is always distinct from a relational property. The third, also problematic, is that a property borne by a concrete particular, such as an individual, is always distinct from a property borne by an abstract particular, such as a state (where I am using the terms "concrete particular" and "abstract particular" in their trope-theoretic sense). If these three assumptions were true, it would follow that the properties picked out by the three reports in the text were metaphysically distinct.

The first distinction is between *creature consciousness* and *state consciousness*. The former is a property of entire persons or organisms or creatures, whereas the latter is a property of particular mental events or states.[6] Thus, the property denoted in (1) and (2) is creature consciousness, since it is ascribed to Jane, a creature, whereas the property denoted in (3) is state consciousness, since it is ascribed to Jane's desire, a state.[7]

I want to adopt Rosenthal's terminology here, but only as a system for keeping track of the aforementioned similarities and dissimilarities in the grammar of "is conscious." I say this because, in the years since Rosenthal introduced the terms "state consciousness" and "creature consciousness," they have tended to be associated with specific doctrines about the nature of the properties they purport to pick out, doctrines that may be true a posteriori but in no way fall out of the grammar. For example, "creature consciousness" is often taken to denote the so-called normal waking state, but this is not how I am going to use the term. The way I use the term, a wakeful zombie lacks creature consciousness, simply because it lacks consciousness and is a creature. In the same vein, "state consciousness" is often taken to denote the property a mental state has just in case its subject is conscious or aware of it. Now, Rosenthal may hold that the property we ascribe to states rather than to creatures is a property states have when their subject is aware of them, but, as I am going to use the term "state consciousness," this is not *definitional* of state consciousness but is rather a substantive claim about it. What is definitional of state consciousness is that it is a consciousness property that it would be a category mistake to attribute to something that is not a state (such as a whole person).[8] Likewise, what is definitional of creature consciousness is that it is a consciousness property that it would be a category mistake to attribute to something that is not a creature (such as a state). These

---

[6] I am going to leave the notion of a mental state unanalyzed at this stage. This seems prudent given the basicness of the notion, which is commonly—and in my opinion, quite unjustifiably—supposed to be unproblematic in contemporary philosophy of mind.

[7] The same distinction can be drawn in different terms. The following appears equivalent to (3): "Jane consciously experiences the rainbow." Here the adverb "consciously" denotes a second-order property of Jane, a property of Jane's property of experiencing the rainbow. We *could*, therefore, recast the distinction between state consciousness and creature consciousness as a distinction between first-order creature consciousness and second-order creature consciousness. The distinction would be the same, but set in different terms.

[8] In a second step, we may extend the definition to allow sensible attribution to entities of ontological categories in the vicinity of "states." Events come to mind, of course, but perhaps also property instantiations and/or states of affairs (if any of those are different from states).

are the only definitions that do nothing but reflect the grammar of "is conscious."

Rosenthal's second distinction is between *transitive consciousness* and *intransitive consciousness*. The former is an ostensibly relational property, denoted by the transitive "conscious of," whereas the latter is an ostensibly intrinsic, non-relational property, denoted by the intransitive "conscious." This is the distinction between consciousness-of and plain consciousness. In the above reports, (1) and (3) employ the intransitive expression, denoting intransitive consciousness, whereas (2) employs the transitive expression, denoting transitive consciousness.

Here again I will adopt Rosenthal's terminology, but again without committing to specific doctrines about the nature of the properties putatively denoted by the terms. In particular, I will later reject Rosenthal's claim that a person can be transitively conscious of something without being in any intransitively conscious state. Conceptual analysis reveals, I maintain, that this is incoherent.

With these two terminological distinctions at hand, we can proceed to label the property denoted in (1), involving a creature's being conscious, *intransitive creature consciousness*; the property denoted in (2), involving a creature's being conscious of something, *transitive creature consciousness*; and the property denoted in (3), involving a state's being conscious, *intransitive state consciousness*.

The reader will have noticed that we did not mention a property of transitive state consciousness, involving a state's being conscious of something. This is because statements of the following form are ungrammatical (or at least nonsensical):

4. * "Jane's desire is conscious of the chocolate."

It is simply a fact about the way "conscious of" works in English that mental states cannot be conscious of anything (in the same sense in which it is a fact about the way "bachelor" works in English that bachelors cannot be married). At the same time, the occurrence of transitive creature consciousness *implicates* a mental state: when Jane is conscious of the chocolate, she is in a certain mental state, and it is in virtue of being in that mental state that she is conscious of the chocolate (as opposed to being conscious of a table, or of nothing at all). We may use the free label "transitive state consciousness" for the property mental states exhibit when, and only when, their subjects are transitively conscious of something in virtue of being in them. Thus, Jane's desire for chocolate is transitively state-conscious because, in virtue of having it, Jane is conscious of the chocolate.[9] More generally, a mental state M of a subject S is transitively state-conscious iff S is transitively creature-conscious in virtue of being in M.

At our disposal now is a symmetric fourfold distinction between properties denoted by the ordinary-language predicate "is conscious." The distinction is represented in Figure 2.1. With this fourfold distinction in place, we can attend to the question of what the relationships between them are—in particular, whether any of them can be analyzed in terms of the others.[10]

According to the Tugendhat–Rosenthal analysis, creature consciousness depends on state consciousness (for both the transitive and intransitive cases), while transitive and intransitive consciousness are mutually independent (for both the state and creatures cases). I will embrace the former claim but reject the latter. The result will be a picture in which the properties of transitive creature consciousness, intransitive creature consciousness, and transitive state consciousness all depend upon the property of intransitive state consciousness, in the sense that none of the former can occur in the absence of the latter. That would make intransitive state consciousness the fundamental ordinary-language concept of consciousness.

---

[9] This claim is not unproblematic. It might be reasonably claimed that being conscious of something is a matter of being in a *cognitive* state, whereas desiring something is a *non-cognitive* state. However, it could also be held that desires, like cognitive states, involve a representation of their object, and that being conscious of something is just a matter of having such a representation. The representation can then turn out to be cognitive or non-cognitive (depending, say, on its direction of fit), so that a desire's being non-cognitive would not make it unfit to make its subject conscious of whatever it is a desire for.

[10] There is arguably one more distinction that is quite pertinent to the everyday use of "consciousness" and its cognates. This is the distinction between *temporally indexed* and *non-temporally-indexed* creature consciousness. Suppose Jane is in a dreamless sleep. It seems to me (though others have reported that this does not resonate with them) that there is a sense in which Jane is unconscious during her dreamless sleep. But there is also a sense in which Jane is conscious, in that she is a conscious being, unlike, say, a chair (or that she is a conscious person, unlike Jill, who is comatose or brain dead). These two senses lead to a distinction between *being conscious* and *being conscious at t*. In her dreamless sleep, Jane instantiates the property of *being conscious*, but not the property of *being conscious at t* (where t is the duration of her dreamless sleep). In other words, the truth conditions of (1) above differ from those of "Jane was conscious at 4:20 last Friday." This case involves *intransitive* creature consciousness. It is a fair question whether the same distinction applies in the *transitive* case. There are complicated issues here, which are not pertinent to our investigation, and so I set them aside, leaving the question unanswered.

	Transitive	Intransitive
Creature	Transitive creature consciousness	Intransitive creature consciousness
State	Transitive state consciousness	Intransitive state consciousness

Figure 2.1. Four consciousness properties

As we have just seen, a person is conscious of something in virtue of being in a certain mental state. This is a definitional matter. So, by definition, a person instantiates transitive creature consciousness only if she is in a mental state that instantiates transitive state consciousness. Therefore, transitive creature consciousness depends upon transitive *state* consciousness.

A similar conceptual dependence is plausible for intransitive consciousness. A person cannot be conscious (instantiate intransitive creature consciousness) if she is incapable of being in mental states that are conscious (instantiate intransitive state consciousness). Thus intransitive *creature* consciousness may be analyzable in terms of intransitive state consciousness, along the following lines: a creature C is intransitively creature-conscious iff there is a mental state M, such that (i) M is intransitively state-conscious and (ii) nomologically possibly, C is in M.[11]

It appears, then, that transitive creature consciousness depends upon transitive state consciousness and intransitive creature consciousness depends upon intransitive state consciousness. We can consolidate and say that

[11] It might be objected that there is yet another kind of intransitive creature consciousness, which does not depend upon state consciousness. Consider the sort of claim we make when we say that orangutans are conscious but snails are not. Here, "conscious" denotes a property of whole species, rather than a particular creature. This property, which we may call *species consciousness*, may not obey the same ascription rules as transitive creature consciousness. However, it seems to me that even species consciousness is dependent upon intransitive state consciousness. For to say of a species that it is conscious is to say that normal specimens are *capable* of being conscious, and, more specifically, that they are capable of being in conscious states. A species of creature that cannot, in principle, have conscious mental states is an unconscious species. Another way to put it is to say that the truthmaker of "orangutans are conscious" consists in many orangutans instantiating creature consciousness, not of the species instantiating a new property.

creature consciousness conceptually depends on state consciousness. I will now argue that, contra Tugendhat and Rosenthal, transitive state consciousness in turn conceptually depends upon intransitive state consciousness.[12]

Recall that transitive state consciousness is the property a mental state M of a creature C has when C is conscious of something in virtue of being in M. The question is, therefore, whether (i) C can be conscious of something even when M is unconscious or (ii) M must be conscious in order to make C conscious of something. The first option seems to run contrary to the normal usage of the terms. If C could be conscious of something in virtue of being in M even when M is unconscious, there would be two ways a person could be conscious of something: consciously or unconsciously. But, as far as the normal usage of the terms is concerned, it is all but incoherent to describe a person as unconsciously conscious of the fact that *p*. In a way, this is just an empirical prediction—namely, that competent English speakers would not accept "Jane is unconsciously conscious of the chocolate" as coherent.[13]

Furthermore, it seems to me that, in the normal usage of the term, a person is conscious of only a limited number of things at any one time. Quite plausibly, however, a person may be properly ascribed innumerably many tacit, hence unconscious, beliefs at any time. If we allowed persons to be conscious of things in virtue of being in unconscious mental states, we would leave open the possibility that each of these tacit beliefs makes its subject conscious of whatever it is about. This would make it possible that people are conscious of innumerably many things at a time, including during their sleep. Again, this strikes me as in dissonance with the normal usage of "conscious" in English. We avoid this result if we deny that a person can be transitively conscious of something in virtue of being in

---

[12] This is where I depart from Tugendhat and Rosenthal. Both hold that transitive and intransitive consciousness are mutually independent notions, and thus that a mental state can be transitively conscious even when it is intransitively unconscious. I will reject this possibility.

[13] It might be objected that one cannot make assertions about dependence relations among different properties, as I have done here, purely on the basis of examining the way we uncritically speak in everyday life. This objection is misguided in the present context, since the properties I have distinguished in this section were separated out, and defined relative to each other, precisely by reference to the linguistic behavior of the everyday term "consciousness." If the properties were defined in terms of grammatical behavior, claims about their interrelations could, and probably should, rest on examination of grammar.

an intransitively unconscious mental state.[14] And to do so is effectively to adopt the view that *transitive* state consciousness cannot occur in the absence of *intransitive* state consciousness. The former is in that sense conceptually dependent upon the latter.[15],[16]

In conclusion, the conceptual analysis of consciousness yields a fourfold distinction between kinds of consciousness, and gives a fundamental place to one of them, intransitive state consciousness. The other three properties are dependent upon intransitive state consciousness, in that none can occur in the latter's absence.[17] It might be objected that intransitive state consciousness cannot possibly be the basic ordinary-language concept of consciousness, since, although we do speak of desires being conscious or unconscious, we do not normally speak of thoughts or experiences being conscious or unconscious. As philosophers, we may say such things as "Jim's thought of Vienna is conscious," but in regular conversation this would be an extremely forced usage of "conscious."[18] This fact

[14] It should be noted that the same absurdity does not arise from allowing unconscious *occurrent* states to make their subject transitively conscious, for certainly a subject does not have innumerably many unconscious occurrent states. So one stable position, as far as the present consideration is concerned, could be that unconscious standing states never make their subject conscious of anything, but unconscious occurrent states at least sometimes do. However, there is something more unified and principled about the position that no unconscious states ever make their subject conscious of anything. This is, moreover, supported by the first consideration I raised in the main text, which applies equally to unconscious occurrent states.

[15] There is no question, of course, that it is possible for a person to be in unconscious intentional states directed at those many things. But we would not use the phrase "conscious of" to describe the person's relation to those things. Thus, we would be reluctant to describe a person as conscious of the fact that 17.3 is greater than 13.9 just because she harbors a tacit belief to that effect. As long as the belief that $17.3 > 13.9$ remains unconscious, we would not say that the person is conscious of the fact that $17.3 > 13.9$ in virtue of that belief. So, when we say that a person is conscious of the fact that $17.3 > 13.9$, we imply that her belief that $17.3 > 13.9$ is conscious.

[16] I happen to think that, conversely, all intransitively conscious states are transitively conscious as well: whenever a mental state is conscious, it makes its subject conscious of something. However, I do not think that this is true a priori or falls out of the grammar of "is conscious." If there is a dependence here, then, it is not a conceptual one.

[17] It might be objected that the notion of *temporally indexed* intransitive creature consciousness, mentioned in n. 10, is even more fundamental than intransitive state consciousness. Plausibly, a mental state cannot be intransitively conscious if its subject is not intransitively conscious *at the time of the state's occurrence*. If so, intransitive state consciousness cannot occur in the absence of temporally indexed intransitive creature consciousness, and in that sense depends thereupon. This observation is accurate, but the dependence runs in the opposite direction as well: a creature cannot be conscious at a time if she is in no conscious state at that time. This two-way dependence suggests that temporally indexed intransitive creature consciousness and intransitive state consciousness are equivalent notions. Thus, what it is like to be Yvette at t is constituted by what it is like for Yvette to be in the maximal conscious state she is in at t, where a person's "maximal conscious state" at a time is the sum of all her conscious states at that time.

[18] Anyone who has taught the subject of consciousness to undergraduates, or for that matter discussed it with his or her fellow barflies, must have noticed how difficult it is to make them wrap their mind

may understandably inspire the suspicion that state consciousness is in reality a technical, theoretically motivated notion, as opposed to creature consciousness, which truly belongs in ordinary language.

However, we should note that, although the construction "Jim's thought of Vienna is conscious" is forced and technical, the construction "Jim is consciously thinking of Vienna" is perfectly ordinary, and the two are equivalent. Since the two constructions are interchangeable, we can with good conscience say that intransitive state consciousness is an ordinary-language concept.

How is intransitive state consciousness related to phenomenal consciousness, the property responsible for generating the mystery of consciousness? Interestingly, in a pre-theoretic mindset, it is most natural to conjure the sense of mystery by appeal to *creature* consciousness. Thus, Nagel's compelling formulation in terms of "what it is like to be a bat" adverted to the bat's creature consciousness. Likewise, Chalmers's more recent formulation in terms of the conceivability of zombies highlights the zombies' (lack of) creature consciousness.[19]

In a more theoretical frame of mind, however, philosophers find it more illuminating to contemplate a specific, preferably simple, moment or episode of conscious experience, such as seeing blue or tasting chocolate or feeling nervous about an upcoming public lecture. As we fix our mind on such momentary and fragmentary conscious experiences, and juxtapose them with the senseless swarming of a thousand electro-chemical pulses in the brain, the mystery of consciousness descends upon us in sharp and acute form. Here, the object of our contemplation is a property of states, not creatures. It is a *kind* of intransitive state consciousness.

2. Phenomenal Consciousness and Access Consciousness

One way to connect the notion of intransitive state consciousness to that of phenomenal consciousness is through the distinction, due to Block (1995),

around the concept of state consciousness. They naturally take the noun "consciousness" to denote a feature of persons, not of particular events or states.

[19] In both cases the focus is on *intransitive* creature consciousness.

between *phenomenal consciousness* and *access consciousness*. Both are kinds of intransitive state consciousness. So the distinction can be thought of as helping to home in on phenomenal consciousness by distinguishing it from other kinds of intransitive state consciousness. Conceptual analysis can take us only so close to the area where the property responsible for the mystery of consciousness lies. Further distinctions, which go beyond folk wisdom, have to be drawn if we are to get nearer. In this section I first introduce Block's distinction and later argue against some of the claims he makes on its basis.

Block introduces the distinction in the context of complaining against current scientific practice in Consciousness Studies. It is frequently remarked that scientific research into consciousness has by and large tended to target the relatively tractable cognitive phenomena surrounding phenomenal consciousness rather than phenomenal consciousness itself. Like the old man who searched for his lost keys under the street light, not because that was where he lost them but because it was the only sufficiently lit place, scientific research sometimes appears to search for the explanation of consciousness where the light is instead of where the explanandum is.

This complaint has been given its clearest articulation by Ned Block, who claims that consciousness research in the cognitive sciences has targeted the wrong phenomenon. Instead of phenomenal consciousness, it has targeted a closely related but crucially different phenomenon, which he calls *access consciousness*.

Block characterizes access consciousness as the property a mental state has just when "it is poised for free use in reasoning and for direct 'rational' control of action and speech" (Block 1995: 382).[20] The idea seems to be that a mental state is access-conscious when the subject has "free" access to its content and can use it in personal-level reasoning. Sometimes the notion of access consciousness is characterized more generally in terms of something like *global accessibility*—that is, availability to a wide range of general-purpose modules, such as executive function, action control, and verbal report. Phenomenal consciousness Block characterizes just as he ought to, in terms of the explanatory gap: "I mentioned the explanatory gap

---

[20] Here, and in what follows, I am quoting from the reprint in Block et al. 1997.

partly by way of pointing to P-consciousness [phenomenal consciousness]: *that's* the entity to which the mentioned explanatory gap applies" (Block 1995: 382; emphasis in original).

From these characterizations, it is clear that the concept of access consciousness is different from the concept of phenomenal consciousness. It is a further question, however, whether the two concepts pick out two numerically distinct properties. Block argues that they do. The argument takes a traditional form, appealing to modal double dissociation (if you please): each property can occur without the other. That is, there are metaphysically possible particulars that instantiate phenomenal consciousness but not access consciousness, and vice versa.[21]

Block's overall argument against current scientific practice in Consciousness Studies has a further step, however. The first step is to show that phenomenal and access consciousness are two distinct properties. But a second step attempts to show that the main research programs in current Consciousness Studies target access consciousness. On the assumption that to target a phenomenon A that is distinct from phenomenon B is not to target B, it follows that these research programs do not target phenomenal consciousness.

In the discussion below, I will argue against the stated assumption. I will argue that, in some cases, one can study B *via* studying A even if A and B are logically (and metaphysically) independent. In particular, that is the case when A is a dispositional property and B is its categorical basis. (Indeed, it is not clear that there is any way to study a categorical property other than by investigating the dispositions for which it is the basis.) The history and practice of scientific inquiry contain many illustrations of this: studies of dispositions that serve as vehicles for trying to understand underlying categorical properties. I will argue that phenomenal consciousness is precisely the categorical basis of access consciousness. If so, the former can be studied via the study of the latter.

One way to organize the dialectic is as follows. Block's argument could be loosely formulated thus:

1. for any properties F and G and research program R, if R targets F, and F ≠ G, then R does not target G;

---

[21] The (plausible) assumption here is that, for property F and property G to be identical, it is necessary (whether or not it is sufficient) that F and G be coextensive in every possible world.

2. phenomenal consciousness $\neq$ access consciousness; therefore,
3. for any research program R, if R targets access consciousness, then R does not target phenomenal consciousness;
4. scientific studies of consciousness have targeted access consciousness; therefore,
5. scientific studies of consciousness have not targeted phenomenal consciousness.

While most of Block's critics (e.g., Dennett 1995, Clark 2000) reject Premise 2 in this argument, I reject Premise 1. My counter-argument is this:

1. for any properties F and G and research program R, if F is the categorical basis of G, and R targets G, then possibly, R targets F;[22]
2. phenomenal consciousness is the categorical basis of access consciousness; therefore,
3. for any research program R, if R targets access consciousness, then possibly, R targets phenomenal consciousness;
4. scientific studies of consciousness have targeted access consciousness; therefore,
5. possibly, scientific studies of consciousness have targeted phenomenal consciousness.

Note that my conclusion is not quite that scientific research into consciousness *has* targeted phenomenal consciousness, but, more modestly, that its doing so is not excluded by the facts that it has targeted access consciousness and that phenomenal and access consciousness are distinct. In the remainder of this section I offer first an exposition of Block's argument, then a case for the first two premises of the counter-argument.

As noted, Block's argument for the distinctness of phenomenal and access consciousness proceeds by modal double dissociation. As a case of phenomenal consciousness without access consciousness, Block adduces absent-minded perception, or, more specifically, the perception of habituated stimuli. Engrossed in heated conversation, a person may not notice the roadwork outside, and consequently auditory information about the drilling noise would not be available for free use in personal-level reasoning

---

[22] The modal force of the "possibly" here is meant to be very strong: physical or nomological possibility at the very least.

and action control. Nonetheless, the person's auditory experience as of drilling is phenomenally conscious.[23] As illustration of access without phenomenal consciousness, Block tells a slightly more fanciful story involving "super-blindsight." Super-blindsight resembles actual blindsight, except that (unlike in actual blindsight) its victims can *prompt themselves* to "guess" what is in their visual field, in a way that makes the prompted information globally accessible. Their visual state instantiates access consciousness but not phenomenal consciousness.[24]

Having thus argued that phenomenal and access consciousness are distinct properties, Block proceeds to survey a number of key research programs in Consciousness Studies and show that their explanandum is more properly construed as access consciousness.[25] The argument, then, is that current scientific research can shed light only on access consciousness, but access consciousness is not the source of the mystery of consciousness. So current scientific theories of consciousness do not contribute toward the demystification of consciousness—that is, toward the explanation of phenomenal consciousness. Let us call this the *access thesis*: current scientific research focuses on access consciousness *to the exclusion of* phenomenal consciousness.

In response, I will now argue for the following alternative picture. Access consciousness is a dispositional property. As such, it must have a categorical basis. In the history of science, oftentimes research programs study dispositional properties in an attempt to understand their categorical bases. Research programs that study access consciousness can be interpreted in this vein, as attempts to understand the categorical basis of access consciousness. Finally, there are good reasons to take phenomenal consciousness to be the categorical basis of access consciousness. This vindicates current research programs as targeting phenomenal consciousness.

---

[23] Thus she may be able to remember at a later time what the drilling sounded like, that it was louder than the hammering, or that it was irritating, by conjuring back up sensory images of the relevant sounds. Her ability to remember these facts need not be taken to *entail* that the state was originally phenomenally conscious. It is certainly *evidence* that it was.

[24] These alleged modal dissociations can be, and certainly have been, disputed. My own critical strategy in this chapter will be different, however, and in any case I do accept that phenomenal and access consciousness are separate properties. Nonetheless, in Chapter 5 I will reconsider the case of the absent-minded hearing of the drill.

[25] He writes (1995: 382; emphasis in original): "it is not easy to see how current approaches to P-consciousness [phenomenal consciousness] *could* yield an account of it. Indeed, what passes for research programs on consciousness just is a combination of cognitive psychology and explorations of neurophysiological syndromes that contain no theoretical perspective on what P-consciousness actually is."

The first thing to note about access consciousness is that it is a dispositional property. Nothing has actually to happen with a mental state or event for it to qualify as access-conscious: the state or event need not actually be access*ed*; it needs only to be access*ible*. To become access-conscious, a mental state need not be *actually* used in the control of reasoning and action, and so on; it need only be *poised for* such use.

Plausibly, dispositional properties are normally surrounded by two kinds of closely related non-dispositional properties. There are, first, what may be called *manifestational* properties: the properties of manifesting the dispositions in question. Thus, mental states are often not only *poised for* use in reasoning and action control, but actually are so used. They are not merely accessible, but accessed. They then instantiate the manifestational property corresponding to access consciousness.

More interestingly, dispositional properties are often taken to require *categorical bases*. A categorical basis is a non-dispositional, occurrent property that accounts for and grounds certain dispositions.[26] When a wine glass is fragile, its fragility is unlikely to be a brute and inexplicable fact. On the contrary, it must be possible to explain why the wine glass is fragile in terms of the physico-chemical properties of the glass it is made of. The glass is fragile—it is disposed to break under relatively lax conditions—*because*, or *in virtue of*, its physico-chemical constitution. Its particular constitution is thus the *reason for* its fragility—the reason *why* it is fragile. In this sense, the glass's physico-chemical constitution is the categorical basis of the glass's fragility.[27]

This applies, of course, to access consciousness. When a mental state is access-conscious, it must also have a categorical property *in virtue of which* it is access-conscious. The state's disposition to be freely used in personal-level cognition cannot be a brute matter. There must be an explanation *why* the state is thus poised, an explanation appealing to non-dispositional properties that *account* for the state's disposition.

---

[26] There is a (harmless) oversimplification here though—see next footnote.

[27] It is possible to hold that the categorical bases of some dispositions are themselves dispositions. These "lower-level" dispositions have their own categorical bases, which may or may not be dispositions. At the bottom level, however, categorical bases cannot be dispositions. They must be non-dispositional properties. At least this is the view I adopt here. For the view that the world consists of dispositions "all the way down," see Shoemaker 1979. A full discussion of this view of properties—a sort of functionalism about everything—and of the problems attending it would take us too far afield. Here, I will assume that this "pure disposition" view is incorrect, and that dispositional properties do require categorical bases—that is, non-dispositional properties whose instantiation *explains why* the dispositional ones are instantiated.

It is quite common in the history of science that scientists labor around a dispositional property by way of trying to learn about its categorical basis. Thus, for centuries geneticists have been studying hereditary properties, which are dispositional, by way of trying to reach an understanding of their categorical basis, which we have only recently identified as DNA. A good example is Huntington's Disease, an inherited neurological degenerative disorder characterized by loss of striatal neurons. Research into Huntington's Disease has led to the discovery in 1993 that a mutation of the CAG gene—a mutation in which the triplet repeats at least 42 times (as opposed to between 11 and 34 times in the normal case)—is what "causes" the disease (see Huntington's Disease Collaborative Research Group 1993). This mutation is effectively the categorical basis of the disposition to suffer from the diseases. In this case, what drove the study of the disposition is a practical interest in identifying what causes the disposition to manifest. But what motivates the study is beside the point. The important fact is that the study resulted in learning more and more about the properties of the disposition's categorical basis, until the particular gene responsible for it could be singled out.

Research into access consciousness can be seen in a similar light. By looking at what causes this disposition's manifestation (the manifestation being the actual use of a state in reasoning and action control), more and more can be learned about the disposition's categorical basis. Thus studies that target the disposition we call access consciousness may well be best understood as attempts to uncover the nature of the categorical basis of access consciousness.

The question, of course, is what the relevant categorical basis is. A natural suggestion is that it is what I called in Chapter 1 for-me-ness, or subjective character. Recall that a mental state has subjective character just in case it is *for* the subject, in the sense that the subject has a certain awareness of it, typically a peripheral and unimposing kind of awareness. What makes this suggestion natural is that subjective character seems to play the right explanatory role vis-à-vis access consciousness. The reason why a mental state is poised for the subject's free use in personal-level reasoning and action control, it is reasonable to suppose, is that the subject is already aware of it. Once the subject is aware of the state, she can freely make use of it in her deliberate reasoning and action control. Thus the state's free usage to those ends can be *explained* in terms of its subjective character or for-me-ness. The subject's awareness of her conscious state is the *reason why* the state is poised for use in reasoning and action control—the *reason for* the state's poise for such use. It is *because* (or *in virtue of* the fact that) I am aware of my bluish experience of the sky that the experience is poised to be freely used in my reasoning about the consistently nice weather and in guiding my vacation plans.[28]

These considerations suggest that subjective character fits the bill to be a categorical basis of access consciousness. They do not rule out, however, that other properties may also fit that bill. Indeed, many properties (for example, fragility) have multiple categorical bases. Other properties have only a single categorical basis. In the case of access consciousness, it is hard to see what other categorical basis it might have (at least at the same level of analysis).[29] In any case, until another potential categorical basis is adduced, we should be entitled to proceed on the assumption that subjective character is the *only* categorical basis of access consciousness—that it is not only *a* categorical basis but *the* categorical basis.

Since the subjective character of a conscious experience is a component of phenomenal character, this view entails that the only categorical basis of access consciousness is a component of phenomenal consciousness. The upshot is that, even if we grant Block that phenomenal and access consciousness are numerically distinct properties, the two may nonetheless be very closely tied. The tie is this: phenomenal consciousness is such that a central component of it is the categorical basis of access consciousness. This is certainly an intimate connection, but observe that it is at the same time only a *contingent* connection, and is thus consistent with Block's modal double dissociation. (More on this below.)

This picture offers at least a partial vindication of current scientific practice. For it suggests that, possibly, in conducting the studies they do, cognitive scientists are not targeting access consciousness *to the exclusion* of phenomenal consciousness, but rather are targeting access consciousness *by way* of studying phenomenal consciousness.

---

[28] Recalling the distinction drawn in Chapter 1 between focal and peripheral awareness, we may say, in short, that the reason my experience is focally access*ible* is that it is peripherally access*ed*.

[29] There may be a neural property N that serves as the categorical basis of access consciousness, but then it may also be that N is precisely the neural correlate, or for that matter the neural reducer, of subjective character.

I will now present three advantages of this vindicatory picture of the relationship between phenomenal and access consciousness over Block's critical picture. To my mind, it is already a major advantage that the present picture *is* vindicatory. I think that, other things being equal, it is always preferable for the philosopher to seek an account of scientific practice that vindicates it rather than debunks it. The history of philosophy is replete with instances of philosophers criticizing scientific practice only to realize later that the critique was based on a naive model of the practice. A much safer goal is to provide conceptual foundations and philosophical underpinnings for scientific practice, trusting that any needed remedy for that practice would come from inside science. Thus, whenever an account of the underpinnings can be provided that illuminates scientific practice and allows us to see why it proceeds the way it does in pursuit of its express goals, this strikes me as preferable to an account that indicts science with malpractice.

Another advantage of the view defended here is that it accounts for the functional role of phenomenal consciousness. Indeed, it accounts for there *being* a functional role to phenomenal consciousness. A problem with Block's distinction is that any function we may wish to attribute to phenomenal consciousness would be more appropriately attributed to access consciousness, leaving phenomenal consciousness devoid of any functional significance it can properly call its own (Chalmers 1997). The source of this unhappy consequence is the picture of phenomenal and access consciousness as two separate properties sitting side by side at the same theoretical level. But if, as I have argued, phenomenal consciousness (or part of it) is the categorical basis of access consciousness, then access consciousness can be readily construed as the functional role *of* phenomenal consciousness. That is, phenomenal consciousness is the *occupant* of a functional role, part of the specification of which is given by access consciousness (namely, the part concerned with poise for free use in personal-level reasoning and action control). Here, the relation between phenomenal and access consciousness is construed as the relation of an occupant to its role: phenomenal consciousness *occupies* access consciousness—phenomenality plays accessibility (if you will). Thus, once we construe phenomenal consciousness as the categorical basis of access consciousness, and access consciousness as the functional role of phenomenal consciousness, we can again attribute certain functions to phenomenal consciousness: the functions are construed as *part* of access consciousness and as *performed by* phenomenal consciousness. This appears to avoid potential conceptual confusions caused by fully divorcing phenomenal from access consciousness.[30]

Yet another advantage of the view is the way it preserves, on the one hand, a metaphysical distinction between phenomenal and access consciousness, and, on the other hand, an intimate connection between the two. It casts the two as metaphysically but not nomologically independent.[31] More specifically, it ensures the nomological supervenience of access consciousness on phenomenal consciousness, but not any modally stronger supervenience. This is because, in general, dispositions cannot occur in the absence of their categorical bases consistently with the natural laws (but can consistently with the "metaphysical laws").[32]

Thus, in a possible world where the laws of psychology are radically different from the actual world's, mental states with subjective character may well not display the disposition to be freely used in reasoning and action control, just as a physically indistinguishable wine glass may not be fragile in some nomologically impossible world.[33] At the same time, there is clearly a nomologically necessary relation between categorical bases and the dispositions for which they are bases. Just as the relevant

[30] It is, of course, open to someone like Block to claim that phenomenal consciousness is in fact devoid of any functional significance (as Velmans 1992 has done) or has very limited functional significance (as Libet 1985 suggests). But I take it that such epiphenomenalism, hard or soft, is a *liability* on a theory of phenomenal consciousness, one better avoided.

[31] This is an advantage because, while it seems that there is a strong connection between phenomenal and access consciousness, Block's argument from modal double dissociation does seem to show that the two are numerically distinct. (For that matter, the simple observation that the one is dispositional whereas the other is non-dispositional suggests this rather forcefully.) Importantly, however, the relationship between a disposition and its categorical basis, although clearly intimate, does not normally hold with metaphysical necessity.

[32] By "metaphysical laws" I refer to the type of a posteriori necessities often recognized in post-Kripkean philosophy. Thus, water's being H_2O would be a metaphysical law. Note that a consequence of what was just noted in the text is that, whenever dispositions have only one categorical basis, they cannot occur in the latter's absence without violating a law of nature. This is what ensures the nomological supervenience of access consciousness on subjective character. What ensures the failure of metaphysical supervenience is the metaphysical possibility of superblindsighters.

[33] The wine glass is fragile in that it is disposed to break in relatively undemanding circumstances. This is so not only due to the physico-chemical constitution of the glass, however, but also in part due to the fact that the actual gravitational constant is what it is. If gravity was a thousand times weaker, the wine glass would be a thousand times less likely to break in any given circumstance, and so would be a thousand times less fragile. In fact, the glass would not *be* fragile—in that its disposition to break would be very limited. (I am assuming here, what may not be uncontroversial, that the glass's being still much more fragile than other objects, say those made of steel, does not suffice to make it fragile in the counterfactual situation we are considering.) Yet the physico-chemical constitution that is the disposition's categorical basis in the actual world would remain the same.

physico-chemical structure yields fragility in all nomologically possible worlds, subjective character yields access consciousness in all. This nomic connection is necessary to license scientific inferences from dispositions (and their manifestations) to the underlying categorical properties.[34],[35]

In summary, it is in general true that a dispositional property and its categorical basis are nomologically but not metaphysically coextensive. So the fact that there are metaphysically possible circumstances in which phenomenal and access consciousness come apart does not militate against the thesis that (a component of) the former is the categorical basis of the latter. There is thus an intimate connection between the two—and, moreover, one that licenses scientific inferences from one to the other—even if they are numerically distinct properties. The fact that the vindicatory picture of the relationship between phenomenal and access consciousness delivers just this kind of connection between the two is the third advantage of the view.

Let me close by considering five objections to the claim that subjective character, hence a component of phenomenal consciousness, is the categorical basis of access consciousness.

An important objection is that subjective character cannot be the basis of access consciousness because, plausibly, infants have phenomenal consciousness, hence subjective character, but not access consciousness. There are two lines of response to this objection. One is to reject the alleged time lag between the onset of phenomenal and access consciousness—either by denying infants phenomenal consciousness or by allowing them access consciousness. A more promising line is to reject the inference from the alleged time lag to the claim that (a component of) phenomenal consciousness is not the basis of access consciousness. As I will argue in Chapter 5, although the minimal form of subjective character *necessary* for phenomenal consciousness may be relatively simple, it is nonetheless *contingently* true that the subjective component of phenomenal consciousness in normal

---

[34] Note, however, that, while categorical bases are always nomologically sufficient for the dispositions they are bases for, (*a*) they are not always nomologically *necessary* for them, and (*b*) they are usually not *metaphysically* sufficient for them. In the case of subjective character, if it is indeed the *only* categorical basis of access consciousness, it is at least actually (and probably nomologically) necessary for access.

[35] As for the converse, consider that some objects are fragile that have a physico-chemical constitution very different from the wine glass's. A vase of completely different constitution can be equally fragile. Thus similar dispositions can have dissimilar categorical bases. Moreover, the functional role occupied by the categorical basis is, like other functional roles, multiply realizable: it allows different occupants to play the exact same role. In similar fashion, access consciousness could readily occur in the absence of its actual categorical basis—if some other categorical properties served as its basis.

human adults is quite rich (involving among other things reference to a self with a personality and a life history). This contingently more sophisticated kind of subjective character is fit to underlie access consciousness in human adults. Since the relationship between a disposition and its categorical basis is contingent, there is no reason to deny that subjective character is (contingently) the categorical basis of access consciousness, even if the former can occur (for example, in infants and animals) in a form too diminished to underlie access consciousness.

Another objection is that categorical bases are to be found at the scientific, "micro" level, whereas subjective character is a property at the commonsensical, "macro" level. But the supposition that a categorical basis *must* be a micro property is misguided. Consider explosiveness, the property of being disposed to explode. To be sure, it has a micro-level categorical basis—namely, the property of containing potassium nitrate. But it *also* has a macro-level categorical basis—the property of containing gun powder. And no doubt gun powder is effective in the way it is precisely because it is constituted by potassium nitrate (at least partially). But in any case it does not follow from the fact that something is explosive in virtue of containing potassium nitrate that it is not explosive in virtue of containing gun powder (in the same sense of "in virtue," the categorical-basis sense). By the same token, it may be that subjective character is a macro-level categorical basis of access consciousness, even though there is also a micro-level categorical basis, in the form of some neural property N, which might well be the neural correlate, neural realizer, or neural reducer of subjective character.[36]

A third objection is that the argument of this section shows only that current research in consciousness science *could be* studying phenomenal consciousness by studying access consciousness, but a closer look suggests that, actually, it does not—actually, current scientific research uses access consciousness as a window on some kind of underlying neural connectivity, not underlying phenomenality. In response, I concede that the argument of this section is intended to show only possibility, not actuality. In a way, what was most important to me in this section was the close nomological connection between access and phenomenal consciousness (as disposition and basis). In any case, I disagree that a closer look at ongoing

[36] As it happens, in Chapter 7 I will offer a hypothesis about what N is.

scientific research reveals that it employs access consciousness across the board to study something other than phenomenal consciousness. If it studies neural connectivity, this may yet be a way of studying phenomenal consciousness—namely, in case the relevant type of neural connectivity is thought to be a correlate, a realizer, or a reducer of phenomenal consciousness or a component thereof. Indeed, if a macro-level analysis cast phenomenal consciousness as the categorical basis of access consciousness, and a micro-level analysis suggested that a certain type of neural connectivity is the categorical basis of access consciousness, this would already constitute evidence that some metaphysical relation such as realization or reduction holds between phenomenal consciousness and the relevant type of neural connectivity.[37]

A fourth objection might be that phenomenal consciousness cannot be the categorical basis of access consciousness, since there are *actual cases* of access consciousness in the absence of phenomenal consciousness. For example, one might hold that long-distance truck drivers have perceptual states that are access-conscious but not phenomenally conscious. In response, note first that, even if there are actual cases of access without phenomenal consciousness, this would only undermine the claim that the latter is the *only* categorical basis of the former, not the claim that it is *a* categorical basis. In any case, however, it is far from obvious that the long-distance truck driver lacks phenomenal consciousness. It is clear that she lacks *something*, but her deficit may have to do with short-term memory rather than phenomenal consciousness: her perceptual states are phenomenally conscious when they occur, but, unlike normal phenomenally conscious states, they are not immediately stored in short-term memory. My own view is that such perceptual states are phenomenally conscious, but are tucked away in the farthest corners of what William James (1890/1918) called "the fringe of consciousness" (more on which in the next section). If, as a result of a cosmic incident, the truck driver became instantaneously colorblind, I contend that she would notice instantaneously a change in the phenomenal character of her perceptual states. Making the case for this

---

[37] None of this is to say that current scientific research into consciousness does not deserve a dash of criticism for its unfocused and often confused practice. My experience with conferences devoted ostensibly to consciousness research is certainly commensurate with the gist of Block's complaint, inasmuch as the great majority of what goes on in consciousness research indeed has little to do with phenomenality, and bears in reality only on learning, short-term memory, unrelated varieties of neural connectivity, etc.

interpretation of the long-distance truck-driver case would take us too far afield, but I hope these remarks make clear the direction I would go in trying to defend the claim that phenomenal consciousness is not only *a*, but *the*, categorical basis of access consciousness.

An objection of a completely different order is that subjective character is not a component of phenomenal character. This matter will be taken up in the next section. It may be worth noting, in any event, that Block himself does accept the existence of subjective character as at least a typical component of phenomenal consciousness: "P-conscious [i.e., phenomenally conscious] states often seem to have a 'me-ishness' about them, the phenomenal content often represents the state as a state of me" (Block 1995: 390).

3. Qualitative Character and Subjective Character

In Chapter 1 I drew a distinction between two aspects, or components, of phenomenal character, which I called qualitative character and subjective character. The distinction is essentially the same as one drawn by Levine (2001: 6–7; emphasis in original):

There are two important dimensions to my having [a] reddish experience. First...there is something it's like for me to have this experience. Not only is it a matter of some state (my experience) having some feature (being reddish) but, being an experience, its being reddish is "for me," a way it's like *for me*...Let's call this the *subjectivity* of conscious experience. The second important *dimension* of experience that requires explanation is qualitative character itself. Subjectivity is the phenomenon of there being *something* it's like for me to see the red diskette case. Qualitative character concerns the "*what*" it's like for me: reddish or greenish, painful and pleasurable, and the like.

The purpose of this section is to say a little more about the notions of qualitative character and subjective character—and about the relationship between them.

Qualitative Character

The bluish character of my visual experience of the blue sky, I said, is its qualitative character. But conscious experiences have not only color-ish qualitative properties. My visual experience of the wall has a whitish quality, but also a rectangular-ish quality; my gustatory experience of honey has a sweetish quality, as well as a smooth-ish quality; my olfactory experience of freshly baked bread has yet another quality, for which I have no words.

The qualitative character of a conscious experience at a time is given by the sum of qualitative properties it instantiates at that time. Thus, the qualitative character of my overall conscious experience as I stare at the wall while eating honey and taking in the scent of the freshly baked bread is given by the sum of the above qualitative properties (whitishness, sweetishness, and so on) and others instantiated contemporaneously.

Qualitative character is not restricted to perceptual experiences. My toothache experiences have a hurt-ish character, my love experiences have a giddy-ish character, and my anxiety experiences have a worry-ish character. All conscious experiences—perceptual, somatic, emotional, and others—have some qualitative character.

It is a further question which types of experience have a *proprietary* qualitative character—that is, a kind of qualitative character that is not merely a composite of other kinds. This question is often very difficult to address introspectively, and may bring to bear a web of considerations only some of which are strictly introspective. For example, do emotional experiences such as feeling disappointed have a proprietary qualitative character, or is their qualitative character merely the mixture of proprioceptive, somatic, and perhaps also cognitive qualitative properties? This is a hard question, but, happily, not one we have to resolve here.

Rejection of the very existence of qualitative character is extremely implausible, although it may be more plausible for some types of experience than others. Denying the existence of a qualitative character of visual experiences, for instance, is almost unintelligible. How can it be denied that there is a qualitative difference between my experience of the sky and a colorblind person's experience of it? It might be thought that rejecting the existence of a qualitative character of emotional experiences, and especially moods, would be more reasonable. Yet intense emotional experiences bring out rather vividly the qualitative character that presumably all emotional experiences possess. Thus, when anger boils over to blind rage, the rage-ish qualitative character is all too evident to the enraged. But, if such intense anger exhibits this rage-ish quality, very mild anger probably exhibits a subdued version of the same. It is perhaps plausible to deny the proprietariness of emotional qualitative character, but not so much its very existence.

Dennett (1988) presents a battery of arguments against the existence of "qualia," which might be thought to apply to our notion of qualitative character. But his arguments depend on a construal of qualia as properties of experience that are ineffable, intrinsic, private, and directly apprehensible. At this stage, let us neither assert nor deny that qualitative characters have those remarkable features. Let us only deny that they have those features *by definition*. More generally, it is worth guarding against defining qualitative characters in a way that imputes on them overly optimistic epistemic features. As long as we do, we will be safe to assume that there exist qualitative characters.

Subjective Character

The other component of phenomenal consciousness is subjective character: the for-me-ness of conscious experiences. What is this for-me-ness? On the view I want to take, it is a form of *awareness*. In virtue of being aware of my experience of the blue sky, there is something it is like *for me* to have that experience. The awareness in question is certainly somewhat elusive. I will attempt to make sense of it—first here and more fully in Chapter 5—in terms of a notion of *peripheral inner awareness*.[38]

Let us distinguish three ways in which a subject S may be related to one of her mental states, M. S may be either (i) focally aware of M, or (ii) peripherally aware of M, or (iii) completely unaware of M. Mental states the subject is completely unaware of are unconscious. Only mental states the subject is aware of can be conscious. Normally, the subject is only *peripherally* aware of her conscious states, though in more reflective moods she may also be *focally* aware of them.[39]

The distinction between focal awareness, peripheral awareness, and unawareness applies not only to awareness of one's mental states, but to all awareness, including awareness of external objects and states of affairs. As

---

[38] I consider it a substantive claim, not a matter of definition, that subjective character amounts normally to peripheral inner awareness. Other construals should in principle be possible, and I will discuss one of them later.

[39] Focal awareness of our conscious states characterizes the more reflective, or introspective, moments of our mental life. When a person introspects, she focuses on her conscious state. When she starts focusing on something else, her state either becomes unconscious, or she retains a peripheral awareness of it.

I look at my laptop, but catch a glimpse of my copy of the *Tractatus* from the corner of my eye, I am related to the *Tractatus* in the second way. I am not related to it, visually, the way I am related to the laptop, but nor am I related to it, visually, as I am to the Brooklyn Bridge all the way in New York. That is, I am neither focally aware of it nor entirely unaware of it. I am related to it, visually, by way of peripheral awareness.[40] Likewise, as I listen to Brahms's Piano Concerto No. 1, I am related to the violas, auditorily, by way of peripheral awareness. I am not related to them as I am to the piano (that is, by way of focal awareness), nor as I am to the frosty winds of Kamchatka's plains (that is, by way of unawareness).

In these two cases, different stimuli compete for the focus of awareness within a single perceptual modality: the *Tractatus* versus the laptop, the violas versus the piano. But the competition for the focus of awareness can be not only intra-modal, but also inter-modal. If I decide to concentrate on the next movement in the concerto, I become focally aware of the piano, and the laptop recedes to an attentional background, where it keeps company with the *Tractatus* and the violas. But I may then "snap out" of the concerto and turn my attention, say, to the copy of the *Tractatus*; the sound of the piano then sinks back, where it joins the violas' sound and the laptop.[41]

Just as competition for the focus of awareness takes place *across*, and not only *within*, perceptual modalities, so it can take place *between* perceptual awareness and non-perceptual awareness. As I listen to Brahms's concerto, I might become increasingly anxious about not having paid last month's electricity bill. In the process, I might move from being focally aware, perceptually, of the piano's sound and only peripherally aware, anxiously, of the fact that I have yet to pay last month's bill, to being focally aware, anxiously, of having to pay the bill, and only peripherally aware, perceptually, of the piano's sound.[42]

---

[40] The case of visual awareness is actually slightly misleading, because, as I will discuss more fully in Chapter 5, there are two different focal/peripheral distinctions that apply to it, one more physiologically based and one more psychologically based.

[41] As these ruminations already bring out, there is an important distinction to draw between two kinds of attention, one that is built into the structure of the sense organs and one that is purely mental. I will say more about this in Chapter 7.

[42] It might be objected that in such a case the piano's sound drops altogether out of awareness. But this need not be the case. Consider the long-distance truck driver, who may become pensive on one of her trips, contemplating ever loftier subjects: yesterday's baseball game, what the new year may have in store, what she hopes to "get from life." The driver is focally aware, intellectually, of yesterday's

These considerations point to the richness of peripheral awareness. The elements stalking the periphery of one's conscious awareness as one stares at a rainbow can be dazzling: the dark shadows below the rainbow, the distant sound of car engines on the highway across the field, the warm and pleasant mood of calm satisfaction, the feel of the moist grass against the back of one's shirt, and the thought of the imminent drive back home, all surround one's strictly visual awareness of the rainbow and make an unmistakable contribution to the overall way it is like for one to have one's overall conscious experience at the time.[43] It was to capture this richness of peripheral awareness and its place in normal conscious experience that William James (1890/1918) introduced the notion of the fringe of consciousness and the phenomenologists the notion of marginal consciousness.[44]

My contention is that another constant element in the fringe of consciousness is awareness of one's concurrent experience. A full list of the peripheral elements in the above rainbow experience would have to include awareness of that very experience. This would be peripheral inner awareness in the normal go of things, though could turn into focal inner awareness when the subject introspects.

Peripheral inner awareness differs from focal inner awareness along a number of dimensions. While focal inner awareness is *rare*, in that our stream of consciousness takes explicit notice of itself relatively infrequently, peripheral inner awareness is virtually *ubiquitous*, in that it "hums" in the background of our stream of consciousness with nearly absolute constancy and is absent only when replaced by focal inner awareness.[45]

game or of the meaning of life. But she is not completely unaware of the cornfields about her and the road before her. Rather, she is peripherally aware, visually, of the fields and road. To see this, compare the overall state of awareness of a colorblind truck driver. Her overall state of awareness appears to be at least somewhat different. This is because the contents of her peripheral perceptual awareness are different, even if the contents of her focal intellectual awareness are the same.

[43] In the nature of things, this is bound to be a very partial list. A full list of the elements in the periphery of the experience would surely run much longer than this.

[44] For the most comprehensive treatment of this notion in the phenomenological tradition, see Gurwitsch 1985 (a draft of which apparently existed already in 1950); also Husserl (1928/1964), who called it *non-thematic consciousness*.

[45] This ubiquity has been noted by philosophers from William James to David Chalmers. James (1961: 42) wrote that "whatever I may be thinking of, I am always at the same time more or less aware of myself, of my personal existence." More recently, Chalmers (1996: 10) has written: "One sometimes feels that there is something to conscious experience that transcends all these specific elements [visual experiences, auditory, olfactory, tactile, and taste experiences, experiences of hot and cold, pain and

Furthermore, while focal inner awareness is ordinarily *voluntary*, peripheral inner awareness is not only not voluntary, but in fact *involuntary*: not only do we not choose to have it; we cannot "shut it down" even if we want to. As well, focal inner awareness is for the most part *effortful*, in that it involves concentration (if ever so slight), whereas peripheral inner awareness is *effortless*, in that it requires no deliberate personal-level decision to initiate or sustain. (This is similar to the difference between, say, calculating and seeing: the former is something one does, the latter something that happens to one.)

I do not mean these observations as definitional of peripheral inner awareness. But the very fact that such observations can be made suggests that there is a genuine subject matter we are talking about—that peripheral inner awareness is a psychologically real phenomenon. My claim, and I do not mean it as trivial or uncontroversial, is that subjective character just is normally peripheral inner awareness. I will say much more on this in Chapter 5. In the remainder of this subsection I wish only to fend off the worry that there is no such thing as subjective character, understood as normally peripheral inner awareness.

To my mind, the best reason to think that there is such a thing as peripheral inner awareness is phenomenological: peripheral inner awareness is simply phenomenologically manifest. I realize, however, that such declamations do not tend to win arguments. Let me, therefore, offer some theoretically based considerations in defense of peripheral inner awareness.[46] These considerations should not be confused, however, for the original motivation for admitting peripheral inner awareness. Rather, they are to be thought of as indirect indicators of something of which I claim we have much more direct knowledge.

A first consideration is that it would be quite odd if, despite applying to all forms of outer awareness, the focal/peripheral distinction did not

---

other bodily sensations, and conscious thoughts]: a kind of background hum, for instance, that is somehow fundamental to consciousness and that is there even when the other components are not. This phenomenology of self is so deep and intangible that it sometimes seems illusory, consisting of nothing over and above specific elements such as those listed above. Still, there seems to be something to the phenomenology of self, even if it is very hard to pin down." See also Kapitan 1999.

[46] Note, however, that these considerations cannot be quite demonstrative. For it is difficult to argue compellingly for the very existence of a mental phenomenon. Thus, I have yet to encounter an effective argument against eliminativism about the propositional attitudes, or about consciousness and qualia, say of the sort espoused by Churchland (1984).

apply to inner awareness. That would cast inner awareness as inexplicably exceptional. More plausibly, just as every other awareness admits of a focal variety and peripheral variety, so inner awareness comes in these two varieties.

Another consideration is that the kind of adaptational/functional advantages commonly attributed to peripheral awareness in general speak in favor of the existence of peripheral awareness of one's conscious experiences. This argument is a complex one, and I will only outline it here; the issue will be discussed more thoroughly in Chapter 7.[47] It is commonly thought that the function of the fringe of consciousness is to augment the availability of some contents (see Mangan 2001). Our capacities for attentive, focused awareness are limited, and, in order not to overburden consciousness and fill it with 'noise', large parts of the contents a person is aware of must remain outside the focus of her awareness. But some contents are important enough not to be excluded from the sphere of consciousness altogether, where their availability for quick and relatively effortless retrieval would be dramatically diminished. These contents are kept in the fringe of consciousness. That is, they become contents of peripheral awareness. My claim is that the functional advantages of keeping information about the peripheries of (say) one's visual field in the fringe of consciousness are at least matched by the advantages of keeping there information about one's concurrent experience.

In addition, considerations that seem to militate against peripheral inner awareness can be explained away. To be sure, peripheral inner awareness is not as phenomenologically impressive as, say, the qualitative character of color experience. But the common tendency to take color experiences as the gold standard of phenomenology may be theoretically limiting inasmuch as it may set the bar too high. For virtually any other phenomenology is bound to be milder.[48]

Furthermore, special difficulties attach to noticing phenomena of peripheral awareness. Suppose a philosopher went eliminativist with respect to peripheral vision, claiming that there is simply no such thing. How would we convince her that there *is* such a thing? We face here a

---

[47] See also Kriegel 2004b.

[48] In this respect, the proponent of peripheral inner awareness is in a similar position to other philosophers who attempt to argue for the existence of a controversial phenomenology. For discussion of these issues, see Kriegel 2007a.

peculiar methodological difficulty, in that, whenever we want to direct our attention to the periphery of our visual awareness, the latter thereby becomes the focal center. And yet we are disinclined to conclude that our eliminativist is right and there really is no such thing as peripheral visual awareness. Similar remarks apply to eliminativism about peripheral inner awareness, as I will press in Chapter 5. If we attempt to turn our attention to it, it inevitably transforms into focal inner awareness. But this should not be taken as grounds for rejecting the existence of peripheral inner awareness.

Further yet, peripheral inner awareness may be singularly elusive among conscious phenomena, because of its ubiquity and involuntariness. These two characteristics may partially explain the fact that peripheral inner awareness does not lend itself to easy noticing. It is in general difficult to notice even stimuli that are constant for a relatively short time, such as the hum of the refrigerator pump. If peripheral inner awareness is indeed ubiquitous, its constancy throughout our waking life would account for the fact that it is so phenomenologically elusive. And the fact that it is involuntary means that we cannot control the conditions of its presence and "compare," as it were, a situation in which it is present with one in which it is absent and bring it into sharper relief. This consideration is intended to explain away any initial appeal there might be to the idea that there is no such thing as peripheral inner awareness.[49]

Qualitative Character, Subjective Character, and Phenomenal Character

Having defended the psychological reality of both qualitative and subjective character as two conceptually distinct components of phenomenal character,

---

[49] One might worry that the notion of peripheral inner awareness is ill defined, in that it is unclear what precisely one is supposed to be aware of when one is peripherally aware of one's current experience. Is one aware of oneself as the subject of experience, or only of the experience itself? Is one aware of the experience itself, or only of its properties? If the latter, is one aware of all the experience's non-relational properties or only, say, of its qualitative properties? Is one aware of the experience's temporal duration, or only of its presence at single instants? However, rather than taking these questions to pose a threat to the soundness of the notion of peripheral inner awareness, we could see them as indicating that peripheral inner awareness is a real phenomenon in need of investigation. These are, in effect, questions about the precise content of peripheral awareness of one's conscious experiences. It would be quite curious for such specific questions to arise if the phenomenon they addressed was a mere illusion. Nonetheless, I will actually address all these questions in Chapter 5.

let me take up the question of their interrelation. In the first instance, we may distinguish four views on the matter:

(*a*) The qualitative and the subjective are mutually inseparable.
(*b*) The qualitative is separable from the subjective, but not conversely.
(*c*) The subjective is separable from the qualitative, but not conversely.
(*d*) The qualitative and the subjective are mutually separable.

I use the term "separable" to indicate the possibility of different extensions. In this sense, F is separable from G if there is a metaphysically possible world in which F is instantiated but G is not.[50]

An even more central question, given present purposes, concerns the interrelations among qualitative, subjective, and phenomenal character. Phenomenal character, recall, is whatever property is responsible for the mystery of consciousness. The question is how this property relates to qualitative character and to subjective character. There are three families of views we need to consider here:

(*e*) *Qualitativism:* phenomenal character is identical with qualitative character.

(*f*) *Subjectivism:* phenomenal character is one and the same as subjective character.

(*g*) *Compresentism:* phenomenal character is a certain compresence of qualitative character and subjective character.

Importantly, these three views play out very differently depending on one's preferences among (*a*)–(*d*). Compare, for example, versions of qualitativism that allow for the separability of qualitative character from subjective character, as in (*b*) and (*d*), with those that disallow it, as in (*a*) and (*c*):

(*e*1) *Separatist Qualitativism:* phenomenal character is identical with qualitative character, which is separable from subjective character.

(*e*2) *Inseparatist Qualitativism:* phenomenal character is identical with qualitative character, which is inseparable from subjective character.

---

[50] It would not follow that G is also separable from F: that would be the case only if there is also a metaphysically possible world in which G is instantiated but F is not.

The same distinction applies to subjectivism. As for compresentism, it could come in four different varieties, depending on which of (a)–(d) is combined with (g).

Tracing out the interrelations among all these different combinations is probably not worthwhile on a cost–benefit analysis, but let me point out some of the major interrelations. Most importantly, the difference between inseparatist qualitativism and inseparatist subjectivism is this: the former is consistent with it being possible that subjective character should occur without qualitative character (whereas the latter is inconsistent with it being possible), but insists that, if such a thing is possible, the free-floating subjective character does not constitute phenomenal character (that is, would not be the kind of thing that generates the mystery of consciousness); by contrast, the latter is consistent (whereas the former is not) with it being possible that qualitative character should occur without subjective character, but insists that, if such a thing is possible, the free-floating qualitative character does not constitute phenomenal character. Now, there is also a version of compresentism, consisting of the combination of (g) and (c), that is consistent with the possibility of free-floating subjective character but insists it would not qualify as phenomenal character. The difference is that that version of compresentism is inconsistent with the impossibility of free-floating subjective character, whereas inseparatist qualitativism is consistent with both its possibility its and impossibility. A parallel exists for inseparatist subjectivism, in the form of the combination of (g) and (b). In addition, however, there is a version of compresentism that is inconsistent with the possibility of any free-floaters—namely, the combination of (g) and (a).

The position I adopted at the end of Chapter 1 is most naturally interpreted as committed to inseparatist subjectivism or a version of compresentism that either combines (g) and (b) or combines (g) and (a). On the scheme I have adopted, bluish-for-me-ness, reddish-for-me-ness, trumpet-ish-for-me-ness, and so on are all phenomenal characters that are determinates of the determinable something-for-me-ness (or plain for-me-ness for short). One can focus the mind purely on subjective character by considering that which remains invariant among all the different determinates, and on qualitative character by considering that which varies among them. This is what accounts for their conceptual distinctness. But either (i) the two are inseparable (in that there can be no for-me-ness in the absence of some qualitative character or other being for me, and there is no qualitative character that is not for me), as in the compresentism combining (g) and (a), or (ii) the qualitative is separable from the subjective but free-floating qualitative character does not qualify as phenomenal character, as in inseparatist subjectivism and the compresentism combining (g) and (b).[51]

Thus my sympathies lie mostly with inseparatist subjectivism and the version of compresentism that combines (g) and (b). I have also some non-negligible sympathy for separatist subjectivism and inseparatist qualitativism and the other two versions of compresentism just mentioned. What I truly have no sympathy for is separatist qualitativism (e1 above). What I want to exclude is the idea that subjective character has no constitutive place in phenomenal character. On the contrary, I hold that phenomenal character necessarily involves subjective character.

This commitment regarding the nature of the explanandum of the theory of phenomenal consciousness may strike some readers as controversial. And indeed it is. Moreover, it is unclear how a case might be made for it. It is notoriously difficult to argue on such matters, and arguments often appear to devolve quickly into more or less egregious question-begging.[52] However, this predicament bedevils all theories of phenomenal consciousness. Thus, proponents of representationalism seem to presuppose separatist qualitativism.[53] Their representational account of phenomenal character is naturally thought of as factorizable into (i) a representational account of qualitative character and (ii) the view that phenomenal character is nothing but qualitative character. Similarly, many proponents of higher-order theory seem to presuppose separatist subjectivism. Their theory can be factorized into (i) a higher-order account of subjective character and (ii) the view that phenomenal character is

---

[51] I offer no argument for this position, because, once we have fixed our ideas on what kind of phenomena qualitative and subjective character are supposed to be, it is more a matter of decision than discovery to determine what is the best way to use them.

[52] As a measure of this, consider that phenomena of absent-minded perception, and phenomena similar to those, have been argued by some representationalists (and their opponents) to demonstrate the falsity of higher-order theories (Dretske 1993, Block 1995)—and by higher-order theorists to demonstrate the opposite (Carruthers 1989, Rosenthal 1991). (In both cases, the argumentation is most naturally construed as targeting the qualitativist or subjectivist factor in the two-factor interpretation of those theories.)

[53] Correspondingly, some of their opponents have embraced the same presupposition. I am thinking mostly of anti-representationalists such as Block (1990a, 1996).

nothing but subjective character.[54] But, arguing in favor of either separatist qualitativism or separatist subjectivism is no easier than arguing for, say, inseparatist subjectivism.

In fact, there is one major advantage in being committed to something like inseparatist subjectivism or compresentism over being committed to separatist qualitativism or separatist subjectivism. This is that the former commitment requires the overall theory of consciousness to produce accounts of both qualitative and subjective character, which means that, if it turns out that one of them is not a component of phenomenal character after all, we are still left with an account of the component that did not drop out of the picture. Thus, in Chapters 3 and 4 I will offer accounts of qualitative and subjective character (respectively). My preference for inseparatist subjectivism or one of the aforementioned two versions of compresentism entails combining these two accounts into an overall theory of phenomenal character in one of three specific ways. But if a reader prefers a different view of the interrelations among qualitative, subjective, and phenomenal character, they could combine the two accounts in a different way (or leave one of the two accounts outside the theory of phenomenal character).

For these reasons, I do not offer here argumentation in support of my preferred view(s) on the interrelations. (Put briskly, the reasons are that it is hard and that it is unnecessary.) Nonetheless, I include an appendix to this book that presents arguments in favor of the thesis that phenomenal consciousness necessarily involves subjective character—that is, that separatist qualitativism is false. I do so only in an appendix, and not in an integral chapter, because I want the reader to keep in mind that representationalists do not typically *support*, but rather *suppose*, their separatist qualitativism, while higher-order theorists do the same with their separatist subjectivism.[55] This is reasonable, given how hard it is to make the phenomenological case for such positions. But, if it is reasonable for

---

[54] A combined account that would allow for inseparatism or compresentism and would capitalize on much of the work that has already been done within a naturalist framework would simply marry a representationalist account of qualitative character with a higher-order account of subjective character. Lycan's theory of consciousness (1996) takes this form. The account I will offer in the chapters that follow will diverge from this template mostly on the side of subjective character. I will embrace a version of representationalism (albeit a peculiar one) about qualitative character, but will reject a higher-order account of subjective character and embrace in its stead a self-representational account.

[55] Or at least they do not support their view and argue for it in a clearly non-question-begging way.

these theorists to proceed in this way, it should also be reasonable for us to do the same here. If they have taken out a loan on phenomenology that they have not repaid, we should be entitled to the same. The fact that in the Appendix I will venture to argue for an inseparatist/compresentist position should not obscure that. And the fact that the arguments are likely to be less than fully compelling (given that argumentation in this area tends to be problematic) should not tempt us to forget that these arguments are in the present context theoretical supererogation.

The main message of this section, in sum, is that the notion of subjective character is central to phenomenal consciousness. This is in opposition to several forms of skepticism about that notion. The most extreme of those is eliminativism about subjective character: the view that there is no such thing. In arguing above for the psychological reality of normally peripheral inner awareness, and taking subjective character to consist therein, I have rejected this view. A less extreme skepticism admits the existence of subjective character but denies that it is universal in phenomenally conscious states. I will address this threat in Chapter 5. Less extreme yet is the view that subjective character is a universal but unnecessary component of phenomenal consciousness. This final threat will be taken up most directly in the Appendix, but, ultimately, I suspect that there is no hope for anything like a *demonstration* in this area.

4. Conclusion: Subjective Consciousness

The approach that arises from the discussion in the last few paragraphs is something like the following. We should start by distinguishing between a notion of *qualitative consciousness* and a notion of *subjective consciousness*, then pursue the theory of each while setting aside their relationship to each other and to *phenomenal* consciousness. If a consensus emerges in the future regarding this additional matter, that consensus could then produce theories of phenomenal consciousness from the existing theories of qualitative and subjective consciousness. Until then, we could conceive of the theory of phenomenal consciousness in terms of a conjunction of conditionals of the form "if separatist qualitativism is true, then p; and if inseparatist qualitativism is true, then q; and if separatist subjectivism is true, then r; and if inseparatist subjectivism is true, then s; and if version one of compresentism is true, then t; and if version two of compresentism is true . . ." and so on and so forth.

With this in mind, this book is devoted almost entirely to subjective consciousness. Nonetheless, the next chapter develops and defends an account of qualitative consciousness. This serves to "cover my bases" regarding qualitative character, even as I pursue most centrally the nature of subjective character. The focus on subjective consciousness is due to a number of factors. First and foremost, it is an expression of my conviction in the greater centrality of subjective character to phenomenal consciousness, as that which is invariant across all phenomenal characters and captures the existence (rather than identity) condition of phenomenality. Secondly, theories of qualitative consciousness that are quite similar to what I want to defend are already available and fairly well developed in the literature, but available well-developed theories of subjective consciousness tend to be very different from the kind of account I want to defend. Thirdly, I simply have much more to say that is new, or relatively new, about subjective consciousness.

To sum up, in this chapter I have made three main claims about phenomenal consciousness. In Section 1 I claimed that phenomenal consciousness is best thought of as a variety of intransitive state consciousness. In Section 2 I claimed that it is distinguishable from, though intimately connected with, access consciousness; more specifically, that its subjective component is the categorical basis of access consciousness. In Section 3 I expanded on the distinction between its qualitative and subjective components, and adopted the view that either phenomenal character is one and the same as subjective character but that subjective character somehow involves qualitative character, or phenomenal consciousness is a certain kind of compresence of qualitative and subjective character.[56]

---

[56] For comments on a draft of this chapter I would like to thank Bill Lycan, Ken Williford, and an anonymous referee. I have also benefited from conversations with David Chalmers, Terry Horgan, Joe Levine, and David Rosenthal.

3

A Representational Account of Qualitative Character

When you have a conscious experience of a red apple, there is a reddish way it is like for you to have your experience; this is the experience's phenomenal character. The experience also represents a red surface; this is its representational content. Many philosophers have recently argued that the phenomenal character of the experience is *one and the same* as its representational content: the reddish way it is like for you to have the experience just is the experience's representation of the apple's red surface. Call this view the *representational theory of phenomenal consciousness*, or *representationalism* for short.

So understood, representationalism comes in two main varieties. One maintains that, although phenomenal character is one and the same as some kind of representational content, the relevant content cannot be understood in non-phenomenal terms (or at least we have no idea how to understand it so); call this *non-reductive representationalism* (McGinn 1988, Horgan and Tienson 2002, Chalmers 2004). Another maintains that not only is phenomenal character one and the same as some representational content, but that content can be understood in purely non-phenomenal terms; call this *reductive representationalism* (Harman 1990, Shoemaker 1994a, 1994c, 2002, Dretske 1995, Tye 1992, 1995, 2000, 2002, Thau 2002). Reductive representationalism is significant, because many believe that the outlines of a reductive theory of representational content in physical terms are already in place. If phenomenal character is nothing but representational content, and representational content is nothing but some sort of physical property, then phenomenal character is nothing but some physical property.

This chapter examines the prospects for reductive representationalism. I will argue that, although reductive representationalism is false as a theory of *phenomenal* character, a special version of it is true as a theory of *qualitative* character. Because my concern in this chapter is almost exclusively with the reductive variety of representationalism, I will drop the qualifier "reductive" unless there is special reason not to. The chapter is divided roughly into two parts. The first spans Sections 1–3: Section 1 introduces reductive representationalism; Section 2 examines the motivation for it; Section 3 notes that it cannot account for the subjective character of experience. The second part spans Sections 4–7: Section 4 introduces the possibility of a representationalism restricted to qualitative character; Section 5 develops an objection to the standard version of representationalism; Section 6 proposes a modified representationalism, which I call *response-dependent representationalism*; Section 7 considers objections to the above.

1. The Representational Theory of Phenomenal Consciousness

Representationalism holds that a conscious experience has reddish phenomenal character only if it represents the red surface or volume of an object in the external world. Thus, your experience of the apple before you is reddish because it represents the apple's red surface, and my experience of a glass of shiraz is reddish because it represents the glass red volume.

The most thorough representational account of phenomenal character is probably Michael Tye's *PANIC theory* (1990, 1995, 2000, 2002). According to PANIC theory, phenomenal character is identical with a specific kind of representational content. The relevant content has four distinguishing characteristics. It is:

(a) poised
(b) abstract
(c) non-conceptual
(d) intentional

We will see what these characteristics are momentarily. Tye calls Poised, Abstract, Non-conceptual, Intentional Content *PANIC*; hence the theory's name. The thesis of PANIC theory is simply that the phenomenal character of a conscious experience is identical with the experience's PANIC.[1] Its PANIC is what makes it the conscious experience it is and a conscious experience at all.

Let us review the four characteristics that make a representational content amount to phenomenal character. First, what is it for a content to be *poised*? Tye (2000: 62) writes:

This condition is essentially a functional role one. The key idea is that experiences and feelings, *qua* bearers of phenomenal character, play a certain distinctive functional role. They . . . stand ready and available to make a direct impact on beliefs and/or desires.

That is, a content C is poised iff C plays a distinctive functional role R—namely, the role of being available for "direct impact" on propositional attitudes.

Next, what is it for a content to be *abstract*? This condition concerns the ontology of contents, and requires that the relevant content involve no concrete constituents. Tye (2000: 62) says that abstract content is "content into which no particular concrete objects or surfaces enter. This is required by the case of hallucinatory experiences . . ." So a content C is abstract just in case only abstract entities can "enter" into it, where "entering into a content C" means being a *constituent* of C. Importantly, the claim is not that a content is abstract if a state that carries it represents abstracta only. The state can represent concreta as well. But it represents those concreta in virtue of standing in a certain relation to abstracta—the "carrying" relation. Thus the abstracta make up that which is carried—that is, the content.

Perhaps the most important characteristic of PANICs is the fact that they are *non-conceptual*, which Tye (2000: 61) explicates as follows:

Color experiences . . . subjectively vary in ways that far outstrip our color concepts. For example the experience of the determinate shade, red_{29}, is phenomenally different from that of the shade, red_{32}. But I have no such concept as red_{29}. So, I cannot see something as red_{29} or recognize that specific shade as such. For example, if I go into a paint store and look at a chart of reds, I cannot pick out red_{29}.

Thus, your conscious experience of a red fire engine represents the fire engine as being a specific shade of red, say red_{17}. Yet you are unlikely to

---

[1] More accurately, Tye holds that conscious experiences normally carry more than one representational content, but, of the various representational contents they carry, only PANIC is identical with their phenomenal character (see Tye 1996, 2000: ch. 4).

distinguish red$_{17}$ from a sample of red$_{18}$ tomorrow, nor pass many of the other standard tests for concept possession. So your experience represents a shade of color for which you have no concept, and is therefore a form of non-conceptual representation.

Finally, what makes a content *intentional*? Content is intentional, we are told, in the sense that it is *intensional* (Tye 2000: 54–5): from the fact that you have a perceptual experience of a red surface, it does not follow that there *is* a red surface of which you have a perceptual experience, and from the facts that you have a perceptual experience of a red surface and that the color red is identical to reflectance property F, it does not follow that you have a perceptual experience of an F surface.

In conclusion, according to Tye, conscious experiences have a representational content that stands ready to make a direct impact on propositional attitudes, has no concrete constituents, represents features for which the subject has no concepts, and is intensional. The phenomenal character of conscious experiences is nothing but this sort of representational content.

PANIC theory is supposed to apply not only to visual experiences, but to all kinds of conscious experience: experiences in other perceptual modalities, somatic experiences, and emotional experiences. It is quite easy to see how it would apply to perceptual experiences in other modalities. Auditory experiences represent the sounds of external objects, olfactory experiences represent their odors, gustatory experiences represent their flavors, and so on. Tye's claim is that these perceptual experiences all have PANICs, with which their phenomenal characters are identical. However, it is more difficult to see how PANIC theory extends to somatic and emotional experiences.

When one has a pain, an itch, or a tickle in one's arm, one's conscious experience has a hurt-ish, itch-ish, or ticklish phenomenal character. Many philosophers have held that such experiences are altogether non-representational: there is nothing they are experiences of. Tye's burden of proof is therefore twofold. He must show, first, that such somatic experiences do represent certain events in the external world, and then, that their having phenomenal character is nothing over and above their doing so.

The first thing to note in this context is that, when we feel a pain or a tickle, we always feel it in a specific region of our body. A toothache is felt in the tooth, a headache in the head, and a stomachache in the stomach. This suggests that the phrase "pain experience" is best understood as shorthand for "experience of pain," where the pain is experienced as in the tooth, the head, or the stomach. So pain experiences are experiences of painful bodily events in the same sense in which color experiences are experiences of colorful surfaces and volumes—that is, in the intentional sense of "of." We can thus say that pain experiences represent painful bodily events.[2] As is to be expected from representations, somatic experiences can also *misrepresent* painful bodily events. For instance, in cases of phantom limb experiences, a person may have an experience of pain in her arm long after the arm had been amputated.[3]

Conscious emotional experiences and moods pose an even sharper intuitive challenge to PANIC theory (and representationalism in general). The peculiar qualities of conscious anger or fear, for instance, do not seem to be qualities of any angering or fearsome worldly objects. Likewise, being depressed is not a matter of representing some depressing object in a way that results in a conscious experience with a depress-ish phenomenal character.

Tye attempts to accommodate conscious emotions and moods again in terms of the representation of bodily events. But, unlike the bodily events represented by somatic experiences, those represented by emotional experiences often take place in internal organs. Thus, "if one feels sudden jealousy, one is likely to feel one's stomach sink, one's heart beat faster, one's blood pressure increase" (Tye 2000: 51). The representation of these internal bodily events accounts for the phenomenal character of conscious jealousy.[4] As for conscious moods, Tye claims that their

---

[2] Here the adjective "painful" modifies not the experience but its object—what is being experienced. This is, of course, the ordinary usage of the word. Such painful events are, at bottom, tissue damages. This does not mean, however, that they must be represented *as* tissue damages, just as colorful objects, although at bottom objects that reflect a certain percentage of the light spectrum (say), need not be represented *as* reflecting the relevant percentage of the light spectrum.

[3] So Tye's claim is that the phenomenal character of somatic experiences is nothing over and above the representation of the relevant bodily events. He writes (Tye 1990: 332): "Now pain experiences, if they are anywhere, are in the head. But in the case of a pain in the leg, what the pain experience tracks, when everything is functioning normally, is tissue damage in the leg. So [it] is a token sensory experience which represents something in the leg is damaged." For details, see Tye 1990, 1995: ch. 4.

[4] Similarly for conscious anger (Tye 1995: 126): "Suppose you suddenly feel extremely angry. Your body will change in all sorts of ways: for example, your blood pressure will rise, your nostrils will flare, your face will flush ... These physical changes are registered in the sensory receptors distributed

phenomenal character is a matter of the representation of bodily changes in oneself as a whole. These attempts at accommodating conscious emotions and moods may or may not be particularly plausible. A more plausible approach to moods might construe their representational content as concerned with changes in the world as a whole, rather than in oneself as a whole.[5] This approach strikes me as capturing better the representational content of conscious moods. But in any case, it does not seem that the case of conscious emotions and moods leaves the representationalist speechless. There is a variety of moves she can make in trying to accommodate them.

A consequence of this sort of representationalism is *externalism* about phenomenal character. Since it is widely thought that there are good reasons to individuate representational content partly by appeal to facts outside the subject's head (Putnam 1975), the identification of phenomenal character with representational content would entail an externalistic individuation of phenomenal character. This sort of *phenomenal externalism* is explicitly embraced by Dretske (1996), Lycan (2001b), and others.

2. Motivations for Representationalism

There are two main motivations for representationalism. The first is its promise to grease the wheels of naturalization. The second is purely phenomenological, and has to do with the so-called transparency of experience.

---

throughout your body. In response to the activity in your receptors, you will mechanically build up a complex representation of how your body has changed, of the new body state you are in ... The feeling you undergo consists in the complex sensory representation of these changes." For details, see the end of Tye 1995: ch. 4. A similar view was propounded by Armstrong (1977: 186) two decades earlier: "it is not so clear whether there really are peculiar qualities associated with the emotions. The different patterns of bodily sensations associated with the different emotions may be sufficient to do phenomenological justice to the emotions." I offer a critical discussion of this approach to emotional experiences in Kriegel 2002d.

[5] Thus, consider the following suggestion by Seager (1999: 183; emphasis in original): "Being depressed is a way of being conscious of things in general: everything seems worthless, or pointless, dull and profitless. That is, more or less, *everything* is represented as being worthless, or pointless, dull and profitless. It is ... impossible for a conscious being to be in a state of consciousness which consists of nothing but unfocused depression; there always remains a host of objects of consciousness and without these objects there would be no remaining state of consciousness."

Representationalism and Naturalization

The reductive strategy of representationalism is to push the mystery allegedly involved in conscious experience out of the mind and into the world. Consider the following passage by Shoemaker (1994a: 23):

[Wittgenstein] talks about the "feeling of an unbridgeable gulf between consciousness and brain processes," which occurs when I "turn my attention in a particular way on to my own consciousness, and, astonished, say to myself: THIS is supposed to be produced by processes in the brain!—as it were clutching my forehead" . . . But we can get much the same puzzle without turning our attention inwards. I look at a shiny red apple and say to myself "THIS is supposed to be a cloud of electrons, protons, etc., scattered through mostly empty space." And, focusing on its color, I say "THIS is supposed to be a reflectance property of the surface of such a cloud of fundamental particles."

What is mystifying about the reddish phenomenal character of your conscious experience is how it could be constituted by the electro-chemical activity of gray matter. Shoemaker's suggestion is that the very same mystery appears to be involved in what your conscious experience is an experience *of*—that is, how the red apple itself could be constituted by a buzzing cloud of molecules. The important point is that it is quite unlikely that we have here two independent mysteries, incidentally brought together through the representation relation holding between reddish experiences and red objects. It is more likely that there is only one mystery, which is then duplicated through representation. Traditional secondary quality theorists have tended to think that the mystery concerns in the first instance the way reddish experiences are constituted by gray matter, and is then duplicated via the experiences' representation of external objects. Representationalists reverse this explanation, claiming that the source of the mystery is the way red objects in the world are constituted by colorless clouds of molecules, and that reddish experiences merely *inherit* this mysterious air by representing red objects (Byrne 2006).[6]

---

[6] The opposite view is what is known as *Projectivism*, the view that worldly objects have no color in and of themselves, but our conscious experiences project their qualitative character onto them (Boghossian and Velleman 1989, Baldwin 1992). Projectivists will claim that the source of mystery is the way our reddish experiences are constituted by brain processes, and red objects merely inherit their mysterious air through the fact that they are represented by reddish experiences.

Once the mystery allegedly involved in conscious experience has thus been pushed out to the represented objects, it remains only to make sure that representational content can be accounted for in unmysterious terms. Thus the project of representationalism is to effect a two-step demystification of phenomenal character: first offer a reductive account of it in terms of representational content, then offer a reductive account of representational content in physical terms. The outlines of a physicalist account of representational content have been developed most fully and convincingly, to my mind, by Fred Dretske (1981, 1986, 1988).[7] In the remainder of this subsection, I offer a quick review of Dretske's strategy for naturalizing representation.

According to Dretske's *teleo-informational semantics*, a subject harbors a mental representation of the fact that it is raining just in case she is in a brain state whose function is to carry information about the fact that it is raining. To understand what this means, we need to understand (i) what *information* is, (ii) what *carrying* information is, and (iii) what having the *function* of carrying information is.

(i) Every event or fact in the world *generates* a certain amount of information. This information consists, in some sense, in the set of all possibilities the event or fact rules out. Thus, when it is raining, this fact rules out the possibilities that it is dry, that it is snowing, and so on. We may think of the information generated by an event or fact in terms of the narrowing of the set of all possible worlds to the set of all possible worlds consistent with its occurrence.

(ii) Some events and facts in the world depend on others, in that they cannot normally take place unless those other events or facts do. Moreover, sometimes this dependence is not accidental, but is due to the laws of nature. That is, some events and facts are *nomically dependent* upon other events and facts. Thus, it is a law of nature (a zoological law, as it happens) that certain kinds of snail do not normally venture out unless it is raining (or has recently been raining). So the fact that Gail the snail ventured out on Sunday at noon is nomically dependent upon the fact that it was raining (or had recently been raining) on Sunday at noon. When fact A nomically depends upon fact B in this way, A is said to *carry information* about B. More

---

[7] For other promising accounts, see Stampe 1977, Millikan 1984, Harman 1987, Fodor 1990, Proust 1997.

specifically, A *carries* the information *generated* by B. The fact that Gail the snail ventured out on Sunday at noon carries the information (generated by the fact) that it was raining (or had recently been raining) on Sunday at noon. Of particular interest to us are certain events in, and facts regarding, the brains of sentient organisms. There are laws of nature—neurobiological laws, this time—that dictate which neurophysiological events take place in a brain under which conditions. Thus, it may be a matter of these laws that a type of neurophysiological event N in Jim's brain cannot normally take place unless it is raining. If so, N is nomically dependent on its raining, and therefore carries the information that it is raining. Thus, if a token N-state took place in Jim's brain on Sunday at noon, it would carry the information that it was raining on Sunday at noon. Thus the present framework allows us to see how a brain state might be said, in rigorous information-theoretic terms, to carry information.

(iii) Some neurophysiological events in the brain are recruited to play a specific functional role in the cerebral economy of the organism, and some are so recruited in virtue of carrying the information they do. Thus, N may be recruited to play the kind of functional role involved in causing Jim to pick up an umbrella or close the window. When a neurophysiological event in the brain is recruited in this way, thanks to the information it carries, it is said to have the *function* of carrying that information.

On Dretske's proposal, a neurophysiological event in the brain that has the function of carrying information about the fact that it is raining represents that fact. More generally, whenever a brain event A has the function of carrying information about B, A constitutes a mental representation of B. B then constitutes the representational content of A. The fact that it is raining is the representational content of the mental state constituted (or realized) by the neurophysiological event nomically dependent thereupon.

Note that this account of mental representation employs physical ingredients exclusively. A is a physical event in, or fact regarding, the subject's brain. B is an event or fact in the subject's physical environment. The relation between A and B is (in an appropriate sense) a physical relation. Hence the physicalistic promise of teleo-informational semantics: the promise to account for mental representation in purely physicalistic terms.

Dretske's account of mental representation is not without its critics.[8] But it has made us quite confident that representational content could eventually yield to a satisfactory account in physical terms. If the phenomenal character of conscious experience could be accounted for in representational terms, then we would be justified in expecting it to yield to a satisfactory account in physical terms. Thus the prospect of reducing phenomenal character to representational content carries with it the promise of an ultimate physicalist reduction of phenomenal character.

Representationalism and Transparency

The second motivation for representationalism is more direct. It has to do not with the payoff of representationalism, but with its grounds: the so-called *transparency of experience*.[9] Conscious experience is transparent, according to several philosophers going back to Moore, in that, whenever we try to introspect one of our experiences, we can become acquainted only with what it is an experience *of* —not with the experiencing itself.[10] We thus cannot help but see the world right through the experience of it, as though the experience were, in itself, transparent. Probably the most influential articulation of the transparency thesis is Gilbert Harman's (1990). Harman (1990: 667) encourages us to perform the following exercise:

Look at a tree and try to turn your attention to intrinsic features of your visual experience. I predict you will find that the only features there to turn your attention to will be features of the presented tree . . .

---

[8] See Millikan 1990, Adams 1991, Dennett 1991, and Kim 1991 for a sample.

[9] After all, representationalism is an initially somewhat unintuitive view, at least to the traditional philosopher. Intuitively, we tend to think of reddish experiences as experiences that do not simply represent red objects, but represent them in a specific *way*—a reddish way. The intuitive outlook has it that the basis of the experience's reddishness is not in *what* the experience represents, but in *how* it represents it. (This is what McGinn (1988: 300) calls the "medium conception" of consciousness: "Consciousness is to its content what a medium of representation is to the message it conveys . . . What it is like to have the experience is thus fixed by intrinsic features of the medium, whereas what the experience is about is fixed by certain extrinsic relations to the world.") According to representationalism, however, the intuitive outlook is simply mistaken. That it is can be seen when we appreciate what has come to be called.

[10] The idea behind the transparency of experience is often traced back to G. E. Moore, though there is some exegetical controversy over this. Moore (1903a: 25) wrote: "the moment we try to fix our attention upon consciousness and to see what, distinctly, it is, it seems to vanish: it seems as if we had before us a mere emptiness. When we try to introspect the sensation of blue, all we can see is the blue: the other element is as it were diaphanous." Or, in slightly different terms (Moore 1903a: 20): "the other element which I have called 'consciousness' . . . seems to escape us: it seems, if I may use the metaphor, to be transparent—we look through it and see nothing but the blue."

Harman's claim is that any subject who would perform this exercise would discover for herself that the only features she can become introspectively aware of are features of what her experience represents, not of the experiencing itself. This is true at least of Eloise, Harman's protagonist (1990: 667):

When Eloise sees a tree before her, the colors she experiences are all experienced as features of the tree and its surroundings. None of them are experienced as intrinsic features of her experience. Nor does she experience any features of anything as intrinsic features of her experience . . .

But it should be true for you too. Even if, when looking at the apple, you decide to stop concentrating on the apple and attend instead to your experience of it, it is still the apple's redness that you are presented with. You do not become suddenly aware of *another* redness, as it were interposed between you and the apple.[11]

To further bring out the transparency of experience, consider the following scenario (adapted from Byrne 2001). Suppose your brain is hooked up to a machine—call it "the inverter"—that can rewire the visual channels in your brain in such a way that, when the operator presses the right button, your color qualia are inverted.[12] Suppose further that, while hooked to the inverter, you are looking at pictures of red apples passing on a monitor for five seconds each. In some cases, the operator lets the picture pass without doing anything. In other cases, after three seconds she alters the picture on the monitor into a picture of a green apple. In yet other cases, after three seconds she presses the button on the inverter, thus inverting your color qualia. From the first-person perspective, you will not be able to tell apart those trials: you will not be able to tell whether the operator changed the apple's color or inverted your qualia. Whether it is

---

[11] As Harman makes clear, the idea is not really new, and has been discussed throughout the twentieth century, but it has just passed unappreciated. Among the philosophers who have repeatedly argued for the transparency of experience, Harman mentions especially Armstrong. Armstrong (1977: 186) writes: "in the case of the phenomenal qualities, it seems plausible to say that they are qualities not of the perception but rather of what it perceived. 'Visual extension' is the shape, size, etc. that some object of visual perception is perceived to have (an object that need not exist). Colour seems to be a quality of that object. And similarly for the other phenomenal qualities."

[12] In this work I use "qualia" in the innocuous sense in which it means the same as "phenomenal properties." Sometimes the term is used to designate properties that by definition cannot be accounted for in terms of functional role or representational content. I am not using the term in this more restrictive sense.

the world that changed or your brain, your experience of the change is the same—it is an experience as of the world changing. This suggests that your experience is inherently directed at the world, that its phenomenal character is inherently representational.

It is important, however, not to conflate the thesis of transparency with representationalism itself. We may formulate the transparency thesis as follows:

> (TE) For any experience e and any feature F, if F is an introspectible feature of e, then F is (part of) the representational content of e.

Representationalism, by contrast, is the following thesis:

> (R) For any experience e and any feature F, if F is the phenomenal character of e, then F is (part of) the representational content of e.

These are different theses. There is, however, a straightforward way to derive the latter from the former—namely, through the following bridge thesis:

> (BT) For any experience e and any feature F, if F is the phenomenal character of e, then F is an introspectible feature of e.

The bridge thesis is highly plausible, since it would be quite odd if there was something it was like for the subject to have her experiences, and yet she could have no introspective access to what it was like for her. The thesis does not say that phenomenal character is necessarily introspected; only that it is necessary that it be *in principle* possible to introspect it. And the notion that phenomenal character must be in principle introspectively accessible seems quite plausible.[13]

With this bridge thesis at hand, we have a straightforward argument from transparency to representationalism: the phenomenal character of an experience is introspectively accessible; the only introspectively accessible aspect of an experience is its representational content; therefore, the

---

[13] Nonetheless, in Chapter 5 I will reject BT, though not in the context of denying representationalism. Note, moreover, that rejecting BT is not yet rejecting representationalism, only a way of rejecting one argument for representationalism. There are probably other arguments for representationalism, including other arguments from transparency to representationalism.

phenomenal character of an experience is its representational content.[14] In other words: (BT) and (TE), therefore (R). Call this the *transparency argument* for representationalism.

An importantly different formulation of the argument from transparency to representationalism is offered by Tye, whose reasoning goes something like this: (1) the thesis of transparency makes a claim about how conscious experience *seems*—namely, that the qualities we are aware of in conscious experience seem to be qualities of the worldly objects being experienced, not qualities of the experiencing of these objects; (2) it is unlikely that there is a radical and fundamental difference between how conscious experience *seems* and how it *is*; therefore, (3) it is unlikely that the qualities we are aware of in conscious experience are qualities not of the worldly objects being experienced, but rather of the experiencing of these objects.[15]

Tye's argument is different from what I have called the transparency argument, but it is quite plausible as well. In any event, the transparency of experience provides a powerful stepping stone to a representationalist account of phenomenal character. It has certainly tilted the debate in favor of representationalism, sociologically speaking.[16] Of particular significance in this development is the fact that the transparency argument is based on a phenomenological observation, rather than being theoretically driven.

3. Representationalism and Subjective Character

In the previous chapter, I distinguished between the qualitative and subjective characters of conscious experience. In the reddish way it is like for

---

[14] This is not quite accurate. Another possibility is that conscious experience does not *have* a phenomenal character. That is, what the premises entail would be more accurately stated as follows: if a conscious experience has a phenomenal character, its phenomenal character is identical to its representational content. To reach representationalism, we must introduce a premise to the effect that all conscious experiences have a phenomenal character. This may be true by stipulation.

[15] Tye (2000: 46) writes: "None of the qualities of which you are directly aware in seeing the various surfaces look to you to be qualities of your experience. You do not experience any of these qualities as qualities of your experience . . . To suppose that the qualities of which perceivers are directly aware in undergoing ordinary, everyday visual experiences are really qualities of the experiences would be to convict such experiences of massive error. This is just not credible."

[16] Several philosophers have denied the transparency of experience, or the support it lends to representationalism (e.g., Block 1996, Rey 1998, Loar 2003). But overall it is my impression that the majority of philosophers of consciousness think today that conscious experience is indeed transparent in the relevant sense, and supports representationalism.

you to have your experience of the red apple, I distinguished the reddish aspect and the for-you aspect. The former is your experience's qualitative character, the latter its subjective character. What I would now like to claim is that representationalism does not even start to account for the subjective character of your experience.

Representationalism does not really address the phenomenon of subjective character. It attempts to account for the reddish character of your experience in terms of the experience's representation of red. But, even if we grant that there is nothing more to your experience's reddishness than the fact that it represents red, this does not even touch on the for-me-ness of your experience.

This is evident from the contrast between conscious and unconscious representations of red. Suppose you subliminally perceived the very same apple. Your perceptual state would represent the apple just as well. But the representation of the red apple would not be *for you*; it would not make the experience's reddishness present *to you*. So the representation of a red surface does not, in itself, guarantee that a perceptual state will exhibit the sort of for-me-ness we find in conscious experiences.

Elsewhere, I have argued that there is an a priori cloud over representationalism, which has to do with the fact that, for any given feature of external objects, it seems possible to represent that feature both consciously and unconsciously (Kriegel 2002b; see also Chalmers 2004). To suppose otherwise is to posit external features that lend themselves only to conscious representation. But why should the world contain features that can be represented only consciously?

If we accept that every feature in the world can be represented both consciously and unconsciously, then it cannot be that an experience's having phenomenal character is just a matter of its representing the right feature. Perhaps it is a matter of representing the right feature *in the right way*, but, in an important sense, this variation would no longer be purely representationalist. For now the difference between phenomenally conscious and unconscious states would come down not to their representational content, what they represent, but to some other feature of theirs.[17]

---

[17] Sometimes one finds in the relevant literature mention of a "Fregean representationalism" according to which phenomenal character is understood not in terms of *what* a conscious experience

We can illustrate this with Tye's PANIC theory. The difference between a conscious and an unconscious representation of red, according to this theory, is that the former carries a PANIC, whereas the latter does not. A PANIC is a poised, abstract, non-conceptual, intentional content. Since both the conscious and the unconscious representation's content is intentional, and since if one's content is abstract then so is the other's, it would seem that only the attributes of poise and non-conceptuality might be suitable to distinguish the two. But, upon closer inspection, both poise and non-conceptuality turn out to be vehicular properties of the representation, rather than content properties. What I mean by this is that a representation is poised or non-conceptual in virtue of properties other than its property of representing what it does. It is poised in virtue of its functional role (in impacting beliefs and desires), and, although it is a vexed issue just what makes a representation non-conceptual, it is also most natural to understand it in terms of functional role (in recognizing, categorizing, and so on). Clearly, a representation is not poised or non-conceptual in virtue of what it represents, since every feature that can be represented with poise can also be represented without poise, and every feature that can be represented non-conceptually can also be represented conceptually.

For the fuller argument, see Kriegel 2002b. The upshot is that the difference between conscious representation and unconscious representation of red is unlikely to be captured in terms of what is represented, and certainly has not been shown to be so captured to date. The natural thought, it seems to me, is that the difference between the two is this: a conscious representation of red has subjective character, whereas an unconscious one does not.[18] That is, the former represents red *to* the subject, whereas the latter represents red *in* the subject, but not *to* her.

This account of the difference between phenomenally conscious and unconscious representations is better than the account in terms of poise

represents but in terms of *how* it represents it (i.e., in terms of the experience's Fregean mode of presentation). Such a Fregean representationalism is not susceptible to the argument just presented in the text. But, as I use the terms, Fregean representationalism is a rubber duck (it is not really a kind of representationalism).

[18] Recall that, on the view suggested in Chapter 1, the subjective character of a conscious experience is what makes it a conscious experience at all. If so, an unconscious representation of red necessarily lacks subjective character. The contrast between conscious and unconscious representation of red is, therefore, a contrast between a mental state with subjective character and a mental state without subjective character.

and/or non-conceptuality in one simple way. Consider first poise. A mental state's poise, as any other functional role property of it, is a *dispositional* property: the mental state instantiates it in virtue of being disposed to bring about (and be brought about by) certain other mental states. As stressed in the previous chapter, however, phenomenal consciousness is *not* a dispositional property; it is an occurrent or manifest or categorical property. Therefore, phenomenal consciousness cannot be identified with poise, so poise cannot account for the difference between phenomenally conscious and unconscious representations. The same argument probably applies to non-conceptuality, because it is highly plausible that non-conceptuality is also a dispositional property. It is not entirely clear what makes a state represent something non-conceptually rather than conceptually, but a natural thought is that it has to do with the representation mobilizing certain capacities—for example, discriminative and recognitional capacities. For example, we might hold that a mental state M of a subject S represents a feature F at a time t conceptually only if S is disposed to recognize an instance of F at a time t^* as an instance of the same feature as the one represented at t. This condition explicitly introduces a dispositional dimension into non-conceptuality.[19]

One philosopher who attempts to capture what is different about conscious representation, and reaches conclusions similar to ours, is Colin McGinn (1988: 300; emphasis added):

I doubt that the self-same kind of content possessed by a conscious perceptual experience, say, could be possessed independently of consciousness; such content seems essentially conscious, shot through with subjectivity. This is because of the Janus-faced character of conscious content: it involves *presence to the subject*, and hence a subjective point of view. Remove the *inward-looking face* [of conscious content] and you remove something integral . . .

That is, phenomenally conscious and unconscious representations are fundamentally different, in that the former involve "presence to the subject," or an "inward-looking face," a characteristic missing from the latter.

---

[19] It is possible for Tye to resist this argument, by proposing a non-dispositional construal of non-conceptuality. However, it is unclear to me how this might be achieved. At the very least, we may think of this challenge as a dilemma: either non-conceptuality is a dispositional property, in which case it cannot capture the difference between phenomenally conscious and unconscious representations, or non-conceptuality is a non-dispositional property, in which case we are owed a plausible account of what it is.

What is this "presence to the subject," which McGinn finds only in conscious representations? My current conscious experience of the laptop before me not only presents the laptop—it presents the laptop *to me*. By contrast, unconscious perception of the laptop (for example, in subliminal vision) would represent the laptop, but it would not represent it to me, at least not in the same sense. So the representational content of my conscious experience of the laptop has two components: its *directedness toward the laptop*, which is its "outward-looking face"; and its *manifestation to me*, which is its "inward-looking face." This double-headed, or Janus-faced, character is unique to conscious representational content, according to McGinn. It should be clear already from these preliminary remarks that McGinn's presence-to-the-subject is probably his way of conceiving of the very same phenomenon we have conceived of here as for-me-ness.

In any event, I hope it is also obvious that a straightforward representationalist account of subjective character is hopeless. Such an account would require that there be some environmental features that it is impossible to represent without representing *to the subject*, features that lend themselves only to subjective representation (in the relevant sense). This seems entirely implausible: it would require that, for a world to become a zombie world, certain environmental features would have to vanish, and, moreover, that it would be their vanishing that would make it a zombie world.[20]

In conclusion, representationalism cannot fully account for phenomenal character, because, although it may be able to account for the identity conditions of phenomenally conscious states, it is incapable of accounting for their existence conditions. That is, although it may account for what makes a phenomenally conscious state the phenomenally conscious state it is, it is unable to account for what makes that state a phenomenally conscious state at all. One might attempt to solve this problem by supplementing one's representationalism about the identity conditions with a sort of functionalism about the existence conditions, as the appeal to poise effectively does, but this implausibly casts the occurrent as dispositional. Much better to think of the existence conditions as given by subjective character, the for-me-ness of conscious experience, and offer an account of the latter

---

[20] In the next chapter I will propose an account of subjective character that is representational in the sense that it adverts only to the representational properties of states endowed with subjective character. But such an account is not representationalist in the sense of the current discussion, because it does not say that a mental state has subjective character in virtue of representing environmental features.

that (i) does not attempt to do so purely in terms of the representation of environmental features and (ii) does not cast it as a dispositional property. Offering an account of this sort is the task of the next chapter.

4. A Representational Theory of Qualitative Character?

It may yet be, however, that the representational theory is workable as a theory of *qualitative character*. Since the failure of representationalism pertains primarily to its inability to account for the existence conditions of phenomenality, and it is independently plausible that qualitative character provides the identity condition of phenomenality (as suggested in Chapter 1), it is natural to suggest representationalism as a plausible account of qualitative character. The idea would be that there is a type of representational content, such that qualitative character is nothing but that content.[21]

This more restricted representationalism, applying only to qualitative character, retains the motivations that supported the more sweeping variety. The prospect of naturalizing qualitative character is still there, and the transparency of experience certainly provides phenomenological evidence in favor of a representational account of qualitative character.[22]

In addition, this scaling-down may neutralize a kind of worry that sometimes inspires non-reductive representationalism. This is the thought that there is something special about the kind of representation we find in conscious experience, something too special to be captured in terms of teleo-informational connections to the environment (McGinn 1988, Levine 2003). The scaled-down version of representationalism, applying only to qualitative character, can accommodate this worry. One way to interpret the idea behind the worry is to say that conscious representation is infused with subjective significance, and that this subjective significance goes beyond any teleo-informational connections between brain states

---

[21] This account could then be plugged into an overall theory of phenomenal character. If phenomenal character were the compresence of qualitative and subjective character, say, the upshot would be that phenomenal character is the compresence of subjective character and the relevant type of representational content.

[22] Indeed, it might be worried that the transparency of experience is a consideration powerful enough to suggest that there is no such thing as subjective character. I will argue in Chapter 5, however, that this is an illusion.

and world states. There may be a *different* naturalistically kosher way to capture this subjective significance, but broadly causal connections to the environment will not do. This interpretation would accommodate the above worry, but would justify a scaled-down reductive representationalism for qualitative character only.

At the same time, there are in the literature myriad arguments by counter-example against representationalism, and those would apply just as well to the scaled-down version.[23] Many opponents of representationalism have indeed attempted to refute it by counter-example (e.g., Peacocke 1983: ch. 1, Boghossian and Velleman 1989, Block 1990a, 1996, 1998, 1999, Loar 2002). These alleged counter-examples fall into three categories:

(a) conscious experiences that allegedly have no representational content;
(b) pairs of conscious experiences that allegedly have different qualitative characters but the same representational content;
(c) pairs of conscious experiences that allegedly have the same qualitative character but different representational contents.

In this section, I discuss the main offers in each category.[24]

In the first category—that of conscious experiences that are allegedly non-representational—many anecdotal counter-examples suggest themselves. Block (1996) points out phosphene experiences: if you rub your eyes long and hard enough, when you open them again you will experience colorful patches floating about in your visual field. Yet your visual experience does not represent any surfaces of floating external objects. Something similar could be claimed about *darkness experiences*: when you are in complete darkness, or your eyes are well shut, you have a conscious experience with a blackish qualitative character. Yet your experience does not represent any black surface.[25]

---

[23] Of course, for a theory to be vulnerable to arguments by counter-example, it must be committed to certain universal propositions. Representationalism about qualitative character is committed to at least three universal propositions. (i) For every conscious experience E, E has a representational content. (ii) For every pair of conscious experiences E and E*, if E and E* have different qualitative characters, then they have different representational contents. (iii) For every pair of conscious experiences E and E*, if E and E* have the same qualitative character, then they have the same representational content. It is accordingly vulnerable to three different kinds of counter-example, as we will see momentarily.

[24] Note that each category targets one of the three universal propositions mentioned in the previous footnote.

[25] This alleged counter-example to representationalism was suggested to me by Michael Pace.

It is unclear, however, that these sorts of experience are not rep-resentational. It seems to me that a phosphene experience does repres-ent—misrepresents—the colorful patches as surfaces of floating external object. It is just that the experience is accompanied by a (true) belief to the effect that one's current experience misrepresents one's surroundings, and that there are in fact no objects with these colorful surfaces in one's surroundings. This belief accounts for the sense that one is not under an illusion when having the phosphene experience, and therefore that it does not seem to one as though there are such objects in one's surroundings. So the reason one is not under an illusion is not that one's experience is not illusory; the experience *is* illusory, but it is accompanied by a belief that ensures one is not under an illusion. One's visual experience does represent phosphene objects; it is just that its representational content is "vetoed," as it were, by the representational content of an accompanying belief.[26] Similarly for darkness experiences: such experiences (mis)represent a black object whose surface covers the subject's entire visual field (or whose volume envelops the subject), but they are normally accompanied by beliefs to the effect that this is not the case.[27]

A less anecdotal and more theoretical case is that of the so-called *Swampman* (Davidson 1987, Block 1998). Through a most unlikely cosmic accident, molecules in a swamp may come together (and remain together) in such a way as to form a human-like creature, which we may call the Swampman. We may stipulate that the molecules in the Swampman's brain are arranged (and function) in the same way as the molecules in my brain. Intuitively, it would seem that the Swampman would have to undergo the same conscious experience I undergo—namely, a bluish experience. However, representational content requires more than just brain activity—it requires a history of systematic interaction with the environment.[28] Because the Swampman has no such history, having come into existence moments ago, its brain cannot support representational

[26] For a representationalist response along these lines, see Tye 2000: ch. 4.

[27] The important point is that the belief does not alter the representational content of the experience itself, but it accounts for the fact that one is not under an illusion as to the way one's surroundings are. In other words, in dealing with darkness or phosphene experiences, it is important to distinguish the representational content of one's visual experience itself from the representational content of one's overall awareness. The latter is determined only partly by the visual experience.

[28] At least this is so according to externalist accounts of representation. Recall that, according to Dretske, a brain state represents an external object only if there are relations of nomic dependency between them.

connections to the environment. Therefore, the Swampman's conscious experience, despite having the same bluish qualitative character that *my* conscious experience has, is unlike my conscious experience in that it does not represent the blue sky. It does not represent anything. So it is possible, if highly unusual, to have conscious experiences that do not represent anything.

Representationalists can deal with the Swampman case in one of two ways. One way is to bite the bullet and deny that the Swampman has any conscious experiences (Dretske 1995: ch. 5). This would entail that conscious experience does not supervene on brain activity, but not that it does not supervene on physical reality altogether. Conscious experience would still supervene on brain activity plus representational connections to the environment (which we are quite confident are physical).

A different way to deal with the Swampman is to adopt an account of representational content that does not require a history of interaction with the environment, and more generally requires only things the Swamp-man has. This is what Tye (2000: ch. 6) opts for. According to Tye, the representational content of a mental state is given by the environmental feature it tracks under normal conditions. For humans, perhaps, "normal conditions" include a history of systematic interaction with the environment. But for Swampmen this may not be so. For Swampmen and similar inhuman creatures, normal conditions are "those in which the creature or system happens to be located or settled, if it is functioning well (for a sufficient period of time) in that environment" (Tye 2000: 122). Whether this response is plausible depends on issues in the theory of content that we cannot go into here. It does suggest, however, that the Swampman fails to constitute a knock-down counter-example to representationalism about qualitative character.

Let us move now to the second category of possible counter-examples, those in which two experiences differ in qualitative character but not in representational content. Perhaps the best-known case in this category is Peacocke's two-tree example (1983: ch. 1). Imagine seeing two equisized trees on two sides of a road ahead of you, such that one is located twenty yards behind the other. According to Peacocke, our conscious experience represents the two trees as being the same size, and yet there is a difference in the qualitative character of the experiencing of the two trees, in that the nearer tree "takes up" more of one's visual field.

The standard response to Peacocke's two-tree case is to claim that the representation of the two trees is different after all: although the trees are represented as being of equal size, the nearer tree is *also* represented as "appearing bigger *from here*"—that is, as subtending a larger visual angle (see Harman 1990, DeBellis 1991, Tye 1992, 1996, 2000: ch. 4).[29] So the difference in qualitative character *is* matched by a difference in representational content.

A different type of alleged counter-example of the same category involves the cases in which the same feature is allegedly represented in different perceptual modalities, producing a pair of experiences that are different in qualitative character but similar in representational content. Thus, Block (1996) compares a visual experience and an auditory experience of "something overhead," and claims that they both represent spatial location, even though what it is like to have a visual experience of an object's location is obviously different from what it is like to have an auditory experience of it. A more sophisticated example is provided by Lopes (2000). Apparently, some blind people can construct representations of shapes in their environment on the basis of auditory information having to do with temporal and level differences in the intensity, frequency, and amplitude of sounds (Lopes 2000: 449). It would seem, then, that they construct auditory representations of shapes. When the same shapes are represented visually, however, the subject's conscious experience has a very different qualitative character. Therefore, Lopes concludes, such experiences are representationally alike but qualitatively different.

One option for the representationalist is to deny that these cases involve *auditory* representation of location and shape. In Block's case, she could claim that, when one hears something overhead, one represents auditorily only the *sound* of the object overhead, and *infers* the location of the source of the sound. The inference need not be conscious, of course; it may be automatic. But there is no way to represent the object's location without that inference. Likewise, Lopes's blind people may have developed the unusual capacity to *infer* information about shapes from auditorily represented information,

---

[29] Peacocke originally opposed this move on the grounds that many subjects who do not possess such concepts as "subtends a larger visual angle" would still experience the two trees differently. However, Peacocke's assumption here is that it is impossible to represent a feature without possessing the relevant concept. That is, the assumption is that there is no such thing as non-conceptual content. Obviously, this is denied by Tye (as well as Harman 1990), according to whom the content of experience is always non-conceptual (recall, this is what the "N" stands for in PANIC).

but that information is not itself auditorily represented.[30] This response is quite promising, but to be complete the representationalist would have to tell us just how the extra information is inferred, and from what. This may not be trivial: it is not easy to see, for example, from what we are supposed to infer the information that the sound is overhead.

Another option for the representationalist is to allow that these are genuine cases of auditory representation, but claim that they fall outside the part of the representational content that constitutes qualitative character. Recall that a representationalist must hold that every qualitative property of experience is identical to some representational property, but need not hold the converse—namely, that every representational property is identical to some qualitative property. She may thus suggest that, although an auditory experience can represent location, the representation of location is not reflected in the qualitative character of the experience. And, indeed, it is hard to imagine two auditory experiences whose qualitative character differs *only* in its locational component. A similar move may be suggested for Lopes's auditory representation of shape: it is not qualitatively reflected representation.

Finally, the representationalist may respond by granting that we can have qualitative auditory representation of location and shape, but claim that it is *not* qualitatively different from qualitative visual representation of location and shape (so that this does not constitute a case of representational constancy with qualitative variation). To be sure, the *overall* qualitative character of seeing location and hearing location is very different, but then again so is their *overall* representational content. There are any number of other properties represented only in the seeing and only in the hearing. The fact that location is represented in both experiences shows that there is some representational *overlap* between the two, but to account for this the representationalist has to demonstrate only qualitative overlap between seeing location and hearing location. As we can see from the difficulty of trying to imagine qualitative characters that differ only in their locational component, it may well be that the contribution of the representation of

---

[30] This seems to be Dretske's response (2000) to Lopes. Dretske (2000: 458) writes: "Why does [Lopes] think that we can both see and hear the shape of distant objects? The only reason I can figure out is because he assumes that if we can *tell* what shape X is via modality M, then we must be M-aware of X's shape...Lopes assumes, in other words, that if S can hear (see, taste, smell) that X is F, if he can know, find out, or discover, in this way that X is F, then S must be hearing (seeing, tasting, smelling) the F-ness of X. It is, perhaps, only necessary to state this assumption to see that it is false."

location to the overall qualitative character is rather subtle, the sharper parts having to do with the representation of other properties. If so, the qualitative contribution of seeing location and hearing location may well be the same.[31]

I now move on to the third category of alleged counter-examples, where conscious experiences with different representational content are claimed to have the same qualitative character. Here is perhaps the best-known argument by counter-example against representationalism, Block's *Inverted Earth* argument (1990a). Suppose there is a planet otherwise like Earth—Inverted Earth—on which every object has the color complementary to the one it has on Earth. On Inverted Earth, fire engines are green, the sky is yellow, and snow is black. One day you are kidnapped by mad scientists, who drug you unconscious, insert spectrum-inverting lenses into your eyes, and transport you to Inverted Earth. You wake up in Inverted Earth and do not notice any difference. Since the inversions due to the way Inverted Earth is and due to your spectrum-inverting lenses cancel each other out, your Inverted Earthly experiences of the sky are still bluish. At the beginning of your tenure on Inverted Earth, your experiences also represent the sky as blue, since experiences of their type nomically depend on a blue sky. However, after living on Inverted Earth for many years, your sky experiences develop a nomic dependence on a yellow sky, and therefore start representing yellow rather than blue. At that point, your Inverted Earthly experiences of the sky become representationally different from your Earthly sky experiences. Yet they remain qualitatively the same: both kinds of experience have a bluish character.[32]

Tye's response (2000: ch. 6) to the argument from Inverted Earth is to claim that your experiences of the sky on Inverted Earth continue to represent the sky as blue, regardless of how long you live there. You are

---

[31] Although it is less natural to apply this point to shape, since the shape component of qualitative character does not seem to be all that subtle, something like it may yet be true. As will be discussed more thoroughly later in the chapter, some representationalists appeal primarily to the representation of appearance properties, and they may hold that the representation of visually apparent shape is very different from that of auditorily apparent shape, and that most of the difference between the shape component of qualitative character is due to the representation of such properties. Much more will have to be said, of course, about the nature of apparent properties and their representation before this suggestion can be assessed.

[32] In a later article, Block (1998) combines this case with the Swampman case, so that a Swampman transported to Inverted Earth allegedly provides a particularly acute counter-example to representationalism. This later argument, and Tye's response (2000: ch. 6) to it, will not concern us here.

doomed to misrepresent the sky on Inverted Earth for the rest of your life. This is because, according to him, what an experience represents is determined not by what it nomically depends upon, but by what it would nomically depend on *under optimal conditions*. The condition of being drugged, having your sensory equipment manipulated, and being transported to a strange faraway planet is far from optimal. Under optimal conditions, your Inverted Earth experiences of the sky would still nomically depend on the presence of blue skies, not yellow skies. Therefore, your Inverted Earthly sky experiences still represent blue skies, and are therefore representationally the same as your old Earthly sky experiences.

This response is unsatisfactory, however, inasmuch as Tye's "optimal conditions" may not succeed in dealing with the following variation on Block's case. Suppose that you yourself never make it to Inverted Earth. However, there happens to be on Inverted Earth a functional Twin of yours. This person is biologically and psychologically exactly like you, except his or her spectrum is inverted relative to yours. If this person lived on Earth, his or her experiences of the sky would be yellowish. But because he or she lives on Inverted Earth, his or her experiences of the sky are bluish. And, of course, your own sky experiences here on Earth are also bluish. So, your Twin's Inverted Earthly sky experiences are qualitatively the same as your Earthly sky experiences. However, by the lights of broadly informational semantics, even of Tye's preferred variety, your Twin's Inverted Earthly experiences of the sky represent yellow rather than blue, since they entertain systematic relations of nomic dependency with a yellow sky, even—it appears—under optimal conditions. Therefore, your Twin's Inverted Earthly sky experiences are representationally different but qualitatively indistinguishable from your Earthly sky experiences.[33]

The representationalist could protest that the fact that the Twin's spectrum is inverted already constitutes a less-than-optimal condition. This would have to be justified, of course, though perhaps the price for justifying that is worth saving representationalism. However, we could stipulate that

---

[33] The difference in this variant is that Tye's "optimal conditions" clause has less clear bearing on the situation. That is, it is less clear that we can claim your Twin is in sub-optimal conditions. For there is nothing out of the ordinary going on with your Twin. He or she is not being manipulated in those radical ways as you are in Block's original tale. The conditions under which your Twin's experiences nomically depend on the yellow sky may therefore be optimal. And yet, his or her experiences of the sky have the same bluish character that your experiences of the sky have. We have a divergence of qualitative character and representational content.

spectrum inversion is rife on Inverted Earth, or even universal, in which case Tye would be forced to declare the whole population of Inverted Earth under sub-optimal conditions and in constant error about the color of objects around them. But perhaps this is not an altogether unacceptable outcome. After all, the Inverted Earthlings have bluish experiences upon looking at yellow objects and yellowish experiences upon looking at blue objects.

At this stage, I would like to remain neutral on whether this variation on the Inverted Earth argument succeeds in counter-exemplifying representationalism about qualitative character. It does seem to me, however, that none of the other arguments by counter-example against representationalism is particularly compelling. Nonetheless, the most straightforward version of representationalism faces a different major objection, as I will now argue.

5. The Shifted Spectrum Objection

According to the representational account of qualitative character under consideration, a conscious experience has bluish qualitative character just in case it represents a blue surface or volume. Shoemaker (1994a, 1994c) developed what is effectively a reductio of this account on the basis of considerations having to do with inverted spectrum scenarios. But as emerges from Shoemaker's later presentation of the argument (2002), the possibility of inverted spectra is not needed for his argument. Below, I will run the argument by appeal to the more mundane phenomenon of *shifted* spectrum.

The phenomenon of shifted spectrum has to do with the fact that different people have color experiences of the same surfaces/volumes that are systematically slightly different. Thus, women apparently perceive surfaces and volumes as ever so slightly darker than how men perceive them. Similar phenomena show up across race and age (Block 1999). Unlike inverted spectra, shifted spectra do not involve functional indistinguishability and are therefore discoverable (and discovered).

Shoemaker's reductio has three premises. The first is that shifted spectra are (metaphysically) *possible*. This is unproblematic, since they are *actual*. Thus we may suppose that there are two normal subjects, Norma and

Norman, whose experiences upon looking at the blue sky are slightly different: Norma has a visual experience with a bluish$_{17}$ qualitative character, whereas Norman has one with a bluish$_{16}$ qualitative character. According to the representational account of qualitative character we are considering, this would mean that Norma's experience represents the sky to be blue$_{17}$ and Norman's represents it to be blue$_{16}$.

The second premise is that, in some circumstances of shifted spectra, neither party can be said to have illusory experiences. Thus, neither Norma nor Norman is misperceiving the sky.[34]

It follows from these two premises that the representational account we have been discussing implies that the sky is both blue$_{17}$ all over and blue$_{16}$ all over at the same time. Since Norma's experience represents the sky to be blue$_{17}$, and is veridical, it follows that the sky *really* is blue$_{17}$; and, since Norman's represents the sky to be blue$_{16}$, and is veridical, it follows that the sky *really* is blue$_{16}$.

The third premise in Shoemaker's argument is simply that it is impossible for anything to be two different colors all over at the same time. Just as a door cannot be white all over and brown all over at the same time, so the sky cannot be blue$_{17}$ all over and blue$_{16}$ all over at the same time. Thus the representational account we have been discussing is reduced to absurdity. Call this the *argument from shifted spectra*.

This does not mean that *every* representational account would lead to contradiction. As we will see momentarily, Shoemaker's own move is to embrace a modified, subtler representational account. Before discussing this, however, let us see what options there are in responding to the argument from shifted spectra.

Denying the first premise is not a real option, at least not for a philosopher. If an *empirical* case could be made against the actuality of shifted spectra, then a philosopher might step in to make a case against their possibility. But the empirical case in favor of their actuality is so overwhelming that the first premise cannot be seriously doubted. Likewise, denying the third premise is also absurd, as it would allow the sky to be two different colors all over at the same time.[35]

---

[34] We may assume that their visual systems are functioning perfectly and the conditions are optimal. *Everything* is optimal! So neither is undergoing an illusion.

[35] Strictly speaking the suggestion is absurd. But perhaps the idea is that there are no such properties as being blue$_{16}$ *simpliciter* and being blue$_{17}$ *simpliciter*. Rather, colors are relativized properties, properties

The only serious option is to deny the second premise, and claim that at least one among spectrum-shifted subjects *does* have an illusory experience—that is, that at most one of Norma and Norman is having a veridical one. The problem with this response, however, is that any choice we might want to make about who it is that perceives the sky veridically would seem entirely arbitrary. Why should it be women and not men, or men and not women, who are designated as the correct perceivers? Can we really justify an error theory for the color perceptions of one gender, as well as some races and many ages? Nor would it be plausible to claim that both Norma and Norman are having illusory experiences. This would resolve the problem of arbitrariness, but it would implicate us with (*a*) an error theory for *all* perception and (*b*) the view that the sky is not only neither $blue_{16}$ nor $blue_{17}$, but colorless (since shifted spectrum scenarios can be constructed with any shade of color).[36]

We can see, then, that none of the three premises in Shoemaker's reductio can be plausibly rejected. Therefore, the representational account we have considered cannot be right. This does not mean, however, that a representational account of qualitative character is unworkable; merely that, if it is to be workable, the properties representation of which would be taken to constitute qualitative character cannot be such straightforward color properties as being $blue_{16}$ and being $blue_{17}$. They must be subtler properties. At the same time, they must be properties that have to do with color. Clearly, the bluish qualitative character of my sky experience cannot be a matter of the experience representing the sky to be, say, rectangular. It must have to do with representation of color-related properties.

Shoemaker's own suggestion is that, while a conscious experience cannot be $bluish_{16}$ in virtue of representing the property of *being* $blue_{16}$, it may well be $bluish_{16}$ in virtue of representing the property of *appearing* $blue_{16}$, or appearing $blue_{16}$ *to me* (Shoemaker 1994a, 1994c). Such "appearance properties" are color-related properties in a very obvious sense, but they

---

such as being $blue_{16}$ relative to observer O and being $blue_{17}$ relative to observer O*. I will return to this idea later on. For now, note only that this idea would not result, strictly speaking, in the sky being *both* $blue_{16}$ and $blue_{17}$ all over at the same time, but rather in its being *neither*. The notion that it might be both is plainly absurd.

[36] This view might be natural for an eliminativist about color (see Hardin 1988, Maund 1995). For she would already be committed to the idea that all our color perceptions are illusory and that the sky is neither $blue_{16}$ nor $blue_{17}$. But, for anyone who accepts the reality of colors, this would seem an untenable option.

do not generate any problem for representationalism. For there is nothing problematic about the sky both *appearing* blue$_{17}$ all over (to Norma) and *appearing* blue$_{16}$ all over (to Norman) at the same time. There is no competition between appearance properties, so the sky can instantiate both at once.[37]

There is a question, of course, as to what exactly appearance properties are, and which appearance properties are represented in experience. I will not dwell here on Shoemaker's own answer to these questions. In the next section I develop my own version of the idea. According to this version, the qualitative character of conscious experiences is a matter of their representing certain *response-dependent properties* of external objects. The motivation for this account is that it has the best chance of accommodating two broadly phenomenological points: the possibility of shifted spectra and the transparency of experience.

6. Response-Dependent Representationalism

What does it mean for the sky to appear blue$_{16}$? In what consists the state of affairs of the sky's appearing blue$_{16}$? Certainly, it consists in the sky instantiating a certain property, an "appearance property." But what is this property? My suggestion is that we construe it as a particular kind of response-dependent property (Wright 1988, Johnston 1989, Pettit 1991).

Response-dependent properties are properties whose instantiation conditions consist in their disposition to elicit certain responses in certain respondents (under certain conditions).[38] Johnston (1989: 145) construes them more precisely in terms of a priori biconditionals of the form "x is C iff x is such as to produce an x-directed response R in a group of subjects S under conditions K." When this sort of biconditional is true a priori, C is a response-dependent property.[39] It is natural to hold, for example,

---

[37] To be sure, there are *some* appearance properties that are in competition and cannot be coinstantiated—e.g., the property of appearing blue$_{17}$ all over to Norma and the property of appearing orange$_{28}$ all over to Norma. But the kind of appearance properties that cannot be coinstantiated are not the kind that generate the original problem, and no new problem can be generated with them, since it is *impossible* for Norma to have a bluish$_{17}$ experience of the sky and a orangish$_{28}$ experience of it at the same time.

[38] For the notion of response-dependent property, see Johnston 1989 and Pettit 1991.

[39] The reason the biconditional is required to be a priori is that a biconditional of this sort could happen to be true of objective, response-independent properties as well—but without being definitive

that artifactual kinds are response-dependent. Thus, for something to be a chair is just for it to be treated as a chair by normal users (in normal circumstances).

To say that the property of appearing blue$_{16}$ is response-dependent is thus to say that there is a certain response R, a certain set of respondents S, and certain conditions K, such that the following biconditional is true a priori: x appears blue$_{16}$ iff x is such as to produce x-directed R in S under K.

In typical response-dependent analyses, the subjects and conditions appealed to are *normal* subjects and conditions; and the responses are perceptual and/or cognitive. But this should not make us forget that there are any number of other response-dependent properties. Thus, there exists also the property of being disposed to elicit in brown-eyed persons the response of sitting under conditions of tiredness. The great majority of chairs have this property, even if some do not; thus this property, while clearly not constituting the property of being a chair, is importantly related to the property of being a chair. In devising a response-dependent account of the properties representing which constitutes qualitative character, we should resort to the response-dependent properties that best suit our theoretical needs.

This is important, because some of the most natural response-dependent properties in this general area turn out to be problematic given our theoretical needs. Consider the property of being disposed to elicit in normal subjects under normal conditions a bluish$_{16}$ experience. This property is doubly unfit to serve as the property representing which constitutes bluish$_{16}$ qualitative character. First, it is defined partly in terms of the bluish$_{16}$ qualitative character, so cannot be used in a reductive account of that property. Secondly, the sky does not *have* this property, since Norma is a normal subject but the sky is not disposed to elicit in her bluish$_{16}$ experiences.[40]

There are two lessons to draw here. First, the right response-dependent properties would not be defined by appeal to responses characterized in terms of qualitative character; otherwise they would be unfit for a reductive

---

of them. For example, things with mass tend to elicit distinctive mass-related responses in normal respondents under specifiable laboratory conditions. Yet this is not what having mass *is*. That is to say, a certain response-dependent biconditional is true of mass, but not a priori.

[40]   This is because, recall, the sky is rather disposed to elicit in Norma bluish$_{17}$ experiences.

account of qualitative character. The designated perceptual responses would have to be characterized in non-qualitative terms. Second, the right response-dependent properties would be defined not in terms of normal respondents, but in terms of something more specific—namely, responses that are shared among groups of subjects for whom it is empirically plausible that they share qualitative character. Individuals of different genders, races, or ages, for example, would not belong to the same groups of designated respondents. A good group of designated respondents might consist in, say, normal human Asian females in their twenties.[41]

We noted that the perceptual responses definitive of the right response-dependent properties cannot be qualitatively characterized. They must be characterized in some other way. Shoemaker's own view characterizes them *functionally*. For him, they are properties of being disposed to elicit a perceptual response with a specific functional role. The problem with this view, as I have argued elsewhere (Kriegel 2002a), is that it cannot accommodate the possibility of inverted spectra. Suppose Twin Norma is a spectrum-inverted functional duplicate of Norma. When she looks at the sky, Twin Norma has a yellowish$_{17}$ experience. Yet the sky is disposed to elicit in Twin Norma a perceptual state with the same functional role as it is disposed to elicit in Norma. So representing this disposition of the sky's should result, according to Shoemaker, in qualitatively indistinguishable experiences in Norma and Twin Norma. But *ex hypothesi* it does not.[42]

In the same place I suggested a different characterization of the relevant responses—namely, in terms of neurophysiological realizers. The idea was that appearing blue$_{16}$ to Norma is the property of being disposed to elicit a perceptual response in Norma that is neurophysiologically realized in a specific way. This is supposed to take care of the spectrum inversion case, because, while spectrum inversion among functional duplicates is

---

[41] Of course, further restrictions would have to be introduced for further factors that turn out to affect the qualitative characters of subjects' experiences. Thus, if it turned out that brown-eyed persons and blue-eyed ones have systematically different qualitative experiences, we would have to split this group into two subgroups, for each type of eye-color subject.

[42] This sort of problem could be fixed by restricting the relevant response-dependent property to *individual* respondents, so that there is one response-dependent property for Norma and another for Twin Norma. The problem with this move is that it will make it impossible for Norma and Twin Norma to have experiences with the *same* qualitative character—and yet surely they sometimes could have such experiences (e.g., when Norma stares at a perfect-blue canvass and Twin Norma stares at a perfect-yellow one).

widely seen to be possible, spectrum inversion among neurophysiological duplicates is more often considered impossible.

The main problem with this version is that it may not accommodate the possibility of multiple realizability. Suppose Venutian Norma undergoes a bluish$_{17}$ experience qualitatively indistinguishable from Norma's experience, but hers is realized in silicon. Since the realizers are different, the relevant response-dependent properties are different, and therefore the representations of those properties are different, so that the theory returns the result that the two experiences are qualitatively different, which is false *ex hypothesi*. In that paper I dealt with this problem by rejecting the orthodoxy on multiple realizability and denying that multiple realizability is possible. Although I still think the case for this position is much stronger than is commonly thought, I am now more inclined to accept the possibility of multiple realizability.

A completely different way to deal with this problem might be to complicate the dispositions that capture the right response-dependent properties. Thus, appearing blue$_{16}$ might be construed as the disposition to produce physical-implementational (neurophysiological) response N in Norma and subjects physically like her within her gender, race, and age group *and* to produce physical-implementational (silicon) response S in Venutian Norma and subjects physically like her within her appropriate group *and . . .* and so on and so forth, for every type of realizer. Perhaps the right response-dependent properties, those whose representation constitutes qualitative character, are *conjunctive dispositions* of this sort.

Such a conjunctive complication is necessary anyway, for the following reason. We supposed that, when Norma and Norman look at the sky in identical circumstances, Norma has a bluish$_{17}$ experience and Norman a bluish$_{16}$ experience. But, of course, Norman is also capable of having bluish$_{17}$ experiences. He just needs to look at the sky in slightly different circumstances, say five minutes later during sunset. That is, there are changes in the sky's color, or rather in the circumstances in which the sky in observed, that would exactly compensate for the perceptual-processing differences between Norma and Norman—where both circumstances are broadly "normal." But, in order for response-dependent representationalism to return the result that Norma and Norman are having qualitatively indistinguishable experiences across these situations, there must be a single response-dependent property, such that each is representing an instantiation of it. This response-dependent property would have to include, then, the disposition to elicit a certain response in Norma and her group members in circumstances C *and* a certain response in Norman and his group members in circumstances C*.

The kind of response-dependent property the theory would ultimately appeal to would thus be conjunctive along several dimensions. It would fold under it the disposition to elicit one physical-implementational response in some subjects and another in other subjects; a response in one type of circumstance in some subjects and in another type of circumstance in other subjects; and so on. What will unify all those dispositions within a conjunctive disposition is, in the first instance, purely our need as theoreticians to home in on a single property that can be represented by all subjects undergoing experiences with the same qualitative character.

There might be a temptation to object that this sort of account cannot explain how coming in contact with this varied bundle of dispositions results in the same qualitative experience in different subjects. But, so formulated, the objection, though motivated by something genuinely troublesome, is wrongheaded. For the claim under consideration is reductive, not causal. The claim is not that coming in contact with the relevant bundle of dispositions *results*, in a causal sense of the term, in having an experience with a specific qualitative character. Rather, it is that coming in contact with that bundle is what having the relevant experience *consists in*. Thus there is nothing the claim has to *explain*; it needs only to return the intuitively correct results on concrete cases.

Nonetheless, the claim smacks of theoretical opportunism. Granted, a conjunctive disposition can be cobbled together, entirely artificially, in such a way that identifying qualitative character with representing it returns all the right results (that is, is extensionally adequate). There still seems to be a certain incongruence between the fact that the disposition is an artificial hodgepodge and the fact that the qualitative character has an obvious sort of inner cohesion.

One way to put this worry is in terms of natural kinds, "homogenous underlying natures," and so on. It would seem that bluish$_{16}$ qualitative character is a natural kind, which carves nature at its joints and has a homogeneous deep nature. By contrast, the sort of conjunctive disposition we have focused on is clearly not, and it seems to follow that the representing of that disposition is likewise a heterogeneous, unnatural property.

On the other hand, perhaps we can resist this last inference. Perhaps we can claim that, however artificial and heterogeneous the disposition represented, the representing of it has the sort of inner cohesion we are inclined to attribute to qualitative character. Indeed, we may take this to capture a grain of truth in the old projectivist view that colors are projected by our experience onto the world. Projectivism is unsatisfying, because the relevant notion of projection is utterly mysterious. But the present apparatus may be thought of as casting projection in a sensible and even plausible light. Impressionistically, the idea is that experience projects a property on the world in the sense that the world has a very diverse way of producing a single kind of internal state, such that the only thing that unifies the world's various dispositions is the nature of the internal state they lead to.[43]

Ultimately, I endorse the response-dependent representational account of qualitative character, if somewhat unhappily (partly because of the worry under consideration and partly because of one of the objections to be raised in the next section). I do so because the alternatives are worse.

There are three kinds of alternative. The first is to embrace response-*independent* representationalism of the sort defended by Tye and Dretske. But this runs into Shoemaker's reductio—that is, is defeated by the argument from the shifted spectrum. The second is to adopt a non-reductive version of representationalism, where the response-dependent property is defined in terms of the qualitative character it elicits. But this is not so much to offer a theory of qualitative character as to make a claim about it; it does not *account* for qualitative character, merely *describes* it. The third alternative is to reject a representational account of qualitative character altogether and pursue a different reductive account of it. But this would be in tension with the transparency of experience. More generally,

---

[43] It should be noted, however, that one of the most disturbing aspects of the present account is that diversity and heterogeneity are to be found both at the cause end and the effect end of the relevant response-dependent properties. The sky can instantiate quite different response-independent color properties and be viewed under quite different circumstances while disposed to elicit an experience with bluish$_{16}$ qualitative character. At the same time, the internal physical-realizer-characterized responses in terms of which the response-dependent property of appearing blue$_{16}$ is defined are also a motley crew of very different states, varying from certain specific neurophysiological responses in actual adult humans to silicon responses in hypothetical Venutian puppies. This aggravates considerably the problem of artificiality. Nonetheless, the relevant (very complicated) response-dependent property defined in terms of these varying reactions to those varying objective external conditions exists, and the thesis on the table is that the bluish$_{16}$ qualitative character is identical to the representation of this property.

for someone who (like me) is seeking a reductive account of qualitative character, and who is impressed by the transparency of experience and the shifted spectrum, the only serious option seems to be response-dependent representationalism. Certain challenges arise around the question of how to construe the relevant response-dependent properties most profitably, and those challenges are quite serious. But there is no real alternative.

An interesting and important consequence of the response-dependent version of representationalism is *internalism about qualitative character* (Kriegel 2002a). We saw at the end of Section 1 that standard representationalism is externalist. This is because representational content is often externalistically individuated. However, the sort of response-dependent content appealed to in my own version of representationalism is locally supervenient, therefore internalistically individuated. It is locally supervenient because the dispositions it designates as represented are defined in terms of their intra-cranial effects, so that two dispositions to elicit different intra-cranial responses *eo ipso* count as different dispositions. Thus, whenever the represented properties are different, there must also be an intra-cranial difference, as per internalism.

In conclusion, the account of qualitative character I am proposing holds that a mental state has the qualitative character it does (and a qualitative character at all) in virtue of representing certain complicated response-dependent properties, characterized in terms of conjunctive dispositions to elicit neurophysiological states in certain subjects under certain conditions. As stressed above, I hold this view with lower credence than is perhaps typical, and for reasons to do not so much with a demonstrative argument as with what seems to me to hit the best overall reflective equilibrium with respect to a number of desiderata. I should add that in the next chapter, and for reasons that will come through only there, I will introduce one more modification into this account of qualitative character.

7. Objections and Replies

There are a number of objections that might come to mind in connection with a response-dependent representationalist account of qualitative character. With the exception of one, these objections are in my opinion satisfactorily answerable.

The objection that impresses me is this. With the transparency of experience, we saw that, when we attend to our ongoing experience, we find
that, in virtue of its qualitative character, an experience puts us in contact
with a property of an external object. But it also seems that it puts us in
contact with a categorical or occurrent property of the external object.
Arguably, dispositional properties such as fragility and solubility are not
strictly speaking perceivable. We can *think* of them, but we cannot *see*
them. However, response-dependent properties are dispositional.[44]

Shoemaker addresses a similar objection: that the properties we are
presented with in perceptual experience seem to be monadic, but his
account construes them as relational. Shoemaker's reply is to embrace
a sort of error theory about this. Weight, he notes, is presented in
tactile perception to be monadic, but we know today that it is relational,
depending as it does on the force of gravity. The relational aspect of weight
is somehow "hidden" from the phenomenology of tactile experience.
Tactile experience *misrepresents* weight as monadic. The same might be
true across the board, Shoemaker suggests, with a relational aspect (of all
perceivable properties) to do with dependence on the subject's responses
being phenomenologically hidden in the same way.

We could adopt the same strategy here, and hold that all conscious
experiences represent response-dependent dispositional properties but misrepresent them as response-independent occurrent properties. But for my
part I find commitment to such all-encompassing error theory unattractive.
I would much rather hold that such error occurs only on special occasions,
such as the case of weight. In addition, it is unclear how well Shoemaker's
reply carries over to the objection regarding dispositional properties. Is
there a similarly intuitive case of a seemingly occurrent property that turns
out to be dispositional? None comes to my mind.[45,46]

---

[44] So, on this objection, the transparency of experience, properly understood, supports not
just a representational account of qualitative character, but a response-independent representational account (unless a response-dependent account could appeal to non-dispositional response-dependent
properties).

[45] It should be stated that, on Shoemaker's own view (1979), all properties are dispositional. So this
version of the objection would not trouble him overmuch—at least not more than it does for his
general theory of properties as universally dispositional.

[46] Perhaps the *extent* of error theory's disattraction could be lessened by drawing certain distinctions
among kinds of error. One distinction is between the error of ascribing to something a property that it
does not have because it has a competing property and the error of ascribing to something a property
that it does not have because it cannot have properties of the relevant kind. Thus, it is one thing to

Another response might be this. Let us say that *weak* error theory is the claim that the properties presented in experience are in fact dispositional, but are not presented as dispositional, and that *strong* error theory is the claim that the properties presented in experience are in fact dispositional, but are presented as non-dispositional. It might be argued that the weak variety is not particularly embarrassing. The properties presented in experience have many features they are not presented as having. Thus, the properties presented in experience, as all properties, are not mango-shaped; yet experience fails to present them as such.[47] The strong variety of error theory is genuinely embarrassing, but also less clearly applies. After all, the claim that the phenomenology itself is simply silent on whether the properties it presents are dispositional or not, rather than committed to their being non-dispositional, is in many ways the safer and more conservative claim in this area. There is some reason to think that phenomenology does not comment on such matters. But in any event the objector who insists that it does would have to offer some procedure by which we might settle the question of whether this is so.

I am not entirely comfortable with this answer, because I do think there is a sense in which the phenomenology does not seem to be silent on the issue of dispositionality. Nonetheless, the considerations just raised seem to me to blunt the initial force of the objection, and to cast it perhaps as a bitable bullet. I now move to consider other objections, which I find less troubling in the last count.

One objection is that it is not clear how perceptual misrepresentation is possible, according to this account. It might be thought that the response-dependent properties highlighted here, being definitionally tied to subjects' responses, are impossible to misrepresent.

The objection is not entirely misguided, in that the response-dependent properties I have focused on are *harder* to misrepresent (by the individual in

---

ascribe greenness to something brown, another to ascribe it to something colorless. Importantly, in some contexts the latter would not comfortably be classified as "error." To say that the sky is green, or triangular, is clearly to say something false. But there is something odd about describing the claim that justice is green, or triangular, as false. The claim seems not so much false as nonsensical. It might be suggested that it is less embarrassing to make the second kind of mistake than the first—that it is more embarrassing to get wrong the color of a colorful thing than wrongly to ascribe color to a colorless thing. The latter is a failure to play by the rules; the former is playing by the rules and losing. It is hard to assess a suggestion of this sort, but it is an example of the strategy of distinguishing kinds of error theory and claiming that some are more acceptable than others.

[47] I am working with the assumptions that (*a*) properties are abstract and (*b*) abstracta are shapeless.

terms of whose responses they are defined) than other properties. But it is nonetheless *possible* to misrepresent them. This is because they are defined in terms of responses in certain broadly normal circumstances, which leaves the possibility of misrepresenting them in clearly abnormal circumstances. Suppose Norma, under the influence of hallucinogens, looks at a $blue_{17}$ canvass but has a $greenish_{78}$ experience of it. The canvass does not instantiate the property of being disposed to elicit the neurophysiological response that realizes $greenish_{78}$ experiences in broadly normal circumstances in Norma and her group members (and other neurophysiological responses in other groups); yet Norma represents that it does. This is misrepresentation.[48]

Another objection is that appealing to response-dependent properties throws a "veil of appearances" over the colors, shapes, flavors, odors, and so on. If all we are presented with in experience are such response-dependent properties as *appearing* $blue_{16}$ (to me), and never with such response-*in*dependent properties as *being* $blue_{16}$, then worldly objective colors are not something we can perceive.

I addressed this objection at length in Kriegel 2002a, developing an account according to which experiences represent "objective" (response-independent) colors *by*, or *in virtue of*, representing the "apparent" (response-dependent) colors. The idea is that there is some kind of response-*independent* shade of blue, such that Norma represents that the sky is that shade by representing that the sky appears $blue_{17}$ (to her and subjects like her) and Norman represents that the sky is that shade by representing that the sky appears $blue_{16}$ (to him and subjects like him). Plausibly, the relevant shade of blue is the categorical basis of both the property of appearing $blue_{17}$ to subjects like Norma and the property of appearing $blue_{16}$ to subjects like Norman—and they represent this categorical basis *by* representing the disposition of which it is the basis. This is, in effect, an unusual version of indirect realism, where objective (here, response-independent) reality is perceived through, or in virtue of, the perception of something like a realm of appearances (here, response-dependent properties). For details, see Kriegel 2002a.

---

[48] To allow misrepresentation in laxer circumstances, we could modify the response-dependent representational account so that it adverts to properties defined, not in terms of normal conditions, but in terms of, say, ideal conditions, or very good conditions, or just good conditions. All these response-dependent properties are legitimate things to appeal to, and it is a question of a technical order which ones it would be wisest for the response-dependent representational account to advert to.

A third objection might be that the response-dependent maneuver cannot help us, because the colors themselves are response-dependent. Thus, according to dispositionalist theories of color (Boghossian and Velleman 1989, Levine 2006), for something to be blue$_{16}$ *just is* for it to appear blue$_{16}$ to certain subjects in certain circumstances.

This objection is doubly misguided. First, although it is true that dispositional accounts of colors cast them as response-dependent properties, they do not cast them as the *same* response-dependent properties as those I have appealed to here. They typically cast, say, redness as the property of being disposed to elicit reddish experiences in normal subjects under normal conditions. This property is very different from the property of being disposed to elicit certain neurophysiological states in certain sets of restricted groups of subjects under certain circumstances that are normal for those subjects. Even if colors are the response-dependent properties dispositional theories say they are, the properties response-dependent representationalism identifies as the properties representation of which constitutes qualitative character are *different* properties.

More importantly, one way to see response-dependent representational-ism is as a way of accounting for qualitative character while staying neutral on the nature of colors, flavors, and so on (Kriegel 2002a). The neutral position allows colors, for example, to be whatever they turn out to be at the end of inquiry, while the properties representation of which constitutes qualitative character are already identified. If it turns out that the colors are just those properties, then it will have turned out that qualitative character is constituted by the representation of colors. But this in itself would not alter the response-dependent representational account of qualitative character.

Finally, it might be objected that there are no such properties as the very specific response-dependent properties our account of qualitative character appeals to. The objector could adopt a sparse conception of properties and complain that the elaborately defined response-dependent properties I have focused on simply do not exist. These properties are not "natural," the objector might insist. If there are no such properties, then our representational account will implicate subjects in massive error after all.

There are two responses to this objection. The easiest response is to reject the sparse conception of properties and adopt a latitudinarian one.

According to a latitudinarian conception of properties, there is a property for every predicate we can devise (modulo certain provisions for contradictory predicates, unintelligible predicates, and so on).[49] Since we can devise predicates that describe and ostensibly denote the kind of properties we have appealed to, those properties exist.

Secondly, even if the entities I have focused on are not properties, we may call them schmoperties, and insist that, as long as experiences put us in contact with these schmoperties in virtue of their qualitative character, they are veridical. After all, there is no question that some worldly particulars are disposed to elicit in Norma the relevant neurophysiological responses. So they have that disposition. Whether that disposition qualifies as a "property" is somewhat irrelevant to the status of the experience representing them.

My own metaphysical inclinations in this area are to claim that there are two notions of property, the "cheap" and the "dear," and to adopt a sparse conception of the latter and a latitudinarian one of the former. For some purposes, cheap properties may not be of interest. But nonetheless they are aspects of the world, and they really are ways things could be. In representing such properties, one might either "get it right" or "get it wrong," and the distinction between the two should be folded under the distinction between veridical and non-veridical representation. As long as the subject, or her experience, "gets right" the relevant cheap property, we should hold that the subject's experience is veridical. Under those terms, subjects will not be implicated in massive error by the response-dependent representational account of qualitative character.

8. Conclusion: The Response-Dependent Representational Account of Qualitative Consciousness

When I have an experience of the blue sky, there is a bluish way it is like for me to have the experience; this is the experience's phenomenal character. The bluish component of this "bluish way it is like for me" is what I have called the experience's qualitative character. A reductive account of qualitative character would seek to account for qualitative

---

[49] The property may not be instantiated in the actual world, but it does exist.

character in non-qualitative terms. In this chapter I have developed such a reductive account, the response-dependent representational account. The nature of this particular account can be appreciated by considering three choice points.

The first choice point concerns the choice between a representational and an anti-representational account of qualitative character. According to the former, but not the latter, an experience's qualitative character is just its representational content, or at least a part or aspect of it. There are two main reasons to adopt such representationalism: the prospect of naturalization and the transparency of experience.

The second choice is between response-dependent and response-independent representationalism. I have chosen the former, on the strength of what I called the *argument from the shifted spectrum*, which was adapted from Shoemaker. The argument is a reductio of response-independent representationalism: two normal subjects in optimal conditions can have slightly different qualitative experiences in the presence of the same worldly object; in such circumstances, it is plausible to ascribe to both a veridical experience; so, if the qualitative character of experience was a matter of its representing response-independent properties, it would follow that the worldly object instantiated two incompatible response-independent properties, which is absurd.

The final choice is between a reductive and a non-reductive version of response-dependent representationalism. According to the reductive version, the response-dependent property representation of which constitutes qualitative character can be specified without appeal to qualitative character, with the result that qualitative character has been accounted for in purely non-qualitative terms. According to the non-reductive version, the response-dependent property is specified partly by appeal to qualitative character, so that no reductive account of qualitative character results. I have banked on the reductive version, just because the purpose of the chapter was to offer an account of qualitative character rather than just describe it.

The account I have defended faces two serious challenges I have no fully satisfactory response to. They concern (i) the heterogeneous underlying nature and (ii) the dispositional nature of the properties representation of which constitutes qualitative character. I nonetheless embrace the account, despite these two problems, because the alternatives are more problematic.

The upshot of the present chapter is a (reductive) response-dependent representational account of the qualitative aspect of phenomenal consciousness. According to this, my experience's bluish qualitative character is nothing but its representing a certain kind of response-dependent property. I have noted, however, that there will be one complication to the account in the next chapter. I have also argued that such representing cannot account for the other component of phenomenal consciousness, the subjective character or for-me-ness of conscious experience. For that, a different story is needed. This is the topic of the next chapter.[50]

[50] For comments on a previous draft of this chapter I would like to thank Bill Lycan, Ken Williford, and an anonymous referee. I have also benefited from relevant conversations with David Chalmers, Joe Levine, and Josh Weisberg.

4

A Self-Representational Account
of Subjective Character

In Chapters 1 and 2 I suggested that a conscious experience's phenomenal character, what makes it the conscious experience it is and a conscious experience at all, involves two properties, qualitative character and subjective character. Roughly, a conscious experience's qualitative character makes it the conscious experience it is, while its subjective character makes it a conscious experience at all. In Chapter 3 I sketched an account of qualitative character. In this chapter I outline an account of subjective character. The outline will then be filled out over the next few chapters. According to the account I defend, conscious states have a subjective character in virtue of representing themselves (in the right way).

1. From Subjective Character to Inner Awareness

One view of subjective character is that it is an unstructured, inexplicable, *sui generis* property, a sort of *intrinsic glow* that attaches to some mental states and not others. On this view, there is very little positive that can be said about subjective character. Certainly there is no prospect for an informative reductive account of it in non-subjective terms.[1]

This "intrinsic-glow" account can be found in some approaches to consciousness in the phenomenological tradition. Thus, according to Husserl (1928/1964), the for-me-ness of conscious episodes involves a *sui generis* form of intentional directedness, which he called *act-intentionality*

---

[1] Perhaps it is possible to offer a brute reduction of this intrinsic glow to some neural property, but a more informative reduction is ruled out.

and contrasted with *object-intentionality*. The idea is that a conscious experience of the sky involves two mutually irreducible kinds of intentionality: an object-intentionality directed toward the sky and an act-intentionality directed toward the mental act itself. Importantly, act-intentionality is not simply object-intentionality that happens to be directed at an intentional act. Rather, it is a *sui generis* form of intentionality found nowhere else in nature and categorically different from regular intentionality.[2]

There is a purely methodological consideration to be made against the intrinsic-glow view. It is that it is generally not recommended to adopt a primitivist account of something, according to which it is a *sui generis* phenomenon inexplicable in terms of anything else, at the *beginning* of inquiry. It may well be that, by the *end* of inquiry, we would be forced to embrace a *sui generis* conception of subjective character. But we should not do so at the *beginning* of inquiry, before at least *trying* to develop a reductive account of the phenomenon. There is, after all, an element of hopelessness about the proposal. To call a phenomenon *sui generis* is not quite the same as to account for it. If an account of subjective character can be developed that casts it in a more familiar light, it is (other things being equal) to be preferred.

It might be objected that not every version of the intrinsic-glow account must cast subjective character as *sui generis* and inexplicable. Thus, Thomasson's *adverbial* treatment (2000) of subjective character might be thought of as an attempt to offer some sort of account of the phenomenon. According to this adverbial account, having a perceptual experience with subjective character is a matter of perceiving, in a certain sort of way, the "subjective" way—just as walking slowly is a matter of walking in a certain sort of way, the slow way.[3]

Arguably, the proposal might be cast in terms of the familiar distinction between content and attitude: we might say that the for-me-ness of a conscious state does not have to do with any extra content the state might carry, but is rather a matter of the attitude the state employs in carrying that content. Under this interpretation, the proposal can be traced back to David Woodruff Smith's seminal paper "The Structure of (Self-)

---

[2] For a much fuller exposition, as well as defense, see Zahavi 1999, 2004 and Drummond 2006.
[3] For endorsements and developments of this adverbial account, see Thomas 2003 and Zahavi 2004.

Consciousness" (1986).[4] On his view, there is not only a difference between seeing a lion and fearing a lion, but also between *subjectively*-seeing a lion and *non-subjectively*-seeing a lion.[5] The difference is that subjectively-seeing is seeing in a way that involves for-me-ness, whereas non-subjectively-seeing is seeing without for-me-ness (for example, in subliminal vision, or blindsight). Thus a conscious experience has subjective character in virtue of employing an intentional attitude of a certain kind, the subjective kind.

I have criticized this view of subjective character in Kriegel 2005. In broad strokes, my argument was the following. First, I noted that the view is not entirely clear, inasmuch as it is not particularly transparent what the attitude of subjectively-seeing would amount to. Next, I considered two accounts of attitude and how they might apply to this notion of subjectively-seeing. One account is in terms of direction of fit, and I argued that it fails to shed light on the notion of subjectively-seeing, because the direction of fit involved in subjectively-seeing is the same as that of non-subjectively-seeing—namely, the mind-to-world (or "thetic") direction of fit. The other account is in terms of functional role, but, as I argued at length in that paper, and will reiterate here in Chapter 6, for-me-ness cannot ultimately be a functional role property, because those are *dispositional*, whereas for-me-ness is most certainly an *occurrent* or *categorical* property.[6]

I still think that this is a good argument against the intrinsic-glow view. But I now think that there is a deeper reason to reject the view.[7] The very suggestion that subjective character is simple and unstructured is

[4] Smith writes (1986: 150): "The reflexive character [of conscious experience] is thus part of the modality [or attitude], and not of the [content], of presentation in the experience. In the modal structure 'in this very experience', the experience is not, strictly speaking, presented . . . Hence, inner awareness does not consist in a second presentation, a presentation of the experience itself . . ." Smith does not use the terminology of "content" and "attitude," but instead uses the terms "mode" and "modality" respectively. However, as he notes (1986: 150 n. 7), these terms are supposed to be interchangeable with Searle's "intentional content" and "psychological mode," which are more recognizably what most now use the terms "content" and "attitude" for. (A historical note: Smith was Thomasson's Ph.D. adviser.)

[5] In some places, Thomas Natsoulas seems to suggest something along the same lines. Consider (Natsoulas 1996: 385): "[There is a] phenomenology of those visual experiences that are a product and part of a kind of seeing that is different from straightforward seeing: a kind of seeing that takes place usually upon adopting an introspective attitude with reference to one's seeing. Elsewhere, I have called such seeing 'reflective seeing'."

[6] Another way to organize the argument is this: the only way to make sense of the attitudinal gloss on subjective character is in terms of functional role; but for-me-ness cannot be a functional role property, because it is non-dispositional; therefore, the difference between subjectively-seeing and non-subjectively-seeing cannot be accounted for in terms of the attitude employed.

[7] This reason is, moreover, independent of the specifics of the attitudinal or adverbial treatment.

quite straightforwardly implausible. It is natural to hold that, in virtue of a conscious experience's subjective character, the subject is *aware of* her experience. It would be quite odd indeed to maintain that an experience is *for* the subject even though the subject is completely unaware of it. Since this awareness is awareness-*of*, it involves an of-ness relation to the experience. To that extent, it cannot be an intrinsic glow, since it is not intrinsic at all, at least not in the sense of being non-relational or of being unstructured. Instead, it involves essentially the subject bearing an epistemic relation to her experience.

In other words, to hold that our conscious states are somehow experientially given to us, in the sense that they possess for-me-ness, but that such experiential givenness involves no epistemic or mental relation between the subject and her experience, is to deny that a conscious state's experiential givenness grounds an *awareness* of the experience by the subject. But, once it is denied that we are aware of our conscious states, it becomes utterly unmotivated, and quite possibly incoherent, to suppose that they are nonetheless experientially given to us in the way suggested by the notion of subjective character.

We can summarize the argument as follows: a conscious experience's subjective character makes the subject *aware of* her experience; but an intrinsic glow would not make the subject *aware of* her experience; therefore, the experience's subjective character cannot consist in an intrinsic glow. More fully and precisely:

> For any subject S and mental state M, such that S is in M and M has subjective character,
> 1. either M has an intrinsic glow or M does not have an intrinsic glow;
> 2. if M does not have an intrinsic glow, M's subjective character is not M's intrinsic glow;
> 3. if M has an intrinsic glow, M's intrinsic glow does not make S aware of M;
> 4. M's subjective character does make S aware of M; therefore,
> 5. if M has an intrinsic glow, M's subjective character is not M's intrinsic glow; therefore,
> 6. M's subjective character is not M's intrinsic glow.

Call this the *argument from awareness-making*. The argument is intended to show that, even if intrinsic glow is not construed as *sui generis* and inexplicable, it cannot account for subjective character, because it is central to subjective character that it enables an epistemic or mental relation between the subject and her experience. (Conversely, the argument does *not* show that subjective character is *not sui generis* or inexplicable; it may well be so, but not in virtue of being an intrinsic glow.)

The argument from awareness-making is my main reason for rejecting an intrinsic-glow account of subjective character. Since the argument is valid, it could be rejected by denying only one of its premises. It is natural to read Thomasson (2005, 2006) as rejecting Premise 4 and Zahavi (2004) as rejecting Premise 3.

Rejecting Premise 4 seems to me hopeless. It may be reasonable for someone to hold that we are *not* aware of our conscious states, which are therefore *not* experientially given to us and do not possess subjective character—that is, to go eliminativist with respect to subjective character. And it is certainly reasonable to hold that we *are* aware of our conscious states, which therefore *are* experientially given to us and *do* possess a subjective character—that is my own view. But the intermediate position, according to which conscious states are experientially given to us and possess a subjective character, and yet we are completely unaware of them, is fundamentally unstable and quite possibly incoherent.

What about Premise 3? On one interpretation, the Husserlian view discussed above is compatible with the idea that our conscious states' subjective character makes us aware of these states. The thought is that act-intentionality is different from familiar awareness-of only in that it is a *non-objectifying* awareness. It *is* awareness-of, just not awareness-of-object. If so, an intrinsic glow might be allowed to make us aware of our conscious experiences, just not in an objectifying manner. In this version, I might be happy with the intrinsic-glow account, but the implications that subjective character is *sui generis* and unstructured, and to that extent inexplicable, no longer follow. In any case, however, the emerging view ultimately strikes me as incoherent, inasmuch as it strikes me as conceptually true that, in the relevant sense of "object," awareness-of is always awareness-of-object.[8] In essence, I am merely reporting here

---

[8] The relevant sense of "object" is that-which-an-intentional-act-is-about. In this sense, "object" does *not* mean "physical object" or "ordinary object." To say that one can be aware of something without that "something" being the intentional object of the awareness is what strikes me as incoherent.

that I cannot really wrap my mind around the notion of non-objectifying awareness.

I conclude that Premises 3 and 4 of the awareness-making argument are highly plausible, and so the argument is quite compelling. A suitable account of subjective character would have to construe subjective character in a way that makes clear how a conscious state's subjective character makes the subject aware of that state. Indeed, the subject's inner awareness of her conscious state could be plausibly taken to *constitute* the state's subjective character. Such an account of subjective character in terms of inner awareness would have to get clear on the nature of the kind of awareness that constitutes subjective character, since certainly not any kind of awareness would do, only a quite special and elusive one.[9] Ideally, we would ultimately obtain an account of the relevant awareness in terms of the more familiar properties of our mental states. I make a start in the next section.

2. From Inner Awareness to (Constituting) Representation

In pursuit of an account of the special and elusive inner awareness we have of our conscious states in terms of familiar properties of mental states, a natural starting point would be to construe such inner awareness in terms of the *representational* properties of mental states.

The promise in such an approach is as follows. It is highly plausible that awareness of anything requires representation of it: to be aware of a tree, for example, involves representing the tree. If so, the obtaining of some kind of representational fact is a *necessary* condition for the occurrence of inner awareness. That is, a subject is aware of her conscious state in the relevant way *only if* the state is represented by the subject. In short, representation is a necessary condition for inner awareness (and therefore, by contraposition,

---

[9] The elusiveness and specialty of the subject's epistemic relation to her conscious states are perhaps the source of the resistance to an inner-awareness approach to subjective character, and the initial appeal of an intrinsic-glow approach. But the elusiveness and specialty might be accounted for in terms of some of the unusual properties of our inner awareness of our conscious states (indicated in Chapter 2), in particular the facts that it is *peripheral* and *ubiquitous*. The case for this claim will be made in Chapter 5, but can also be found in Kriegel 2004a.

inner awareness is a sufficient condition for representation).[10] Moreover, it might be thought to be the core condition, in the sense that it is the kind of necessary condition that can yield a sufficient condition once a number of appropriate qualifiers are attached to it.[11] This would yield a reductive account of subjective character of the following form: for a mental state M of a subject S to have subjective character is for M to be represented by S in a way that satisfies conditions C1, C2, and so on—in other words, for M to be the target of a representation of kind K.

The key issue for an account of this form is to specify C1, C2, and so on, or K, in a way that generates a satisfactory theory. I will address this issue incrementally as we go alone, and most thematically in Section 6. In this section I want to consider a more fundamental threat to this representational approach to inner awareness. This is the potential objection that the special and elusive awareness we have of our conscious states cannot be accounted for in representational terms at all—that representation is not even a necessary condition for this form of inner awareness.

The thought behind this objection is that the relationship between one's inner awareness and what one is thereby aware of is more intimate than the relationship between a representation and what it represents. To be sure, most types of awareness can be understood along the above representational lines. But the inner awareness that constitutes subjective character or for-me-ness is not like that. In that kind of awareness, there is not the kind of gap between the awareness and that of which one is aware that calls for a representational treatment. There is not the gap between vehicle and content that we expect from standard cases of representation.

Something like this objection is aired in the recent literature by Levine (2001, 2006) and Hellie (2007). The objection takes a slightly different form

---

[10] See Lycan 2001a. Lycan proceeds to argue for a higher-order representationalist story, but this is because he seems to presuppose that a self-representational view is not an option; this will be the topic of the next section.

[11] The notion of a "core necessary condition" is a pragmatic one. Usually (though not always), in the analysis of a notion, there is a condition that seems more central or salient than the others, a necessary condition that would yield a sufficient condition if the right qualifications were added but also seems more salient than other conditions. Thus, let us agree, for the sake of argument, that knowledge is true, justified, Gettier-proof belief. There seems to be a clear sense in which being a belief is the *core* necessary condition of being knowledge. Even though being a truth would yield knowledge if the right qualifiers were added, it somehow seems less central to the notion of belief. To repeat, this is a pragmatic notion—we can imagine creatures for whom a different condition may seem salient.

in each case, but in both versions it appears to be animated by sensibility to what I have just described: the strong sense that the relationship between inner awareness and that of which it makes one aware is more intimate than the relationship between a representation and that which it represents. We may call this the *objection from intimacy*.

The term "acquaintance" is sometimes applied to the kind of epistemic relationship we seem to have on our hands here, a relationship reminiscent of representation but lacking the typical gap between representor and represented.[12] The objection from intimacy can be thought of simply as the claim that the phenomenological facts about inner awareness support an account of inner awareness in terms of an acquaintance relation rather than a representation relation (see Hellie 2007).

In assessing the objection from intimacy, it is necessary to get clearer on just what the intimacy claim amounts to. I will address this issue below. But, in any event, there are three possible responses to the objection. The first is to deny the datum: insist that the relevant type of inner awareness is not intimate in the way suggested by the objector. On most reasonable construals of intimacy, I do not wish to adopt this response. The second and third responses do not contest the datum; both accept that intimacy is a real phenomenon. One of them will emerge only at the end of Section 4. The other is pursued in the remainder of this section.

The idea of intimacy is sometimes cast in terms of the thought that there could be no gap between how a conscious experience is and how it appears to one to be—between the qualitative properties the experience actually has and the qualitative properties one is aware of it as having, at least where the relevant kind of inner awareness is concerned. Although we might get wrong the various features of our experience (including its qualitative ones) in a variety of explicit introspective tasks, we cannot get them wrong in the kind of inner awareness that constitutes for-me-ness. It cannot be that, upon looking at the sky, my visual experience has a bluish qualitative character, but I am aware of it as having a greenish qualitative character. That kind of gap between real and apparent qualitative character simply makes no sense.

---

[12] Sometimes "acquaintance" is used more liberally, to cover whatever special awareness constitutes for-me-ness, whether or not it is endowed with intimacy. I will use the term in its more restrictive usage, as indicated in the text.

If this is how we understand the phenomenon of intimacy, then I think there is nothing about the phenomenon that rules out a representational treatment. For starters, we could hold that, for whatever specialized reasons, the kind of representation involved in inner awareness turns out to be infallible. Indeed, the idea of infallibility is one traditionally appealed to by philosophers responsive to the sensibility that animates the objection from intimacy. So, if the sensibility can be placated or spoken to by an account that construes inner awareness as infallible representation, then, given that, pending a compelling account of the relevant type of infallibility, representation is a more familiar and less inherently mysterious notion than acquaintance, we should embrace the infallible-representation account.

It would probably be objected, however, that ultimately the animating sensibility is not placated by appeal to infallible representation, because the idea of intimacy involves more than just the impossibility of inner awareness "getting wrong" the qualitative properties of experience. It involves the thought that there is not a gap to begin with between the awareness and what one is aware of. In infallible representation, the vehicle of representation and the content of representation are still wholly distinct entities (just as in true belief there is still a clear numeric distinction between the believing and what is believed). It is this element of "whole distinction" that intimacy banishes but infallible representation does not.

It may be possible, however, to capture both (*a*) the impossibility of "getting wrong" qualitative properties in the right kind of inner awareness, and (*b*) the lack of "whole distinction" between that awareness and what one is thereby aware of, by construing inner awareness in terms of *constituting* representation. The idea is that qualitative properties are *constituted* by the inner awareness representation of the conscious state.

To make sense of this, we must distinguish two kinds of property—the properties represented and the properties constituted by the representation. We may call the former schmalitative properties and the latter qualitative properties. Just as there is a distinction between being 6 foot tall and being represented to be 6 foot tall, so there is a difference between being schmalitatively bluish and being represented to be schmalitatively bluish. The question then is which of these two properties ought to be identified with the property of being qualitatively bluish. What I am proposing is that being qualitatively bluish ought to be identified with being represented to be schmalitatively bluish.[13] For a conscious state C to be qualitatively bluish is just for C to be represented to be schmalitatively bluish in the right kind of inner awareness.

What the schmalitative properties are is not immensely important in the present context, but obviously I would like to use the response-dependent representational story from the previous chapter to account for them. For a conscious state to be schmalitatively bluish, on this view, is for it to represent the right response-dependent property. For the state to be *qualitatively* bluish is for it to be *represented* to represent the right response-dependent property.

I mentioned in the previous chapter that in this one I will modify the response-dependent representational account of qualitative character. This is the modification I had in mind: that account may be better thought of as an account of schmalitative character; qualitative character is appropriately represented schmalitative character.[14]

On the view under consideration, inner awareness need not be infallible. One can misrepresent to oneself the schmalitative properties of one's conscious experience; but these schmalitative properties are not part of the experience's phenomenal character, indeed are not phenomenologically manifest in any way. The phenomenologically manifest properties, those that do form part of phenomenal character, are the qualitative properties. Those cannot be misrepresented in the relevant kind of inner awareness, not because of any *cognitive achievement* involved in the relevant awareness, but simply because they are *constituted by* the contents of that awareness.[15]

---

[13] The idea is then that the qualitative properties of a conscious state are constituted by the way the state's schmalitative properties are represented. More strongly even, a state's qualitative property *just is* its represented schmalitative property qua represented through inner awareness.

[14] We could also adopt a different system of bookkeeping, where this qualitative/schmalitative distinction is replaced by phenomenal/qualitative. Under this terminological regime, a conscious state's qualitative character is its representing the right kind of response-dependent property and its phenomenal character is its represented qualitative character. There is something to be said for this regime, inasmuch as it casts the representation and the represented as two seamlessly conjoined aspects of phenomenal character. The downside is that it casts qualitative character as external to phenomenal character, whereas in Chapters 1–3 we have treated qualitative character as a component of phenomenal character. For this last reason, I will stick with the previous regime, whereby qualitative character is a component of phenomenal character that is constituted by the representation of some other properties (schmalitative ones), with the representing itself constituting subjective character.

[15] At the same time, the fact that the relevant inner awareness need not be infallible does not imply that it cannot be, let alone that there is no infallibility involved in our relation to our stream of consciousness. Terry Horgan and I argue for such limited infallibility in Horgan and Kriegel 2007. But

Thus the construal of the kind of inner awareness that constitutes subjective character as a constituting representation delivers the results that (*a*) inner awareness cannot get wrong the qualitative properties of the conscious state one is thereby aware of and (*b*) there is not a gap between the awareness and what one is aware of—the two are not wholly distinct. All this falls out of the idea that the relevant element one is aware of—the qualitative properties—is constituted by one's awareness of it. To that extent, the constituting-representation account captures everything we want to capture in the phenomenon of intimacy, while still being more familiar than anything like acquaintance. For these reasons, I prefer construing subjective character in terms of such constituting representation than in terms of acquaintance.

It may be objected that the phenomenon of intimacy requires something stronger than either (*a*) or (*b*) above. It requires something like (*b*) but involving a genuine *cognitive achievement*, of the sort captured (for example) in infallibility theses.[16] In the constituting-representation account, however, there is no genuine representational achievement. There is only the theoretician's decision to focus on properties that are definitionally tied to representation. My response to this objection is that, if something as strong as this is built into intimacy, it becomes more plausible to adopt the first response to the objection from intimacy—that is, to deny the "datum."[17]

A more general objection may be that there is no substantive difference between the constituting-representation view and the acquaintance view. The immediate response, however, is that, if the two collapse into the same, then we need not worry about the acquaintance view presenting a genuine alternative to the constituting-representation view.

it is important to emphasize that the claims made here are independent of, and do not rest upon, any infallibility claim.

[16] The achievement may not need to be as impressive as infallibility, but the objector would insist that the phenomenon of intimacy requires that our special awareness of qualitative character involve *some* cognitive achievement on the subject's part, an achievement that results in a lack of numeric distinction between the awareness and what one is thereby aware of, rather than be the artifact of a constituting relation between the representation and the properties we focus on.

[17] In addition, it may also be possible to meet this stronger requirement in purely representational terms—namely, by combining the thesis that qualitative character is constituted by represented schmalitative character with the thesis that the relevant representation of schmalitative character is infallible. The constitution claim would deliver a lack of numeric distinction between awareness and that which one is aware of, while the infallibility claim would deliver the dimension of cognitive achievement. I personally do not think that the representation of schmalitative properties is infallible, so do not endorse this response.

Nonetheless, somehow they do not seem to collapse. Both views rest on some constitutive relationship between the awareness and what one is aware of, but perhaps there is a sense in which the "order of constitution" is opposite: in the acquaintance view, what one is aware of somehow constitutes one's awareness, whereas, in the constituting-representation view, the awareness constitutes what one is aware of. One option is to frame the issue in terms of the following Euthyphro-style question: when one has the special and elusive awareness of one's concurrent experience as bluish, is the experience bluish because the awareness is as of a bluish experience, or is the awareness as of a bluish experience because the experience is bluish? The representation-friendly view is that one's experience is bluish because one has an awareness as of a bluish experience. The acquaintance-friendly view is that one's awareness is as of a bluish experience because one's experience is bluish. If this is the contrast, then the representation-friendly view strikes me as more antecedently plausible than the acquaintance-friendly view, though I cannot say that this is so with overwhelming confidence.

The main reason to prefer the representational model, however, is the issue of familiarity. The notion of representation is familiar and well behaved, whereas that of acquaintance is unfamiliar and somewhat mysterious. One way to bring this out is to note the way "acquainted with," in the relevant sense, is supposed to be a *basic* factive mental verb—something of which there is no other example. Since there is no other example of this, the relation denoted by "acquainted with" is unique and deeply unfamiliar.[18]

Let me explain the notion of a basic factive mental verb. There are, of course, many factive mental verbs, most notably "knows." But, in those, the relations denoted are always asymmetrically dependent on other relations denoted by non-factive mental verbs. In the case of "knows," the denoted relation depends asymmetrically on the relation denoted by "believes," which is a non-factive verb.[19] But this is not supposed to be the case with "acquainted with": there is no non-factive relation on which the acquaintance relation depends asymmetrically. It is in this sense that

[18] By "deeply unfamiliar," I mean that its unfamiliarity is not a matter of the theoreticians failing to use it more frequently or in an earlier stage of inquiry. Rather, it is bound to be unfamiliar because of its own properties. This is a kind of metaphysical as opposed to epistemic unfamiliarity.

[19] Williamson (2000) notwithstanding.

"acquainted with" is a *basic* factive mental verb. If I am right that it is the only one, this would make it deeply unfamiliar.

In other words, acquaintance seems to be the only exception to the following principle:

(NBF) For any mental relation R denoted by a verb V, if V is factive, then there is a mental relation R*, denoted by a verb V*, such that (i) R is asymmetrically dependent upon R* and (ii) V* is non-factive.

My claim is that we should hold onto this principle—call it the *principle of no basic factivity* (NBF)—as universal and exceptionless. Since acquaintance is by definition a basic factive relation, it follows that there is no such thing as acquaintance.

The overall argument of this section is this: the view that inner awareness is a constituting representation is preferable to the view that it is acquaintance, because a constituting representation can accommodate the phenomena of intimacy characteristic of the inner awareness that constitutes subjective character, while still being more familiar than acquaintance in the very specific sense of being consistent with NBF. Call this the *argument from familiarity*.

The upshot of the last two sections is that the bluish way it is like for me to have an experience of the sky is a matter of my constitutingly representing my experience to be bluish. Recall, however, that such constituting representation is merely a necessary condition for subjective character, and further qualifications would be needed to obtain a sufficient condition.

3. From Representation to Self-Representation: I. *Via Positiva*

We have reached the conclusion that every conscious state, in virtue of its subjective character, is represented by its subject. Now, it is plausible to maintain that, whenever a subject represents something, she does so in virtue of being in a mental state that represents that thing. If I represent the sky, then there is a mental state M, such that I am in M and M is a representation of the sky. The same should apply to the kind of constituting representation that constitutes subjective character: if I represent my sky experience, M, then there is a mental state M*, such that I am in M* and M* is a representation of M.[20]

At this point, there are three options regarding the relationship between M and M*: either (i) M* is always identical to M, or (ii) M* is always numerically distinct from M, or (iii) sometimes M* and M are identical and sometimes they are different.[21] More formally:

(i) For any conscious mental state M of a subject S, necessarily, there is a mental state M*, such that S is in M*, M* represents M, and M* = M.

(ii) For any conscious mental state M of a subject S, necessarily, there is a mental state M*, such that S is in M*, M* represents M, and M* ≠ M.

(iii) For any conscious mental state M of a subject S, necessarily, there is a mental state M*, such that S is in M* and M* represents M; for some M, M* ≠ M, and for some M, M* = M.

That is, either (i) every conscious state is represented by itself, or (ii) every conscious state is represented by a mental state numerically distinct from it, or (iii) some conscious states are self-represented and some other-represented. Option (i) is a *self-representational account* of subjective character. Option (ii) is a *higher-order representational account*. Option (iii) is a *hybrid account*. In this section and the next I argue for option (i). That is, I argue for a broadly self-representational account of subjective character: the thesis that every conscious state, in virtue of its subjective character, self-represents.

Before starting, a few words on option (ii). In the relevant literature, one often comes across higher-order representation accounts, which are typically divided into *higher-order thought* and *higher-order perception* accounts. These higher-order accounts are typically construed as theories of *consciousness*, not of subjective character.[22] But I think they are most plausible when

---

[20] Farid Masrour has recently made the case to me that perhaps this step is less innocuous than it appears, and in fact what is so special about for-me-ness might have to do partly with the fact that for-me-ness is based in a *sui generis* representation relation in which it is *the subject*, and not one of her *states*, that stands in a relation to the conscious state endowed with subjective character.

[21] By "always" and "sometimes" I mean here "for all values of the variable" and "for some values of the variable."

[22] Sometimes they are more specifically construed as accounts of *state* consciousness, which is then typically taken to be the same as *phenomenal* consciousness by proponents of the account and often taken

seen as motivated by the thought that consciousness *consists in* subjective character, or at least that subjective character is the core of consciousness. That is, the motivation for higher-order theories of consciousness can be factorized into two components: (*a*) the thesis that consciousness amounts to subjective character and (*b*) a higher-order representation account of subjective character. For this reason, my discussion will move freely back and forth from talk of subjective character to talk of consciousness.[23]

In the next section I will argue that such higher-order representation accounts are bedeviled by too many problems, which then affect the hybrid account as well; this would provide an argument for a self-representational account *via negativa*. In the present section I want to develop an argument in favor of self-representationalism *via positiva*. The argument I will present, cryptically put, is that only self-representationalism can account for the epistemology of consciousness. For this reason, I call it the *epistemic argument* for self-representationalism. It proceeds as follows: (1) every conscious state is not just represented, but *consciously* represented; (2) if that is the case, then it must be that every conscious state is *self*-represented; it follows that (3) every conscious state is self-represented.[24]

The First Premise

Let us start by again distinguishing three options: either (iv) every conscious state is represented consciously, (v) every conscious state is represented unconsciously, or (vi) some conscious states are represented consciously and some unconsciously. More formally:

- (iv) For any conscious mental state M of a subject S, necessarily, there is a mental state M*, such that S is in M*, M* represents M, and M* is conscious.
- (v) For any conscious mental state M of a subject S, necessarily, there is a mental state M*, such that S is in M*, M* represents M, and M* is unconscious.

to be different from phenomenal consciousness by its opponents. I discussed these issues in Chapter 2, and will not revisit them here.

[23] In any case, for any higher-order theory of consciousness out there, we can formulate a parallel higher-order account of subjective character, in which the explanandum may or may not be the same but the explanans is certainly the same.

[24] If you will: (1) every conscious state is consciously represented; (2) if (1), then (3); therefore, (3) every conscious state is self-represented.

(vi) For any conscious mental state M of a subject S, necessarily, there is a mental state M*, such that S is in M* and M* represents M; for some M, M* is conscious, and for some M, M* is unconscious.

It seems to me that (iv) is the most phenomenologically adequate view. The subjective character of a conscious experience is after all a component of its phenomenal character, so, on the assumption that a component of phenomenal character must be phenomenologically manifest, subjective character must be phenomenologically manifest.[25] The most important reason to think that all conscious states are consciously represented, however, is not so much phenomenological as epistemic. It is, in a nutshell, that, if there is any evidence for conscious states being represented, or being *for the subject*, it must be *direct phenomenological evidence*—and only of the conscious can we have direct phenomenological evidence.

By "direct" phenomenological evidence, I mean that what we have phenomenological evidence for is the very same thing whose existence we are trying to establish. Consider a perceptual analogy. Suppose we are seeking perceptual evidence for the existence of parrots in the neighborhood. One kind of perceptual evidence is that we saw parrot nests in a number of trees in the neighborhood. A very different kind of perceptual evidence is that we saw *parrots* in a number of trees in the neighborhood. The former is *indirect* perceptual evidence for the existence of parrots in the neighborhood; the latter is *direct* perceptual evidence. By the same token, direct phenomenological evidence for the existence of a representation R would be constituted by the fact that R itself is phenomenologically manifest; indirect phenomenological evidence would be constituted by some phenomenological fact P, such that P is not identical to, but

---

[25] There might be an objection to the principle that a component of phenomenal character must be phenomenologically manifest. Part of the issue in assessing this principle is to get clear on what "phenomenologically manifest" (an expression I use quite impressionistically here) involves, something we will not do until Chapter 5. But, setting that apart, and assuming that every phenomenal property is phenomenologically manifest, we may see that the principle is highly plausible, inasmuch as it requires that every component of a phenomenal character be itself a phenomenal property. It is unclear how someone might argue against this principle. Suppose I have an experience of square and circle side by side. If the phenomenal character of my experience is square-and-circle-ish, so that both the square and the circle are part of the phenomenal character, it would seem that each must be phenomenologically manifest. What is true "horizontally" is also true "vertically": if both qualitative and subjective character are components of phenomenal character, each must be phenomenologically manifest. (Another possible objection might be that subjective character is shown not to be phenomenologically manifest by consideration of the transparency of experience. I think this is a mistake, and will attempt to show that it is in the next chapter.)

makes probable, the fact that R exists. My argument in this subsection is this: if there is any evidence for the proposition that all conscious states are represented, it is direct phenomenological evidence; only conscious states are such that there can be direct phenomenological evidence for their existence; therefore, if there is any evidence for the proposition that all conscious states are represented, it is because all conscious states are consciously represented.

Suppose conscious states are always consciously represented. Then, since their representation is always conscious, it would always be phenomenologically manifest. That is, it would be phenomenologically manifest to us that our conscious states are always represented. More precisely, for any subject S, for each conscious mental state M of S, it would be phenomenologically manifest to S that M is represented. So S would have *direct* phenomenological evidence for the representations of each of her conscious states, and therefore for the proposition that all of S's conscious states are represented. S could then infer from this—by analogy or by inference to the best explanation—the more general proposition that all conscious states, including others', are represented.

If conscious states are not always consciously represented, however, then there cannot be *direct* phenomenological evidence for their always being represented (at all). For, in that scenario, even if all conscious states are represented, at least some are unconsciously represented. Since their representation is unconscious, there will be no direct phenomenological evidence of it. The evidence must be different. I will now consider four possible alternative sources of evidence: indirect phenomenological evidence, a posteriori experimental evidence, a priori conceptual-analysis evidence, and philosophical principles. After arguing against each possibility, I will conclude that, if there is *any* evidence for the proposition that all conscious states are represented, it must be direct phenomenological evidence. Since the only way there could be direct phenomenological evidence for all conscious states being represented is if all conscious states were *consciously* represented, I will conclude that all conscious states are consciously represented.

Start with the idea of indirect phenomenological evidence. Suppose that not all conscious states are consciously represented, but that there are some other phenomenological data, such that the best explanation of those other data is that all conscious states are represented. In these circumstances, those other data would constitute *indirect* phenomenological evidence for the proposition that all conscious states are represented. The evidence would be "indirect" in the sense that what we would have phenomenological evidence for would *not* be the very thing whose existence we were trying to establish.

There is an argument of Rosenthal's (1990) that takes this form—or at least can be interpreted along these lines. Rosenthal notes that a wine connoisseur and a novice can have very different gustatory experiences upon tasting some new wine, even if the strictly sensory component of their experiences is the same. The best explanation for this, he claims, is that the connoisseur possesses higher-order concepts the novice lacks, which help her classify her experiences more finely, in a way that makes a difference, via higher-order representations, to the experience's phenomenal character. A central plank of this explanation is the claim that when the connoisseur and the novice have their gustatory experiences, they have higher-order representations of them. In this argument, the phenomenological data regarding the experiential difference between the connoisseur and the novice constitute indirect phenomenological evidence for the proposition that all conscious states are represented.

However, this is the only argument I know of that takes this form, and it is probably unsound. It is unclear why the experiential difference between the connoisseur and the novice could not be explained purely in terms of first-order concepts, or even just first-order discriminative abilities: the connoisseur can classify *wines* in ways that the novice cannot, thus attributing *to the wine itself* properties that the novice cannot attribute. To obtain a compelling argument from inference to the best explanation here, Rosenthal would have to argue that his explanation is better than this alternative. It seems to me, however, that it is *worse*: the two explanations account for the data equally well, as far as I can tell, but the appeal to first-order concepts/abilities is superior with regards to its theoretical virtues, especially simplicity.[26]

There may be another form of argument based on indirect phenomenological evidence that we should consider. Even if not *all* conscious states are *consciously* represented, one may still hold that *some* are. If some conscious

---

[26] I am assuming here that, if the same data can be explained by the representational content of a conscious state, instead of in terms of the conscious state being represented, then this would be simpler.

states are consciously represented, one might use some kind of ampliative inference to the conclusion that all conscious states are represented (either consciously or unconsciously). For example, one might hold that all—and only—*introspected* conscious states are consciously represented (Rosenthal 1990, 2002a).[27] One might reason, say by enumerative induction, that, since all the conscious states one has actively introspected have been represented, it is plausible that all conscious states are represented, including those that have not been actively introspected.[28]

The obvious objection to this form of reasoning is that the inductive sample is wildly biased. *Of course* all the conscious states in the sample would be represented if what makes them belong to the sample is that they are introspected. The deep problem here is that the introspecting itself constitutes the representing, so the very criterion for selecting the sample adverts to representedness. Furthermore, if the inductive inference were warranted for the conclusion that all conscious states are represented, it would also be warranted for the conclusion that they are all *consciously* represented, since all the instances in the sample are consciously represented.

Moving on to the second alternative source of evidence, what sort of a posteriori experimental evidence might require the postulation of higher-order representations involved in consciousness? Suppose neuro-imaging studies revealed that, whenever a subject appears to be conscious, the part of the brain usually responsible for internal monitoring is activated. This would constitute strong evidence in favor of the proposition that all conscious states are represented.

The problem, however, is that there is not currently any serious evidence of this sort.[29] It is illuminating, in any case, that no philosopher has ever made the case for conscious states always being represented on such experimental grounds. The thought is rather that there is something intuitive, hence (presumably) altogether pre-theoretic, about the idea that, as Rosenthal

---

[27] On Rosenthal's view, conscious states that are not explicitly introspected are only unconsciously represented (we will see why later in the section). But explicitly introspected ones are *consciously* represented, while the introspecting itself is unconsciously represented.

[28] I am not familiar with any philosopher who holds that all conscious states are represented on these grounds. But the *possibility* of doing so has been suggested to me, somewhat coyly, by John Pollock.

[29] In Chapter 7 I will suggest that there may be, but that will be mostly by way of prediction, not by way of retrodiction.

(1990) puts it, "conscious states are states we are conscious of." This idea would not be *intuitive*, however, if the reasons to believe it were purely experimental.

Perhaps the motivation for thinking that all conscious states are represented, and the reason it is intuitive that conscious states are states we are conscious of, is broadly verbal, or conceptual. This would be our third potential alternative source of evidence, based on some sort of a priori conceptual analysis. It might be claimed, for example, that it is just a contingent fact about the English word "conscious" that it applies appropriately only to states of which we are aware (and hence represent). On this view, the evidence for the proposition that all conscious states are represented is of the same kind as the evidence that all bachelors are unmarried: it simply falls out of the meaning of the terms.

The problem with this line of thought is that the proposition that all conscious states are represented is supposed to apply to conscious states in the phenomenal sense of "conscious," not in the mundane sense. In the phenomenal sense, what makes a mental state conscious is that it exhibits the feature responsible for the explanatory gap, or more generally the relevant philosophical conundrum. It is not verbally or conceptually true that a state cannot exhibit this property unless it is represented. More pointedly, as subjective character may turn out to be an aspect of consciousness only in the phenomenal sense, and not in the everyday sense, it is unclear that conscious states' being represented in the everyday sense is relevant to the understanding of subjective character.

It might be claimed that consciousness in the mundane sense of the word *just is* phenomenal consciousness. But presumably we would have to be convinced of that. What fixes the reference of "phenomenal consciousness" is the property of generating the explanatory gap, or the mystery of consciousness, *not* (at least not necessarily) the property of being denoted by the English word "consciousness" and its cognates. A claim about the latter property would also be a claim about the former only on the outside chance that there is a necessary coextension between the two, something I have seen no argument for and which is almost certainly false.[30]

---

[30] Relatedly, it is sometimes charged that certain views of consciousness are really views about *access* consciousness, not *phenomenal* consciousness. Higher-order representationalists routinely reject the charge (Rosenthal 2002b), but the reason the charge sticks is that they have failed to cast their posited higher-order representations as in any way relevant to the phenomenology. This is because

Finally, it might be suggested that the way we reach the proposition that all conscious states are represented is by some sort of philosophical reasoning from first principles (whatever turns out to be involved in such reasoning). Indeed, the very discussion of the past two sections provides one such reasoning: phenomenal consciousness involves for-me-ness, which is better accounted for in terms of representation than in terms of intrinsic glow or acquaintance, so all phenomenally conscious states are represented. Such reasoning from first principles is ubiquitous in philosophy, and provides the most natural support for the proposition that all conscious states are represented.

Here the problem is that, when the support for a proposition is grounded in first principles, the ultimate evidence for that proposition is whatever is the evidence for the principles. Thus if the first principles themselves are baseless, there is ultimately no evidence for the proposition. So to identify the evidence for the proposition, we must identify the evidence for the first principles. In the present case, the question is what evidence we have for accepting the claim that all phenomenal consciousness involves for-me-ness. I claim that, if there is any evidence for this, it is direct phenomenological evidence.[31] If my opponent wishes to contest this claim, she must suggest another kind of evidence for the thesis that all phenomenal consciousness involves for-me-ness. Indirect phenomenological evidence, experimental evidence, and conceptual-analysis evidence do not seem to be forthcoming, and it is unclear what other evidence might be assessed.[32] So the appeal to philosophical reasoning from first principles is unlikely to generate a source of evidence that is genuinely an *alternative* to direct phenomenological evidence.

---

they construe the higher-order representations as typically external to the phenomenology. If a phenomenological story were told about our inner awareness of our conscious states, the force of the charge would dissolve. But, once such a phenomenological story is told, one must construe the awareness of our conscious states as conscious and internal to the phenomenology—that is, one must claim that all conscious states are consciously represented.

[31] Of course, I assert the antecedent, and therefore hold that there actually is such direct phenomenological evidence. As discussed in Chapter 2, however, I realize that it is hard to convince others with such assertions, wherefore I adopted the cluster-of-conditionals approach to the theory of consciousness at the end of that chapter.

[32] Certainly there is no experimental evidence that I know of to show that phenomenal consciousness involves for-me-ness. And conceptual analysis would again be irrelevant. For my part, nor can I think of relevant indirect phenomenological evidence, though perhaps someone could come up with such evidence.

In conclusion, I have argued that we do have direct phenomenological evidence for the proposition that all our conscious states are represented, and that we do not have any other serious evidence for this. The upshot is that, if there is any evidence for the proposition that all conscious states are represented, it must be direct phenomenological evidence—which is the first premise of the epistemic argument. Next I will argue for the second premise of the epistemic argument: that the only way there could be such direct phenomenological evidence is if every conscious state is consciously represented. Before doing so, however, let me consider some objections to my argument for the first premise.

One objection is that the proposition that all conscious states are represented is supported not by a single type of evidence, but rather by a loose array of considerations. The proposition may not be the best explanation of any one kind of consideration and yet be the best account of the lot. If so, it is fallacious to infer, as I did above, that, unless conscious states are consciously represented, there is no reason to suppose they are represented at all.

However, even if the support for the proposition comes from a loose array of considerations, it must be possible to separate the various considerations and assess the individual support each lends to the proposition. And, while there could be a scenario where one proposition is better supported by a set of considerations than its competitors even though for each consideration there is a competitor it supports better, in practice that kind of scenario requires that many of the considerations individually lend significant support to the proposition. Otherwise it would be hard for their cumulative support to add up in the right way. But the present case does not seem to bear these characteristics. The conceptual-analysis consideration raised above lends *no* support, upon inspection, to the proposition that all conscious states are represented; the experimental consideration lends negligible support; while the indirect phenomenological evidence lends either no support (in the case of the induction from introspected states) or non-negligible but far from overwhelming support (in the case of the difference between connoisseurs and novices). The cumulative support for the proposition cannot be very impressive.

Another objection in the same vein is that the thesis that all conscious states are represented is one we ought to adopt not because there is specific and isolable evidence in its favor, but because it is part of the most attractive package deal when it comes to the theory of consciousness. To put it crudely, the evidence is not foundational but coherentist: the reason to believe that all conscious states are represented is that this coheres well with other things we have good reason to believe, not because there is an independent reason to believe it.

However, it would be quite hard to make this objection work. The objector would have to show two things: (i) that the relevant package deal is indeed the most attractive, and (ii) that, even though the proposition is not itself supported by the evidence, removing it from the package decreases significantly the package's attraction. The second element in particular presents an outstanding challenge.[33]

A different objection might target my claim that there *is* direct phenomenological evidence for conscious states being always represented. The objection is that there can be no direct phenomenological evidence for a universal generalization. By the nature of things, only the truth of singular and existential propositions can be phenomenologically revealed. We can reach the universal proposition only by inductive inference from those singular propositions. What is phenomenologically manifest, then, does not support the proposition that *all* conscious states are represented more than the proposition that *most* are. The latter proposition, being the more modest one, is therefore the one we should adopt on the strength of the direct phenomenological evidence.

The force of this objection depends on a misguided model of how we reach the universal proposition from the phenomenological data, a model in which inductive reasoning plays the crucial role. I have suggested an alternative model, however, involving two steps neither of which implicates enumerative induction. In the first step, the theoretician reaches the conclusion that all *her* conscious states are represented, and, in the second, she reasons that this must be the case with others as well. The first step does not involve inductive inference, because the for-me-ness of every conscious state is phenomenologically manifest and thus provides to its subject direct phenomenological evidence that that state is represented.

---

[33] In the present context, the most natural version of this objection would maintain that the best overall theory of consciousness is the higher-order theory, and that the proposition that all conscious states are represented is an ineliminable tenet of that theory. In this case, the proposition is so central to the package deal that it is unclear how the package could be so strongly supported by the evidence without the proposition being individually supported.

At this stage there is no inductive inference, even though a universal generalization is established: it is akin to establishing that all ravens are black by observing each and every raven.[34] The second stage does not involve enumerative induction either, since the sample is too small (one) to support any such induction. Rather, it is a sort of analogical inference, or perhaps inference to the best explanation, based on the thought that it would be quite the coincidence if it turned out that one was exceptional in having all one's conscious states represented (in this phenomenologically manifest manner no less). Under this model, what is phenomenologically manifest does seem to support the proposition that all conscious states are represented more than the proposition that most are.

I conclude that, if there is any evidence that all conscious states are represented at all, then the evidence is that they are all consciously represented. I now move to the next stage of the argument: the claim that, if all conscious states are consciously represented, then all conscious states are self-represented—that is, (i) above.

The Second Premise

My claim in this subsection will be that (ii) and (iii) are incompatible with the proposition that all conscious states are consciously represented. The argument is simply that, conjoined with said proposition, (ii) and (iii) lead to most unlovely consequences.

Take first (ii), the claim that every conscious state is represented by a numerically distinct state. Combined with (iv), the proposition that every conscious state is consciously represented, it entails this: For any conscious mental state M of a subject S, there is a mental state M*, such that S is in M*, M* represents M, M* ≠ M, and M* is conscious. What this means, however, is that, whenever a subject is in a conscious state, either (*a*) she harbors an infinite hierarchy of mental states, each representing the one before it, or (*b*) she harbors a finite number of mental states that form a closed cycle. It is highly implausible—perhaps even impossible—that being in a single conscious state involves being in infinitely many, as per (*a*).[35] As

---

[34] It is important to note here that the phenomenological evidence is provided without need of introspective examination of each and every conscious state: each and every conscious state is phenomenologically manifest, even though not all of them are introspectively examined. How this could be will emerge in Chapter 5.

[35] Whether it is impossible depends partly on one's ontology of states. If states are bare particulars, it is probably impossible for a person to be in infinitely many mental states at one time, since it is

for the possibility brought up in (b), the existence of *large* cycles implicated in a person being in a single conscious state is empirically problematic, assuming that generating every representational state has its cost in terms of taxing the subject's cognitive resources. The leanest and most plausible version of (b) would posit a two-state cycle, in which M_1 is represented by M_2 and M_2 is represented by M_1.[36] On the one hand, this view can in many ways be seen as a version of self-representationalism, and so I am not very concerned to rebut it.[37] At the same time, while the phenomenological reality of for-me-ness supports the idea that M_1 is represented by M_2, it does not seem to support the idea that M_2 is represented by M_1, and to that extent the suggestion may involve a superfluous element it would be better to do without. Furthermore, (i) is essentially a one-state cycle, which is that much more economical than a two-state cycle.

The combination of (iii) and (iv) leads to slightly more complicated results, but essentially the same dialectic arises. The claim in (iii) is that some conscious states are self-represented and some are other-represented. The self-represented ones do not generate any regress, but the other-represented ones will generate a regress that can be stopped only by either a closed cycle or a self-representing state. If the stopping is through a closed cycle, the above considerations will apply here again. If it is through a self-representing state, then Aristotle's wise observation in *De Anima* II.3 would apply: if we have to cap a regress of representing states with a self-representing one, we might as well do so at the floor level and let the first-order state represent itself.[38]

---

probably impossible to harbor infinitely many bare particulars (though I can imagine some moves to accommodate such a possibility). If states are rather dated property exemplifications, then, given that a particular can relatively plausibly exemplify infinitely many properties at a time, it is more plausible that a person should be in infinitely many mental states at a time.

[36] The reason this is the most plausible version can be seen by extension from the point made by Aristotle to be mentioned in the next paragraph. The pressure to posit cycles is theoretically driven, not driven by observation of certain phenomena, so there is no reason to posit any cycle larger than the minimum necessary to meet the theoretical demands. The minimal cycle is a two-state one, so that is what we should posit.

[37] Indeed, the view is defended by Williford (2006), a staunch self-representationalist, and in Chapter 6 we will encounter a number of views quite similar to it.

[38] For discussion of this, see Caston (2002). The key passage in Aristotle is translated by Caston as follows: "Since we perceive that we see and hear, it is necessarily either by means of seeing that one perceives that one sees or by another perception. But the same perception will be both of the seeing and of the color that underlies it, with the result that either two perceptions will be of the same thing, or it [sc. the perception] will be of itself. Further, if the perception of vision is a different perception,

In addition, the hybrid view captured in (iii) introduces an untoward heterogeneity in the underlying nature of consciousness. It is rather implausible, on the face of it, that some conscious states are conscious in virtue of being represented one way, while others are conscious in virtue of being represented another way. One would expect a certain underlying unity, at a reasonable degree of abstraction, among conscious states. Indeed, if conscious states form a natural kind, as they probably do, they should boast a relatively concrete "underlying nature" common to all of them. The only thing the hybrid view can appeal to is the fact that all conscious states are represented. But, first, this commonality seems to lie too high in the order of abstraction, and, second, it cannot be that conscious states are conscious in virtue of being represented, since many unconscious mental states are represented as well.

It might be objected that some sort of regress attaches to the combination of (i) and (iv) as well. Suppose every conscious state represents itself. Something must make the state's self-representation conscious. According to self-representationalism, this would have to be the fact that conscious states represent themselves to represent themselves. But their representing themselves to represent themselves is also conscious, which requires accounting for. So now, although we have avoided a regress of conscious *states*, we are still saddled with a different kind of regress, a regress of conscious *contents*.

This objection rests on a fallacy, however.[39] The fallacy is to suppose that we can apply the attributes of consciousness and unconsciousness to contents just as we do to states, and that the account of content consciousness must be the same as that of state consciousness. But one view is that the attributes of consciousness and unconsciousness do not apply to contents at all, *only* to states. On this view, it is simply false that something must make a state's self-representation conscious. This view may not be plausible, but something very close to it probably is: that for a content to be conscious is not at all for it to be represented by itself, or for the mental state that carries it to represent itself to carry it, or anything in

either this will proceed to infinity or some perception will be of itself; so that we ought to posit this in the first place."

[39] For a much more thorough treatment of this regress charge, see Williford 2006. My treatment owes much to him. In Kriegel 2003a I offered a response to this objection that is in the same general vein but not nearly as accurate.

the vicinity; rather, for a content to be conscious is simply for it to be carried by a conscious state. On the self-representational view, that would entail that what it is for a mental content to be conscious is for it to be carried by a self-representing state. The idea is that we start by trying to understand what makes a mental state conscious, and then by extension speak of contents as conscious when they are carried by conscious states. But content consciousness is merely derivative and does not involve substantive addition to the theory of consciousness. So it is simply false that a mental state's representation of itself is conscious in virtue of the state representing itself to represent itself, as the objection states above.

The point may be put more precisely as follows. Compare and contrast the following two theses:

(S) Necessarily, for any mental state S, S is conscious iff S represents itself.

(C) Necessarily, for any mental content C, C is conscious iff C represents itself.

(S) is an account of what makes mental *states* conscious, (C) an account of what makes mental *contents* conscious. I grant that (C) leads to infinite regress of contents. But self-representationalism as such, and certainly (i) above, is not committed to (C), only to (S). (S) can then be combined with the following thesis about conscious *contents*:

(C−) Necessarily, for any mental content C, C is conscious iff there is a mental state S, such that (i) C is the content of S and (ii) S is conscious.

The conjunction of (S) and (C−) does *not* lead to infinite regress. What it leads to is this: necessarily, for any mental content C, C is conscious iff there is a mental state S, such that (i) C is the content of S and (ii) S represents itself. There is no regress here.

There would still be some threat of regress if we required conscious states not just to represent themselves, but to represent their own representational properties—*all* their representational properties. Thus the following indeed leads to an infinite regress:

(S+) Necessarily, for any mental state S and any mental content C, such that S has C, S is conscious iff S represents itself to have C.

But, again, (i) above, and more generally self-representationalism, are not committed to (S+) at all (Williford 2006). They require that conscious states represent themselves, but not that they represent themselves to have their self-representational properties. Minimally, conscious states may simply represent themselves to have their schmalitative properties.

In conclusion, the regress-of-contents charge is successful only if self-representationalism is committed either to (C) or to (S+), but in fact it is committed to neither. By contrast, if we adopt (iv), the claim that every conscious state is consciously represented (that is, represented by a conscious state), there is a threat of regress involved in (ii) and (iii). The regress can be stopped by a closed cycle, which in its most plausible version does not present a deep alternative to, and certainly not an improvement upon, (i). So, if we adopt (iv), we should also adopt (i). And I have argued in the previous subsection that we should adopt (iv).

All Together Now

To repeat, the argument of this section—the "epistemic argument," as I have called it—has been this: (1) all conscious states are consciously represented; (2) if all conscious states are consciously represented, then they are all self-represented; therefore, (3) all conscious states are self-represented. The sub-argument for Premise 1 of the epistemic argument is this: (1) we have evidence that all conscious states are represented; (2) if we have any evidence that all conscious states are represented, it must be direct phenomenological evidence; (3) we have direct phenomenological evidence that all conscious states are represented only if all conscious states consciously represented; therefore, (4) all conscious states are consciously represented. The sub-argument for Premise 2 of the epistemic argument is this: (1) either all conscious states are self-represented, or they are all other-represented, or some are self-represented and some are other-represented; (2) if all conscious states are consciously represented, then all are self-represented (on pain of vicious regress); (3) all conscious states are consciously represented; therefore, (4) it is much more plausible that all conscious states are self-represented than that some or all are other-represented. So the overall argument is this:

1. we have evidence that all conscious states are represented;
2. if we have evidence that all conscious states are represented, it must be direct phenomenological evidence;
3. we have direct phenomenological evidence that all conscious states are represented only if all conscious states are consciously represented; therefore,
4. all conscious states are consciously represented;
5. if all conscious states are consciously represented, then they are all self-represented; therefore,
6. all conscious states are self-represented.

This is my *via positiva* case for a self-representational account of subjective character. In the next section I offer a complementary *via negativa* case.

4. From Representation to Self-Representation: II. *Via Negativa*

The *via negativa* case is, in essence, an argument by elimination. I will argue that (ii) and (iii) above are riddled with problems. More specifically, I will present four problems for higher-order representationalism, and will note that they afflict the hybrid view as well, but not self-representationalism. I will conclude that we should adopt self-representationalism.

The Problem of Targetless Higher-Order Representations

The first problem for higher-order representationalism draws on the possibility of targetlesss higher-order representations.[40] The basic idea is simple: higher-order representationalism gets into trouble when we consider (suitable) higher-order *misrepresentations*. Just what the trouble is changes from one presentation of the argument to another. Let me offer one way of understanding what the trouble is.

---

[40] The argument is developed in Byrne (1997) and Neander (1998). See also Levine 2001: ch. 3, Caston 2002, and Kriegel 2003a.

There are two ways the higher-order state M^* may misrepresent M: (i) by representing that M is F when in reality M is not F, or (ii) by representing that M is F when in reality M does not exist. Let us call misrepresentations of the latter type "targetless" higher-order representations. The argument I will pursue in this subsection is that higher-order representationalism (as well as the hybrid view) cannot handle suitable targetless higher-order representations, whereas self-representationalism can.

Let M be the state type of undergoing a bluish experience and M^* the state type of suitably representing that one is undergoing a bluish experience. If M and M^* are distinct existences, then M can be tokened without M^* being tokened and vice versa. Then let S_1 and S_2 be two subjects, such that (i) both S_1 and S_2 harbor a token of M^* at t, (ii) S_1 does but S_2 does not harbor a token of M at t (nor roughly contemporaneously with t), and (iii) neither is in any *other* suitably represented mental state. Higher-order representationalism faces a dilemma: either (*a*) what it is like to be S_1 at t is the same as what it is like to be S_2 at t, or (*b*) what it is like is *not* the same. Both options are unpalatable.

Let us start with (*a*), since this is the horn Rosenthal (1990: 744; emphasis added) embraces explicitly in print:[41]

Strictly speaking, having a HOT [higher-order thought] cannot of course result in a mental state's being conscious if that mental state does not even exist . . . Still, a case in which one has a HOT along with a mental state it is about may be *subjectively indistinguishable* from a case in which the HOT occurs but not the mental state. If so, folk psychology would count both as cases of conscious states.

The problem with this response can be set out as follows: the combination of higher-order representationalism and (*a*) is inconsistent with the following obvious truism:

(OT) For any subject S and time t, there is something it is like to be S at t iff there is a mental state M, such that (i) S is in M at t and (ii) M is conscious at t.

In other words, if higher-order representationalism takes the first horn of the dilemma, it entails that OT is false. I take this to be an unacceptable consequence.

---

[41] Quoting this very passage, Levine (2001: 109 n. 24) comments: "But doesn't this give the game away?"

To see that higher-order representationalism and (*a*) are inconsistent with OT, let us construct a reductio of the conjunction of all three. *Ex hypothesi*, at *t* S_1 is in M and M is suitably represented by M*. According to higher-order representationalism, this means that S_1 is in a conscious state at *t*. By OT, it follows that there is something it is like to be S_1 at *t*. Since, according to (*a*), what it is like to be S_1 at *t* is the same as what it is like to be S_2 at *t*, it follows that there is something it is like to be S_2 at *t*. From this it follows, by OT, that S_2 is in a conscious state at *t*. According to higher-order representationalism, this means that there is a mental state M, such that at *t* S_2 is in M and M is suitably represented by a higher-order state. But *ex hypothesi* there is no such state. So the conjunction of higher-order representationalism, (*a*), and OT entails that, at *t*, there both is and is not a mental state M, such that S_2 is in M and M is suitably represented by a higher-order state.[42]

To relieve the contradiction, we must reject either higher-order representationalism, or (*a*), or OT. I take it that OT is a truism that cannot be seriously rejected. This leaves open rejecting either higher-order representationalism or (*a*). Higher-order representationalists would prefer rejecting (*a*), obviously. This amounts to embracing the second horn of the dilemma, (*b*). According to this horn, what it is like to be S_1 at *t* is *not* the same as what it is like to be S_2 at *t*.

The problem with embracing (*b*) is the reason Rosenthal avoids it: it forsakes the higher-order representationalist ambition to have the phenomenal character of conscious states *fixed* by the way these states are higher-order represented. If the higher-order representations harbored by S_1 and S_2 at *t* are the same, and yet what it is like to be S_1 at *t* and what it is like to be S_2 at *t* are not the same, then either what it is like to be S_1 at *t* or what it is like to be S_2 at *t* is not fully *determined* by the higher-order representations harbored by S_1 and S_2 at *t*.

---

[42] We can run the reductio from the opposite direction. *Ex hypothesi*, there is no mental state M, such that at *t* S_2 is in M and M is suitably higher-order represented. According to higher-order representationalism, it follows that there is no conscious state that S_2 is in at *t*. By OT, it follows that there is nothing it is like to be S_2 at *t*. Given (*a*), it follows that there is nothing it is like to be S_1 at *t*. From this it follows, by OT, that there is no conscious state that S_1 is in at *t*. According to higher-order representationalism, this means that there is no mental state M, such that at *t* S_1 is in M and M is suitably higher-order represented. But *ex hypothesi* there is such a state. So again the conjunction of higher-order representationalism, (*a*), and OT entails a contradiction.

To put it in terms of our own discussion in this chapter, embracing (*b*) conflicts with what we have argued for in Section 2 above—namely, that the inner awareness we have of our conscious experiences must be a *constituting* representation. The idea was that, since there cannot be a gap between the qualitative character of a bluish experience and the immediate inner awareness we have of the experience's qualitative character, the experience's qualitative character must be constituted by the way other properties of the experience ("schmalitative properties") are represented.[43] It follows from this that the only way there could be a difference between what it is like to be S_1 and S_2 at t is if there is a difference in how their current mental states' schmalitative properties are represented. This would require a difference in the representational properties of their respective tokens of M*. But *ex hypothesi* there is no such difference.[44]

So: if the higher-order representationalist embraces (*b*), she must forsake her ambition to give an account of phenomenal consciousness, or what it is like to be in a conscious state, in terms of higher-order representation; but, if she embraces (*a*), she must deny OT, the truism that there is something it is like to be someone at a certain time just in case that someone is in a conscious state at that time. Both options being unpalatable, the only open avenue for the higher-order representationalist is to modify her account in such a way that targetless higher-order representations no longer present an embarrassment to the account but the account's spirit is preserved. Let us consider a few options along these lines.

First, higher-order representationalists may claim that, when M* is targetless, the property of being conscious, although not instantiated by M, is instantiated by M*. However, this would pose a new dilemma: either M* is suitably higher-order represented, or it is not. If it is, then the problem of targetless higher-order representations would recur for the higher-order representation of M*. If it is not, then (i) the resulting view is independently implausible, inasmuch as it seems to offer no unified account of what it takes for a mental state to be conscious, and (ii) it does not seem that the resulting view preserves the spirit of higher-order representationalism

---

[43] Recall, I have suggested that a conscious experience's qualitative character is identical to its represented schmalitative character.

[44] I have assumed a representational type-individuation of higher-order states, such that what makes a token state a token of M* is precisely that it has the representational properties it does.

(as it involves discarding the thesis that all conscious states are suitably higher-order represented).

Secondly, higher-order representationalists might claim that the property of being conscious is, in reality, not a property of the discrete state M, but rather attaches to the compound of M and M*.[45] Thus, if M* exists but M does not, then the compound does not exist, and consciousness is not instantiated. Here the resulting view does not strike me immediately as independently implausible, as in the previous proposed modification, but nor does it seem to preserve the spirit of higher-order representationalism. For again phenomenal character is no longer fixed by the higher-order representation: the higher-order representation can remain exactly the same, but, because it is not integrated into a compound, there is no consciousness. The view is in many ways more akin in spirit to self-representationalism than higher-order representationalism. Indeed, in Chapter 6 I will consider a number of versions of self-representationalism, and one of them will be more or less the view under consideration.

Thirdly, it might be claimed that consciousness is in the first instance a property of creatures, not of states. On this diagnosis, the problem of targetless higher-order representations arises because we are attached to a model that construes phenomenal state consciousness as more basic than phenomenal creature consciousness (as we saw in Chapter 2). Once we renounce this, we can formulate higher-order representationalism as the thesis that a creature instantiates phenomenal consciousness at a time t just in case the creature is in a mental state such as M* (whether or not it is also in M). However, this reversal of the explanatory order between state and creature consciousness would not solve the problem unless we reject the highly plausible principle that a creature instantiates consciousness iff the creature is in a state that instantiates consciousness—that is, OT. As long as this principle holds, even if consciousness is in the first instance a property of creatures, it may still be, in a second instance, a property of states. The question would then arise as to what makes a state instantiate this property, and again a dilemma would arise: either (a) higher-order representations have nothing to do with a state's instantiating the property,

---

[45] This proposal is sometimes aired by Rosenthal, and was presented to me by him once in conversation.

and the spirit of the view is not preserved, or (*b*) they do, and the prospects of targetless higher-order representations re-emerges. In other words, for this modification of higher-order representationalism to solve the problem, it would have to claim something fairly strong, such as that it is a category mistake to attribute consciousness to individual mental states, or that such attribution would not follow from attribution of consciousness to creatures at times.

Fourthly, it might be proposed that the property of being conscious is instantiated, in the first instance, by the *intentional object* of M*. In cases in which M exists, M will *be* the intentional object of M*, and therefore will instantiate consciousness. But, in cases of targetless higher-order representation, no *real* object coincides with M*'s intentional object, which therefore would be a *mere* intentional object. Nonetheless, just as unicorns can have properties (for example, being horned), so could this mere intentional object of M*.[46] However, it is unclear that this modification would help the higher-order representationalist. My response is twofold. First of all, I deny that there are merely intentional objects (see Kriegel 2008). Secondly, even if there are, the fact that a mere intentional object is a certain way, hence "has a property," cannot entail that a property has been *instantiated*. I could hallucinate a lion, and the lion I hallucinated could be beige, but it would not follow that beigeness had been instantiated—that there is one more instance of beigeness in the world.[47] There might be instances of beige in the (actual) world, but not on account of my hallucinated lion's being beige. Similarly, even if the merely intentional object of M* could be conscious, it would not follow that consciousness has been instantiated. Thus, a world in which all higher-order representations are targetless would still be a zombie world.

Fifthly, and finally, proponents of higher-order representationalism might deny that there is a substantive distinction between misrepresentation of a lower-order state's *properties* and misrepresentation of its *existence*. They might claim that a person is always in *some* lower-order state or another, even if it is a lower-order state entirely unconnected with any

---

[46] Something at least very much like this has been presented to me, by way of defense of higher-order theory, by Josh Weisberg.

[47] This is actually rejected by some Meinongians, who maintain that properties *are* instantiated when had by non-existent objects (see, e.g., Priest 2005). But presumably it is bad news for higher-order representationalism if its plausibility ultimately depends on this doctrine.

higher-order state. If so, a higher-order state could always be interpreted as misrepresenting the properties of some such unrelated lower-order state.[48] However, although it is very improbable that any actual person has ever harbored higher-order states while lacking *any* first-order ones, this is surely just a contingent matter, and, as long as first- and higher-order states are distinct existences, it ought to be metaphysically possible for someone to have the latter without the former. Compare the case of targetless first-order hallucinations. It is very improbable that anyone has ever hallucinated a worldly object in an otherwise empty world, but that has never stopped philosophers of perception from taking seriously the possibility of such hallucination. It is no solution to the problem of hallucination to claim that all hallucinations are in fact covert illusions.[49] Moreover, even if there happens to be an unrelated lower-order state when someone is in a higher-order state, there are facts of the matter pertaining to what makes the latter represent something—we cannot just "interpret" it to represent the former in the absence of any relationship between them. Compare again first-order hallucinations. If I hallucinate a beige lion, it is not equally legitimate to say that I have simply misperceived the Eiffel Tower as being beige and leonine. There are facts of the matter that make it the case that this "interpretation" is incorrect.[50] There is thus very certainly a substantive distinction between targetless higher-order representations and higher-order misrepresentations of lower-order states' properties.[51]

One response that is *not* available to higher-order representationalists, and that has never been pursued by any of them, is to say that the occurrence of targetless higher-order representation is bound to be a rare affair, and therefore nothing to worry about. The mere possibility of even a single

[48] David Rosenthal suggested this to me as a possible response many years ago (in conversation). I am not sure how serious he was, much less if he believes today that this is a viable response to explore.

[49] I am following here the common practice of distinguishing between hallucination and illusion, the former involving misperception of an object's existence, the latter misperception of an object's properties.

[50] What these are may or may not be an independently interesting matter, but there surely are some such facts of the matter.

[51] More generally, it is clear that there are various ways in which the higher-order representationalist may try to accommodate targetless higher-order representations. But many of them are starkly implausible and all of them complicate the theory considerably. One of the initial attractions of higher-order representationalism is its clarity, elegance, and relative simplicity. Once the view is modified along any of the lines sketched above, it becomes significantly less clear, elegant, and simple. To that extent, it is bound to be considerably less attractive than it initially appeared.

targetless higher-order representation is sufficient to embroil the view in the theoretical crisis we have been discussing.

For this reason, the problem of targetless higher-order representations applies with equal force to the hybrid view presented in the previous section, according to which *some* (rather than *all*) conscious states have their subjective character, and therefore are conscious, in virtue of being targeted by higher-order representations. Since the hybrid view allows that some conscious states are conscious in virtue of being other-represented, it is vulnerable to the occurrence of some targetless higher-order representations.

The problem does not affect the self-representational account at all, however (Caston 2002, Kriegel 2003a). According to the self-representational account, all conscious states have their subjective character, and therefore are conscious, in virtue of being self-represented. It is perfectly coherent to suppose that a mental state may represent itself to be a certain way when in reality it is not that way, or even that it may represent itself not to exist when in reality it does exist. But it is incoherent to suppose that a mental state may represent itself to exist when in reality it does not exist. If it does not exist, it cannot represent itself—it cannot represent anything. In supposing that the state represents something, we are supposing that it exists. Thus a targetless self-representation is logically impossible.

It might be objected that self-representationalism, although invulnerable to a problem of targetless self-representations, nonetheless faces serious difficulties when handling self-misrepresentations of the other varieties. Thus, there are some implausibilities associated with the possibility of a state representing itself to have properties it does not have, or representing itself not to exist.

The response to this objection is twofold. First of all, if the possibility of such misrepresentations creates a *prima facie* problem for self-representationalism, it surely creates the very same problem for higher-order representationalism and the hybrid view. Thus there is no advantage to be sought here for either over self-representationalism.[52] But self-representationalism maintains its advantage over the competition with respect to the possibility of targetless higher-order representation. Thus the

---

[52] Recall the goal of the argument *via negativa*: after formulating (i)–(iii) as an exhaustive list of options, we sought considerations that would eliminate two among them, thus leaving one option as the most plausible. For the purposes of *this* argument, it does not matter if all three options are ultimately implausible, as long as one among them is significantly more plausible than the others.

fact that (i)–(iii) share certain problems does not diminish the fact that (ii) and (iii) face tremendous problems (i) does not.

In any case, it strikes me as simply false that self-representationalism faces any serious problems with respect to those other varieties of self-misrepresentation. Self-representationalism is not thrown into any instability by their possibility, but instead renders a clear verdict on them that is fully consistent with intuition.

Recall that inner awareness is a constituting representation: the qualitative character of a conscious experience is constituted by the schmalitative properties it is represented to have in the kind of representation that constitutes inner awareness. Self-representationalism claims that the relevant kind of representation is self-representation. So, if a mental state misrepresents itself to be F when in reality it is G, where F and G are schmalitative properties, then self-representationalism's verdict is that the state is merely schmalitatively G but qualitatively F. For what it means for a state to be qualitatively F is that it represents itself to be F. The point is that self-representationalism cannot face a problem with the self-misrepresentation of qualitative properties, since those cannot be self-misrepresented on the view that the self-representation is constituting.

It may be pressed that there is still a problem with the self-misrepresentation of schmalitative properties. We may even imagine a case where state M does not have *any* schmalitative properties but represents itself to be F (where F is a schmalitative property). This may be taken to constitute a serious embarrassment for self-representationalism. However, I do not see that it is. Again self-representationalism turns in a verdict that is clear and unproblematic. The verdict is that M is qualitatively F. It is unclear what intuitions, or for that matter what theoretical considerations, are supposed to militate against this verdict. Recall that schmalitative properties are not phenomenologically manifest, so their misrepresentation would not result in an unacceptable difference between the schmalitative properties a state has and those it seems to have, since in the relevant sense the state does not *seem* to have *any* schmalitative properties.[53]

More generally, it is unclear to me what problem the misrepresentation of a state's properties is supposed to present, even in the case of higher-order

---

[53] Compare: a state may misrepresent itself to occur on a Tuesday when in reality it occurs on a Wednesday, but, since there is no such thing as Tuesday phenomenology anyway, none of this makes a difference to the state's phenomenal character.

representationalism. When presenting the argument from targetless higher-order representations, I considered the case of two subjects, S_1 and S_2, who are both in a state M^* but where only S_1 is in M, and I asked whether what it is like for them at the time is the same or different. The problem for higher-order representationalism was that answering "different" involved forsaking the idea that the phenomenal character of a state is fixed by how it is represented, but answering "same" entailed $\sim$OT. The same problem does not seem to arise when we consider radical but not targetless higher-order misrepresentations. Suppose two subjects, S_1 and S_2, are such that both are in M and in both cases M is represented to be F, but in S_1's case M is G whereas in S_2's case M is F (where F and G are schmalitative properties). The question is whether what it is like to be S_1 at the time is the same as, or different from, what it is like to be S_2. Here the higher-order representationalist can answer "same" without committing to $\sim$OT, so it is unclear what problem the case generates. Perhaps there is some other obvious truth that the answer "same" conflicts with, but it is unclear to me what that may be.

This is to suggest that the possibility of radical but not targetless higher-order misrepresentation or self-misrepresentation is not problematic for any of the views in this area—self-representationalism, higher-order representationalism, or the hybrid view. Certainly I do not see how it is problematic for self-representationalism. And, as I stressed at the beginning of this discussion, even if this possibility is problematic for all three views, this does not diminish the fact that the possibility of targetless higher-order misrepresentation is a major problem for higher-order representationalism and the hybrid view but not for self-representationalism.

As for the case of a state that misrepresents itself to be non-existent, self-representationalism may simply say that this kind of self-representation is not a sufficient condition for subjective character, and so the mental state in question remains unconscious. Recall that, at this stage, we are merely zooming in more and more specifically on a necessary condition for subjective character. We have determined in Section 1 that subjective character must be inner awareness, and in Section 2 that it must be a constituting representation, and in Sections 3–4 we have been arguing that that it must be a constituting *self*-representation. Our hope is that the necessary condition can be narrowed down enough that it may also become a sufficient condition, and we will return to the issue of sufficient condition in Section 6. But for now we can simply note that, if a state represents itself to be non-existent, that sort of self-representation would not suffice to make the state *for the subject*, hence not endowed with subjective character.

I conclude that the other varieties of self-misrepresentation do not pose a serious threat to self-representationalism, and, even if they did, that would not affect the *via negativa* argument for self-representationalism, which seeks only *some* advantages for the latter over its competition. Since targetless self-representation is impossible, but targetless higher-order representation is possible, we have here one very serious advantage for self-representationalism over its competition.

The Problem(s) of Extrinsicness

According to higher-order representationalism, all conscious states have their subjective character, and thus are conscious, in virtue of being related in the right way to *other* mental states—namely, their relevant higher-order representations. Thus subjective character is construed as an *extrinsic* property of conscious states. In the present context, a property is extrinsic just in case its bearer instantiates it in virtue of standing in a relation to something else: F is extrinsic iff for any x, if x is F, then there is a y, such that y does not overlap x (where "overlap" is used in its classical-mereological sense of sharing a part, so that x overlaps y iff there is a z, such that z is part of x and z is part of y).[54]

Some philosophers find the notion that consciousness is an extrinsic property counter-intuitive. What it is like to be in a given conscious state must be an intrinsic property of the state, they insist. For some, this alone is a ground for rejecting higher-order representationalism (Smith 1989, Gennaro 1996, Natsoulas 1999). In this section, I will argue that construing consciousness as extrinsic not only is counter-intuitive, but also brings up the specter of two serious problems, problems that affect both higher-order representationalism and the hybrid view. This constitutes another advantage for self-representationalism, since, as I will argue toward the end, these problems do *not* affect self-representationalism, which construes consciousness as an intrinsic property in the relevant sense (namely, the

---

[54] Given that consciousness is construed as subjective character by higher-order representationalists, and that I take subjective character to capture the existence condition of consciousness, it follows both for them and for me that consciousness is an extrinsic property.

sense in which F is intrinsic just in case, for any x, x's being F does not entail that there is a y, such that y does not overlap x).

Let us start with the first problem with extrinsicness. Two decades ago, perhaps the most widely discussed problem in the philosophy of mind concerned the causal efficacy of mental content. After externalist accounts of content—which construed content as an extrinsic property of mental states—became popular, it was observed that this appears to render mental content causally inert.[55] The reasoning was this: only intrinsic properties of a mental state contribute to its fund of causal powers, because causation is a local affair; so, if content is an extrinsic property, it makes no contribution to the state's causal powers; therefore, if externalism about content is true, then content is causally inert, or epiphenomenal.

That problem was never resolved to everybody's satisfaction. Different solutions, of different merits, have been offered, but no agreement is in sight.[56] One thing many participants accepted was the thesis that the causal powers of a mental state reside fully in its intrinsic properties, since it is hard to see how intrinsic duplicates could differ in their capacity to influence the world (see especially Kim 1982).[57] This thesis is not uncontroversial, and some philosophers have rejected it (e.g., Dretske 1988). But, if we accept the thesis, we have a straightforward argument against higher-order representationalism, since the latter construes consciousness as extrinsic. Crudely put, the argument would be this: extrinsic properties are epiphenomenal; higher-order representationalism entails that consciousness is extrinsic; therefore, higher-order representationalism

[55] Perhaps the most poignant presentation of the problem is Stich's (1979), but see also Kim 1982 and Fodor 1987.

[56] Perhaps the most common approach was to claim that, even if mental content lacks causal powers, it is nonetheless *explanatorily* relevant in psychology (see Burge 1989). Another popular strategy, identified with the internalist camp, was to construct a notion of *narrow content*—that is, content that is fully determined by the intrinsic properties of the state whose content it is (see Fodor 1987)—and to claim that this narrow content is the causally efficacious content.

[57] Sometimes, it has been claimed not that causal efficacy resides solely in *intrinsic properties*, but that it resides solely in properties that *supervene* on intrinsic properties ("locally supervenient" properties). This does not make a difference to the present argument, though. The present argument is based on the fact that higher-order representationalism construes consciousness as an extrinsic, relational property. But higher-order representationalism *also* construes consciousness as not locally supervenient. Thus, according to higher-order representationalism, two mental states that are intrinsically indistinguishable can differ in consciousness: one is conscious and one is not (because one is appropriately represented and one is not). If so, the property of being conscious is not locally supervenient.

entails that consciousness is epiphenomenal (see Dretske 1995: 117 for an argument along these lines).

(Some readers might find the thesis that extrinsic properties are epi-phenomenal counter-intuitive: holding a hammer is an extrinsic property, but certainly increases one's causal powers. However, it is only when we talk loosely that we say such things. Clearly, strictly speaking it is only the sum of oneself and one's hammer that boasts the increased causal powers, not oneself in isolation from one's hammer. And the sum's causal powers are due entirely to its intrinsic properties. Other readers might be tempted to suspect that something must be wrong with the thesis, since it threatens so many other plausible claims—for example, that intentional properties can causally influence behavior. But the thesis will never threaten such claims all by itself—it requires conspiracy with an extrinsic construal of some properties. For example, it threatens the claim that intentional properties are causally efficacious only in conspiracy with the idea that intentional properties are extrinsic—that is, in conspiracy with externalism about intentionality. To my mind, this is a fair consideration in favor of internalism about intentionality.)

As noted, some would be inclined to reject the premise that extrinsic properties are epiphenomenal. Discussing this matter will take us too far afield, so I propose instead to offer the argument only to those readers whose credence in the thesis that causal powers reside in intrinsic properties is non-negligible. My claim is that they should attach the same credence to the thesis that higher-order representationalism leads to epiphenomenalism. Such epiphenomenalism can be rejected, however, both on commonsense grounds and on the grounds that it violates what has come to be known as *Alexander's dictum* (Kim 1998): to be is to be causally effective.[58] Surely a theory of consciousness would be better

---

[58] There may also be an epistemological problem involved in epiphenomenalism: if genuine knowledge requires causal interaction, as some philosophers have maintained (e.g., Goldman 1967), there can be no knowledge of epiphenomenal entities or phenomena. This would make higher-order representationalism entail the absurdity that we cannot, in principle, have any knowledge of the existence of consciousness. I do not wish to press this problem because, on my view, our knowledge of consciousness is not causally mediated (more on this in Chapter 8). But this view is motivated partly by the self-representational account of consciousness. For someone who does not think that conscious states necessarily self-represent, it is more likely that knowledge of conscious state requires some causal interaction with them.

off if it could legitimately assign some causal powers to consciousness. Higher-order representationalism fails to do so.

This is, by all appearances, a serious problem for higher-order representationalism. Why have philosophers failed to press this problem more consistently? My guess is that we are tempted to slide into a causal reading of higher-order representationalism, according to which M* *produces* the consciousness of M, by impressing upon M a certain *modification*. Such a reading does make sense of the causal efficacy of consciousness: after M* modifies M, this intrinsic modification alters M's causal powers. But, of course, this is a *misreading* of higher-order representationalism. It is important to keep in mind that higher-order representationalism is a *constitutive*, not a *causal*, thesis. Its claim is *not* that the presence of an appropriate higher-order representation *yields*, or *gives rise to*, or *produces*, M's being conscious. Rather, the claim is that the presence of an appropriate higher-order representation *constitutes* M's being conscious. It is not that, by representing M, M* *modifies* M in such a way as to make M conscious. Rather, M's being conscious simply *consists in* its being represented by M*.

A person *could*, of course, propound higher-order representationalism as a causal thesis. But such a person would not be offering an account of consciousness itself; merely an account of the *causal origin* of consciousness. To the extent that higher-order representationalism is meant as an account of consciousness itself, it puts in jeopardy the causal efficacy of consciousness.

When proponents of higher-order representationalism have taken this problem into account, they have typically responded by downplaying the causal efficacy of consciousness.[59] But, if the intention is to bite the bullet, *downplaying* the causal efficacy is insufficient—what is needed is *nullifying* the efficacy. The charge at hand is not that higher-order representationalism may turn out to assign consciousness too small a fund of causal powers, but that it may deny it *any* causal powers.[60]

The first extrinsicness problem for higher-order representationalism is, therefore, that it appears to entail epiphenomenalism about consciousness.

---

[59] Thus Rosenthal (2002a: 416; emphasis added): "It's easy to *overestimate* the degree to which a state's being conscious does actually play any [causal] role . . . [In fact,] whether or not a state is conscious will not affect the state's [causal] role in planning and reasoning."

[60] So to be clear: to bite the bullet, higher-order representationalists must embrace epiphenomenalism about consciousness.

The second problem is that it has no principled way of ruling out conscious non-mental states. This, or something very much like it, is sometimes referred to as the *generality problem* (Dretske 1995, Van Gulick 2001, 2006, Gennaro 2004).

According to higher-order representationalism, M's property of being conscious is just the property of being represented by the right kind of mental state. But some states of our skin are represented by the right mental states, and yet none is conscious (Dretske 1995: 97).[61] Thus higher-order representationalism appears to allow non-mental states to be conscious.[62]

It might be replied that it need not be part of higher-order representationalism that *any* internal state of an organism can become conscious upon being appropriately represented. The higher-order representationalist may hold that not any old internal state lends itself to such representation, only *mental* states (perhaps only mental states of a certain *kind*) do. Only they are such as to become conscious upon being suitably represented by another internal state.[63]

This reply has less merit to it than may initially appear. Again, the problem is that we are tempted to read higher-order representationalism causally instead of constitutively. If M* *gave rise* to consciousness by modifying M, then it would make a difference what characteristics M has (for example, being mental). It could be claimed that only states with the right characteristics can be modified by being appropriately represented in such a way as to become conscious. But then we must keep in mind that, according to higher-order theory, conscious states do *not* undergo any (non-Cambridge) change in response to the fact that they

---

[61] Dretske (1995: 97) writes: "Some people have cancer and they are conscious of having it. Others have it, but are not conscious of having it. Are there, then, two forms of cancer: conscious and unconscious cancer?...Experiences are, in this respect, like cancers. Some of them we are conscious of having. Others we are not. But the difference is not a difference in the experience. It is a difference in the experiencer—a difference in what the person knows about the experience he or she is having."

[62] Note that none of Rosenthal's conditions (1990) for a higher-order representation being *appropriate* would rule this out. These are that the higher-order representation be (i) non-inferential, (ii) roughly simultaneous with M, (iii) assertoric, and (iv) with *de se* content. All these conditions can be met by representations of one's skin states.

[63] Thus Lycan (1996: 758–9; I am quoting from the reprint in Block et al. 1997): "What is it that is so special about physical states of that certain sort, that consciousness of them makes them 'conscious'? That they are themselves mental...It seems psychological states are called 'conscious' states when we are conscious of them, but nonpsychological things are not." Lycan's view is particularly implausible, as he seems to hold that there is nothing substantially different about mental states that makes them conscious upon being suitably represented—it is simply that we are unwilling to *call* non-mental internal states conscious when they are suitably represented.

are appropriately represented. Their being conscious is *constituted* by their being appropriately represented. It is not so clear, then, what difference it makes whether an internal state has certain characteristics or not. Thus higher-order representationalism leaves it unexplained why only a certain kind of internal state is "the right kind" of state for becoming conscious upon being appropriately represented even though nothing has to happen with that state when it is thus represented.[64]

It might be claimed that raising this sort of consideration against higher-order representationalism misfires, because it misses out on a certain deflationary spirit in which the theory is offered. The theory's spirit is precisely that the difference between a mental state we call conscious and one we do not is "no big deal"—it is somewhat arbitrary and does not capture a deep difference between the two. This is probably a justifiable observation, though its characterization of the spirit in which higher-order theory is offered is probably more accurate of some proponents than others (Lycan more than Rosenthal, for example). In any case, we have to keep in mind that here we are interested in higher-order representationalism only insofar as it is a theory of *phenomenal* consciousness—that is, of the property responsible for the explanatory gap (or, more generally, the philosophical mystery surrounding consciousness). In its deflationary form the theory is unlikely to address *that* phenomenon.[65] We can, therefore, treat higher-order representationalism in the present discussion as though it is not offered in this deflationary spirit.

In summary, the extrinsic construal of consciousness lands its proponents in significant trouble. It appears to cast consciousness as causally inert and suggests that consciousness is a ubiquitous property in nature, including inanimate nature. No doubt the proponents of higher-order theory may devise ways of dealing with these problems. Those are likely, however, to

---

[64] After all, as we can see with Lycan's view (see the previous footnote), there is nothing theoretically (or explanatorily) relevant in the fact that these states are mental. The upshot must be that there is an arbitrary fact that makes suitably represented mental states, but not other suitably represented internal states, conscious. In Lycan's case the arbitrary fact in question is the fact that we are willing to *call* the former, but not the latter, "conscious." This line of rejoinder, if seriously pursued, would be at odds with the fact that conscious states most probably constitute a *natural kind*, and in any event seem to share something objective that is common and peculiar to them.

[65] Thus, Lycan often seems to me to think that the deep mystery pertains primarily to qualitative character, and the need to incorporate a higher-order component derives mostly from how we happen to use consciousness talk in everyday life, not from pressures to account for whatever is responsible for the mystery of consciousness.

complicate the theory considerably, and in any case it is clearly preferable to avoid the problems altogether.

The problems are avoided by any account of consciousness that construes it as an intrinsic property. Self-representationalism is such an account. According to it, M is conscious in virtue of representing itself, so it does not bear a relation to anything that does not overlap it, and is therefore intrinsic in our sense.

It might be objected that self-representationalism would face the very same problems because, even though it construes consciousness as an intrinsic property, it also construes it as a relational property, and the same problems will apply to relational properties. The objector is exploiting a distinction between extrinsic and relational properties. My property of having an arm is a relational property, but it is not an extrinsic property. It is relational because I instantiate it in virtue of standing in a relation to *something*—namely, my arm. But it is not extrinsic because I do not instantiate it in virtue of standing in a relation *to something that does not overlap me*. Likewise, a mental state's property of representing itself may be said to be intrinsic but relational. If a case could then be made that it is not only extrinsic properties that are epiphenomenal, but also relational ones, then the problem of epiphenomenalism would arise for self-representationalism as well. The higher-order theorist could present the following *tu quoque*: relational properties are epiphenomenal; self-representationalism entails that consciousness is relational; therefore, self-representationalism entails that consciousness is epiphenomenal.

One response is to deny that relational properties are epiphenomenal. The question is whether non-relational duplicates must share causal powers. More specifically, the question is whether two items that share all their non-relational properties but differ in some relations they bear to themselves would necessarily have the same causal powers. At present there is no argument I know of to suggest that this is so, though I recognize that it might be possible to generate such an argument. In any case, personally I would deny the second premise in the objector's argument—namely, that self-representationalism entails that consciousness is a relational property—because I deny a relational account of representation across the board (Kriegel 2007b, 2008); I would also apply it to self-representation. I thus reject the claim that self-representationalism construes consciousness as a relational property.

Before closing, let me note that the specters of epiphenomenal and non-mental conscious states infect the hybrid view as well. On this view, the property of being conscious is an extrinsic property of some conscious states and an intrinsic one of others. There are serious questions as to whether such a view is coherent, but let that slide. If *some* states can be conscious in virtue of standing in a relation to something that does not overlap them, then *some* states' consciousness is epiphenomenal, and some non-mental states may still be conscious. Furthermore, the view involves a further implausibility with respect to causal efficacy: it entails that two phenomenally indistinguishable token conscious states may have different causal powers: if one is self-represented and the other is other-represented, the former's property of being conscious may contribute to its fund of causal powers while the latter's cannot.

To summarize, the fact that self-representationalism construes consciousness as an intrinsic property of all conscious states, whereas higher-order theory construes it as an extrinsic property of all of them and the hybrid view construes it as an extrinsic property of some of them, provides an important advantage for self-representationalism over its competition.

Intimacy Revisited

In Section 2, we discussed the intimacy of inner awareness. One facet of this phenomenon is the alleged fact that, in the inner awareness constitutive of subjective character, the awareness and that of which one is aware do not seem to be wholly distinct. This was brought up as a challenge to the representational account of subjective character, and I noted that there are two responses to it. One of them was developed there, but now we are ready to note the other. It is simply to point out that, if a subject is aware of her conscious state in virtue of the state representing itself, then there truly is no numeric distinction between the awareness and that of which one is aware: the representing state and the represented state, and hence the awareness and that of which one is aware, are one and the same.

Thus the self-representational account of subjective character delivers the central facet of intimacy straightforwardly. Higher-order theory and the hybrid accounts do not—at least not very straightforwardly. For them, there are at least *some* conscious states that are numerically distinct from the awareness of them. This, too, is an advantage of the self-representational account over its competition.

This consideration is unlikely, however, to impress higher-order theorists, who would be tempted to deny that inner awareness and that of which one is therewith aware are wholly distinct. Moreover, they may protest—justifiably, in this context—that assuming otherwise amounts to begging the question against them. What the higher-order representationalist can do is offer a different gloss on intimacy. This would be to preserve a sense of intimacy in the theory but deny that it amounts to the lack of numeric distinction. Typically, the alternative gloss is in terms of *immediacy*: the inner awareness we have of our conscious states is in some sense immediate. As I will now argue, however, self-representationalism is better positioned to account even for this deflated conception of intimacy.[66] Let me explain what the notion of immediacy is, how higher-order theories propose to account for it, and why they fail.

If a subject is of reflective disposition, she may infer that she must be distressed or anxious about something on the basis of how unfocused and unproductive she has been, or how lightly she has been sleeping. But, even if she really is distressed or anxious about something (for example, a looming banquet with the in-laws), her newfound awareness of it would not make the distress or anxiety conscious in the relevant, phenomenal sense. Likewise, when a therapist tells a subject that she has an unresolved anger at her father, the subject becomes aware of her anger, but the anger may not be phenomenally conscious yet. These cases show that not any awareness of a mental state would guarantee the state's being conscious. Some mental states the subject is aware of are conscious and some are unconscious. The question is what makes the difference between an awareness of M that guarantees M's being conscious and an awareness that does *not*. The proposal under consideration is that awareness of M makes M conscious if it is *immediate* awareness, and fails to make M conscious if it is *not* immediate.

So one requirement on an "appropriate" or "suitable" representation of a mental state M of a subject S is that it make S not just aware of M, but aware of M with the requisite immediacy. There are two ways higher-order representationalists have tried to capture this immediacy. The first is by construing the higher-order representation as quasi-perceptual,

---

[66] Goldman 1993a, Natsoulas 1993, Moran 2001, and (most effectively, in my opinion) Kobes 1995 also argue against the higher-order treatment of intimacy. Natsoulas and Kobes come close to doing so in pursuit of a self-representational alternative.

the second by construing it as non-inferential. I will now argue that it is unclear how the first maneuver might work and that it is clear that the second will not. In both cases I will not offer a philosophical knock-down argument, but rather will offer non-demonstrative considerations.

According to higher-order perception theories of consciousness (Armstrong 1968, Lycan 1996), mental states are conscious when and only when they are suitably targeted by higher-order representations that are "quasi-perceptual." The main motivation for construing the higher-order representations as quasi-perceptual is precisely that this is more likely to capture the immediacy with which we are aware of our conscious states. Just as perceptual first-order representations put us in direct contact with tables and chairs, such that these targets of theirs are immediately present to us, so quasi-perceptual higher-order representations would put us in direct contact with conscious states, making them *for us* in the relevantly immediate way. The greatest challenge for this maneuver, of course, is to explicate the notion of "quasi-perceptual" representation—in a way that sheds light on the immediacy of inner awareness.

Van Gulick (2001) and Lycan (2004) point out a number of contrasts between perceptual and non-perceptual representations in the light of which we might consider whether or not the relevant higher-order representations are quasi-perceptual.[67] Some of these contrasts do not seem to underwrite any kind of immediacy.[68] But some may. They fall into two broad groups: those that appeal to phenomenology and those that appeal to mechanics.

The first option is to appeal to a putative phenomenological similarity between higher-order representations and perceptual representations. There is a phenomenological difference between, on the one hand, *perceiving* a table, and, on the other, standing in front of the table with one's eyes closed and *thinking* about it. Perhaps the phenomenology of appropriate higher-order representations is more akin to the former than to the latter.

---

[67] Lycan concludes that the relevant higher-order representations are indeed quasi-perceptual, while Van Gulick issues a "tie" verdict.

[68] For example, both Van Gulick and Lycan point out that the content of perceptual representation is involuntary or beyond our control. Lycan proceeds to argue that the appropriate higher-order representations share this feature in a way that higher-order thoughts would not, whereas Van Gulick holds that both kinds of higher-order thoughts can accommodate this phenomenon. This dispute does not concern us here. The point is that whether or not higher-order representations are involuntary in this sense does not bear on whether they constitute *immediate* awareness of their objects.

The problem with this answer is that the main difference between perceiving something and thinking about it in its presence seems to be that only the perceiving has qualitative character.[69] If so, what would make a higher-order representation quasi-perceptual is a distinctive qualitative (or at least quasi-qualitative) character. But, as Rosenthal (1990) notes, there seems to be no such thing.[70]

There may be a subtler variation on this phenomenological answer. Above, we were asked to contrast perceiving a table and thinking of it with eyes closed. The variation would employ the contrast between, on the one hand, perceiving a table, and, on the other, thinking of it *and visualizing it* with eyes closed. We may, moreover, stipulate that the appropriate visualization is qualitatively just as vivid as a perception. It might be claimed that, since we know that our eyes are closed and we are not actually perceiving the table, there is still a phenomenological difference here—and that the relevant higher-order representations are phenomenologically more akin to perception than to thought accompanied by vivid visualization.

This answer strikes me as not altogether implausible. However, its proponent faces a number of challenges. First, if Rosenthal is right and there is no qualitative character associated with higher-order representations, it will not be a trivial task to show that such representations have *any* phenomenology. The proponent will have to point out a kind of non-qualitative phenomenology. For, if there is no phenomenology associated with higher-order representations, it will be impossible to distinguish quasi-perceptual from non-perceptual ones phenomenologically. Secondly, even if we concede a phenomenology of higher-order representation, there is some difficulty with the idea that the difference between perceiving and thinking-cum-visualizing is indeed a phenomenological one. An alternative account of the difference, which we may call the *doxastic account*, would have it that the difference is in the surrounding beliefs: perceiving is accompanied by a belief to the effect that one is in direct contact with the table, whereas

[69] According to most philosophers, thoughts about tables do not have a qualitative character at all (I too have defended this view—in Kriegel 2003c). But, even if there is a qualitative character of thoughts, it is certainly different from the qualitative character of perceptions. We might state the difference by saying that perceptions have a sensory qualitative character, whereas thoughts have a non-sensory one if at all.

[70] We seem to be able to tell this by simple introspection. Or rather: since we do not introspect such a higher-order qualitative character as much as we try, we conclude that there is none.

thinking-cum-visualizing is not so accompanied.[71] It will have to be shown, then, that the phenomenological account of the difference between perceiving and thinking-cum-visualizing is superior to the doxastic account. Personally, I think the difference is genuinely phenomenological, but, when I try to get clear on what the phenomenological difference exactly is, the answer that arises most naturally is that the former's object is immediately present in a way the latter's is not. But the account before us cannot appeal so directly to the phenomenology of immediacy (of the immediate presence of the represented), on pain of circularity. Thus another challenge faced by the present proposal is to identify the relevant phenomenology other than in terms of immediacy.

A completely different approach would appeal to the mechanisms that produce the relevant higher-order representations. There seems to be a clear-cut difference between the mechanisms that produce perceptual representations of tables and those that produce thoughts about (and visualizations of) tables. If the mechanisms that produce the relevant higher-order representations are more like the former than the latter, then those representations would have earned their qualification as quasi-perceptual. The question at this point, though, is how to understand the relevant mechanical difference.

One option is to say that the former are exogenous, triggered by processes that start outside the cognitive system, whereas the latter are endogenous, in the complementary sense. This is problematic, however, inasmuch as some types of perceptual hallucination are endogenous. Still, it might be thought that perceptual representations are formed *in the normal case* responsively to external forces, whereas non-perceptual representations are not so formed even in the normal case. This sounds right, but also seems to be purely contingent. In a sufficiently bizarre world, perceptual representations would not in the normal case be formed responsively to external occurrences. It might be objected that in such a world the relevant representations would disqualify as perceptual. But this does not entail that they would disqualify as representations of the kind that delivers an immediate presence of the object—and it is this feature that we are trying to capture.

---

[71] Note that on this account there may still be a phenomenological difference between the subjects' overall conscious states—namely, if the phenomenology of those surrounding beliefs is different.

Another option would be to construe the production mechanisms characteristic of perception as involving something like *transduction*.[72] Perceptual representations are produced by mechanisms that employ specialized transducers, whereas non-perceptual, purely intellectual ones do not. There are two problems with this proposal, however. First, the notion of transduction is unclear. Secondly, and more problematically, empirically speaking there is no reason to believe in the existence of second-order transducers. This means that, if we stick with this model, empirically the likelihood that there *are* quasi-perceptual higher-order representations is slim.

More generally, higher-order perception theories, and more pointedly the attempt to account for the immediacy of inner awareness in terms of the quasi-perceptual status of higher-order representations, are beholden to empirical matters in a way the self-representational account of immediacy is not. For the former to be viable, there would have to exist higher-order transducers or a phenomenology of immediacy. The viability of self-representationalism is contingent on no such commitment. To that extent, the latter is *mutatis mutandis* preferable to the former. I conclude that self-representationalism is preferable to a higher-order perception account of subjective character in terms of accounting for immediacy. I now turn to consider whether an account of immediacy in terms of non-inferentiality could help the higher-order theorist.

According to higher-order thought theories of consciousness (Rosenthal 1990, 2002a, 2005), the relevant higher-order representations are not quasi-perceptual, but thoughts. Crucially, however, they are *non-inferential* thoughts. According to Rosenthal (1990), what is required for a subject S's awareness of a mental state M to be immediate is not that the formation of the higher-order state M* *be* unmediated, but rather that it *seem* unmediated *to* S. Or, perhaps even more minimally, the formation of M* must not seem mediated to S. As long as it does not seem to S that the formation of M* is mediated, her awareness of M will be immediate. (Note that, the way I am using the terms "immediate" and "unmediated," the two are *not* synonymous, at least as applied to awareness. An awareness that

---

[72] This is similar to Van Gulick's point (2001) that perceptual representations are usually based in the operation of a dedicated organ. I am focusing here on transducers rather than organs because, even though the two seem to go hand in hand, if they parted it would be the presence of specialized transducers that would seem more pertinent to a representation's status as perceptual.

is immediate may not be unmediated, for example, when an awareness is mediated by processes of which the subject is unaware.)

There are two ways the formation of M* may not seem mediated to S. One is when the formation of M* *really is* unmediated. Another is when the formation of M* is mediated, but the processes by which it is mediated are processes S is completely unaware of. If S is completely unaware of the processes that mediate the formation of M*, M*'s formation will seem unmediated to S, or at least it will not seem mediated to her. Rosenthal's claim is that, while it is true that the formation of M* may be mediated by a causal process—presumably one starting with M and ending in the formation of M*—the subject is completely unaware of this process, and therefore her awareness of M is immediate, in that it does not seem mediated to her.[73]

To meet the requirement of immediacy, Rosenthal therefore claims that an "appropriate" higher-order representation must be *non-inferential*, where this means that the higher-order representation is not formed through a conscious inference. For such a *conscious* inference would be a mediating process of which the subject *would be* aware (since it is conscious).[74] In other words, where P is the process leading from M to the formation of M*, M is conscious just in case P is unconscious; when P is conscious, M is unconscious.

(Note that, the way Rosenthal uses the terms, inference is by definition conscious. To be sure, we could call certain unconscious cognitive processes "inferences," and so allow for unconscious inference. But this is not how Rosenthal uses the term. He allows that there may be unconscious

---

[73] A word on the causal process. Suppose S has a conscious perception of a tree. According to higher-order representationalism, the perception, M, is conscious because S has another mental state, M*, which is an appropriate higher-order representation of M. Now, surely M normally has a role in the causal process leading up to the formation of M*. Just as the tree normally has a central role in the causal process leading up to the perception of it, so the perception itself normally has a central role in the causal process leading up to the higher-order representation of it. Arguably, M* would not *be* a representation of M if that were not the case. This means, of course, that the formation of M* is not exactly simultaneous with the formation of M. Rather, there is some sort of (temporally extended) causal process starting with M and ending in the formation of M*. It is worth noting, however, that there are places where Rosenthal claims explicitly that there is normally *no* causal connection between M and M* (e.g., Rosenthal 1990: 744). These comments are sporadic and unmotivated, however. The resulting higher-order account is, if anything, less plausible than it could be (see Kobes 1995).

[74] The reason the subject would necessarily be aware of this process is that it is conscious, and conscious states and processes are states and processes the subject is aware of having or undergoing.

processes resembling inference in every other respect, but reserves the term "inference" to those that are conscious. For the sake of clarity, I will align my usage with Rosenthal's. To refer to the unconscious cognitive processes that are otherwise just like inference, I will use the expression "unconscious inferential processes."[75])

Rosenthal's treatment of the problem of immediacy may initially appear satisfactory, but it does not withstand scrutiny. Let us start by adopting a certain principle regarding inferential processes. The principle is that a conscious inference can start only from conscious "premises."[76] More literally, for any process P leading from mental state M_1 to the formation of mental state M_2, P is conscious only if M_1 is conscious. If M_1 is unconscious, then P will necessarily be unconscious.[77] My claim is that, once we have adopted this principle, Rosenthal's account of immediacy leads to an unacceptable consequence.

The consequence I have in mind is that it is impossible for there to be an unconscious state M of which one is aware, such that the awareness of M has been formed by a process emanating or starting from M. This is implausible, but follows from Rosenthal's account of immediacy. Suppose for reductio that M is an unconscious state of subject S, such that (i) S is aware of M and (ii) S's awareness of M has been formed by a process starting from M. Given the principle that conscious processes must start from conscious "premises," since M is unconscious, the process by which S becomes aware of M must be an unconscious process.[78] But, since the process is unconscious, the awareness of M in which it results is non-inferential. Since it is non-inferential, S is immediately aware of M, and therefore M qualifies as conscious by Rosenthal's standard. But *ex hypothesi*

[75] It is important to stress that no substantive issue is at stake here, only a verbal one. If we insist that there are unconscious inferences, Rosenthal would need only to rephrase his thesis. Instead of claiming that M* is an appropriate representation of M only if it is non-inferential, he could claim that that M* is an appropriate representation of M only if it is non-schminferential, where "schminference" is a conscious inference.

[76] I am using scare quotes because all I mean by "premise" in the present context is the initial state in a process. The principle is simply that a process can be conscious only if it starts in a conscious state.

[77] It is important to distinguish here between a process being conscious and the process's product being conscious. There are certainly inferential processes whose product is conscious even though the "premises" are not. But that is not the same as the inferential processes being themselves conscious.

[78] Recall that it is definitional of the state from which the process emanates that it serves as a "premise" in the inferential process—the way I am using the term "premise" here.

M is unconscious. So M is both conscious and unconscious. Thus what we have supposed for reductio leads to a contradiction. Rosenthal's account implies that there cannot be an unconscious mental state M of which the subject is aware, such that the awareness of M has been formed by a process starting from M. To repeat, this is empirically implausible. More probably, there are *some* unconscious states of which we are aware but the awareness of which is formed responsively to those states—or at least there *could* be.

I conclude that neither the quasi-perceptual maneuver nor the non-inferential maneuver can help the higher-order theorist account for immediacy.[79] Since immediacy is a *universal* feature of all our awareness of our conscious states—or, more accurately, all awareness that constitutes subjective character—the inability of higher-order representationalism to account for it infects also the hybrid view, which will be unable to account for the immediacy of our awareness of our conscious states in *some* cases (namely, those where the conscious state is not self-representing).

Self-representationalism, by contrast, accounts for this immediacy straightforwardly.[80] It is clear that according to self-representationalism there is no causal process that mediates the formation of S's awareness of M: M *comes with* the awareness of it, if you will. In the case of self-representationalism, our awareness of our conscious states is immediate in the most straightforward sense. It is not that the awareness does not seem mediated to us, or even that it seems unmediated to us. Rather, it actually *is* unmediated. The problem evaporates.[81]

---

[79] A higher-order representationalist could, of course, retreat to the view that immediacy is *not* what distinguishes the awareness we have of our conscious states from that we have of our unconscious states. But this, beside being *prima facie* implausible and quite ad hoc, would leave higher-order representationalism without an account of the difference between conscious and unconscious states of which we are aware. Furthermore, arguably the immediacy that characterizes our awareness of our conscious states is a phenomenon that calls for explanation regardless of its theoretical role within the theory of consciousness.

[80] Rosenthal admits as much when he writes (1993: 157; emphasis added): "One way to answer the question about immediacy is just to stipulate that one's being [aware] of a conscious mental state is *internal to* that state itself. Immediacy is thus guaranteed. Our being [aware] of the state would be a *part or aspect of* the state itself, so nothing could mediate between the state and one's being [aware] of it." The phrases "internal to" and "part or aspect of" are naturally understood along the lines of self-representationalism.

[81] Even if self-representationalism construes M as having two parts, a lower-order part $M^{\diamond}$ and a higher-order part M^{*}—an idea we will play with in Chapter 6—the problem does not arise. $M^{\diamond}$ would normally have a causal role in the process leading up to the formation of M^{*}. But, until M^{*} is formed, the conscious state M does not exist yet. M comes into existence only upon the completion of the causal process leading up to the formation of M^{*}. Once M comes into existence, it already

Recall, furthermore, that immediacy was supposed to be a watered-down gloss on the phenomenon of intimacy, which on the face of it appeared to involve something more than immediacy—namely, something to do with the lack of whole distinction between the awareness and what one is aware of. Certainly higher-order theory does not have a satisfactory account of intimacy understood in this robust way, whereas self-representationalism does.

In conclusion, self-representationalism faces no serious difficulty in its attempt to account for the intimacy that characterizes the awareness we have of our conscious states (and does not characterize the awareness we have of our unconscious states), whereas higher-order representationalism and the hybrid view face corrosive difficulties in this area. This is, again, a serious advantage for self-representationalism over its competition.

5. Taking Stock: Self-Representation as a Core Necessary Condition for Subjective Character

We have just surveyed four advantages of self-representationalism over higher-order and hybrid accounts of subjective character: the possibility of targetless higher-order representations, the prospects of epiphenomenal and non-mental conscious states, and the difficulties accounting for intimacy bedevil the latter but not the former. In addition, as we saw in the previous section, the epistemology of consciousness virtually compels us to self-representationalism. It is, therefore, highly likely that mental states have subjective character in virtue of representing themselves in a certain way. Such self-representation seems to be the core necessary condition of subjective character.[82]

Recall that, in pursuit of a general account of subjective character, I have taken the approach of first identifying the core necessary condition for subjective character and then seeking the right qualifications that would

envelops within it $M^\diamond$ and M^*; no further causal process is required. So M itself does not play a causal role in the process leading up to the formation of M^*. For M does not exist before M^* does. Thus, once S enters the conscious state M, S's awareness of $M^\diamond$ is not mediated in any way. In other words, once M comes into existence, no further process is needed that would mediate the formation of M^*. The awareness constituted by M^* is therefore immediate.

[82] I explain the notion of a core necessary condition in n. 11 above.

generate a sufficient condition as well. It is by pursuing this strategy that I have reached the conclusion that the core necessary condition of subjective character is self-representation.

The overall argument proceeded in three main phases. First, I argued that subjective character must implicate the subject's awareness of her mental state (since it involves for-me-ness and a state can be for the subject only if the subject is aware of that state). Secondly, I argued that the subject's awareness of her mental state must involve her having a representation of it (since the only serious alternative—the subject's being acquainted with her state—fails to account for anything the representation view cannot account for, and at the same time is inconsistent with the highly plausible principle of no basic factivity). Thirdly, I argued that the subject's representation of her mental state must be grounded in that state itself, such that the state is self-representing (since the alternatives—the higher-order representation and hybrid views—are inconsistent with the fact that the representation of the mental state must be always conscious, and moreover run into four problems that do not affect the self-representation view).

We can summarize this argument more formally, if somewhat lengthily, as follows:

1. For any mental state M of a subject S, M has subjective character iff M is for S. (Stipulative)
2. For any mental state M of a subject S, M is for S only if S is aware of M. (Argument of Section 1)
3. For any entity X and any subject S, S is aware of X only if X is represented by S. (Argument of Section 2)
4. For any entity X and any subject S, X represents S only if there is a mental state M*, such that (i) S is in M* and (ii) M* is a representation of X. (Innocuous principle) Therefore,
5. For any mental state M of a subject S, M has subjective character only if there is a mental state M*, such that (i) S is in M* and (ii) M* is a representation of M. (From 1–4)
6. Either (a) for any mental state M of a subject S, M has subjective character only if there is a mental state M*, such that (i) S is in M*, (ii) M* is a representation of M, and (iii) M* = M; or (b) for any mental state M of a subject S, M has subjective character only if there is a mental state M*, such that (i) S is in M*, (ii) M* is a representation

of M, and (iii) $M^* \neq M$; or (*c*) for some mental state M of a subject S, M has subjective character only if there is a mental state M^*, such that (i) S is in M^*, (ii) M^* is a representation of M, and (iii) $M^* = M$ and for some M of S, M has subjective character only if there is a mental state M^*, such that (i) S is in M^*, (ii) M^* is a representation of M, and (iii) $M^* \neq M$. (Excluded middle)

7. (*a*) is greatly preferable to (*b*) and (*c*). (Argument of Sections 3–4) Therefore,

8. For any mental state M of a subject S, M has subjective character only if there is a mental state M^*, such that (i) S is in M^*, (ii) M^* is a representation of M, and (iii) $M^* = M$. (From 5–7)

Call this the *master argument for the necessity of self-representation*. If we accept this argument, it remains to seek the kinds of qualification of self-representation that would yield a *sufficient* condition for subjective character.

6. In Search of a Sufficient Condition

It seems conceivable, on the face of it, that a zombie should harbor self-representing internal states. These states would represent themselves but would not be conscious. If so, one might reason, self-representation is insufficient for subjective character. Similarly, the explanatory gap and the hard problem seem, on the face of it, to have equal bite when applied specifically to self-representing states. This may suggest, again, that self-representation, while necessary for consciousness, is insufficient.

We will consider issues of this sort in more depth in Chapter 8, which is dedicated to the reducibility of consciousness. In this chapter I want to consider more immediately tractable challenges to the notion that self-representation might be a sufficient condition for subjective character and hence consciousness. Dealing with these challenges will allow us to produce the kind of qualifications that might eventually render self-representation a sufficient condition for for-me-ness. Until now, I have formulated the self-representational account as holding that mental states are conscious when they represent themselves *in the right way*. This section effectively cashes out "the right way."

Non-Derivative Self-Representation

Consider the sentence "this very sentence is written in Garamond." It is a self-representing sentence, but, like every sentence, it is not conscious and is not *for* anyone. This is a counter-example to the claim that self-representation is sufficient for consciousness.

One response to this counter-example is to claim that the sentence cannot be conscious because it is not a mental entity, and only mental entities can be conscious. This is effectively to suggest a modification of the sufficiency claim to the effect that *mental* self-representation is sufficient for consciousness.

I prefer to avoid this response, because my own view is that the notion of mentality is ultimately derivative from the notion of phenomenal consciousness (see Horgan and Kriegel 2008). On this view, something is a mental state just in case it is appropriately related to a conscious state. This view renders the appeal to *mental* self-representation in the account of consciousness circular.

The response I propose to this problem appeals to the distinction between derivative and non-derivative representation. It is often noted that some representations appear to have their content in and of themselves, while others owe their contents to interpretation. Thus, the concatenation of symbols c^a^t does not represent cats in and of itself, since the very same concatenation might represent two-headed space elephants in a language yet to be invented. The word "cat" means what it means because we interpret it the way we interpret it. By contrast, a thought about cats seems to represent cats in and of itself, and not because of the way we interpret it: we interpret it the way we interpret it because it represents what it represents, not the other way round.[83] To mark this distinction, we may say that symbols that represent what they do (and at all) only thanks to interpretation are *derivative* representations, whereas ones that represent what they do (and at all) in and of themselves are *non-derivative* representations.[84]

---

[83] Many philosophers have held that, in general, linguistic expressions derive their representational content from mental representations. However, the claim that linguistic representations are derivative representations is not entirely uncontroversial, and has been denied by Millikan (1984) among others. But I will assume here that it is true.

[84] It is important to note that the conceptual distinction itself is independent of the claims that linguistic representation is derivative and that mental representation is non-derivative. At this point, I am using examples that presuppose something like those claims only as illustrations, and just because the

Importantly, there is a way to grasp the notion of non-derivative representation without appeal to consciousness: non-derivative representation is interpretation-independent representation. Once all the facts about a certain self-representation are known, we can determine whether it is non-derivative by considering whether it has its content independently of any interpretation. Thus the appeal to non-derivative self-representation is not circular in the way the appeal to mental self-representation is against the background of the view that the notion of mentality cannot be grasped independently of the notion of consciousness.[85]

Given that natural-language sentences are most certainly merely derivative representations, the claim that non-derivative self-representation is sufficient for subjective character rules out the counter-example with which we opened: "This very sentence is written in Garamond" is not conscious because it does not represent itself non-derivatively.

Specific Self-Representation

Consider the sentence "all the sentences in this book are English sentences." This sentence refers to itself, in the sense that it falls under the extension of the predicate "is a sentence in this book," which is a constituent of it itself. Call this *generic self-representation*. It seems fairly easy to imagine unconscious mental states that are generically self-representing. Thus, some educated laypersons, and certainly many philosophers, nowadays hold the tacit belief that all their beliefs are neurophysiologically realized. This belief is generically self-representing in the same way the above sentence is: it falls in the extension of the concept of being neurophysiologically realized. But *ex hypothesi* it is an *unconscious* belief. It is thus a counter-example to the claim that self-representation is sufficient for consciousness.

To rule out this counter-example, I propose to say that only *specific* self-representation may be sufficient for subjective character. Let a *specific*

examples are intuitively compelling. That the examples are intuitively compelling is in turn suggestive of the intuitiveness of the general claims, but I am not presupposing at this stage the truth of those claims.

[85] This is so despite the fact that, on my view, only conscious states are non-derivative representations (Kriegel 2003d, 2007b). What matters is that we have a way of homing in on the notion of non-derivative representation that does not appeal to consciousness. That is, non-derivative representation is not *definitionally* connected to the notion of consciousness even if, as it turns out, it is *necessarily* connected.

representation be a representation that purports to represent a particular.[86] Then a mental representation M is *specifically self-representing* just in case M has a (proper or improper) constituent C, such that (i) C is a specific representation and (ii) C represents M.[87] My claim is that only specifically self-representing states have subjective character. That is: for any mental state M, M has subjective character only if M has a constituent C, such that (i) C is a specific representation and (ii) C represents M. The existence of generically self-representing unconscious states is irrelevant to the truth of this claim.

More generally, there is good reason to believe that specific self-representation is sufficient for consciousness. This is because most unconscious states are generic representations. The great majority of specific representations are *occurrent* states (and quite possibly *all* representations of *dated* particulars, such as events and states, are), and the great majority of occurrent states are conscious. I do have tacit beliefs about my mother, and, since she is a particular, those tacit beliefs are specific representations; and I do have unconscious occurrent states in, say, the dorsal stream of my visual system. But, by and large, there are relatively few unconscious yet specific mental representations. Thus the likelihood that a counter-example could be produced of an unconscious state that self-represents specifically ought to be very low. Of course, all that is needed to refute the thesis that specific self-representation is sufficient for consciousness is one counter-example, and I have done nothing to rule out the possibility of such a counter-example. I am offering the present consideration simply by way of indicating that finding such a counter-example may prove difficult. In any case, I do not actually endorse the thesis that specific self-representation is sufficient for consciousness. The sufficiency thesis I endorse will emerge at the end of this section.

---

[86] Two clarifications: first, I use the term "particular" in a trope-theoretic vein, to cover both concrete particulars, such as chairs and leptons, and abstract particulars, such as events, states, facts, processes, etc. (e.g., the arrival of the train, or the sky's being blue); secondly, there is a close relationship between specific representation in the present sense and singular representation in the sense typically used in philosophy of language and mind, but there are certain commitments built into the latter that I am not building into the former.

[87] I use the terms "proper constituent" and "improper constituent" analogously to the way we use the terms "proper part" and "improper part": C is a proper constituent of W if there is a C*, such that (i) C* is a constituent of W and (ii) C* ≠ C (if (i) but not (ii), then C* is an improper constituent of C).

Essential Self-Representation

It is important to distinguish a thing's representing what happens in fact to be itself and its representing itself *qua* itself. In a story now famous, Perry (1979) tells of the time he was walking around the supermarket with a torn bag of sugar and, noting the sugar trail on the floor, thinking to himself "the person with the torn bag is making a mess." Only later did he realize that he himself was the person with the torn bag, whereupon he thought what was surely a *new* thought, "I am making a mess." The story brings out the difference between, on the one hand, representing what happens to be oneself, and, on the other hand, representing oneself *as oneself*.

The pertinent distinction is not just between *contingent* and *necessary* self-representation. If Perry thought to himself "my mother's nieceless brother's only nephew is making a mess," he might be thinking about what is *necessarily* himself, but still he would not be thinking about himself *as himself*. Thus, just as Perry did not know he was the person with the torn bag, so he might not know that he was his mother's nieceless brother's only nephew—even though he might necessarily be. So this is not a distinction between contingent and necessary self-representation.

One way to draw the distinction that it really is is in terms of *epistemic* modality: the self-representation in "my mother's nieceless brother's only nephew is making a mess" is *epistemically contingent*, whereas that in "I am making a mess" is *epistemically necessary*. This would capture the fact that the former is a posteriori self-representing, whereas the latter is a priori self-representing. For the sake of convenience, I will say instead that the former is *accidentally* self-representing, whereas the latter is *essentially* self-representing.

Perry (1979) argued that no mental state that we would report using the direct reflexive "I" is type-identical with any mental state that we could report without an indexical expression. Castañeda (1966) argued (earlier but much more austerely) for the generalized form of this claim: that no mental state report using a reflexive could be paraphrased into a report that did not use a reflexive. This included also (third-person) reports using indirect reflexives, as in "Perry thinks that he himself is making a mess," where "he himself" functions as an indirect reflexive.

Let us now say that, while expressions such as "I" and "he himself" function (in some central uses) as (respectively) direct and indirect *utterer-reflexives*, the expressions "this very" and "that very" function (in some central uses) as (respectively) direct and indirect *utterance-reflexives*. Thus, we can imagine that, in the middle of an important business meeting, a Turrets patient exclaims, truly no less, "this very sentence is making a mess."[88] With this utterance we would have an essentially self-representing utterance.[89]

We may suppose that there is a type of mental representation constituent that functions as a mental direct utterance-reflexive. Adopting for the sake of presentation the idea that there is a language of thought (Fodor 1975), *Mentalese*, we may say that there is a Mentalese expression that translates the English "this very" (in the relevant use). This Mentalese direct reflexive would be the relevant mental representation constituent type. But, regardless of whether we adopt the Language of Thought hypothesis, we may say with some confidence that there is probably a mental representation constituent type C, such that, for any mental state M, if a token of C is a constituent of M, then M is essentially self-representing.

I belabor this point here because it seems quite reasonable, *prima facie*, that a mental state's self-representing accidentally would not suffice to make it conscious. If a mental state has a representational content that it itself happens to satisfy, but the state does not in some (obviously metaphorical) sense "mean" to pick out itself, then the subject's inner awareness of the state would not be of the right sort to make the subject aware of it as the state she is currently and thereby in. This suggests that only *essential* self-representation may be sufficient for subjective character and hence consciousness. The thesis I want actually to endorse, however, is that non-derivative specific essential self-representation is sufficient for consciousness.

Displays and Summaries

Suppose you peacefully drive on a bridge, when you suddenly see the words "under construction" painted on the road. It is most likely that,

---

[88] This example is a little far-fetched, of course, but it is so only in a brave attempt to use "making a mess" in the example. The utterance "this very sentence is spoken on a Thursday" would do just as well, and is not far-fetched at all, as I have just uttered it aloud.

[89] For the sake of symmetry, we could say that in someone who utters "I am making a mess" we have an essentially self-representing *utterer*.

when you read these words, a *complete* thought occurs to you, a thought with the full propositional content that you would express by saying "this bridge is under construction." It is the same thought as would occur to you if you heard an officer shouting "this bridge is under construction."

How can the words "under construction" vehicle a full-blown proposition, when they do not constitute a full-blown sentence?[90] The answer is that they cannot. Rather, it is the combination of the words and the bridge whereupon they are painted that vehicles the full-blown proposition. The bridge itself functions as the subject term in the *sentence* that vehicles the proposition that makes up your thought's content. This suggests that there *is* before you a full-blown sentence, albeit with an unusual ontology: whereas the sentence shouted by the officer has as constituents only sounds, and the sentence that might be posted on a sign would have as constituents only ink marks, the sentence you are confronted with when driving onto the bridge has as constituents ink marks and a bridge.

Eddy Zemach (1985) calls sentences of this sort *display sentences*, because in them, he claims, the object predicated is *displayed* rather than *referred to*. But the notion that there are two kinds of sentence, those that refer to their object and those that display it, is needlessly radical, and initially implausible. Better to hold that the bridge *is* referred to by a specific constituent of the sentence. It is just that that constituent is itself. We can still retain the term "display sentence" to mark sentences with this unusual ontology, but the claim would now be that display sentences are such that their object is referred to by (constituents of) themselves. Thus display sentences use the same referential mechanism that regular sentences do. It is just that, in a regular sentence, the bridge would be referred to by a *different* entity, which would *stand for* it, whereas that is not the case in a display sentence.[91]

We might hypothesize that all and only non-derivatively, specifically, and essentially self-representing states are *Mentalese display sentences*. Thus,

---

[90] Note that, if you only heard or saw "construction," no complete thought would occur to you; instead, only an "idea" of construction would. But the paint on the road somehow succeeds to vehicle a whole proposition.

[91] Another way to look at it may be this: whereas in a regular sentence the bridge is *represented*, in the display sentence it is *presented*. Just as I can either present myself at the meeting or send my representative, who cannot present me but can represent me, so when the bridge is a constituent of a sentence it can present itself, whereas the word "bridge" can only represent the bridge but not present it. (This analogy is due to Michael Gill.) I will not pursue this line of thought any further.

consider a thought whose content is "this very thought is being thought by the mess-maker." Here the property of being thought by the mess-maker is predicated of a certain thought, T, which is also self-representationally referred to by the Mentalese direct reflexive "this very," which is non-derivative and specific. We may imagine that to *have* this kind of thought is to have a certain internal occurrence or token with the Mentalese "being thought by the mess-maker" so to speak "posted" on it, in a way analogous to the English "under construction" being posted on the bridge.[92]

I am not sure I endorse this model—it is just an idea, as they say. I bring it up mainly because one can appreciate that there is something special and unusual going on in display-like self-representation, which might help us *feel* a "quantum leap" to something that might indeed be sufficient for subjective character. Thus a claim to the effect that display-like self-representation is sufficient for subjective character seems intuitively plausible. But, if it does, then, against the background of the hypothesis that all and only non-derivatively, specifically, and essentially self-representing states are Mentalese display sentences, this intuitive plausibility should transfer, to some degree at least, to the claim that non-derivative, specific, and essential self-representation is sufficient for subjective character and hence consciousness.

On this basis, that is the thesis I am prepared to assert at this point: that non-derivative specific essential self-representation is sufficient for subjective character, and hence consciousness. Putting this together with what we have established in Section 5, we can state the following: necessarily, for any mental state M of a subject S, M has subjective character both if and only if there is a mental state M^*, such that (i) S is in M^*, (ii) M^* is a non-derivative representation of M, (iii) M^* is a specific representation of M, (iv) M^* is an essential representation of M, and (v) $M^* = M$. More economically:

(SR)   Necessarily, for any mental state M, M has subjective character iff M is non-derivatively, specifically, and essentially self-representing.

Call this the *self-representational account of subjective character*.

---

[92] This is analogous to the case of the words on the bridge. Just as the latter in fact constitutes the English display sentence "This very bridge is under construction," so the mental occurrence in question constitutes the Mentalese display sentence "This very thought is being thought by the mess-maker."

7. Conclusion: Subjective Character and Phenomenal Consciousness

In Chapter 2, I claimed that the phenomenal character of a conscious state—what makes it the conscious state it is and a conscious state at all—has two components: qualitative character and subjective character. We now have on our hands representational accounts of both. Indeed, we have a single account that brings them together in the sort of intimate way they in fact seem to be connected. The account is that the phenomenal character of a conscious state is constituted by the state's non-derivative, specific, and essential representation of its own representation of the right external response-dependent property. (The state need not represent itself *as* representing a response-dependent property; it just needs to represent itself to have a property that *in fact* is the property of representing a response-dependent property.) Thus, for there to be a bluish way it is like for me to have my visual experience of the sky is for my experience to represent itself non-derivatively, specifically, and essentially to represent the right response-dependent property of the sky. The experience has its bluishness (qualitative character) in virtue of non-derivatively, specifically, and essentially representing itself to represent the specific response-dependent property it does represent itself to represent; and it has its for-me-ness (subjective character) in virtue of non-derivatively, specifically, and essentially representing itself at all.

Call this the *self-representational theory of phenomenal consciousness*, or *self-representationalism* for short. In the next three chapters we will consider the way self-representationalism illuminates the phenomenological, ontological, and scientific nature of phenomenal consciousness.[93]

---

[93] For comments on a previous draft of this chapter I would like to thank David Chalmers, Bill Lycan, Ken Williford, and an anonymous referee. I also benefited from conversations with Benj Hellie, Leon Leontyev, Joe Levine, David Rosenthal, Susanna Siegel, and Josh Weisberg.

5

Self-Representationalism and the Phenomenology of Consciousness

It is perhaps the most poorly kept secret in discussions of consciousness that positive theories of consciousness are strongly influenced by the conception of the phenomenology of consciousness their proponents presuppose. In reductive explanation as elsewhere, one's conception of the explanandum constrains one's thinking about the explanans. But in the theory of consciousness *more* than elsewhere, one's conception of the explanandum often bubbles up to the explanans-level surface, so that one's explanatory theory is just the outer expression of one's prior commitments about the nature of the explanandum. In this chapter I lay my cards on the table. I describe my own conception of the phenomenology (Sections 1–2), defend it (Section 3), and argue that only self-representationalism can accommodate the phenomenology so understood (Section 4).

The secretive nature of phenomenological commitments is understandable. To the extent that one's theory of consciousness rests on phenomenological observations that are not entirely pedestrian, it is open to glib rejection. All an opponent would have to do is profess that the unpedestrian phenomenological pronouncements do not resonate with her. At the background here is a very real and important worry about the rational resolvability of phenomenological disputes. Yet there are certainly facts of the matter pertaining to phenomenology. For all the difficulty associated with developing rational standards for evaluation of unpedestrian phenomenological claims, some of these claims are true and some are false. When they are true, the one true theory of consciousness should be able to accommodate them.[1]

---

[1] Again, this is so regardless of whether we possess the standards to evaluate the accommodation attempt. In Kriegel 2007a, I suggest ways of getting at the phenomenology. But these were intended

In Sections 1–2 I will make some unpedestrian phenomenological assertions, in a rather dogmatic spirit. In Section 4 I will argue that only self-representationalism can accommodate these; the main thesis of that section can thus be construed as a conditional: *if* the phenomenology has the features I say it does, *then* self-representationalism is true. To use this conditional in a *modus ponens* for self-representationalism, I would need to argue that its antecedent is true—that the phenomenology is indeed the way I say it is. Unfortunately, as just noted, we do not at present possess clear guidelines for defending positive phenomenological claims that are not entirely pedestrian. Short of offering a positive argument for the antecedent, then, what I will attempt to do in Section 3 is argue against arguments *against* the antecedent. If successful, such argumentation should at least establish that there are no good reasons to reject the antecedent. The upshot will be this: there is an argument for self-representationalism that we have no good reasons not to accept—since we have good reasons to accept its major premise and no good reasons to reject its minor premise.

1. Conscious Experience: A Phenomenological Description

Let us start with the pedestrian observations. When you look at the blue sky on a sunny day, you undergo a visual experience. There is a bluish way it is like for you to have this experience. This bluish way it is like for you captures your visual experience's phenomenology.

Other perceptual experiences are associated with other phenomenologies. There is a distinctive way it is like to have auditory experiences, such as hearing a bagpipe; olfactory experiences, such as smelling freshly brewed coffee; gustatory experiences, such as tasting ripe raspberries; or tactile experiences, such as feeling the sassy resistance of velvet stroked against its grain. There is even such a thing as proprioceptive phenomenology, which can be brought to the fore by extreme exertion.

as preliminary sketches of some options, not as worked-out methods we could actually start using. Here I wish only to stress that the question of the availability of such methods and standards should be distinguished from the question of the existence of phenomenological facts of the matter. This is just to distinguish between truth and justification for phenomenological propositions.

There is also a phenomenology associated with non-perceptual experiences. Bodily experiences such as tickles and orgasms have their own phenomenologies, as do emotional experiences such as being angry with your Internet provider or being disappointed about a date standing you up.[2] Relatedly, there is the phenomenology of mood, such as feeling calm satisfaction at the end of a long day of work or subdued excitement immediately after watching a powerful film.

Let us move now to less pedestrian varieties of phenomenology. Those involve mostly new categories of phenomenology, going beyond perceptual, bodily, and emotional phenomenology. But there are also phenomenological exotica already within those categories. Some people report that, upon looking at the stars on a clear night, they have a curious phenomenology as of *seeing the past*. Personally, I am somewhat skeptical of this description of their phenomenology. But I have encountered my own phenomenological exotica, perhaps most vividly with moods. When I was young and foolish, I once spent nearly two months in an Israeli prison on charges of military desertion; I will never forget the first 5–6 hours after being released, when I could vividly and viscerally feel in every fiber of my being something that could only be described as a *phenomenology of freedom*.

Regarding other phenomenological categories, it has also been claimed that there is a distinctive phenomenology associated with more intellectual experiences, such as occurrently thinking that the weather is nice, recalling that tomorrow is one's sibling's birthday, or suspecting that there is a suppressed premise in one's argument. These mental states could lack the sensuous quality of perceptual, bodily, and emotional experiences, and there would still be something it is like to be in them. That is, there is a *proprietary* phenomenology such cognitive states boast—a phenomenology that goes beyond the sum of perceptual, bodily, and emotional phenomenologies associated with them. In other words, there is a proprietary cognitive phenomenology.[3]

---

[2] I am assuming here, for the sake of exposition, that bodily and emotional experiences are not perceptual. It has been argued of each type of experience that it *is* perceptual. I do not wish to take a substantive stance on this matter here. (However, if "perceptual" just means "representational," then I am certainly in agreement, since I take bodily and emotional experiences to be representational, as per Chapter 3.)

[3] I will not argue for this here. For arguments in favor of cognitive phenomenology, see Goldman 1993b, Strawson 1994: ch. 1, Peacocke 1998, Siewert 1998, Horgan and Tienson 2002, Kriegel 2003c, and especially Pitt 2004. For expressions of sympathy, see Flanagan 1992 and Chalmers 1996.

Thinking, recalling, and suspecting are cognitive states. There may also be a proprietary phenomenology associated with *conative* states, such as deciding to buy a new private jet, or, somewhat less glamorously, intending to do the dishes soon.[4] Such states have a world-to-mind rather than mind-to-world direction of fit, in the sense that their function is to *change* the world rather than *reflect* it. Personally, I am less confident that conative phenomenology is proprietary rather than a variety of emotional phenomenology. Although discussions of belief–desire psychology in the philosophy of mind have tended to treat desire as a non-emotional state (on a par with belief), pre-theoretically (and, to my mind, also post-theoretically) desire is just one kind of emotional state.

Within the conative realm, there may also be an *agential* phenomenology that goes beyond the purely conative phenomenology. Thus, *trying* to open the window feels different from *deciding* to open it.[5] What it is like actually to *do* the dishes is alas different from what it is like to *intend* to do them. The difference between agential conative phenomenology and intellectual conative phenomenology presumably parallels the difference between perceptual phenomenology and cognitive phenomenology. Just as perceptual phenomenology has a "sensuous" component missing from cognitive phenomenology, so agential phenomenology has a "muscular" component missing from conative phenomenology.

The phenomenological elements we have surveyed thus far are all at the "floor level" of phenomenology. But there is also a phenomenology associated with inner awareness and self-awareness.[6] When you start staring at the sky and marvel at its deep blueness, you might be absorbed in the sight and take no notice of yourself. As the novelty (such as it is) wears thin, your awareness of yourself as the subject of the ongoing experience of the sky comes a little more to the fore. Likewise, there is a felt difference between asking a lady out on a date in a spontaneous, non-premeditated way (say, at the end of a long and naturally flowing conversation) and doing

---

[4] The existence of a phenomenology of agency is defended by Horgan et al. (2003), Siegel (2005), and Bayne and Levy (2006).

[5] I am assuming here that trying is at least partially a mental phenomenon. It may be natural on first glance to think of trying as a purely physical endeavor. But, when we attend to the presuppositions that go into trying attributions, we can see that a mindless robot cannot really be said, in any literal sense, to be trying to do something. Trying is in that respect akin to Searle's "intention-in-action" (1983).

[6] For recent exponents, see Zahavi 1999, Levine 2001, Kriegel 2004a, and Horgan et al. 2006. As in previous chapters, I use "inner awareness" to indicate awareness of one's internal *states*, and "self-awareness" to indicate awareness of *oneself*.

so in a very deliberate and self-conscious way (when one is too nervous and tongue-tied to make conversation). We can imagine circumstances in which everything in one's phenomenology is held constant except the degree of self-consciousness.

So far we have mentioned the phenomenology of different mental *states*. But there is also a phenomenology associated with mental *processes*. There is something it is like visually to track a passing Porsche; gustatorily to attend to the unfolding taste of a single-malt scotch; auditorily to follow a Flii Stylz melody; to deliberate about what birthday present to buy for one's sibling; or to calculate a 15 percent tip on a $67 bill.

The above unpedestrian phenomenological observations might strike you as problematic, and so they should. It is a legitimate view that there is no cognitive phenomenology beyond the visual and auditory imagery that normally accompanies thinking; that there is no conative nor agential phenomenology beyond the sensuous deliverances of proprioception; that there is no phenomenology of self-awareness beyond the rapid transitions from attending to the world and attending to one's emotions; and that there is no process phenomenology beyond the sum of phenomenologies associated with a process momentary stages. These more deflationary views attempt to rein in the scope of phenomenology, and they are perfectly legitimate.

The deflationary views are "legitimate" in the sense that they are not by any means obviously false. I will not offer any argumentation against them. However, some of the motivation for adopting them should disappear when we are careful to separate the ontology and the epistemology of consciousness. One is tempted to adopt the deflationary claims when one is presented with an unpedestrian phenomenological claim and is unsure how to even start assessing its plausibility. But the difficulties associated with assessment of phenomenological claims do not entail anything about the truth of those claims. There is a fact of the matter regarding the existence of conative phenomenology, for example, regardless of how hard it is to get at that fact. To move from epistemological difficulty to ontological deflation is to presuppose that, if it is a phenomenological fact that p, then it should be immediately and effortlessly evident to one that p upon consideration of whether p. Ironically, ontological deflationism in this area is thus largely motivated by an inflationist epistemology (perhaps with Cartesian overtones).

My own test for an unusual phenomenology derives from my construal of phenomenal consciousness as the property for which there is (an appearance of) an explanatory gap. I can imagine a world with creatures who have no perceptual, bodily, or emotional experiences but a rich stream of intellectual consciousness. (It would be a very bizarre world, but that is neither here nor there.) When I contemplate this world, I find that the problem of the explanatory gap rationally arises for it as well. Hence my inclination to embrace a proprietary cognitive phenomenology.

This test tends to yield relatively inflationist results. To my mind, some mental phenomena have a rich and acute phenomenology, and are not easily understood in separation from this phenomenology, and yet their phenomenology is quite exotic, in that it exhibits several unpedestrian aspects. A case in point is concentration. Concentrating involves some sort of harnessing of cognitive energies. The agent applies herself to the cognitive task at hand in a way that makes her internal goings-on more intense and more "present" in some elusive sense. The phenomenology of concentration—this feel of intensified cognitive energies—features cognitive, agential, and process elements. Thus concentration is a piece of phenomenological exotica. But to understand concentration without taking into account this phenomenology would be almost hopeless. Imagine trying to explain to a French-speaking zombie what the English word "concentration" means.

The notion of phenomenal intensity just brought up introduces a whole new layer of complexity to the phenomenology. In line with the previous observation, we may say that, when eating a peanut-butter-and-jelly sandwich, the gustatory experience of jelly is more phenomenally intense when one concentrates on the jelly, less intense when one concentrates on the peanut butter. When one concentrates on the violas in a symphony, one's auditory experience of them is more phenomenally intense. Beyond concentration, one toothache can be more phenomenally intense than another in a straightforward way: it hurts more. In a more subtle way, one realization that there is a suppressed premise in one's argument can be more phenomenally intense than another. This may involve something like a clearer and more distinct presence to the mind, whatever that means.

Changing one's overall phenomenology by modulating the phenomenal intensity of one of the items in the phenomenology is unlike changing the phenomenology by adding or subtracting an item. Phenomenal intensity is not an extra item in the phenomenology, alongside bluishness, nervousness, and so on. Yet it makes a difference to what the overall phenomenology is. It is in this sense that phenomenal intensity introduces a new layer of complexity to the phenomenology. Once we take it into account, we can appreciate that a person's overall phenomenology at a time is not fully determined by the collection of items in it. There are other axes along which the phenomenology varies. We may flag this by saying that phenomenal intensity is a *structural feature* of phenomenology. Something is a structural feature of phenomenology if it is an *aspect of* it—if it makes a difference to the phenomenology—without being an *item in* it. There are other structural features of phenomenology—other than intensity, that is. A central one is *unity*, both *at* a time and *across* time.[7] As I stare at the blue sky and undergo my bluish visual experience, I also at the same time hear the roar of car engines passing by; can feel the seat under me, as well as the soles of my shoes; am faintly aware, in an unpleasantly anxious sort of way, that I have yet to pay last month's telephone bill, which I keep forgetting to pay; and am even more faintly aware of my having this very bluish-roarish-anxious experience. Some of these items are more phenomenally pronounced than others, but each contributes *something* to the overall phenomenology. If the feeling of the soles of my shoes were to suddenly disappear (say, because my foot nerves were incapacitated), I would notice a change in my overall phenomenology. What I want to stress here is that my overall phenomenology is unified at the time (that is, it is *synchronically* unified), in that it does not feel like just so many unconnected items, but rather like a single cohesive "field of experience." Moreover, phenomenology is often also unified *across* time (that is, *diachronically* unified). Listening to a melody is experientially unlike hearing a sequence of unrelated notes.

These forms of unity are not themselves phenomenological items, but they make a difference to one's overall phenomenology. To the extent that we can imagine a conscious experience that is disunified synchronically or diachronically, it would seem to feel quite different.[8] The difference I have

---

[7] Among those who develop accounts of *phenomenal* unity are Bayne and Chalmers 2003, Tye 2003, and Masrour 2008.

[8] To the extent that we cannot, this might suggest that the phenomenology would dissolve altogether in the absence of these structural features; but, of course, holding off the total dissolution of phenomenology is a form of "making a difference to the phenomenology."

in mind here is contributed by unity not causally but constitutively. It is not just that the unity *causes* a change in the phenomenal items (although it very well may). The very presence of unity feels different.

When describing my overall phenomenology at a single conscious moment just now, I noted that some items in my phenomenology are more "pronounced" than others. This seems to do again with phenomenal intensity. It is noteworthy that the distribution of this sort of "pronounced-ness," or intensity, is itself structured. Usually, the phenomenological field has a center/periphery structure. In the experience described above, the focal center is occupied by the bluishness, while the periphery is populated by the roarishness, the subtle sense of anxiety, and the even subtler sense of myself as the subject of experience. If a different item displaced the bluishness at the center—say, if I started paying more attention to my growing anxiety and in some sense "lost sight" of the blue sky—the overall phenomenology would change, even though no addition or subtraction is made to the inventory of phenomenal items.

Normally, the center/periphery distinction applies not only globally, across one's entire experience, but also locally, within modality-specific "compartments" thereof. Thus, in my current visual experience I am focally aware of the laptop before me and only peripherally aware of the bonsai to my left and the coffee to my right. If one listens to a piano concerto, one's auditory experience is liable to involve focal awareness of the piano and merely peripheral awareness of the cellos, the violas, and for that matter the sound of raindrops on the roof. Likewise for awareness in other perceptual modalities: every form of perceptual phenomenology comes in two varieties, focal and peripheral.[9]

It might be thought that cognitive phenomenology cannot involve a center/periphery structure, because intellectual activity is fundamentally different from perceptual activity. The thought might be encouraged by a conception of intellectual activity as involving the orderly succession of discrete mental states bearing discrete propositional contents. In such propositional content, it might be thought, there is no place for a distinction between parts of the proposition one is focally aware of and parts one is peripherally aware of. Rather, one is fully aware of the proposition as a whole.

---

[9] I will discuss these matters in more detail in Chapter 7. See also Williford 2006.

A moment's reflection, however, should convince us of the poverty of this conception of intellectual activity. Thinking is not a sequence of successive discrete states that take a single proposition as their object. As many philosophers have noted (e.g., James 1890/1918, Ryle 1949), thinking is rather like a stream, flowing sometimes in succession oftentimes in parallel, sometimes peacefully oftentimes gushingly. If we could examine in detail a stretch of this stream, we would be liable to find a number of propositions before the mind at any one time. Thus, as I focally think of tomorrow's lecture, I may also peripherally think that I have yet to pay last month's electricity bill.

Moreover, although initially plausible, the notion that a center/periphery structure cannot distribute over a proposition may well be false. There seems to be a phenomenological difference between propositions expressed in the active voice and in the passive voice. We can readily imagine circumstances in which there would be an important difference between the reports "the pianist believes that her husband is carrying the piano" and "the pianist believes that the piano is being carried by her husband." In some circumstances, the first report might betray the pianist's concern that her husband will not be hurt in the process of carrying the piano, the second her concern that her instrument will not be harmed in the process of being carried. Arguably, the ascribed state's propositional content is the same in both cases, but in the former case the pianist is focally aware of her husband and only peripherally aware of the piano, whereas in the latter case she is focally aware of her piano and only peripherally aware of the husband.

We have considered the distinction between structural and non-structural features of phenomenology. An even more fundamental distinction is between constitutive and non-constitutive aspects. Most aspects of phenomenology are purely contingent. Thus, it is a contingent fact that most of us have an auditory phenomenology. It also seems contingent that phenomenology is diachronically unified: we can envisage a creature existing for a single moment and yet enjoying splendid purplish phenomenology. The center/periphery structure also appears contingent: we can imagine a centerless field of equally vivid experiences.

What are the constitutive aspects of phenomenology? This question cannot be easier to answer than "What are the aspects of phenomenology?" And, yet, again there are most certainly facts of the matter. There must be aspects of the phenomenology that are constant and universal, and moreover in the absence of which all phenomenology dissolves entirely. In trying to get at the facts regarding such constitutive phenomenology, the most natural place to start is trying to imagine a phenomenology without a given aspect. If we find that we cannot envisage what such a phenomenology would be like, this should be taken as evidence (doubtless defeasible) that the relevant aspect of phenomenology is constitutive.

For my part, I can attest that I cannot envisage what it would be like to have a phenomenology lacking synchronic unity. Thus synchronic unity may be a constitutive aspect of phenomenology.[10]

Likewise, I cannot envisage what it would be like to have a phenomenology lacking the kind of inner awareness that constitutes for-me-ness. Even the simplest visual experience—say, a homogenously bluish experience—folds within it an outer awareness of blue and an inner awareness of that very outer awareness.[11]

In addition, it seems to me that the existence of at least one floor-level non-structural feature is a necessary condition for the existence of any phenomenology: I cannot envisage a phenomenology consisting in nothing but inner awareness, unity, and so on.[12] If so, it is a constitutive aspect of phenomenology that it contains some floor-level non-structural item(s).

Other than these three elements—synchronic unity, inner awareness, and a floor-level item—nothing strikes me as *constitutive* of phenomenology. Even some aspects that are *ubiquitous* in the phenomenology seem to lack something extra that would make them *constitutive*. I have in mind diachronic unity as a case in point: all our experiences are diachronically unified as a matter of fact, but it does not seem to be necessary that they be. The accompaniment of mood may well be another example: mood seems to be an aspect of all our experiences, but there seems to be no necessity in this.

[10] It should be noted that the possibility of a single-item phenomenology should not be taken as a counter-example. There is a sense in which such phenomenology is unified, indeed the most unified we can imagine, even if it does not involve unification of several items.

[11] This issue has already come up in Chapter 2, and we will return to it in the Appendix. But, on the view that I hold, it is the mark of conscious awareness that it involves an elusive fusion of world-awareness and self-awareness, or at least of outer awareness and inner awareness.

[12] Such a state of pure, contentless awareness is the state that certain meditative techniques are supposed to lead to. Certainly the state in question has been described along these lines by some practitioners. It is nonetheless open to the theoretician to challenge the practitioner's own description of the state she is in.

Toward the end of this chapter I will argue that self-representationalism is the only theory of consciousness that can accommodate the constitutive inner-awareness aspect phenomenology. Because the phenomenology of for-me-ness, or inner awareness, is central to this reasoning, let me pause to discuss in more detail the nature of this phenomenon. This is the topic of the next section.

2. The Phenomenology of Peripheral Inner Awareness

The nature of the phenomenon under consideration has been discussed extensively in the phenomenological tradition, in connection with what is commonly referred to within that tradition as "pre-reflective self-consciousness." The term denotes the kind of self-consciousness one enjoys when one does *not* explicitly reflect on oneself and one's internal goings-on. Different accounts of pre-reflective self-consciousness can be found in the writings of Husserl (1928/1964), Sartre (1936, 1943: ch. 1), Merleau-Ponty (1945), Gurwitsch (1985), Henry (1963/1973), and others. My favorite description of this phenomenon is nonetheless by a philosopher outside the phenomenological tradition, Alvin Goldman (1970: 96):[13]

[Consider] the case of thinking about x or attending to x. In the process of thinking about x there is already an implicit awareness that one is thinking about x. There is no need for reflection here, for taking a step back from thinking about x in order to examine it . . . When we are thinking about x, the mind is focused on x, not on our *thinking* of x. Nevertheless, the process of thinking about x carries with it a non-reflective self-awareness.

Goldman's "non-reflective self-awareness" and the phenomenologists' "pre-reflective self-consciousness" are very much in line with what I have in mind in speaking of the subjective character or for-me-ness of experience.

Recall that in Chapter 2 (Section 3) I characterized subjective character in terms of peripheral inner awareness. Although most phenomenologists would reject any construal of pre-reflective self-consciousness as peripheral

---

[13] My thanks to Cybele Tom for pointing out to me this passage (c. Mar. 2001).

inner awareness (see, e.g., Zahavi 2004), parallel debates to those they have conducted concerning the nature of pre-reflective self-consciousness can be formulated with regard to peripheral inner awareness. In this section I use some of their contributions in this way.[14]

The phenomenologists' accounts of pre-reflective self-consciousness differ in how richly they construe the content of this sort of self-consciousness. As far as I can tell, general standards for the evaluation and comparison of these competing accounts are no more developed in the phenomenological tradition than in analytic philosophy of mind. But the multitude of accounts it features is useful in clarifying the different options for understanding peripheral inner awareness.

The first question that arises in this context is whether pre-reflective self-consciousness involves only the subject's awareness of her experiences or also her awareness of herself. Is the content of the awareness constituted fully by a state or also partially by the subject? Does it have the relatively thin form "this mental state is occurring" or the more robust "I am in this mental state"? The latter makes reference to the self, whereas the former does not. In the terms I have been using up till now, the question is whether peripheral inner awareness is *mere* inner awareness or is also *self*-awareness.[15]

In the phenomenological tradition, the leaner view—sometimes referred to as the *non-egological* conception of pre-reflective self-consciousness—has found a fierce proponent in Sartre (1936, 1943: ch. 1). If I were to make another unpedestrian phenomenological assertion, I would say that my current experience's pre-reflective self-consciousness strikes me as egological—that is, as a form of peripheral *self*-awareness. My peripheral awareness of my current experience is awareness of it *as mine*. There is an elusive sense of self-presence or self-manifestation inherent in even a simple conscious experience of the blue sky. It is less clear to me, however, that this feature of peripheral inner awareness—its being *self*-awareness and not *mere* inner awareness—is *constitutive* of phenomenology. Thus one position on the matter is that peripheral inner awareness takes a more robust form as

---

[14] An exception among phenomenologists may be Aron Gurwitsch, whose views on this subject (and others, as it happens) are very close to mine. In particular, he seems to understand pre-reflective self-consciousness in terms of marginal consciousness, which is virtually the same notion as peripheral awareness.

[15] Clearly, the term "pre-reflective self-consciousness" suggests the more robust, self-involving variety. But we can treat the term as a mere tag, without any descriptive purport.

peripheral *self*-awareness in normal human adults, but may retain a leaner form as *mere* inner awareness in other cases (for example, with infants and animals). On this view, the only *necessary* condition for phenomenology is inner awareness, though this inner awareness *can* take on extra elements of a more contingent nature. The view is that pre-reflective self-consciousness is *often* egological, but not *constitutively* so.

There might be an argument to the effect that inner awareness *must* be self-awareness, that is, for a full-fledged "egological" view of pre-reflective self-consciousness. The argument I have in mind is adapted from Rosenthal (1990: 741).[16] It starts from the observation that one's awareness of one's concurrent conscious state is awareness of it as a particular *token* mental state, not as a *type* of mental state. According to Rosenthal, such awareness of a state as a particular requires awareness of the subject of the state. As I have my bluish experience of the sky, it is possible to be aware of the general *kind* of experience—bluish experience of the sky—in abstraction from its being *someone*'s experience, but it is not possible to be aware of it as an unrepeatable *particular* instance of a bluish experience of the sky in abstraction from its being this or that person's experience. Rosenthal asserts this requirement without argument, but perhaps the thought is that (*a*) token states are necessarily someone's and (*b*) the only thing that distinguishes different tokens of the same experience type is that they occur in different subjects (and/or at different times, presumably). In that case, being aware of a token state as the token it is would require being aware of whose state it is (and what time it occurs, relative to the time of awareness).

It is not entirely clear to me that token mental states are necessarily someone's, if the necessity in question is stronger than nomological. Furthermore, I am not sure that, in order to be aware of a token state as a particular, one must be aware of that which makes it the token state it is. Perhaps this is plausible when the awareness is purely intellectual, and of course, according to Rosenthal, the relevant kind of inner awareness is. That is, it may well be plausible that one cannot *think* about a mental state as a particular without thinking about the subject whose state it is. But it

---

[16] Rosenthal (1990: 741): "Independent considerations point to the same conclusion. One cannot think about a particular mental-state token, as opposed to thinking simply about a type of mental state, unless what one thinks is that some individual creature is in that mental state. So [our awareness of our conscious states] will not be about mental-state tokens unless [its] content is that one is, oneself, in the mental state."

may nonetheless be *implausible* that one cannot quasi-perceive a token state as a particular without quasi-perceiving it as someone's. As I wish to remain neutral on the question of whether this inner awareness is intellectual or quasi-perceptual, I remain neutral on the question of the merit of this argument for the egological view of pre-reflective self-consciousness.

Within the family of egological views, there are further questions that arise regarding the *way* the self or subject is presented in pre-reflective self-consciousness. A thin view is that the presented self is purely "logical": it is that which has or undergoes the experiences. On this view, I am aware of my conscious experiences as mine, but I am not aware of the "me" there in any personal way. A more robust view of pre-reflective self-consciousness casts this "me" precisely as a personal me, with all its idiosyncratic memories, emotional attachments, and self-conceptions. It is fairly obvious that, in being aware of one's bluish experiences, one is not thereby aware of all of one's memories, attachments, self-conceptions, and so on. But it may still be that one is aware of oneself *as the sort of thing* that has those memories, attachments, and self-conceptions. This is sometimes referred to as the *autobiographical* view of pre-reflective self-consciousness. I am not sure what to say about this, except that something in the autobiographical picture strikes me as vaguely correct.

Within the family of non-egological views, different questions arise. Consider again my overall conscious experience as I stare at the blue sky, hear the car engines, feel the soles of my shoes, and anxiously think of the unpaid bill. Another item in this phenomenology is my peripheral inner awareness of this very experience. But which of the "floor-level" items does this inner awareness attach to?

One view is that it attaches to each and every item. Thus, in addition to the four items comprising the visual experience of the sky, the auditory experience of the cars, the tactile experience of the soles, and the intellectual-cum-emotional experience of the unpaid bill, there are four other items—namely, the peripheral awareness of the visual experience of the sky, the peripheral awareness of the auditory experience of the cars, and so on. For every floor-level item in the phenomenology, there is a corresponding item in the form of an awareness of it. This seems somehow too baroque, as well as psychologically inexpedient.

A leaner view is that the peripheral inner awareness attaches only to whichever floor-level item occupies the focal center of the overall phenomenology. In the present case, the visual experience of the blue sky is the focal floor-level item. So, on this view, there is only a fifth item in addition to the four floor-level ones—namely, the peripheral awareness of the visual experience of the blue sky. This view can still make sense of the notion that peripheral inner awareness is a constitutive aspect of conscious experience. It can maintain that a mental state counts as an experience only if it is synchronically unified with at least one mental state that is the object of peripheral inner awareness. If so, it is still a necessary condition on something's being an experience that it bears the right relation to peripheral inner awareness. At the same time, it is hard to see how this view can be motivated: whatever argument there is for thinking that we are aware of each of our conscious states will probably extend to thinking that we are aware of each phenomenal item in each of our conscious states.

An intermediate view might be that there is only a fifth item of peripheral inner awareness, but that its content encompasses all four other items. The object of a single item of peripheral inner awareness need not be a single "floor-level" item. It may be the sum of a number of such items. Perhaps the underlying psychological mechanism involves first the synchronic unification of the floor-level items and then their synchronic unification with a peripheral awareness of their unity (see Williford 2006: 128–9). This view strikes me as the most plausible of the ones we have considered thus far, though that will not matter for our discussion here.

We have seen a great number of different views of the phenomenology of pre-reflective self-consciousness, which can translate into views on peripheral inner awareness. These views are certainly anything but pedestrian. Given the lack of clear standards for evaluating such views, it is extremely difficult to take a position on them. But I hope that the discussion in this section has shown that the issue can be discussed in an intelligible way, and that intelligible distinctions can be drawn and a map of options be intelligibly sketched out.[17]

---

[17] For my part, I find myself attracted to the view that pre-reflective self-consciousness in normal human adults is a genuine form of awareness-of, which takes as its object a unity of floor-level items as well as oneself as (potentially autobiographical) subject of the unity. I am much less confident of this claim, however, than of the claim that peripheral inner awareness is a constitutive aspect of phenomenology.

In any event, here I wish to defend only the minimal claim that one (constitutive) aspect of phenomenology is peripheral inner awareness. The leaner claim may be formulated as follows:

(UIA) For any mental state M of a subject S, if M is conscious at t, then (i) S is aware of M at t and (ii) S's awareness of M is part of S's overall phenomenology at t.

Call this the *Ubiquity of Inner Awareness* thesis. It is the thesis I will now defend. Note well: I use "defend" advisedly: as stated in Chapter 1, I will not offer a positive argument for UIA, only defend it against counter-arguments.

3. The Transparency of Experience and Other Challenges

The Ubiquity Thesis and the Transparency of Experience

In Chapter 3 we encountered the phenomenon of transparency: the fact that the only introspectively accessible properties of conscious experience are its representational properties. Of course, the intent behind the transparency thesis is not to include the self-representational properties of experiences, but rather to confine the introspectively accessible to floor-level, first-order representational properties.

For present purposes, then, we may amend the transparency thesis from Chapter 3 to read as follows:

(TE) For any experience e and any feature F, if F is an introspectible feature of e, then F is (part of) the first-order representational content of e.

A first-order representational content is a content involving neither representations nor representational properties. What is purportedly represented is neither a representation nor something's representational properties. If a content C involves representations or representational properties, then C is *not* a first-order representational content.

As we have seen in Chapter 3, TE carries intuitive conviction. But it seems on the face of it to conflict with UIA. UIA claims that there is a phenomenological element in conscious experiences that does not have to do with their first-order representational content—namely, peripheral inner awareness—but TE claims that no such thing appears to introspection. This certainly seems like a conflict, so, to the extent that TE seems intuitive, UIA should seem counter-intuitive. In fact, TE seems to be in conflict even with the weaker *existential* (as opposed to universal) thesis that *some* conscious states involve a phenomenologically manifest awareness of them.

More precisely, we may construct the following argument from transparency to the phenomenological unreality of peripheral inner awareness: the only introspectively accessible aspect of a phenomenal experience is its first-order representational content; peripheral inner awareness involves no first-order representational content; therefore, peripheral inner awareness is not an introspectively accessible aspect of phenomenal experience. Call this the *transparency argument against UIA*.

To defend UIA, one must argue either (i) that TE is false or (ii) that TE is *not* in conflict with UIA, despite appearances. Here I will pursue the latter strategy. As should be clear from the discussion in Chapter 3, I am quite sympathetic to TE. What I want to do in this subsection is argue that, despite initial appearances to the contrary, self-representationalism is *compatible* with the transparency thesis. In fact, I will argue that, combined with a natural account of introspection, self-representationalism actually *predicts* that peripheral inner awareness is not introspectible.

Note, to begin with, that TE does not say that there *are* no elements in the phenomenology that go beyond first-order representational contents. Rather, it says that no such elements are *introspectively accessible*. This leaves open the possibility that there are introspectively *inaccessible* elements in the phenomenology that go beyond such world-directed representational content. In fact, TE does not even say that there are no *phenomenologically manifest* elements in the phenomenology beyond world-directed representational contents; merely that, if there are, it is not through introspection that they are manifest.[18]

---

[18] I bring up the notion of phenomenological manifestness to accommodate the possibility that some aspects of the phenomenology are completely opaque to the subject, who bears no epistemic relation to them whatsoever. This view strikes me as extremely implausible, but it appears to be coherent. What I want to argue, in any case, is that peripheral inner awareness is such that, although we cannot introspect it, we do bear some epistemic relation to it, in virtue of which it is phenomenologically manifest to us.

For most putative elements in the phenomenology, it would be odd to claim that, though they are phenomenologically manifest, they are not introspectively accessible.[19] But what I want to argue is that the case of peripheral inner awareness is an exception: peripheral inner awareness is phenomenologically manifest, yet not introspectible.

To see how this could be, consider what is involved in introspecting one's concurrent conscious experience. According to one model, when one introspects one's current experience, one enters a new representational state, a state of introspective awareness, that takes one's current experience as its object. But, for someone who believes UIA, a more natural model of introspecting suggests itself. On this model, introspecting one's current experience does not involve entering a completely new representational state. Rather, it involves reorganizing the center/periphery structure of one's overall experience, by transforming one's peripheral inner awareness of one's current experience into a focal one. Consider my visual experience of the laptop before me and the bonsai to my left. Before the introspecting, my visual awareness of the laptop is focal, whereas (a) my visual awareness of the bonsai and (b) my inner awareness of my overall experience are peripheral. When I introspect, what happens is that the inner awareness displaces the visual awareness of the laptop in the focal center. Now the inner awareness is focal, whereas both the visual awareness of the laptop and the visual awareness of the bonsai are peripheral. We may call this the *attention-shift model* of introspecting.[20]

The attention-shift model of introspecting is more natural for the ubiquity theorist, because she holds that all conscious experiences—and not only the explicitly introspected ones—are objects of awareness. It also has the added advantage of illuminating the fact that introspecting does not feel, phenomenologically, like performing a "dramatic" mental act, an act that creates an altogether new representation (as, say, visualizing a cat does).

---

[19] They may not be introspectively accessed most of the time, but to claim that they are not accessible in principle may appear to stretch credulity. On some views, this may be downright incoherent.

[20] It is also worth noting that, in the case of visual awareness, there may be two focal/peripheral distinctions that could be confused. One lines up with the (cognitively based) attentive/non-attentive distinction, but the other lines up with the (physiologically based) foveal/non-foveal distinction. Thus one can attend to something in one's visual field that one is not foveating. In that case, one would be focally visually aware of that thing in one sense but not in the other. The distinction that is relevant to our present purposes is between attentive/inattentive visual awareness. So, in the case described in the text, I am peripherally aware of both the laptop and the bonsai, though the laptop I am also foveating, whereas the bonsai I am not.

Instead, it feels more like shifting around one's attention, and attending more carefully to contents that were already previously there.

My claim is that the attention-shift model predicts that peripheral inner awareness is not introspectible. On this model, introspection cannot *reveal* peripheral inner awareness, because it *supplants* it. Introspecting one's current experience is a matter of having focal inner awareness of it. But, once one enters the state of focal inner awareness, the state of *peripheral* inner awareness that existed prior to the introspecting has gone out of existence; or, rather, it has "graduated" to focal awareness. This is because, on the present model, it is one and the same awareness that is peripheral before the act of introspecting is performed and focal thereafter. Thus introspecting cannot reveal peripheral inner awareness because it *annihilates* it (by supplanting it). All this is to say that, for someone who believes in the phenomenology of peripheral inner awareness, and embraces the attention-shift model of introspecting, the right—indeed, only—prediction to make is that peripheral inner awareness is not introspectible.

The apparent tension between TE and UIA is based on an attachment to a model of introspection as involving the production of a new awareness of that which is being introspected. That model is perhaps natural for someone who holds that there are conscious experiences of which one is unaware. But the ubiquity theorist denies this, and therefore that model of introspection is unnatural for her. The natural model for her is the attention-shift model, according to which no new awareness is produced, but rather attention is shifted from one pre-existing awareness to another. Once we adopt the attention-shift model, we see that UIA predicts that peripheral inner awareness is non-introspectible. This makes it compatible with TE. If the transparency theorist is right—as I think she is (see Chapter 3)—that all the other elements in a conscious experience's phenomenology are presented to introspection as first-order representational contents, and the ubiquity theorist is right that peripheral inner awareness is non-introspectible, then it follows that TE is true.[21]

---

[21] Self-representationalism is in itself silent on the truth of the antecedent, of course, but my own version of self-representationalism, including the representational account of qualitative character defended in Chapter 3, is certainly in line with the transparency theorist's. (This holds, on my view, even for what I called in Section 1 the "structural" aspects of phenomenology, such as synchronic unity: they are just representations of response-dependent relations among items represented by other items in the phenomenology.) In any case, what the present reasoning shows is that self-representationalism is certainly *compatible* with TE.

Let us dwell on this point a little longer. If the transparency theorist is right on the nature of all the aspects of phenomenology other than peripheral inner awareness, then, according to the view defended here, before I introspect my experience of the laptop before me and the bonsai to my left, all the phenomenological components of my experience *but one* are representations of the external world (or at least present themselves this way to introspection). Once I introspect the experience, the introspecting destroys that sole item, leaving only the representations of the external world standing. What I become aware of when I introspect is thus that the experience represents the world to be so and thus—and of nothing more. This is just what the transparency thesis claims. Thus the transparency theorist ought to have no qualms about embracing UIA.

If peripheral inner awareness is not introspectively accessible, in what sense is it phenomenologically manifest? More generally, how can any mental phenomenon be phenomenologically manifest but not through introspection? This is a good question, and one for which I do not have a general answer. But note that a parallel quandary could be raised for peripheral *outer* awareness. As you listen to the piano concerto, you can decide to attend to the cellos rather than the piano. What you cannot do, however, is attend to the cellos qua peripherally experienced. For that would amount to attending to the cellos qua unattended to, or become focally aware of cellos qua objects of non-focal awareness—a manifest contradiction.[22] Yet few would infer that the sound of cellos is something you are unaware of. For, despite the fact that we cannot attend to the periphery qua periphery, we have a general impression of this periphery from our ordinary everyday phenomenology. Just how we have such an impression, and what is its nature, are important questions that ultimately should be addressed; but there is certainly such an impression. The same situation, I maintain, applies to peripheral *inner* awareness. We cannot attend to peripheral inner awareness qua peripheral, because that would amount to attending to it qua unattended to, which is logically impossible.

---

[22] In the case of visual awareness, the duality of focal/peripheral distinctions noted above (in n. 20) may tempt us to think that I can attend to the visual periphery qua periphery after all—say, because I can attend to a bonsai without foveating it. But this would be merely attending to the foveal periphery qua foveal periphery. It would not be attending to the attentional periphery qua attentional periphery. It is the latter kind we are concerned with, however, since the relevant focal/peripheral distinction, as drawn in Section 2, is drawn in terms of attention distribution.

But we do have a general impression of peripheral inner awareness from our ordinary, non-introspective consciousness.

To be sure, this talk of a "general impression" is, as it stands, somewhat mysterious. What is this general impression? How come we have one, given that we cannot attend to that of which we allegedly have a general impression? Is the general impression grounded in a higher-order representation or not, and how is all this supposed to work? These too are good questions, but I think we would do well to treat them here as material for future investigation. As the case of peripheral auditory awareness just discussed shows, there clearly *is* some way this all works. The fact that it is not clear *how* should not blind us to this fact.[23]

All this is to claim that the transparency thesis does not by itself pose a threat to the phenomenological reality of peripheral inner awareness. There may also be, in addition, a more positive piece of evidence for that phenomenological reality. As I noted above, introspecting feels more like a phenomenologically light shifting around of attention than like a dramatic mental act that produces a completely new awareness. Indeed, it feels very much like shifting one's attention from piano to cellos, rather than creating a previously non-existent awareness of cellos. This may be taken to constitute phenomenological evidence that, prior to the introspecting, there was already inner awareness of the conscious experience, albeit peripheral—just as it suggests that, prior to attending to the cellos, there was already an auditory awareness of them, albeit peripheral. If the inner awareness was altogether outside the phenomenology, introspecting would be phenomenologically more dramatic than it actually is: it would feel like the introduction of a new item into the phenomenology, not like a reorganization of the center/periphery structure over already existing items.[24]

---

[23] Moreover, my purpose here is only to show that TE is not in tension with UIA. And the above discussion should suffice to establish that. The discussion suggests that at most UIA is in tension with the conjunction of TE and the further claim that there can be no general impressions of things to which we cannot attend. But first, it is not in tension with TE *by itself*, and, second, it is surely false that there can be no general impression of things to which we cannot attend, again as the case of peripheral auditory awareness shows.

[24] This consideration also suggests that the self-representational account of the phenomenology of introspective consciousness is more accurate than the higher-order representational account, which requires the appearance in the phenomenology of a representation that was previously not there.

Returning to the transparency argument against UIA, the response is that the ubiquity theorist can actually accept the argument's conclusion—namely, that peripheral inner awareness is not introspectible. What she rejects is the implication that peripheral inner awareness is not phenomenologically manifest (let alone that it is not phenomenologically real). This depends, of course, on finding daylight between introspective accessibility and phenomenological manifestness. The above discussion, in particular the adopted model of introspecting, is supposed to show that there is such daylight. The combination of the attention-shift model and UIA allows us to see how there could be a peripheral inner awareness that is both phenomenologically manifest and non-introspectible. An opponent of UIA would thus have to do more than just assert (and defend) the transparency of experience; she would also have to argue either against the attention-shift model of introspecting or against the claim that it illuminates the status of peripheral inner awareness as both phenomenologically manifest and non-introspectible. I conclude that there is no conflict between TE and UIA—the two are perfectly compatible against the background of the attention-shift model of introspecting. Before closing this part of the discussion, let me address a handful of objections to this attempt to reconcile UIA and TE.

First, it might be objected that, even if the above discussion establishes the compatibility of UIA with TE, most transparency theorists would insist on a version of the transparency thesis that is stronger than TE, and with which UIA is incompatible. TE's antecedent is formulated in terms of introspectible properties of experience—that is, properties of which we are introspectively aware. However, a stronger transparency thesis could be formulated in terms of phenomenologically manifest properties.

The objector may be right that UIA is incompatible with the stronger transparency thesis, but the stronger transparency thesis may also be stronger than is plausible. While it is plausible that all properties presented to introspective awareness are first-order representational properties, it is not all that clear that this is the case also for properties presented in non-introspective awareness. At any rate, I have not heard an argument to suggest that the force of the observation regarding introspectible properties carries over to non-introspectible ones.[25, 26]

A second objection can be presented as a dilemma. Either the general impression of which I speak is a form of awareness or it is not. If it is, then we may have on our hands a regress problem, as the question will arise whether the general-impression-constituting awareness is something of which we are aware, with unappealing implications either way. If it is not, then another embarrassing question arises: if the peripheral inner awareness of which we have a general impression is something of which we are unaware, and yet is a component of the phenomenology, does it not follow that there is a component of the phenomenology of which we are unaware?

My response is that this general impression is most certainly an awareness, but there is no regress, for the reasons we have already explored in the previous chapter. As I noted there, this kind of regress is precisely the sort of problem to avert which we have to embrace a self-representation rather than higher-order account of subjective character. Thus the awareness that constitutes the peripheral inner awareness, and that which constitutes the general impression thereof, are in fact one and the same—it is an awareness that is partly an awareness of itself.

A third objection is that the view defended here implies, implausibly, that an introspected experience and an unintrospected experience cannot have the same phenomenology, because there will be at least this difference between them, that one involves peripheral inner awareness whereas the other involves focal inner awareness. This in turn has the untoward consequence that one and the same token conscious state cannot be unintrospected at one time and introspected at another. The objector's reasoning might be this: if a token experience e_1 at a time t_1 and a token experience e_2 at t_2 have different phenomenologies, then e_1 and e_2 are numerically distinct experiences; self-representationalism implies

---

[25] It seems to me that TE is so compelling partly because introspection is often under our voluntary control, which gives us control over the examination of introspectible properties. But non-introspective inner awareness is involuntary and uncontrollable, so we cannot straightforwardly compare what happens when it is present and when it is absent.

[26] Also, the objector seems to assume that peripheral inner awareness is an element of our phenomenology of which we are aware. But it is an open question whether it is. Above, I did not assert that it is. What I said is that it is something we have a general impression of. It would follow that we are aware of it only if there is no way to have a general impression of something without being aware of it. Admittedly, part of the problem is that I did not clarify what that general impression exactly is.

that introspected and unintrospected experiences always have different phenomenologies (since the latter does, but the former does not, involve peripheral inner awareness); therefore, self-representationalism implies that introspected and unintrospected experiences are always numerically distinct.

My response is disjunctive and depends on one's view of the metaphysics of experiences (and states generally)—whether one takes them to be property exemplifications or bare particulars. If they are property exemplifications, then most certainly they are phenomenal-property exemplifications. Given that the property exemplified in introspected and unintrospected experiences is different, it would indeed follow that introspected and unintrospected experiences must be numerically distinct. But under this metaphysic of experiences this result is actually independently plausible. Christopher Hill (1988) notes, very plausibly, that introspection appears to function as a "volume control" of phenomenology: an introspected toothache hurts more than an unintrospected one, and does so *because* it is introspected. Thus there is always a difference in phenomenal intensity between introspected and unintrospected experiences. So, if experiences are phenomenal-property exemplifications, then introspected and unintrospected experiences must be token-different independently of self-representationalism. On the other hand, if experiences are bare particular, then they can persist through change in their phenomenal properties, with the result that one and the same experience can be unintrospected one moment and introspected the next.[27]

A fourth objection is that it is misleading to construe subjective character as "peripheral" inner awareness, because it suggests that there is a center/periphery distinction for inner awareness that behaves in the same way as the center/periphery distinction for outer awareness. That this suggestion is false can be seen from the fact that items in outer awareness compete for the focus of attention, but there is no such competition between items of outer and inner awareness: one can attend to one's attending to the piano sound. It appears, then, that there is not a single field of experience with a

---

[27] Scenarios involving phenomenal sorites support the bare-particular view: one and the same token experience can change, by a series of indiscriminable changes, from being yellowish to being reddish. It is true that on this view one and the same phenomenal token may fall under different phenomenal types at different times, but, although this is certainly unusual, it should not be deemed impossible. Thus, it is plausible to maintain that one and the same concrete particular can be a caterpillar at one time and a butterfly at another, thus falling (quite essentially) under two different kinds at different times.

center/periphery structure that encompasses both outer and inner awareness, and more generally there is something confused about the notion of
peripheral inner awareness.

It is true that I have assumed thus far that there is competition for the
focus of attention between objects of outer and inner awareness. However,
this assumption seems unnecessary for most of my purposes. In particular,
it does not undermine the construal of subjective character in terms of
the notion of peripheral inner awareness. Even if there is no competition
for attentional focus between objects of outer and inner awareness, as
long as there *is* such competition among the objects of inner awareness,
inner awareness has its own center/periphery structure and is to that
extent analogous to outer awareness. We could also suppose that outer
and inner awareness do form a unified field, but one with two center
points rather than one. What makes it unified is after all not only—not
even chiefly—the existence of a single center, but rather the synchronic
unity of the items within it. In addition, I am not so sure that it is in
fact possible to attend to one's attending to some external item. Perhaps
we can only rapidly move back and forth from attending to the external
item to attending to that attending—so rapidly, in fact, that it may seem
superficially as though one attends to one's attending.[28]

Finally, it might be objected that the attention-shift model of introspecting entails that there are conscious experiences that do *not* involve peripheral
inner awareness—namely, explicitly introspected conscious experiences.
Since in those experiences the peripheral inner awareness has been destroyed, they must lack peripheral inner awareness.

My response is simply to agree with the objector. UIA, and more
generally the phenomenological view I am defending here, should not
be understood to claim that all conscious experiences involve specifically
peripheral inner awareness. What they all involve is inner awareness. *Ordinarily*, that is, in cases of non-introspective consciousness, that awareness is
peripheral. *Sometimes*, namely in cases of introspective consciousness, that
awareness is focal. In both cases, on the view defended in this book, this
involves the conscious experience representing itself. The difference is in
how attention resources are distributed among the experience's different
representational properties.

---

[28] On the other hand, perhaps such dual attending is really possible. I could go either way on this.

Other Challenges to the Ubiquity Thesis

Opponents of UIA sometimes offer more direct arguments against it. Consider the following argument, due to Charles Siewert (1998: ch. 7). As you read a breathtaking mystery novel, there is "silent speech" taking place in the back of your mind. This episode of silent speech appears to have a conscious feel, a phenomenal character. But suppose now that you decide to turn your attention away from the tales you read and onto your silent speech episode. Some psychologically real event is taking place. How are we to characterize this psychologically real event? According to Siewert, the only plausible way to construe this event is as follows: upon turning your attention to the silent speech episode, you become aware of something of which you were previously unaware. This means that, before thus turning your attention, the episode had a phenomenal character of which you were unaware. So there are such.

There are two ways to defend UIA here. The first is to deny that the episode had a phenomenal character prior to the attention turning; that strikes me as implausible. The second is to deny that you were unaware of the episode prior to the *attention-turning*; that is plausible. Siewert claims that the only way to construe the psychological event that takes place when you turn your attention to the silent episode is to say that you become aware of something of which you were previously unaware. But another way to construe it is as follows: upon turning your attention, you become *focally* and attentively aware of what you were previously only *peripherally* and inattentively aware of. The latter construal is fully in line with UIA.

Siewert's is perhaps the best of a series of alleged counter-examples that advert to cases of *absent-minded* experience. In Chapter 2 we encountered Block's story (1995) of being engrossed in heated conversation and not noticing a drilling outside one's window. The story was originally suggested by Block, or at least commonly interpreted as intended, to show that the auditory experience of the drilling is phenomenally conscious even though there is no awareness of it. However, again it seems to me that the more accurate description is that, while engrossed in conversation, Block has a very peripheral awareness of his auditory experience—but he is aware of it nonetheless. Whence else Block's confidence that he had had the experience at the time it took place?[29] Block's latest position on stories of this kind (2007) is that they show that the absent-minded perception can be phenomenally conscious even when it is not introspectively accessible, though the subject may have a subtler and more elusive awareness of it.

Perhaps the cleverest attempt at a counter-example is Dretske's (1993).[30] Suppose you are presented with a "baker's dozen" of bagels. Then one bagel is surreptitiously removed and you are presented with an otherwise identical arrangement of a (non-baker's) dozen bagels.[31] Call the removed bagel "the baker's bagel." If you are allowed to stare at the two arrangements long enough, you will be able to tell the difference between them. If you are allowed to look at them for only a very short time, you might not see the baker's bagel to begin with. But there is an intermediate length of time such that, if you were allowed to look at the two arrangements for just that long, you would be unable to tell the difference between them, despite seeing the baker's bagel.[32]

One way to interpret the argument is as follows. When allowed to stare at the arrangements for just the right length of time, your experience of the baker's dozen is different from your experience of the dozen, but you are unaware of the difference.[33] So there is a difference between your experiences of which you are unaware.

On this interpretation, however, the argument does not really threaten UIA. UIA is a thesis about individual conscious states, not about relations *between* them, such as relations of similarity and difference. It claims that there are no phenomenally conscious states of which we are unaware. It does not claim in addition that there are no phenomenal relations between conscious states of which we are unaware.[34]

---

[29] For a similar line of response, see Dennett 1995.

[30] The example I will provide is not exactly Dretske's, but is rather a text-friendly variation on Dretske's that retains the same structure.

[31] For those unaccustomed to bagel-involving examples: a baker's dozen numbers thirteen.

[32] This is particularly plausible if we accept something like George Miller's "seven plus or minus two" principle (1956), according to which the number of items that can be retained in a normal subject's working and short-term memory is 5–9—so less than a dozen.

[33] If you had been aware of the difference between your experiences of the two arrangements, you would be able to tell they differed (which you are not). And, if your experiences did not differ, you would not have seen the baker's bagel (which you did).

[34] It may be that when there is a phenomenal relation between two conscious states, each state also has a relational phenomenal property. But nor does UIA claim that we are aware of *all* the properties of our conscious states, only that we are aware of those states themselves. Arguably, for this to hold there must be awareness of *some* properties of the states, such as some qualitative properties. Certainly,

A better interpretation of Dretske's argument is this. When looking at the baker's dozen the right length of time, you had a conscious experience of the baker's bagel, but you were unaware of having that experience. Therefore, there are conscious experiences of which one is unaware. More rigorously, for some subject S looking at the baker's dozen bagels long enough,

1. S has a conscious experience of the baker's bagel at t;
2. S is not aware of S's experience of the baker's bagel at t; therefore,
3. S has conscious experiences of which S is not aware.

If so, UIA is false. What supports Premise 1 in this argument is the fact that S saw the baker's bagel (at t). What supports Premise 2 is the fact that S could not tell the difference between the two arrangements (at t).[35]

Both premises are objectionable, however. Premise 2 is particularly implausible. The fact that S could not tell the difference between the two arrangements would support it only on the assumption that awareness of x must be awareness of it *as x*. Without this assumption, we can say that S is aware of her experience of the baker's bagel even though S is not aware of it *as* an experience of the baker's bagel, let alone as *the difference between her experiences of the baker's dozen and the dozen*.[36]

Premise 1 is more plausible but not beyond dispute. An assumption behind it is that every part of an experience is itself an experience. If S has at t a conscious experience e, and e^* is a part of e, then S has at t a conscious experience e^*. It is only under this assumption that the fact that S has an experience of the baker's dozen (at t) entails that S also has an experience of the baker's bagel (at t). This assumption is questionable, however. It tempts us in the case of visual experience because of the spatial layout of visual contents: we are tempted to suppose that a part of an experience is itself an experience, just as a part of a spatial region is itself

however, we can exclude any relational properties of the sort currently under consideration from this privileged group.

[35] There are other ways to interpret Dretske's argument. For instance: (1) S is unaware of the difference between S's experience of the baker's dozen and S's experience of the dozen; (2) the difference between S's experience of the baker's dozen and S's experience of the dozen is (identical with) S's experience of the baker's bagel; therefore, (3) S is unaware of S's experience of the baker's bagel; therefore, (4) there are experiences of S that S is not aware of. This argument is invalid, however, as it substitutes "the difference between S's experience of the baker's dozen and S's experience of the dozen" and "S's experience of the baker's bagel" in an intensional context.

[36] This response is developed more fully in Rosenthal 2000.

a spatial region. But the supposition becomes more tendentious when we consider other modalities. Thus, part of my olfactory experience of the blueberry pie is the smell of dough, but it is not obvious that I can thereby be said to have an olfactory experience of dough. Note that, without the assumption in question, Dretske's argument can establish only that there are experience-*parts* of which the subject is unaware. But UIA says nothing about experience-parts. At the same time, the spirit of UIA may well extend to experience-parts, so personally I am disinclined to adopt this objection to Dretske's argument. Instead I rely on the previous paragraph's objection.

I conclude that, even under its most plausible interpretation, Dretske's argument against UIA fails.

Let me close this section with a discussion of what is perhaps the most worrisome cloud over UIA. This is the suspicion that it may be overly demanding. Certain animals, as well as human neonates and infants, appear (on the one hand) to have phenomenally conscious states but (on the other hand) to lack the capacity to be aware of their internal states. If so, while awareness of one's conscious states may be *characteristic* of adult human consciousness, it cannot be a *necessary condition* of consciousness as such.[37]

In support of the claim that animals and infants have conscious states, intuition is adduced, as well as the consideration that folk-psychological explanations of their behavior invoke conscious experiences (see Lurz 1999). In support of the claim that animals and infants have no awareness of their conscious states, intuitions are proffered, as well as experimental findings to the effect that animals and infants possess little metacognitive capacities.[38] To take the paradigmatic experimental measure of self-awareness, the mirror self-recognition test, successes are few and far between: humans younger than eighteen months fail, and the only (adult) animals known to pass are the chimpanzee, the orangutan, the bottlenose dolphin, and the Asian elephant (while even gorillas and gibbons fail).[39] In another set of paradigmatic findings, most animals and all human infants and

[37] This worry was raised originally by proponents of UIA, actually—see Rosenthal 1986 and Carruthers 1989. Dretske (1995) was among the first to work this worry as an argument against UIA. For review and discussion, see Lurz 1999.

[38] The notion of metacognition is employed in cognitive science to denote second-order cognition. It seems to have been introduced into psychological discourse by John Flavell (see, e.g., Flavell 1979). We will discuss it more thoroughly in Chapter 7.

[39] For the findings on mirror self-recognition in human infants and toddlers, see Amsterdam 1972. For its lack in gorillas, see Suarez and Gallup 1981. For the successes of dolphins, see Reiss and Marino 2001, and, for those of Asian elephants, see Plotnik, de Waal, and Reiss 2006. Gallup was the first

toddlers younger than 3 seem to lack the concepts of believing and seeing: they cannot ascribe—not even to themselves—false beliefs or non-veridical visual experiences; which suggests that they do not understand the difference between believing/seeing and that which is believed/seen.[40] These facts paint a bleak picture of animal and infant metacognition.

There are generally two responses to this challenge. The first is simply to deny that metacognitively challenged animals and infants have conscious states (Carruthers 1999, 2000). The second is to reject the claim that animals and infants cannot be aware of their conscious states. The latter response comes in two varieties: one might either (i) undermine the force of experimental findings about metacognition (typically on methodological grounds), thus denying that animals and infants are metacognitively challenged, or (ii) undercut the inference from these findings, thus denying that the metacognitively challenged cannot be aware of their conscious states. Version (i) of the second response seems the most widely pursued among proponents of UIA. Rosenthal (2000, 2002a) pursues it particularly vigorously, although he also pursues a subsidiary line of defense that focuses on version (ii).[41]

To my mind, version (ii) of the second response is the most plausible. Rosenthal (2002a) notes that, even if animals and infants cannot be aware of their beliefs and experiences in a way that employs the concepts of belief and experience, they may still be aware of their beliefs and experiences in a way that employs cruder concepts. A metacognitively challenged subject may lack the concepts of belief and experience but possess the concepts of truebelief and veridicalexperience (if you will). Such a subject could still be aware of her internal states, even if not in the way adult humans are.

More radically, animals and infants may be aware of their beliefs and experiences in a way that does not employ *any* concept. It is consistent with UIA that their awareness of their conscious states is altogether *non-conceptual*. Such non-conceptual self-awareness would require minimal

to conduct mirror self-recognition experiments (Gallup 1970), and later offered them as capturing an operational definition of self-awareness (Gallup 1975).

[40] For first studies of inabilities to ascribe false belief in humans, see Perner et al. 1987. For application of the issue to *self-ascription* of false beliefs, see Gopnik and Astington 1988. For chimpanzees' inability to ascribe knowledge, see Povinelli et al. 1994. There is some recent evidence, however, that chimpanzees can distinguish what conspecifics can see from what is the case (Tomasello and Call 2005).

[41] Version (i) can be pursued not only on methodological grounds, but also by citing such counter-evidence as is found in Tomasello and Call 2005.

metacognitive capacities, of the sort not really questioned by current experimental evidence.

Furthermore, note that most metacognition involves *focal* self-awareness, whereas UIA need not implicate anything more than *peripheral* self-awareness. It is reasonable to suppose that the latter requires weaker cognitive capacities than the former. An unsophisticated creature may not have enough attention resources to allocate to awareness of its own inner activity to sustain something like focal inner awareness, but have just enough to allocate the kind of resources needed to sustain peripheral inner awareness.[42]

These considerations point to the paucity of metacognitive capacities required by UIA. The limited capacities possessed by animals and infants probably suffice to meet the requirement. Thus none of the challenges to UIA we have examined in this subsection seems particularly compelling.

This concludes my case against the case against UIA.

4. From Phenomenology to Self-Representationalism

If I am right in my defense of UIA, we have no good reason not to accept that the overall phenomenology of a conscious subject at a time always and necessarily includes an element of inner awareness. This is important because, once we accept the phenomenological reality and necessity of inner awareness, there is a straightforward argument that forces self-representationalism on us.

The argument takes the same form as the master argument from Chapter 4, but reaches its conclusion much faster. Recall that UIA states the following:

(UIA)   For any mental state M of a subject S, if M is conscious at t, then (i) S is aware of M at t and (ii) S's awareness of M is part of S's overall phenomenology at t.

---

[42] This response faces some problems. It is quite a plausible principle that a creature is capable of peripheral awareness of some type only if it is at least in principle capable of focal awareness of that type. This principle is especially plausible if we suppose that the central function of peripheral awareness is to

Adding to this the assumption that a subject S is aware of a mental state M only if there is a mental state M*, such that (i) S is in M* and (ii) M* represents M, we reach:

(UMR) For any mental state M of a subject S, if M is conscious at *t*, then there is a mental state M*, such that (i) S is in M* at *t*, (ii) M* represents M at *t*, and (iii) M* is part of S's overall phenomenology at *t*.

Now we add the assumption that a mental state M is part of the overall phenomenology of a subject S at a time *t* only if M is conscious at *t*, and we reach:

(UCR) For any mental state M of a subject S, if M is conscious at *t*, then there is a mental state M*, such that (i) S is in M*, (ii) M* represents M at *t*, and (iii) M* is conscious.

For reasons covered in Chapter 4, Section 3, UCR eventually rules out higher-order representationalism and the hybrid view on pain of vicious regress. The upshot is:

(USR) For any mental state M of a subject S, if M is conscious at *t*, then there is a mental state M*, such that (i) S is in M, (ii) M* represents M at *t*, and (iii) M* = M.

This is self-representationalism.

I hesitate to cast this as an independent argument for self-representation-alism, since it relies so heavily on a phenomenological assertion that is very much self-representationalist in spirit, and for which I have not provided independent positive arguments. The primary purpose of this chapter has been to flesh out the phenomenological component of self-representationalism. At the end of this chapter we can appreciate, I hope, that self-representationalism has a specific and rich story to tell about the exact phenomenology of our stream of consciousness. This should at least cast self-representationalism as a fruitful and potentially lively research program.

---

facilitate focal awareness in some way. And, indeed, I will argue for something like that in Chapter 7. So I am disinclined to embrace this response myself.

5. Conclusion

As just noted, the discussion in this chapter does not quite provide a genuinely independent and positive argument *in favor* of self-representationalism. But it does, to my mind, provide indirect support for self-representationalism—in three ways.

First, it shows that, while the lack of widely accepted standards for evaluating phenomenological claims may understandably tempt us to greet with suspicion the claim that inner awareness is a constitutive aspect of phenomenology, on reflection there are no good reasons to do so. Although the claim is not pedestrian, it does not face any formidable theoretical challenges. Thus, the phenomenological claim at the center of this chapter is not one that comes with an unlovely theoretical price we can point to.

Secondly, it is worth noting that, although I have set myself the goal of arguing against arguments against my phenomenological claim, rather than of positively arguing in favor of the claim, I did cite in passing a positive piece of evidence in its favor. This was the idea that introspecting one's concurrent conscious experience feels more like shifting attention around than like forming an altogether new representation. The thought is that we would expect this to be so only on the supposition that we have *some* awareness (though not attentive) of our conscious states even before they are explicitly introspected.

Finally, the discussion in this chapter shows that the self-representational theory has a natural and interesting story to tell about the phenomenology, rather than being theoretically insulated from the flesh-and-blood matter of phenomenology.[43] Unlike some of its competitors, the self-representational theory is crafted sensitively to a phenomenological position that is far from clinically neutral. Thus self-representationalism offers a cohesive outlook on the nature and the phenomenology of consciousness. In the next chapter I attempt to do something similar with respect to the

---

[43] This is in contrast to the higher-order theory—see Ch. 4, n. 30.

ontology of consciousness: to show that self-representationalism has an interesting and meaty story to tell about the ontological structure of consciousness.[44]

[44] For comments on a previous draft of this chapter I would like to thank Bill Lycan, Ken Williford, and an anonymous referee. I have also benefited from conversations with and/or feedback on parts of this material from Miri Albahari, Ned Block, Fred Dretske, Terry Horgan, Bernie Kobes, Robert Lurz, Farid Masrour, Bob Van Gulick, and Dan Zahavi.

6

Self-Representationalism and the Ontology of Consciousness

In the previous chapter we described the overall *phenomenological* structure of an ordinary conscious experience. The present chapter's topic is the *ontological* structure of a conscious experience. The two are not unrelated: it is a desideratum of an ontological account that it reflect the phenomenology. Another desideratum, at least for many philosophers, is that the account "ready" consciousness for naturalization. A third one is that it appeal to sound, well-behaved ontological notions.

In what follows, I am guided mainly by these three desiderata in seeking an account of the ontology of consciousness. By an account of the "ontology," I mean an account of the sort of property consciousness is. According to self-representationalism, consciousness is a mental state's property of representing itself in the right way—that is, non-derivatively, specifically, and essentially. But there are many different ways this could play out, as far as the ontological structure of the property is concerned. The purpose of this chapter is to go through some of these ways and home in on the best of them.

There is a straightforward suggestion for the ontology of consciousness, which casts it as a relation some mental states bear to themselves, but which unfortunately also faces serious difficulties; it will be considered in Section 1. An alternative that construes consciousness as a disposition will be examined in Section 2, and found wanting as well. A more promising family of proposals, appealing to mereological notions, will be explored in Section 3.

1. The Straightforward Representational Account

In trying to clarify the ontology of self-representation, it is natural to look at the ontology of representation in general. We have fairly well worked out accounts of representation at our disposal, and moreover ones that are amenable to naturalist treatment. It is natural to hope that the familiar ontology of representation could be used to understand the special case of self-representation.

The common view of representation casts it as a relation between two items: the representing item and the represented item. The former is the *vehicle* of representation, the latter the *content* of representation. The question is how to specify the relation R that holds between, and only between, vehicle and content.

Naturalists have offered a number of approaches to this question. As a first step, they construe both the vehicle and the content as physical entities. In the case of mental representation, the vehicle is a neurophysiological state of the subject's brain and the content is a feature in the subject's physical environment (body included). It now remains to be seen only what the physical relation R is that holds between a neurophysiological state of a subject's brain and a state of her physical environment when, and only when, it is the case that the former represents the latter.[1]

The account of self-representation suggested by these considerations is straightforward. Whatever the physical relation R underlying representation in general, a mental state that would bear R to itself would be a mental state that represented itself. It would be self-representing. Call this the *straight representational suggestion*.

This account has the virtue of being ontologically unproblematic. All it requires us to posit is an a-reflexive relation—that is, a relation that *some* entities may bear to themselves. A-reflexive relations lie between reflexive and anti-reflexive relations. Reflexive relations are relations that everything bears to itself; they will not do, because it is important in the present context

---

[1] At least this is the model for mental representation of *concrete objects*. For mental representation of abstract entities, if such there be, certain complications will have to be introduced.

that *at most* some things self-represent. Anti-reflexive relations are relations that nothing bears to itself; they will not do either, because it is important in the present context that *at least* some things self-represent. A-reflexive relations are those that some, but not all, things bear to themselves. Such relations are rife. Being-the-accountant-of is an example: some people are their own accountants; some have other people as their accountants.

The straight representational suggestion fares well, then, in terms of the desideratum of ontological soundness. Let us consider how it fares on the other two fronts, to do with phenomenological adequacy and naturalizability potential.

There is an argument, due to Joseph Levine (2001: 171–3), which may be used to show that the straight representational account fares poorly on the phenomenological front. Levine's own target is slightly different: he does not so much attempt to show that this straight representational version of self-representationalism is phenomenologically inadequate, as that it fails to yield a kind of self-representation that would be special enough to illuminate the sense of explanatory gap between consciousness and physical properties. However, since in parts of the argument the failure to illuminate the explanatory gap is blamed on inability to capture the phenomenology, the argument could be interpreted—or rather a parallel argument could be generated—as concerned with the phenomenological adequacy of the straight representational version of self-representationalism.

The Levinean argument is a trilemma, and proceeds as follows. When a bluish conscious experience E, which is realized by a neurophysiological state of the brain B, represents itself, there are three descriptions under which it might represent itself. It might (i) represent itself qua the brain state B; (ii) represent itself qua the bluish experience E; or (iii) represent itself indexically—that is, *qua* whatever is doing the representing. All three options, however, yield unsatisfactory portraits of inner awareness.

The first option Levine dismisses on the grounds that inner awareness does not "deliver a neurophysiological description" of the state it represents (Levine 2001: 172). The experience is not presented in inner awareness as a neurophysiological state, so the suggestion that conscious states represent themselves as neurophysiological states is phenomenologically inadequate.

The second horn of the trilemma has a bluish experience representing itself with a phenomenal (rather than neurophysiological) description, "bluish experience." Against it, Levine argues that if the bluish experience's self-representation employed such a general description, there would be nothing special in its self-representation. It would represent itself simply by falling under the extension of the description it employs. It would represent itself in the same sense in which the word "word" may be said to represent itself. And just as the word "word" is not conscious, so the bluish experience ought not to become conscious by representing itself in this way.[2, 3]

The third horn has the experience represent itself in an altogether non-descriptive way. Instead the experience represents itself *indexically*. Levine argues that this option likewise gives the wrong account of how the experience is presented in inner awareness.[4] An indexical represents what it does in a blank sort of way, not through any specific information about what it represents. Thus, a token of "I" refers to the person who produced it, *whoever it may be*. Similarly, if the bluish experience represented itself indexically, it would represent itself as the state that is doing the representing, *whatever state it may be*. But, according to Levine, the inner awareness of the bluish experience is not an awareness of it as *whatever it may be*. Rather, it is an awareness of it as *bluish*. So the inner awareness built into the experience cannot quite be captured by indexical self-representation.

Levine's argumentation against these three options strikes me as cogent.[5] But, as an argument by elimination, it suffers from the problem that there

---

[2] One problem with Levine's argument here is that "word" represents itself in a derivative way, whereas a bluish experience that would represent itself as a bluish experience would do so intrinsically. I am not going to dwell on this difficulty, though, because I think Levine is ultimately right to maintain that this sort of self-representation is somehow insufficient for inner awareness. This issue overlaps some of the issues that were discussed toward the end of Chapter 4.

[3] This part of Levine's argument is the least amenable to interpretation as an argument against the phenomenological adequacy of the straight representational version of self-representationalism, but I will do so nonetheless for the sake of completeness.

[4] Levine couches this horn of the trilemma in terms of what he calls our *substantive and determinate* awareness of our conscious experiences. This feature Levine attributes to conscious experiences is apparently very important to him. I cannot discuss it in detail here. The general idea is that the mode of presentation of qualia is substantive, in the sense of employing the very quale it presents in presenting it; and it is determinate, in that it presents the quale independently of anything else the quale may be related to.

[5] There is a response to the argument against the third option that I hesitate to endorse, but can see someone whose view is not too far from mine making. This is to claim that the peripheral inner awareness I have of my bluish experience does not in fact present it as a bluish experience. Rather, the bluishness is contributed (so to speak) by another item in the overall phenomenology. In the previous chapter we construed the overall phenomenology of a global conscious experience as involving a number of different items, only one of which is inner awareness. The bluishness is a separate item. It may well be that the inner awareness presents the experience simply *as occurring*, therefore precisely in that blank way described in the second option. But when this inner awareness of the experience *as occurring* is unified or fused with the other items, including the bluishness, the sense emerges of an

is a fourth option he does not consider. This fourth option essentially combines the second and third, casting the experience as representing itself *both* indexically *and* with a phenomenal description. Thus, the experience may represent itself both qua bluish experience *and* qua the thing that does the representing.[6] That is, it might represent itself qua the bluish thing that does the representing, say by employing the indexical definite description "this very bluish experience." This description ensures that a representation using it would not have the blankness of sheer indexical representation but at the same time would feature the particularity lacking in indefinite-descriptive representation.[7, 8]

However, even this fourth option faces another phenomenological problem—namely, that it lacks a way to capture the internal structure of a global conscious experience. As described in the previous chapter, the phenomenology of a global conscious experience is structured and articulated: there are discernible different items, there are specific relations among those items, and so on. None of this is captured in the notion of a single mental state that represents itself. Thus the straight representational suggestion involves the whole conscious experience representing its–whole-self. But the phenomenology is different. It is one in which there is a particular item within the whole that represents the whole. To that extent, the straight representational suggestion is phenomenologically deficient.

It is important to note that the deficiency is not just a matter of not capturing the particular view of the phenomenology that I took in the

overall phenomenology that involves inner awareness of the experience as bluish (among other things). This way of viewing things would vindicate the third option targeted by Levine, and is quite hard to rule out as *phenomenologically* inadequate. Nonetheless, it is *theoretically* problematic, inasmuch as the fusion or unification of the bluishness and inner awareness remains unexplained. The suggestion is also in conflict with the kind of view of the relationship between qualitative character and subjective character taken in Chapters 1 and 2. For these reasons, I do not myself endorse this response.

[6] More generally, then, Levine fails to consider the possibility of self-representation in accordance with more than one of the three options. The particular combination I cite in the text—self-representation along the lines of both the second and the third option—strikes me as particularly plausible, but other combinations are logically possible as well.

[7] What seems to be missing in the second option, as presented by Levine, is a way for the experience to represent itself qua *particular* experience, as opposed to qua experience of a certain *type* (e.g., bluish). It seems that, when a bluish experience represents itself, it represents itself not just qua bluish experience but qua one particular bluish experience. So the suggestion might be that the experience represents itself not under the indefinite description "a bluish experience," but under the definite indexical description "this bluish experience."

[8] In addition, it might be special enough as to overcome Levine's own misgivings, concerning the illumination of the explanatory gap, especially if construed along the lines of Mentalese display sentences, as per the end of Chapter 4.

previous chapter. It is a matter of lacking the resources to reflect any kind of internal structure involved in self-representation. The only way the present account could be phenomenologically adequate is if the way we were aware of our conscious experiences just in virtue of having them indeed lacked any internal structure. But that sounds implausible.

To summarize the point, a phenomenologically adequate account of the ontology of consciousness must have the resources to reflect an internal structure in self-representation; the straight representational suggestion does not; therefore, the straight representational suggestion is phenomenologically inadequate.

Graver problems yet may attend its prospects for naturalizability. On the face of it, the suggestion might be thought to lend itself to naturalization quite handily, since it is based on an approach to mental representation that has several naturalist versions. However, on closer inspection the naturalistic credentials of these accounts appear to be in conflict with the possibility of self-representation. Roughly, the problem is that these accounts offer a reductive explanation of representation in terms of broadly causal relations, but causal relations are *anti-reflexive* (they never hold between a thing and itself).[9] Thus no mental state can bring about its own occurrence, which seems to preclude a physicalistically kosher self-representation.

A naturalist account is built on the notion of general concomitant variation between the representor and the represented (the vehicle and the content). Thus, the number of rings on a tree's trunk represents the tree's age because there is a general covariation between rings and age (Stampe 1977). However, in order to introduce asymmetry into the representation relation, so that the rings could be said to represent the age but not the other way round, some kind of causal relation is introduced. The rings represent the age, and not the other way round, because the rings are caused by the age, and not the other way round. On a simple causal-covariational account of representation, then, x represents y just in case x betokens a type Tx and y betokens a type Ty, such that (i) tokens of Tx covary with tokens of Ty, and (ii) tokens of Ty cause tokens of Tx.

This simple account of representation makes self-representation impossible. For x to represent itself, it would have to betoken a type whose

---

[9] Some naturalist theories do not revolve around a broadly causal relation between representor and represented, but instead around the representor's functional role within a web of representors. I will discuss this option in the next section.

tokens (i) covary with themselves and (ii) cause themselves. Although (i) is easily met, (ii) cannot be met. No event, fact, or state can cause its own occurrence. Thus the simple causal–covariational account renders self-representation impossible.

On the other hand, if the causal requirement is lifted, then self-representation becomes cheap—too cheap to account for consciousness. Since every event, fact, or state covaries with itself, every event, fact, or state would self-represent. A self-representational account of consciousness cannot accept this, since it designates self-representation as the factor that distinguishes the conscious from the non-conscious. The promiscuous conception of self-representation under consideration would make non-conscious mental states, as well as altogether non-mental states, self-represent.

This dilemma is particularly clear in the case of the simple causal–covariational account, but other naturalist accounts of mental representation are in the same bind: with a powerful causal condition, they allow *nothing* to self-represent; without such a condition, they allow *everything* to self-represent. The intermediate position, where some things self-represent and some do not, cannot be delivered by naturalist accounts. And yet that is the position self-representationalism is committed to. I cannot discuss each and every naturalist account of mental representation here, let alone every *possible* naturalist account. But let me make the case for my claim by considering the two main ones, *informational semantics* and *teleological semantics*.

According to Dretske's informational semantics (Dretske 1981, 1986, 1988), one thing represents another when it has the function of carrying information about it. More precisely, x represents y just in case x is recruited to do a certain job within a certain system in virtue of the fact that x carries information about y, where x's carrying information about y means that x betokens a type Tx and y betokens a type Ty, such that Tx is nomically dependent upon Ty. Nomic dependence may be loosely defined as follows: Tx nomically depends upon Ty just in case, in every nomologically possible world in which Tx is tokened, that tokening of Tx is caused by a tokening of Ty. The upshot, then, is that x represents y just in case: x betokens a type Tx and y betokens a type Ty, such that, (i) in every nomologically possible world in which Tx is tokened, that tokening of Tx is caused by a tokening of Ty, and (ii) there exists a system S and a functional role R, such that x occupies R in S in virtue of (i) being the case.

Within this framework, for x to represent itself, x would have to be recruited to do a certain job in a certain system in virtue of tokening a type Tx that nomically depends upon itself. The problem is that, for Tx nomically to depend upon itself, nomically possible tokens of Tx would have to cause their own occurrence. But that is impossible. Thus Dretske's informational semantics entails the impossibility of self-representation. There might be a different understanding of nomic dependence that is kinder to self-representation. Suppose that x is nomically dependent upon y just in case there is no nomologically possible world in which Tx is tokened but Ty is not. The problem here, however, is that, while this take on nomic dependence does not make self-representation impossible, it makes it necessary. Since there is no nomologically possible world in which an event takes place but also does not, it follows that, on this understanding of nomic dependence, every event is nomically dependent upon itself.

It might be thought that self-representation could still be made sense of if we adopted this understanding of nomic dependence and accepted that every mental state is nomically self-dependent, but then insisted that *some* of these nomically self-dependent mental states, but not *all*, are recruited to do some job on the basis of the fact that they nomically self-depend. If this were indeed so, then only *some* mental states would be self-representing, consistently with self-representationalism.

However, it is hard to see how a mental state *could* be recruited to do a certain job in virtue of being nomically self-dependent in this way. After all, on that understanding being nomically self-dependent does not amount to anything useful, and therefore not to anything worth recruiting in virtue of. The problem here is that there is something very trivial about the way in which mental states nomically self-depend. It becomes something of a logical truth that everything is nomically self-dependent. But such logical properties are not the kind that can be crucial to the performance of a certain function. Just as no entity has ever been recruited to perform a job on the basis of being self-identical, so we should not expect any to be recruited on the basis of being nomically self-dependent.

There are other versions of informational semantics. We cannot cover all of them, but the best known is probably Fodor's "asymmetric dependence" account (1990, 1994). According to it, x represents y iff x betokens a type Tx and y a type Ty, such that (i) it is a law of nature that tokens of Ty cause tokens of Tx, (ii) some tokens of Ty actually cause some tokens of

Tx, and (iii), if anything other than tokens of Ty cause tokens of Tx, the fact that it does is asymmetrically dependent on the fact that tokens of Ty cause tokens of Tx. It is clear that the second clause in this account excludes self-representation, for the reasons covered above. Here as well, certain modifications might be made to weaken the second clause, but the same dialectic is likely to arise again.

Let us move, then, to teleological approaches to representation. The general idea (Millikan 1984, 1993, McGinn 1989b, Papineau 1993) can be put thus: x represents y more or less just in case Tx has been selected by evolutionary processes to covary with Ty. Here the impossibility of self-representation is even more evident. For x to represent itself, Tx would have to have been selected by evolutionary processes to covary with itself. But, since everything covaries with itself independently of, and prior to the introduction of, any evolutionary pressures, nothing can be selected *to* covary with itself.[10]

There are subtler versions of teleosemantics that may be thought to fare better. According to Millikan's "biosemantics" (1989), for example, one thing is a representation of another when there is a consumer system that uses it as such. More precisely, x represents y just in case x betokens Tx and y betokens Ty, and there is a system S, such that (i) S consumes present tokens of Tx, (ii) past tokens of Tx occurred mostly when tokens of Ty occurred, and (iii) S can perform its biological proper function (whatever it may be) because (i) and (ii) are the case. Here self-representation appears to be ruled out by the third clause: although every state covaries with itself, it is unclear how this fact could enable or in any way facilitate a system's performing its biological function.

This is, as I warned, a very partial discussion of naturalist semantics and their resources for accounting for self-representation. But the general problem for such theories accommodating self-representation should be evident: simple covariation is too weak to rule *out* any self-representation, but the causal or evolutionary/teleological dimension added to covariation is too strong to rule *in* any self-representation. The upshot is that, given our best naturalist accounts of representation in general, there is no way

---

[10] Saying that Tx is selected to covary with Ty implies that there is a time before which tokens of Tx did not co-occur with tokens of Ty (except accidentally)—namely, the time before the selecting had been completed. But there is no time before which tokens of Tx did not co-occur with themselves. So no Tx has been selected to covary with itself.

to cast self-representation as naturalizable yet useful for the theory of consciousness.

I conclude that the straight representational suggestion for understanding self-representation, although ontologically sound, does not fare well with regard to the phenomenological adequacy and potential naturalizability desiderata. In the next section I consider an alternative account with a more functionalist inspiration.

2. A Functionalist Alternative

The gravest problem for the straight representational account was its inability to naturalize self-representation. On that front, functionalism has long been a reliable friend of the naturalist's. In this section I consider a specific account of self-representation in functionalist terms.

The basic idea behind the functionalist account is drawn from Shoemaker (1994b: 288–9). According to self-representationalism, a bluish conscious experience represents both a blue object (surface, volume) and itself. It represents the blue object in virtue of a floor-level perceptual component, and represents itself in virtue of a peripheral inner awareness component. Each of these components can be functionalized: we can readily specify the functional role of a perception of blue and the functional role of an awareness of a perception of blue. On a functionalist approach, a mental state that would play the former functional role would be a perception of blue, and a mental state that would play the latter functional role would be an awareness of a perception of blue. The key step arrives now: a mental state that would play *both* functional roles would be *both* a perception of blue *and* an awareness of a perception of blue. It would thus bear the kind of representational content the self-representationalist seeks in a bluish experience.

This account can be regimented in a number of ways, depending on one's preferred brand of functionalism. In Lewis-style *analytic* functionalism, the functional role is specified by Ramsification over platitudes (see Lewis 1966, 1972). Thus, to produce the functional role of, say, the property of being a rainbow, we collect all the everyday platitudes about rainbows, string them together not into a long conjunction of all of them but into an even longer disjunction of all conjunctions of most of them, replace occurrences of "rainbow" with a free variable, and prefix the whole thing with an existential quantifier. The result is an existential proposition that states that there is something that matches most of our pre-theoretic conception of rainbows.[11]

This apparatus could be used to capture a more mature, scientific conception of rainbows as well. Instead of collecting *platitudes* about rainbows, we might collect all the *scientifically accepted claims* about rainbows. The result would be an existential proposition that would state that there is a something that matches most of our scientific conception of rainbows. Using Ramsey sentences of this sort to functionalize mental properties yields *psycho*-functionalism, which is distinguished from analytic functionalism in that it appeals to empirical psychology rather than folk psychology. Another version of functionalism, embraced by Lewis (1994) himself later in his career, instructs us to collect *both* platitudes *and* scientific claims.

Applied to bluish conscious experiences, the proposal might play out in a number of ways, but the most natural one is the following. In a first stage, we collect all the platitudes and/or scientific claims about perception of blue, and produce a disjunction of the conjunctions of most of them. In a second stage, we collect all the platitudes and/or scientific claims about awareness of perception of blue and do the same. In a third stage, we introduce a conjunction of these two disjunctions. Finally, we replace all occurrences of *both* "perception of blue" *and* "awareness of perception of blue" with *the same* free variable, and prefix with the existential quantifier.[12] The result would be an existential proposition stating that there is something that matches most of our pre-scientific and/or scientific conception of both perception of blue and awareness of such perception. That "something" is the property of being a self-representing perception.

This is one functionalist construal of self-representation. Another strand in the functionalist tradition specifies the functional role of a mental state by abstracting from the state's total set of causal relations to its causes and effects. The abstraction is called for because, if two mental states M_1 and M_2

---

[11] The point of going with disjunctions of conjunctions of most platitudes rather than with conjunctions of all platitudes is to allow that not all our platitudes about rainbows have to be true for there to be rainbows.

[12] Another way to produce the Ramsey sentence of interest might skip the segregation of platitudes and/or scientific claims about perception of blue and awareness of perception of blue, and simply produce one long disjunction of conjunctions of most platitudes and/or scientific claims about either of them.

bring about the same effect E, but M_1 takes three milliseconds more than M_2 to do so, we want to abstract from this psychologically insignificant difference and maintain that the functional roles of M_1 and M_2 are the same (as far as their relation to E is concerned).[13] The question for a functionalist is *how much* to abstract from the concrete causal interactions of mental states. Different functionalist accounts of mental states follow from different abstraction policies.

One popular policy is to abstract from anything that does not bear on the *inferential relations* among mental states. A belief that p tends to bring about a belief that q, when conjoined with a belief that if p then q, and tends to be brought about by a belief that r, when conjoined with a belief that either $\sim r$ or p. Not only is it psychologically inconsequential whether it takes half a second or a full second for the belief that p to bring about, and be brought about by, these other beliefs—anything about these causal relations that does not bear on inferential connections should be abstracted from.

On this view, functional role is *inferential role*. This notion of inferential role has been regimented most seriously by Field (1977), in confirmation-theoretic terms. But a simpler version of the idea would be this: the inferential role of a mental state M is fully characterized by an ordered quadruple of sets $<S_1, S_2, S_3, S_4>$. S_1 is the set of all mental states from which M can be inferred deductively; S_2 is the set of all mental states from which M can be inferred non-deductively (inductively, abductively, by inference to the best explanation, and so on); S_3 is the set of all mental states that can be deductively inferred from M; and S_4 is the set of all mental states that can be non-deductively inferred from M. M_1 and M_2 have the same inferential role iff each quadruplet in the inferential role of M_1 is equivalent to the corresponding quadruplet in the inferential role of M_2. Using the present apparatus, we can formulate a functionalist construal of self-representation as follows. Suppose we exhaustively characterize the inferential role of the perception of blue in terms of the ordered quadruple $<S_1, S_2, S_3, S_4>$ and then the inferential role of the awareness of the perception of blue in terms of the ordered quadruple $<S_1^*, S_2^*, S_3^*, S_4^*>$. We can then produce the *intersection* of each pair of corresponding quadruplets. Thus, $S_1 \cap S_1^*$, the intersection of S_1 and S_1^*, includes all the mental states from which *both* a perception of blue *and* an awareness of a perception of blue can be deductively inferred.[14] Similarly for the other quadruplets. The ordered quadruple we thus define, $<S_1 \cap S_1^*, S_2 \cap S_2^*, S_3 \cap S_3^*, S_4 \cap S_4^*>$, captures the inferential role of a mental state that is both a perception of blue and an awareness of a perception of blue.[15] A state that would occupy this inferential role would be both a perception of blue and an awareness of such a perception, and thus would bear the self-representational character of a bluish conscious experience.

It is, of course, an empirical question whether any neurophysiological state of the brain occupies this inferential role. But the fact that we can produce a characterization of the relevant inferential role means that there is no *conceptual*, or *principled*, difficulty for naturalizability associated with the notion of self-representation, once we embrace the functionalist account thereof. The same observation applies to the Ramsification functionalism described before. Both deliver a procedure for characterizing self-representing states in a naturalistically kosher way. In this respect, then, the functionalist proposal is superior to the straight representational proposal from the previous section.

On the phenomenology front, however, prospects look bleaker. A functionalist account might well be able to account for the internal structuredness of phenomenology that eluded the straight representational account. On the other hand, it faces a problem similar to the one pointed out in the second horn of Levine's trilemma. What the functionalist account secures is a mental state that is both a bluish experience and an awareness of a bluish experience. This does *not* secure that the awareness is of *that very* bluish experience.[16]

There is, in any case, an even deeper phenomenological problem for the functionalist account. The problem is that the functionalist account attempts to account for self-representation (hence consciousness) in terms of a *dispositional* property, whereas, as I have already noted in passing in Chapter 4, consciousness (thence self-representation) is most certainly a *manifest* or *categorical* or *occurrent* property.

---

[14] There may not be any—but that is immaterial to the *definition* of the inferential role.

[15] A plausible functionalist account could require less than full intersection of the relevant pairs of quadruplets. Thus it could require no more than significant *overlap* between the functional role characteristic of a perception of blue and the functional role characteristic of awareness of a perception of blue to characterize the functional role distinctive of a conscious experience. That seems to be what Shoemaker (1994b) in fact requires—significant overlap rather than full intersection.

[16] Thanks to Bill Lycan for pointing this out to me.

is augmented with tools that are supposed to help capture the phenomenological structure and articulation of a global conscious experience.

3. A Crooked Representational Account

The phenomenological problem with the straight representational account
examined in Section 1 was its inability to account for the internal structure
of the phenomenology of a self-representing global conscious experience.
In describing the phenomenology in Chapter 5, I noted that the inner
awareness of a conscious experience is one phenomenal item among others.
In this sense, the inner awareness is *part* of the overall phenomenology.
And, since a conscious experience represents itself in virtue of that inner
awareness, it represents itself in virtue of one part of itself. This fact could
not be captured in the straight representational account, which casts the
experience as wholly representing its-whole-self, as I put it. The thought
guiding the present section is that a representational account with the
sensitivity to capture the fact that experience represents itself in virtue of
one of its parts doing the representing would be at least phenomenologically
adequate.

Another aspect of the main idea will involve a distinction between direct
and indirect representation. I will suggest that only direct representation
requires the broadly causal relations mandated in naturalistic accounts of
representation, but that self-representation is indirect. This will allow the
account to meet the potential naturalization desideratum. The upshot will
be an account according to which conscious states have a part that represents
directly another part, and in virtue of that represents indirectly the whole
state. This will be formulated more precisely as we go along.

Logical Parthood

I have consistently spoken of parts of conscious states as though this is an
unproblematic notion. But what kind of part are we talking about here?
Certainly the inner awareness is not a *spatial* part of the overall conscious
state, at least not in the first instance. Nor is it a *temporal* part, since it
is fully synchronous with the global conscious experience of which it is
a part. I propose that we construe it as a *logical* part. The account I will
explore in the present section combines regular representational notions

with a mereological notion of a logical part to try and account for the self-representational character of conscious experiences. To distinguish it from the straight representational account of Section 1, I call it the *crooked representational account*. There are complicated questions surrounding the explication of the notion of logical part, questions to which justice cannot be done here. But let me start with some preliminary remarks on the subject.[20]

There are many everyday examples of talk of parts that does not seem to be talk of spatial or temporal parts and is more naturally construed as having to do with logical parts. We say that the department of philosophy is part of the university; not a spatial or temporal part, though.[21] Likewise, we might say that some radical group is part of a neo-Marxist alliance, or that Kramerica Inc. is part of Vandelay Industries. Again, spatial and temporal parthoods seem irrelevant. Closer to our area of interest, when I am *glad* that the weather is nice, I necessarily also *believe* that the weather is nice, but my belief that the weather is nice is not an extra mental act, which occurs *in addition to* my gladness. Rather, the belief is somehow *inherent in*, or *built into*, the gladness. It is natural to say that my belief is *part of* my gladness, in a logical sense of "part of." So my believing that the weather is nice is a *logical part* of my being glad that the weather is nice.[22]

Ultimately, what I want to claim is that consciousness and inner awareness provide another example. When I have a conscious experience of blue, I am aware of my experience. But the awareness is not an extra mental act, which occurs *in addition to* the experience. Rather, the awareness is *inherent in*—it is *built into*—the experience. It is in this sense that the inner awareness of a conscious experience is a logical part of that very experience.

Examples aside, however, what *is* a logical part? Paul (2002) explores the notion of logical part and its potential serviceability in modern metaphysics in a way that construes logical parts simply as *properties*.[23] There may be no need, however, to restrict logical parts to properties from the outset.

---

[20] For discussion of the logical part–whole relation, see Smith and Mulligan 1983, Mulligan and Smith 1985, Simons 1987, Lewis 1991, Smith 1994, and Paul 2002. For a recent discussion of the related mathematical part–whole relation, see Bell 2004.

[21] Perhaps we can say that the department is a *legal* part of the university, but that may just be one kind of logical part.

[22] More examples of this sort are provided by Smith (1994: ch. 3).

[23] She argues that appeal to logical parts can resuscitate a version of the bundle theory of concrete particulars, where particulars would be identified with sums of logical parts; that it helps explain the token-identity of universals at different places and times; as well as shed light on material constitution

In a way, "what is a logical part?" is the wrong question. The answer to *that* question is simply "whatever can bear the logical parthood relation."[24] Perhaps only properties can bear that relation, perhaps other kinds of entity can as well. The real question is not "what is a logical part?," but "what is the logical parthood relation?" I propose that we answer, to a first approximation, by defining a relation R that (i) obeys those axioms of classical mereology that pertain to the parthood relation in general and (ii) is neither spatial parthood nor temporal parthood, and identify logical parthood with R.

In classical mereology, the relation of parthood is treated as a primitive and undefined relation used in turn to define other notions, such as those of proper parthood, overlap, composition, and simplicity.[25] As is customary with primitive notions within formal systems, its nature is captured entirely by the axioms that apply to it. The meaning of "part of" is thus exhausted by, and is to be gleaned from, the expression's theoretical role within the system, which of course follows from the system's axioms. Some of these axioms pertain to ordering: they stipulate that parthood is reflexive, transitive, and anti-symmetric, and that proper parthood is irreflexive, transitive, and asymmetric. Then there is the axiom of supplementation, which states that, if x is a proper part of y, then there is a z, such that z is part of y and z does not overlap x. Finally, classical mereology includes two more problematic axioms, which guarantee extensionality and unrestricted composition: if x and y have all the same parts, then $x = y$ and, if there exist x and y, then there also exists a z that is their sum.

Non-classical mereological systems could be formulated as well, for example, that do not include the axiom of unrestricted composition. But in any case the notion of parthood is a primitive understood purely and entirely in terms of the axioms in which it figures. My suggestion is that

and identity across time. The main purpose of the exercise is to show that we can, quite profitably, do a mereology of properties, in addition to the more familiar mereology of particulars.

[24] Note that the relation is asymmetric (in the sense that only some things may bear it things that reciprocally bear it to them), so that a logical part is not just any admissible relatum of the logical parthood relation, but only any bearer of the relational property of *being a logical part of*. That excludes entities that cannot bear that relation but can bear the relational property of having something as their logical parts.

[25] Thus, x is a proper part of y iff x is a part of y and $x \neq y$; x overlaps y iff there is a z, such that z is both part of x and part of y; x and y are disjoint iff there is no such z; x is a sum of (composed by) y and z iff both y and z are parts of x and every part of x overlaps either y or z; and x is simple iff there is no z, such that z is part of x.

we use the notion of parthood thus understood, and stipulate that *logical* parthood is parthood that is neither spatial nor temporal. This definition requires, of course, that we have an understanding of the notions of spatial and temporal parthood, but here I think it is safe to assume that we have a sufficiently robust intuitive grasp on these notions to meet the requirement. Whether the definition is ultimately appropriate will depend on whether it accords with our pre-theoretic intuitions, if such there be, as to what should count as a logical part.[26]

With this definition of logical parthood at our disposal, we can make more concrete sense of the claim that inner awareness of a conscious experience is a *logical part* of that conscious experience. Since these are *states*, the logical parthood relation would have to be the kind of relation that *states* can bear. (If we insist that only properties can bear that relation, and that states are not properties, then the point would have to be made not in terms of experience and the awareness of it, but in terms of the property of being some particular experience and the property of being the awareness of that particular experience.[27] Nothing of substance would be lost in this formulation, but, since it is inelegant, I will conduct my discussion using the formulation in terms of states.)

The central idea behind the crooked representational account might be initially formulated as follows, then:

(CR1)   For any mental state M of a subject S, M is conscious iff there is an M*, such that (i) M* is an appropriate representation of M and (ii) M* is a proper *part of* M.

---

[26] If we have no pre-theoretic intuitions about logical parthood, the issue will become pragmatic. The proposed definition will be judged by its serviceability and whether there is a genuine commonality among (and peculiarity of) all instances of non-spatial and non-temporal parthood. If we do have such intuitions, then the definition will be appropriate only if spatial, temporal, and logical parthood turn out to be intuitively exhaustive and exclusive—that is, if intuitively any parthood that is neither spatial nor temporal is logical and no logical parthood is also temporal or spatial. It seems to me that such intuitions do exist: the property of being unmarried is intuitively a logical part of the property of being a bachelor in a way that the property of being either square or not is not. There are technical questions surrounding how to separate out such cases. This is not the place to tackle these questions, but I should note that they have parallels in the theory of confirmation that have been treated quite rigorously. The confirmation-theoretic question is how to separate some proposition *p* that is intuitively part of the "logical content" of, say, quantum mechanics from the disjunction of *p* and the proposition that the absolute is way cool. There are currently three main approaches to this question, discussion of which would take us too far afield (see Schurz 1991 and Gemes 1998).

[27] The properties in question would be so-called concrete universals, such as being Socrates or being the Sydney Opera House.

In this formulation, it is explicitly required that M^* be a *proper* part of M. This is intended to ensure that the crooked representational account be exclusive of the straight representational account. For the straight account is:

> (CR2) For any mental state M of a subject S, M is conscious iff there is an M^*, such that (i) M^* is an appropriate representation of M and (ii) $M^* = M$.[28]

However, a thesis can be formulated that will remain silent on whether M^* is a proper or improper part of M, thus covering both the crooked and straight accounts:

> (CR3) For any mental state M of a subject S, M is conscious iff there is an M^*, such that (i) M^* is an appropriate representation of M and (ii) M^* is a (proper or improper) part of M.

When M^* is a *proper* part of M, CR3 accords with CR1; when it is an *improper* part, it accords with CR2. But CR3 itself allows both structures to be involved in conscious states, and is therefore different from both CR1 and CR2.

A disjunctive claim such as CR3 is always *safer* than a non-disjunctive one, in the sense that it is less likely to come out false.[29] At the same time, the disjunctive nature of CR3 seems a liability in the present context. For consciousness appears to be a natural kind property. If so, there should be an underlying unity in the phenomenon—something that ensures that the class of conscious states exhibits a strong homogeneity, and at a reasonable level of abstraction. CR3 may be unfit to accommodate this homogeneity.

CR1 faces its own problems, however. The reasons we moved away from CR2 had to do with naturalizability and phenomenology. The former consideration may still apply, however, to CR1. Recall that the problem with the straight representational account was that it was unclear how a mental state could bear a genuine causal relation to itself, in virtue of which

---

[28] Note that this is the straight representational account, so the label "CR" is in fact a mislabel. I use it nonetheless for smoothness of exposition.

[29] CR3 is disjunctive in nature not in that it is the disjunction of CR1 and CR2—it is not—but in that it involves a disjunctive conjunct corresponding to the CR1 and CR2 (see the second clause). This could be brought out by formulating CR3 as follows: For any mental state M of a subject S, M is conscious iff there is an M^*, such that (i) M^* is an appropriate representation of M and (ii) either M^* is a proper part of M or $M^* = M$. This formulation is, of course, logically equivalent to the one in the main text.

it might represent itself. But it is no clearer how a mental state could bear a genuine causal relation to its logical part. Just as my being glad that the weather is nice does not and cannot bear a causal relation to its belief component, so my bluish experience cannot bear a causal relation to its inner-awareness component.

We do say that the philosophy department bears a causal relation to the university of which it is a part. But what we mean by that is that the philosophy department bears a causal relation to *the rest* of the university—that is, to the university's complementary part. By analogy, we might suggest that the relevant causal relation holds between two separate logical parts of a conscious state. The idea would be that a conscious state has *two* parts, such that one represents the other:

> (CR4) For any mental state M of a subject S, M is conscious iff there are M^* and $M^\Diamond$, such that (i) M^* is a proper part of M, (ii) $M^\Diamond$ is a proper part of M, and (iii) M^* is an appropriate representation of $M^\Diamond$.

Here the conscious state involves the "mereological sum" of a representing state and a represented state.[30]

It might be objected that causal relations cannot hold among logical parts of the same particular any more than between the particular and itself. And, indeed, there seems to be something problematic about the idea of a causal relation between two logical parts of one and the same particular. Yet there are cases that are naturally described in just that way. Consider a hard-boiled egg. It is natural to think of the egg's hardness and its boiledness as logical parts of its being a hard-boiled egg, and yet the former is causally related to the latter: the egg is a hard egg *because* it is a boiled egg (in a causal sense of "because"). Here there is a property, the property of being a hard-boiled egg, of which two logical parts—the property of being hard and the property of being boiled—are causally related. Similarly, one model may be that the property of being a qualitatively bluish conscious state has two

---

[30] The clearest proponent of this sort of view is Gennaro (1996, 2002). He writes (1996: 23; emphasis added): "We can understand consciousness as involving the property of 'accompanied by a MET [meta-psychological thought]'...But we might individuate conscious states 'widely'—i.e., in a way that treats consciousness as an intrinsic property of those states. On this account, the MET is *part* of the conscious state."

logical parts, the property of being in a schmalitatively bluish state and the property of being at least peripherally aware of that schmalitatively bluish state, such that the two are causally related.[31]

CR4 faces another problem, however: it appears to be only *superficially different* from a higher-order theory, according to which there are two separate states involved in a conscious experience. Having posited a represented and a representor, it is not clear that there is a *substantive* difference between treating them as separate states and treating them as separate parts of a single state. Both CR4 and higher-order theory require only the compresence of a represented state and a representing state. The only difference is that the former *calls* "conscious state" not just the represented but the compound of both the represented and representor. The difference thus appears to be largely verbal. Call this the "problem of insubstantial distinction."

It may be insisted that, if logical parts of states are not themselves states, then the appeal to logical parts of a single state will be non-trivially different from the appeal to different states. But, even so, it seems that CR4 does not have the resources to capture the notion that conscious states are self-representational, and, moreover, that it probably inherits all the problems associated with higher-order theory covered in Chapter 4.

In addressing the problem of insubstantial distinction, we might appeal to a mereological distinction between two kinds of wholes: *sums* and *complexes* (Simons 1987: ch. 9). A complex is a whole whose parts are *essentially* interconnected, or bound, in a certain way. A sum is a whole whose parts are interconnected contingently if at all. The interconnection between the parts is thus an identity and existence condition of a complex, but not of a sum. For example, a molecule is a complex of atoms rather than a sum, since for the atoms to constitute a molecule they *must* be interconnected in a certain way. Likewise, the state of Hawaii (as distinguished from the geographic location) is not merely a sum of seven islands. It is also a matter of their political interconnection as answering to the same State Government. If that government dissolved permanently, the *state* of Hawaii (though not the location) would go out of existence, despite the persistence of all its parts. So Hawaii is a complex of islands, not merely a sum.

[31] I am grateful to Amie Thomasson for raising this objection to CR4, and to Keith Lehrer for offering the rejoinder. I was fortunate to be present to record the proceedings.

The key difference between sums and complexes is that, for a sum to go out of existence, it is necessary that one of its parts go out of existence, whereas a complex can go out of existence even if none of its parts goes out of existence (namely, in case the relationship or interconnection among its parts is destroyed).[32] Thus, suppose W is a whole comprising components $C_1, \ldots, C_n$; then W is merely a sum just in case W's going out of existence entails a C_i's going out of existence; W is a complex just in case W's going out of existence does *not* entail a C_i's going out of existence.

This mereological distinction is important, because it suggests the thought that a conscious experience similarly involves a *complex*, rather than a *sum*, of the representing state and the represented state. The two are unified in a way that genuinely makes them parts of a single complex, not an arbitrary collection or sum of two inherently unrelated items. When I have a perceptual experience of the blue sky, the perception of blue and the awareness of that perception are unified by some psychologically real relation whose dissolution would entail the destruction of the experience.

This psychologically real relation is effectively the synchronic unity of consciousness. Accounts of synchronic unity are offered sometimes at the phenomenal level, where a phenomenal feature is sought that distinguishes apparently unified experiences from apparently disunified ones, and sometimes at the sub-personal level, where sub-personal causal processes are sought to do that work. There are various reasons to prefer a sub-personal account (see, e.g., Hurley 1998), especially in the present context.[33] In the next chapter I will adopt a neural synchrony account of the relevant kind of unity; this would be an account at the sub-personal level.

Once an account of the relevant unity is adopted, the notion of a mereological complex becomes clearer, and we can propose the following:

(CR5) For any mental state M of a subject S, M is conscious iff there are M^* and $M^{\lozenge}$, such that (i) M^* is a proper part of M, (ii) $M^{\lozenge}$

---

[32] The notion of a complex-making relation, as opposed to a mere sum, is similar to Levey's notion (1997) of "principles of composition." According to Levey, objects are not just sums of disparate parts, but the parts put together in accordance with a *principle of composition*.

[33] Hurley argued against any account of the unity of consciousness in phenomenal terms, claiming that, for any phenomenal feature that might be offered as corresponding to the unity of consciousness, we could ask what unifies *it* with its instantiator's *other* phenomenal properties. This is known as the "just more content" argument. (I have, in any case, no particular preference among accounts of the phenomenal unity of consciousness, and am happy to adopt whatever would please the reader.)

is a proper part of M, (iii) M is a *complex* of M^* and $M^\lozenge$, and (iv) M^* is an appropriate representation of $M^\lozenge$.

CR5 is to be distinguished from a parallel thesis that would *require* M to be a mere sum of M^* and $M^\lozenge$, and from CR4, which *allows* M to be such a sum. In contrast to these theses, CR5 *disallows* M to be a mere sum—it requires that M be a complex.[34]

There are illustrations in the literature of the sum and complex views. As far as I can tell, according to Gennaro's "Wide Intrinsicality View" (1996: ch. 2, 2002), what makes M^* and $M^\lozenge$ two parts of a single mental state is simply our decision to treat them as such. There is no psychologically real relation between them that unites them into a single, cohesive mental state. By contrast, according to Van Gulick's Higher-Order Global States theory (2001, 2004, 2006), what makes M^* and $M^\lozenge$ two parts of a single state is the fact that they are integrated and unified through a psychologically real cognitive process of information integration.[35] So a conscious state arises, on this view, when a mental event ($M^\lozenge$) and the subject's awareness of it (M^*) are integrated into a single unity through the relevant sort of cognitive process. Gennaro's view seems to construe M as a mere *sum* of M^* and $M^\lozenge$, whereas Van Gulick's appears to construe it as a *complex* of M^* and $M^\lozenge$.[36]

---

[34] It may be objected that the sum view is not really a coherent position, since, despite characterizing M as a mere sum of M^* and $M^\lozenge$, it does postulate an essential relationship between them—namely, the relation of representation that M^* bears to $M^\lozenge$. The objection is that a view such as Gennaro's in fact construes M as a complex, not a mere sum. However, the representational relation M^* bears to $M^\lozenge$ is essential to the identity of M^*: M^* would not be the state that it is if it did not represent $M^\lozenge$. So, if M^* did not bear the representational relation to $M^\lozenge$, it would go out of existence. It would then fail to be the case that M's two parts continue to exist but M itself ceased to exist—as is required for M to qualify as a complex and not a mere sum. (This brings into sharper focus the relationship R that has to hold among the parts of a whole in order to make the whole a complex rather than a mere sum. For R to be a complex-making relation, R must be (i) an existence (and identity) condition of the whole, but (ii) neither an existence condition nor an identity condition of any of the parts.) A similar objection may be that Gennaro's view, in order to be at all plausible, must require that M^* and $M^\lozenge$ be roughly simultaneous and occur in the same subject's head, but such relations would make his view a complex view rather than a sum view. In response, it may be claimed that temporal and spatial relations are not substantive enough to be complex-making.

[35] I too have defended a view of this sort—e.g., in Kriegel 2002c, 2003b, and 2005. And I too focused on cognitive integration of the different parts into a complex. I now think that most of this integration belongs at the level of the sub-personal mechanisms that sustain consciousness. We will see how exactly this works in the next chapter.

[36] At least this is how I understand Gennaro's and Van Gulick's views as they appear in print. It is quite possible that I am misinterpreting one or both of them. My primary interest, however, is in the views themselves, not so much in the exegesis of Gennaro's and Van Gulick's work. In particular, some passages in Gennaro's work may suggest that he is more of a complex theorist than a sum theorist

This is because the latter view requires that there be a specific relationship between M^* and $M^\Diamond$ for them to constitute a conscious state—namely, the relation effected by their cognitive integration. M^* and $M^\Diamond$ would fail to constitute a conscious state if this relationship failed to obtain, and would go out of existence if the relevant relation was destroyed. There is no such provision in Gennaro's view: the only way for M to go out of existence is for either M^* or $M^\Diamond$ to go out of existence.

I belabor this point because CR5 clearly presents a genuine—that is, substantive rather than verbal—alternative to a higher-order theory. It introduces an element absent in higher-order theories—namely, the essential relation between the representing and represented states.[37] This overcomes the problem of whole distinction, thereby enabling a natur-alistically kosher ontological assay of consciousness. Since CR5 is also phenomenologically accurate, at least inasmuch as it has the resources to capture the internal structure of a global conscious experience, we may have here a satisfactory account of the ontological structure of conscious states.

Indirect (Self-)Representation

The problem with CR5 is that it is unclear how it might capture the notion of self-representation. There is a clear sense in which a mental state with two unified parts one of which represents the other is not quite a self-representing state. To overcome this difficulty, I now want to introduce a distinction (perhaps familiar) between direct and indirect representation, and claim that, although there is no *direct* self-representation in conscious states, there *is indirect* self-representation.

The notion of indirect representation is familiar in philosophical dis-cussions mainly from "indirect realism" or "representative theories" of perception (see, e.g., Jackson 1977). In such theories, mental particu-lars (such as sense data) are posited, and it is claimed that perception represents *directly* only such mental particulars, but in addition can also represent *indirectly* non-mental particulars; in fact, often perceptions will

---

(see especially Gennaro 1996: 29–30). More explicitly, responding to my accusation (in Kriegel 2006a) that his view is a mere sum view, Gennaro (2006) argues that it is in fact a complex view.

[37] This new element should make a tangible difference: if the two states are unified through a *psycho-logically real* process, that process would presumably affect the causal powers of the whole—something that would not happen if the two states were arbitrarily "summed up." (I am indebted to Paul Raymont for pointing this out to me.)

represent non-mental particulars *by*, or *in virtue of*, representing mental particulars. For example, perceiving the table at which I eat involves indirectly representing the table in virtue of, or by, directly representing a tablesque mental particular.

Indirect realism about perception is widely regarded as bankrupt, but it is important to realize that its distinction between direct and indirect representation is really just an extension (if the critics are right, an over-extension) of a more mundane and much less controversial distinction. For example, we may say that a painting depicts a house even though a portion of the house is occluded by a bush in the corner. It is natural to describe this as a case where a painting represents an entire house by, or in virtue of, representing a big part of it; the entire house is represented indirectly, its big part is represented directly. Likewise, a visual perception may represent an apple by representing its front surface and an olfactory perception may represent an apple pie by representing its odor; the surface and odor are directly represented, the apple and pie indirectly represented.

In this mundane sense, it seems that x may sometime represent y in virtue of representing z because z is a part of y. The unoccluded portion of the house is obviously a spatial part of the house. Likewise, the surface of an apple is part of the apple. The odor of apple pie is not a spatial part of the apple pie, but it is a logical part, inasmuch as the odor is a property of the pie in a way that complies with mereological axioms.

Certainly, one thing's being part of another does not guarantee that by representing the former we can represent the latter. The apple and its surface are part of our galaxy, but by having a perceptual experience of the apple or its surface one does not thereby represent the galaxy. Thus further conditions must be met if something is to represent another thing in virtue of representing its part. But it is clearly a central feature of indirect representation that it is mediated by direct representation of parts.

In this respect, the "in virtue of" locution behaves in representational contexts as it does in others. It is natural to say that I live in Arizona in virtue of living in Tucson, and that Jimmy punched Johnny in virtue of punching his nose. The facts that Tucson is part of Arizona and that Johnny's nose is part of Johnny are central to the applicability of the "in virtue of" locution in such contexts.

An important question is what distinguishes cases in which representation of a part serves as basis for representing the whole and cases in which it does not so serve. I will return to this question toward the end of this subsection. But, first, I want to apply this discussion of indirect representation to the crooked representational account. According to CR4, a conscious state is a whole, M, one of whose parts, M^*, represents the other, $M^\Diamond$. The problem we started this subsection with is that this does not seem to amount to self-representation. The above discussion may help with this problem.

Since $M^\Diamond$ is part of M, it may be that, *by* representing $M^\Diamond$, M^* represents M. In that case, M^* would represent indirectly M in virtue of representing directly $M^\Diamond$. This would cast a conscious state as a state part of which represents its whole self. This is surely genuine self-representation, albeit indirect. This could be formulated as a specific version of CR4:

(CR6) For any mental state M of a subject S, M is conscious iff there are M^* and $M^\Diamond$, such that (i) M^* is a proper part of M, (ii) $M^\Diamond$ is a proper part of M, and (iii) M^* represents M *by* representing $M^\Diamond$.

In CR6, M is self-represented in the sense that it is represented by a part of itself.

The fact that the self-representation here is only indirect, being as it is mediated by representation of one thing by another, can help us reconcile it with naturalist semantics. The key is to maintain that the broadly causal or teleological relation between representations and representata is necessary only for *direct* representation. Indirect representation does not have to involve any such relation. Rather, indirect representation is based on the combination of two relations: (i) the relevant naturalistic relation between the representation and *part of* the represented and (ii) the relevant parthood relation between the part of the represented and the represented. Both relations being naturalistically kosher, we have here the makings of a naturalistic account of indirect representation. But it is an account that is fully consistent with self-representation. In our case, the broadly causal relation holds between M^* and $M^\Diamond$, but it does not hold between M^* and the whole of M. Rather, M^* represents M because (i) it bears the relevant causal relation to $M^\Diamond$ and (ii) $M^\Diamond$ bears the relevant parthood relation to M.

The point is that naturalist semantics can be understood to apply to "direct representation," while indirect representation is understood to be based on direct representation in some way that does not require any causal relation between representor and represented. A very simple naturalist semantics might combine the following two claims: (*a*) *x* represents *y* directly just in case y causes x; (b) x represents y indirectly just in case there is a z, such that (i) z is part of y and (ii) z causes x. A more sophisticated naturalist semantics would posit a much more complex relation to account for direct representation (for example, a teleo-informational relation) and would ground indirect representation in a much more complicated mereological relation.

Let us return to the question of the conditions under which representation of a part is a basis for indirect representation of the whole. A full account of the matter will probably require its own volume, but a key seems to be that the part is suitably integrated into the whole. Visual perception of the apple's surface serves as a basis for perception of the apple, but not for perception of the whole galaxy, because the apple's surface is integrated into the apple in a much tighter way than into the galaxy, in that the interconnections between an apple's surface and the rest of the apple are deep and cohesive in a way they are not between a galaxy and the surface of an apple therein.

Again, this is how the "in-virtue-of" locution works in other contexts as well. By punching Johnny's nose, Jimmy punches Johnny, but does not punch the galaxy, because Johnny's nose is integrated into Johnny in a way it is not into the galaxy: the interconnections between Johnny's nose and the rest of Johnny are very tight relative to the interconnections between Johnny's nose and the rest of the galaxy.

Thus one view might be that x represents y in virtue of representing z if (i) x represents z, (ii) z is part of y, and (iii) z is highly integrated into y. I hesitate to endorse this claim, because I would not be all that surprised if there turn out to be cases where high integration does not bring in its train indirect representation, and moreover there is something vague and obscure about the notion of "high integration." But we may suppose that something *like* the above analysis is probably right and more precisely expressible. This would be good news, because the kind of view captured in CR5, which requires M to be a *complex* rather than a mere *sum* of its parts, is based on the idea that there is a real psychological relation that integrates M's parts.

If so, part of the answer to the question of what makes it the case that, in virtue of directly representing $M^{\Diamond}$, M^* also indirectly represents M, is precisely that M^* and $M^{\Diamond}$ form a complex. When a painting represents something that happens to be a component of a mere sum, it is not guaranteed, and is in fact quite doubtful (other things being equal), that the painting also represents the sum. But, if it represents something that is a component of a complex, then, unless there is some special reason not to do so, it is natural to regard the painting as a representation of the complex.[38], [39]

The fact that complexes make it easier, if nothing else, to represent a whole in virtue of representing its part suggests combining CR5 and CR6 into a single thesis. The result would be:

(CR7)   For any mental state M of a subject S, M is conscious iff there are M^* and $M^{\lozenge}$, such that (i) M^* is a proper part of M, (ii) $M^{\lozenge}$ is a proper part of M, (iii) M is a complex of M^* and $M^{\lozenge}$, and (iv) M^* represents M by representing $M^{\lozenge}$.

CR7 is my proposed account of the ontology of consciousness. It is a genuinely self-representational account, which, I claim, is naturalistically, phenomenologically, and ontologically adequate. I close with discussion of some objections to this account.

Some Objections and Replies

First, it might be worried that the possibility of infinite regress might raise its ugly head again. As we saw in Chapters 4 and 5, the inner awareness of a conscious experience is itself conscious. This means that not only M is conscious, but also M^*. According to CR7, a mental state is conscious just in case it is an appropriate complex of two state parts. It follows that not only M, but also M^*, is a complex of the sort. We may say that M^* is a complex of M^{**} and $M^{*\lozenge}$, where M^{**} represents

---

[38] If a cabinet could be a mere sum of its door and its frame, without the two being necessarily connected in a certain way, then representation of the door could not constitute also a representation of the whole cabinet. But, since the door and the frame must be connected in a specific way in order for their whole to function in the way a cabinet does, representation of the door can double as representation of the larger unit of which the door is a part.

[39] At least this is so if the part is "big enough." What counts as big enough is of course a complicated question, but I think in the present case there are good reasons to suspect that $M^{\lozenge}$ is a big enough part of M. In general, the floor-level items that comprise a global conscious experience at a moment greatly outnumber the inner-awareness item, which is always only one. Thus $M^{\lozenge}$ is probably big enough a part of M to make it possible for M^* to represent M indirectly in virtue of representing $M^{\lozenge}$ directly. (Consider the global experience we considered in the previous chapter, with its four floor-level items to the one inner-awareness item. In some obviously oversimplified way, we can say that the $M^{\lozenge}$ comprises 80% of M, so that representing $M^{\lozenge}$ directly should suffice for representing M indirectly.)

M* by representing $M^{*\Diamond}$. But then M^{**} is itself conscious, and would therefore implicate an appropriate complex as well. And so on and so forth.

The first thing to note about this objection is that it has a suppressed premise. This is that M* is a mental state. Observe, however, that CR7 does not state that M* is a mental state.[40] I concede, however, that there are independent reasons to treat M* as a state. But I also think that this only forces us a terminological reshuffling of sorts.

In the previous chapter I offered a phenomenological description of a global conscious experience—that is, the maximal conscious state a person is in at a time t. That global experience, or maximal conscious state, was claimed to have many distinguishable parts, which we are now conceding to be conscious states in their own right. We are led into trouble if we offer CR7 as an account of conscious states in general. But really CR7 is best thought of as an account of the ontological structure of the *global* experience/*maximal* conscious state. As for sub-maximal conscious states, what makes *them* conscious is simply that they are logical parts of a maximal conscious state—that is, logical parts of a mental state that conforms to CR7 (or, at least, they are the right kinds of such logical parts). We can capture this with the following assay:

> (CR8) For any mental state M of a subject S, M is a maximal conscious state iff there are mental states M* and $M^{\Diamond}$, such that (i) M* is a proper part of M, (ii) $M^{\Diamond}$ is a proper part of M, (iii) M is a complex of M* and $M^{\Diamond}$, and (iv) M* represents M by representing $M^{\Diamond}$; M is a sub-maximal conscious state iff there are mental states $M^{\aleph}$, M*, and $M^{\Diamond}$, such that (i) M* is a proper part of $M^{\aleph}$, (ii) $M^{\Diamond}$ is a proper part of $M^{\aleph}$, (iii) $M^{\aleph}$ is a complex of M* and $M^{\Diamond}$, (iv) M* represents $M^{\aleph}$ by representing $M^{\Diamond}$, and (v) M is an appropriate part of $M^{\aleph}$.

This can be further unpacked by construing a "maximal" conscious state as a conscious state which is not part of any other conscious state. In other words, $M^{\aleph}$ is a *maximal* conscious state just in case $M^{\aleph}$ is a conscious state

---

[40] What CR7 states is that M* is a *logical part of a mental state*. And, although CR7 states that a conscious mental state involves an appropriate complex, it does not say that a conscious mental-state-part involves such a complex. In other words, to obtain an infinite regress from CR7, we would have to assume that every mental state part is a mental state.

and there is no M^a, such that M^a is also a conscious state and $M^\aleph$ is part of M^a. We thus obtain:

> (CR9) For any mental state M of a subject S, M is conscious iff there are mental states $M^\aleph$, M^*, and $M^\lozenge$, such that (i) M^* is a proper part of $M^\aleph$, (ii) $M^\lozenge$ is a proper part of $M^\aleph$, (iii) $M^\aleph$ is a complex of M^* and $M^\lozenge$, (iv) M^* represents $M^\aleph$ by representing $M^\lozenge$, (v) there is no mental state M^a, such that M^a satisfies (i)–(iv) and $M^\aleph$ is a logical part of M^a, and (vi) either (vi_a) $M = M^\aleph$ or (vi_b) M is an appropriate part of $M^\aleph$.

CR9 is much less elegant than CR7, but has the virtue of being consistent with the possibility of M^* being a state in its own right. It is, if you please, the "official" thesis of this chapter.

A completely different objection is more phenomenological. One may worry that what is indirectly represented is not strictly given in consciousness, and so that the indirect content (if you will) of M^* would not show up in the phenomenology. This would mean that M^* itself, as well as M, would not show up in the phenomenology.

This is a very interesting objection, and I am not sure how I want to respond to it. My inclination is to contest the claim that the indirect content of a representation does not show up in the phenomenology. Given the account of indirect representation sketched in the previous subsection, one might be tempted to hold that a normal perceptual experience of the sky represents the sky by representing a blue expanse, and yet it seems that both are phenomenologically manifest; or that an olfactory experience of freshly brewed coffee represents the coffee by representing its odor, where, again, it seems that both are manifest in the phenomenology. However, by the lights of the principle that only direct content enters the phenomenology, the sky and the coffee would have to be non-phenomenal. So the principle must be rejected.[41]

Another objection is that, contrary to what I argue above, Gennaro's wide intrinsicality view could be seen as requiring the conscious state to be

---

[41] Another response, which I am not sympathetic to but which might appeal to some readers, is simply to accept that M^*'s representation of M, being indirect, does not enter the phenomenology of consciousness. On this view, the only thing that enters the phenomenology is M^*'s representation of $M^\lozenge$, the lower-level component of the conscious state. I am not sympathetic to this on phenomenological grounds, but the phenomenology suggested by this view might resonate with some readers.

the complex of its two parts rather than their sum. After all, on Gennaro's view the lower-order part of a conscious state *causes* the higher-order part of that state. This causal connection is psychologically real, so there *is* a difference between a conscious state and a mere sum of two unconnected parts.

In response, I should first say that, although Gennaro holds that there is a causal connection between the two parts of a conscious state, that causal connection does not enter the main presentations of the wide intrinsicality view on what *makes* a mental state conscious. One position is that conscious states have two parts that happen to be causally connected, but they are conscious states purely in virtue of the fact that they have two parts, and not at all in virtue of the fact that those parts are causally connected. On this position, there is a causal connection between the parts of a conscious state, but it is accidental to the state's being conscious. Such a position does not qualify as a "complex" view as I understand it here. A "complex" view would *require* the parts of a conscious state to be causally connected. Ultimately, however, I should note that, if Gennaro's wide intrinsicality view is suitably modified that it includes such an explicit requirement, then the view *would* qualify as a "complex" view and I would have no ontological objection to it. I would still have a phenomenological objection to it, inasmuch as Gennaro (2006, 2008) insists that the higher-order part of a conscious state is itself phenomenally *unconscious*, whereas I hold that it is phenomenally conscious; but that would be a separate objection.

4. Conclusion

I conclude that the account I proposed for the ontology of consciousness—CR9—satisfies, or at least is well positioned to satisfy, the ontological desideratum mentioned at the beginning of this chapter. The account also satisfies the phenomenological desideratum. On the one hand, it reflects quite faithfully the internal structure of a global conscious experience, as that structure is described in the previous chapter. At the same time, it does so while appealing only to occurrent, non-dispositional features. Finally, the account overcomes the straight representational account's difficulties with naturalizability, as it ensures that no element in a global conscious experience directly represents itself. The case for the naturalizability of self-representation, as construed in the account I propose, is completed in the next chapter, where a concrete proposal regarding the neural correlate of consciousness is made on the basis of CR7. The upshot of this chapter, then, is a view on which a mental state is phenomenally conscious when it conforms to the ontological structure described in CR9.[42]

[42] For comments on a previous draft of this chapter I would like to thank Bill Lycan, Kristie Miller, Ken Williford, and an anonymous referee. I have also benefited from exchanges with Ermanno Bencivenga, Terry Horgan, Keith Lehrer, Leon Leontyev, Joe Levine, Luca Moretti, Paul Raymont, Sydney Shoemaker, (Buffalo's) Barry Smith, (Sydney's) Nick Smith, Amie Thomasson, and Josh Weisberg.

7

Self-Representationalism
and the Science of Consciousness

In the scientific study of consciousness, there are two outstanding questions. The first concerns the neural correlate of consciousness: what is the neural condition that is present whenever one is conscious and absent whenever one is not? The second concerns the function of consciousness: what is consciousness good for; what is it exactly that it does? In this chapter I show that self-representationalism delivers quite precise answers to both questions. In Section 1 I address the question of neural correlate, in Section 2 that of functional significance.

1. The Neural Correlate of Consciousness:
A Cross-Order Integration Hypothesis

In the previous chapter we developed an account of the rather complex ontological structure involved in consciousness. The basic elements, however, were (i) a first-order representation, (ii) a higher-order representation of that first-order representation, and (iii) some relationship of cognitive unity between the two, in virtue of which they form a complex.[1] To identify the neural correlate of consciousness (NCC), we should seek, to a first approximation, a neural triad of correlates to match these three elements. Once the triad has been designated, the general shape of the NCC should become evident.

---

[1] The conscious states involve a first-order representation only when we are dealing with a first-order conscious state, of course. The general claim should be that the three elements are (i) a n-order representation, (ii) a $n + 1$-order representation of that n-order representation, and (iii) a relationship of cognitive unity between the two.

The first element in our neural triad, however, falls outside the purview of the theory of consciousness proper. Depending on which kind of conscious state we are dealing with, different parts of cognitive neuropsychology would have to be "fielded" to match the appropriate neural correlate of the first element. For an experience of blue, the first-order representation would consist in neural activation in some subpopulation of neurons in V4, since V4 is dedicated to the representation of color (Zeki et al. 1991). But, for a conscious experience of recognizing a friend's face it would be activation in the fusiform gyrus (Kanwisher 2000), for an auditory conscious experience it would have to be activation in the auditory cortex, and so on. These are essential components of the neural correlates of specific conscious states, but none of them correlates with consciousness in general, since each has to do with a particular *kind* of conscious state. We can think of these floor-level representations as determining the specific *contents* of consciousness once consciousness is present, rather than as ensuring the presence of consciousness in the first place.[2] However, the search for the NCC is in the first instance a search for the correlate of consciousness as such, not of specific contents of consciousness.[3]

The second element in the triad is the neural correlate of higher-order representation. Presumably, it would have to be seated in an area of the brain that is associated with quite sophisticated cognition, since higher-order representations require the ability to direct the cognitive system onto itself and engage in what is known in the cognitive-scientific literature as *metacognition*. A good preliminary guess is that the neural substrate of such metacognitive activity is to be found in the prefrontal cortex, which is associated with executive function and other forms of sophisticated cognition.

---

[2] It may be worth pausing to stress the distinction between the contents of consciousness and consciousness as such. The contents of consciousness vary across different conscious experiences: a visual experience of blue, a visual experience of a friend's face, and an auditory experience of a bagpipe have different contents. But they also share something—they are all conscious experiences! There is something that is invariable across all conscious experiences, which we may therefore call consciousness-as-such.

[3] Chalmers (2000) argues that the ultimate goal of the search for the NCC is to identify the neural correlates of the *contents* of consciousness. But the fact that the contents of consciousness vary across different conscious experiences, whereas the NCC should be the element that is invariable across all conscious experiences, suggests that this is the wrong methodological priority. The search for the NCC should be a search for the neural signature of consciousness—that is to say, the correlate of consciousness-as-such, of consciousness *per se*.

The third element in our triad is the cognitive unification of the two representations. This cognitive unification would probably involve a sort of functional integration of the first-order and second-order representations. By "functional integration," I mean a process of unifying disparate bits of information into a single representation in a functionally significant way—that is, in such a way that the functional role of the single representation is in some sense more than the sum of the functional roles of the different bits making it up. Imagine a creature that engages in some activity only when it is cold and muggy; then the process by which a representation that it is cold and a representation that it is muggy are integrated into a single representation of it being cold and muggy is a process of functional integration.

There are many forms of functional integration in the cognitive system. The neural mechanisms underlying them may inspire different analogies for the functional integration of a conscious experience and one's awareness of that experience. By far the most extensively studied of those, at least in recent years, is the kind of functional integration involved in so-called feature binding. When a person perceives a blue patch moving from left to right, the patch's blueness is represented in V4, but its left-to-right motion is represented in MT. V4 and MT are not spatially adjacent brain areas (nor would it particularly help if they were), so something must "tell" the brain that the blueness and the motion belong together as two features of one and the same object, and this "something" is the binding mechanism.[4] A natural place to start looking for the third element in our triad is this binding mechanism, in the hope that something like it would also subserve the functional integration of a floor-level representation and its higher-order representation.[5]

To generate a concrete hypothesis about the NCC, then, what is needed is evidence about the concrete brain structures and mechanisms involved in

[4] The brain must find a way to represent that the blueness and the motion belong together as two features of one and the same stimulus. We will see that there is something particularly problematic about this sort of representation in due course.

[5] This third element introduces, in all probability, a non-anatomical aspect to the NCC. Although one model of integrating two pieces of information might involve sending both to some special place in the brain where "it all comes together," a more psychologically plausible model involves only a special relationship between the two pieces of information—for example, a relationship created by the binding mechanism. If so, there is no *neuroanatomical* correlate of consciousness. Activity (over baseline) in the brain areas responsible for the floor-level and higher-order representations is not sufficient for consciousness. A further element is the relationship between them that guarantees their functional integration.

higher-order representation and functional integration. We noted that the most natural places to look for these are in studies of the neural mechanisms underlying, respectively, metacognition and binding: metacognition creates higher-order representations, binding produces cognitive integration. In the next two subsections, I pursue these ideas in more detail.

The general approach we are looking at is to pinpoint the neural mechanisms underlying the integration of first- and higher-order representations. This is a form of what we might call *cross-order integration*. For this reason, I call the hypothesis I will end up with the *cross-order integration hypothesis*, or the COI hypothesis for short.

The COI hypothesis is meant somewhat coyly, inasmuch as currently the knowledge we have of the relevant structures and mechanisms, and the conceptual contact they make with the psychological and phenomenological phenomena, are too limited to produce a hypothesis we could responsibly commit to in earnest. What follows is in many ways wildly speculative and incomplete. The point of the exercise is mostly to illustrate how a concrete hypothesis about the NCC *could* be produced from the philosophical and phenomenological theory of self-representationalism.

Neural Correlates of Higher-Order Representation

Imaging studies of metacognition have found, with remarkable consistency, that activity in the prefrontal cortex, especially in the right lobe, is associated with cognition of one's psychological states and character traits. More specifically, there is a remarkable convergence on the medial prefrontal cortex (mPFC), with relevant activity in the anterior cingulate cortex (ACC) as well.[6] Thus it might be thought that the natural hypothesis is that mPFC activity, perhaps aided by ACC activity, corresponds to the second element in our neural triad.

There is, however, a problem with these studies that may undermine their relevance to our present project. The problem is that many of the areas associated with metacognition appear to be associated with other tasks as well, especially those involving social cognition. This problem is particularly acute because both metacognition and social cognition involve

---

[6] For mPFC relevance, see Lane et al. 1997, Craik et al. 1999, Gusnard et al. 2001, Johnson et al. 2002, and Kelley et al. 2002. For ACC relevance, see Johnson et al. 2002 and Kelley et al. 2002.

cognition of psychological states; the difference is that metacognition is directed at psychological states of *oneself*, whereas social cognition is directed at psychological states of *others*. If the mPFC is activated both in metacognition and social cognition, the natural inference is that the mPFC subserves the cognition of psychological states in general, rather than more specifically cognition of one's *own* psychological states. Thus it may be that the mPFC subserves Theory of Mind (ToM)-related activity rather than metacognition proper. Metacognition is one kind of application of ToM—namely, to oneself—but social cognition is another.[7]

A recent study that targeted precisely the difference between cognition of psychological features of oneself and those of a significant other has found that, while in both tasks the mPFC was activated, it was also activated equally, hence non-differentially, in both. What was activated differentially was rather the dorsolateral prefrontal cortex (dlPFC), which was significantly more active during cognition of one's own psychological features than during cognition of the significant other's (Schmitz et al. 2004). If so, it may in the end be the dlPFC that is the better candidate for capturing the second element in our triad.

Clinical studies of subjects with deficits in metacognitive assessment of their own features and abilities provide convergent evidence. For starters, it has been found that schizophrenics unaware of their condition tend to have reduced gray matter volume in the dlPFC relative to schizophrenics with a more accurate understanding of their condition (Flashman et al. 2001). Similarly, patients who have a distorted assessment of their abilities after traumatic brain injury have been shown to exhibit lower activity in the medial and right dorsolateral PFC relative to traumatic-brain-injury patients with a more accurate assessment of their abilities (Schmitz et al. 2006).

A further problem, however, threatens to undermine the relevance of all these results. Many of the non-clinical studies in this area are based on a paradigm in which subjects are asked to state whether some trait adjectives describe them accurately. For example, the subject is presented with the adjective "honest," or "polite," and is asked to state whether

---

[7] That is, the involvement of the mPFC in both metacognition and social cognition suggests that the mPFC does not subserve metacognition as such, but whatever is common between metacognition and social cognition—which is to say cognition of psychological states. See Frith and Frith 1999 for a review of the connection between mPFC and ToM.

he or she is indeed honest, or polite. The metacognitive judgment the subject is asked to render is a judgment not about a particular occurrent mental state, then, but rather about a standing feature of her overall personality. Let us call the former kind of judgment *state metacognition* and the latter *trait metacognition*. The problem is that these studies tell us rather about the neural mechanisms underlying trait metacognition, whereas the mechanisms relevant to consciousness are those underlying state metacognition.[8] Likewise for the clinical studies, which are also focused on metacognition of standing abilities as opposed to occurrent states. It is conceivable, of course, that the mechanisms underlying metacognition of occurrent states are the same as those underlying standing features and abilities, but there is no a priori necessity that this be so, and in fact no a priori reason to suspect it to be so.

What are needed, then, are studies that target state metacognition while making sure that they dissociate it from what we might call *state social cognition*: the cognition of psychological states of others. Progress in this area is sure to be made over the next few years, and we may then learn more about what exactly subserves state metacognition. But it is reasonable to expect the relevant area to be in the prefrontal cortex, most probably medial or dorsolateral, perhaps with assistance from the anterior cingulate.

To get another angle on state metacognition, we might consider taking into account research on so-called attentional control. Large parts of this literature are concerned with error detection and conflict resolution in the cognitive system. When the cognitive system's activity produces what appear to be erroneous results, or conflicting results, some correction of the error, or resolution of the conflict, is in order. The system thus needs mechanisms for (i) detecting such problems and (ii) fixing them.

There are two highly plausible assumptions that would make these mechanisms relevant to our present purposes. The first is that the mechanism in charge of detecting the problems is probably engaged in ongoing monitoring of activity in the system. The second is that a mechanism engaged in ongoing monitoring produces higher-order representations. Against the background of these two assumptions, it seems that the

---

[8] In fact, it may not be just any kind of state metacognition that is relevant, but a particular kind, which may or may not share the same "neural seat" with other kinds.

mechanism in charge of detecting error and conflict in the system produces higher-order representations.

Note that our interest here is not just in any old higher-order representations, but in specifically conscious and yet non-introspective higher-order representations. Happily, however, the attention–shift model of the relationship between focal, peripheral, and unconscious higher-order representations suggests that all three varieties have the same neuroanatomical seat. For the difference between such representations is not intrinsic to them, but rather has to do with the attention resources dedicated to them. Against the background of that model of introspecting, then, evidence for the location of any kind of higher-order representation is also evidence for the location of the kind of conscious but non-introspective higher-order representations we are interested in.

The most straightforward experimental paradigm in the study of attentional control employs the Stroop task (Stroop 1935), in which subjects who are asked to state the color in which a color word is inked are presented sometimes with words whose meaning and color are congruent (e.g., "yellow" written in yellow) and sometimes with words whose meaning and color are incongruent (e.g., "red" written in yellow). Reaction times are consistently greater in the incongruent cases (this is the "Stroop effect"). This suggests that there is some sort of interference from the lexical processing of the words in the performance of the task, which concerns only the color in which the word is displayed. This sort of interference is an instance of cognitive conflict, and is thought to be the main trigger for deployment of "cognitive control" (Botvinik et al. 2001), whose job is to resolve the conflict by assigning greater cognitive resources to the task at hand (this is the exercise of "attentional control").[9]

Interestingly, research on cognitive control has homed in on two of the three brain areas we have already met: the ACC and the dlPFC. The leading model, due to Cohen, Carter, and collaborators, is fairly

---

[9] Note that the kind of metacognitive representation involved in the Stroop effect is unconscious, whereas the kind we are ultimately looking for, in the light of CR7 from the previous chapter, is conscious. But, as noted above, there is good reason to think that the neural seat of conscious and unconscious higher-order representations is the same. More generally, in any case, it should be stressed that the evidence we currently possess about such things is insufficient to get at exactly the kind of higher-order representations cited in CR7. But getting at *some* kind of higher-order representation is a first step toward producing an ever more precise hypothesis about the neural correlate of consciousness from the self-representational theory.

straightforward. In a nutshell, the model says that the ACC is in charge of detecting conflict and error, and when it does, it sends the information regarding the problem to the dlPFC, which proceeds to fix the problem.[10] The model draws a neat division of labor between the ACC and the dlPFC: the ACC is in charge of *detecting* problems, the dlPFC in charge of *fixing* them (MacDonald et al. 2000). If we embrace this model, then this research would suggest that the ACC is the monitoring mechanism that produces higher-order representations.

Others have argued against the one-directional model of Cohen et al., suggesting that both the ACC and the dlPFC are involved in both the detecting and the fixing of problems (Gehring and Knight 2000). It is not very important for our purposes which model is favored by the evidence. If the Cohen et al. model is correct, then the evidence from research on attentional control is that only the ACC produces higher-order representations, whereas the dlPFC does not.[11] If the alternative model is correct, then the evidence from research on attentional control is that both the ACC and the dlPFC are involved in producing higher-order representations. What is interesting is that this evidence is in line with evidence from metacognitive evaluation research, inasmuch as some of the same brain areas appear to be implicated. Thus we may conclude with some confidence that it is highly probable that higher-order representations are produced by the ACC, mPFC, and/or dlPFC.[12]

This evidence offers seven different options for the COI hypothesis regarding the neural correlates of higher-order representations: three hypotheses that identify a single neuroanatomical seat (ACC, dlPFC, or mPFC); three that identify two neuroanatomical seats (ACC + dlPFC, ACC + mPFC, and dlPFC + mPFC); and one that identifies three seats (ACC + dlPFC + mPFC). At this relatively early stage of inquiry, there is no particular reason for the COI theorist to be attached to one of these hypotheses rather than another. Whichever of them finds most independent support as hypothesis about a component of the NCC is the one the COI theorist should embrace.

---

[10] See Botvinik et al. 2001, Milham et al. 2001, and Milham et al. 2003.

[11] Note well, though: there may still be evidence from *other* research that the dlPFC produces higher-order representations.

[12] At the same time, this does not rule out the possibility that higher-order representations are produced independently in other areas.

Arguably, such independent evidence favors the dlPFC. There are two particular studies that have found clear differential activation in the dlPFC between a conscious condition and a non-conscious condition.

The first study focused on blindsight. Saharaie et al. (1997) used fMRI to compare overall brain activation during stimulus detection by blindsight patient GY in (i) the blind part of his visual field and (ii) the normal part of his visual field. The most significant difference between the two conditions, and by most measures the only significant one, was activation in the dlPFC in the conscious condition but not in the non-conscious condition.[13]

The second study is more recent and focused on metacontrast masking (Lau and Passingham 2006). Subjects were presented with a shape stimulus—a square or a diamond—that was masked by a later stimulus at varying intervals. The subjects were asked, first, to judge whether the stimulus was a diamond or a square, and second, to report whether their judgment was based on what they saw or was just a guess. Lau and Passingham looked for a pair of different intervals separating the target stimulus from the masking stimulus, such that the first answers were correct at more or less the same frequency in both, but the second answers differed importantly, so that in one interval subjects reported merely guessing significantly more often than in the other. And indeed they found two such intervals: 33 ms and 100 ms. Judgments about the shape were correct 68 percent of the time when the interval was 33 ms and 70 percent when it was 100 ms (so the difference was statistically insignificant). But subjects reported just guessing 51 percent of the time in the 33 ms interval and only 40 percent of the time in the 100 ms interval (so the difference was statistically much more significant). On the assumptions that (*a*) above-chance correct judgments about the stimulus indicate that the subject did *perceive* the stimulus, and (*b*) reports of just guessing indicate that the subject did not *consciously* perceive it, these results suggest that, at these two intervals, there is no significant difference in the quality of subjects' perception of the stimulus (or at least in the quality of their task performance), but there is significant difference in the presence of consciousness (with greater presence in the

[13] I have been told by more than one expert that this study is less technically sound than would be ideal. This suggests to me that, on its own, it would present little evidence for an NCC hypothesis. But, in a supporting role, treated as subsidiary evidence to back more central evidence, it need not be disregarded.

100 ms interval).[14] Lau and Passingham then compared brain activity in subjects performing the task in the two intervals and found only one brain area that was significantly more active in the 100 ms one—the dlPFC.[15]

These studies support the concrete hypothesis that the dlPFC is the sole anatomical seat of higher-order representations of one's own occurrent mental states. There is evidence against the dlPFC as well, however. It comes from sleep research, where it has been known for some time that the dlPFC is strongly *deactivated* during REM sleep, hence during dreams. On the assumption that dreams are conscious experiences, this constitutes counter-evidence against the hypothesis that dlPFC is a component of the NCC. The most straightforward way the COI theorist can accommodate this piece of evidence is to adopt one of the other seven possible hypotheses about the neural correlates of higher-order representations, since those do not give the dlPFC the exclusive function of producing higher-order representations.[16] In particular, the option of giving a central, but not exclusive, place to dlPFC activity as the neural correlate of higher-order representations of one's own occurrent mental states, as a component of the NCC, is still open to the COI theorist, and is well supported by currently available evidence. As noted above, this does not matter a great deal for our present purposes. Further research on state metacognition, as opposed to both trait metacognition and (what we called) state social cognition, should shed further light on the second element in our neural triad.

---

[14] The second assumption could use some justification, because it may well be that reports of just guessing are due not to the absence of consciousness but rather to the absence of short-term memory. Ultimately, some experimental design would have to be generated to control for this alternative explanation in terms of memory deficit. Nonetheless, the simpler explanation is probably the one that adverts to consciousness deficits, and anyway that explanation is certainly *confirmed* by reports of merely guessing (even if it is not confirmed *better than every alternative*).

[15] This result can be co-opted by the COI theorist, then, according to whom a perceptual state becomes conscious only when it is represented by a higher-order representation with which it is functionally integrated. If this higher-order representation is implemented in the dlPFC, this would explain why two perceptual states can (no doubt, in unusual circumstances) be just as perceptually reliable while only one state is conscious.

[16] Probably the most plausible of these other hypotheses would be the hypothesis that higher-order representations are produced by the dlPFC and ACC. Perhaps the claim could be that both brain areas can produce higher-order representations, and, while the dlPFC produces most of them, especially in standard circumstances (in some suitable sense of "standard"), the ACC produces some of them, especially in less standard circumstances. The response, then, is that, although dream research provides evidence against the supposition that the dlPFC is the sole producer of higher-order representations, the COI hypothesis as such is not wedded to the view that it is.

In conclusion, in search for the second element in our neural triad, the neural correlate of higher-order representation, we have found three brain areas of particular interest. The most central one is the dlPFC, the second is the ACC, and a third one of some interest is the mPFC. It is quite plausible that one or more of these subserve(s) higher-order representation.

Neural Correlates of Functional Integration

Let us turn now to the third element in our neural triad—the correlate of cognitive unification, or functional integration. It was noted above that studies of the binding mechanism are a good place to start looking for it. In a series of seminal studies, Treisman has shown that some patients exhibit "illusory conjunctions" (see Treisman and Schmidt 1982). When presented with a green square and red circle, they may perceive a green circle and red square. Their perceptual system represents all the right features, but puts them together in the wrong way. Such "misbinding" shows that a distinctive mechanism must be involved in the "putting-together" of stimuli.

The "binding problem" is the problem of how the brain executes such feature binding (see Treisman 1996). A representation of a red circle involves three representational elements: (i) a representation of the redness, (ii) a representation of the circularity, and (iii) a representation of their togetherness as two aspects of a single object. The first two elements involve straightforward activation of subpopulations of neurons in dedicated parts of the brain, say V4 and V2 respectively. The relevant neurons fire their electrical impulse at some baseline rate, say 10 Hz (once every 100 ms) in V4 and 15 Hz (every 67 ms) in V2. When the system detects redness and circularity, these neurons fire their electrical impulse at an increased rate, say 25 Hz (every 40 ms) in V4 and 50 Hz (every 20 ms) in V2. Thus the increased rates of firing in the V4 and V2 subpopulations represent the redness and the circularity. But what represents their togetherness? It cannot be a similar event of increased firing rate in a different part of the brain, for that event would then need to be itself bound with the other two. Some "cleverer" mechanism must be in place for representation of togetherness.[17]

---

[17] The problem is especially evident when the system is presented with two objects, say a red circle and a green square. There may be two representations of togetherness in the brain, but something must

The leading (though certainly not uncontested) model of the neuro-physiological process underlying feature binding is the neural synchrony model.[18] The idea was first proposed by von der Malsburg (1981). In the illustration above, each of the two subpopulations in V4 and V2 fires its electrical impulse at an increased rate. But the rates are different. Von der Malsburg's idea was that the brain could represent the togetherness of two features by *synchronizing* the firing rates: when two features belong together, the brain activities that represent them involve firing rates that are not only increased relative to baseline, but also more or less equal to one another. In the illustration above, the firing rate in V4 might be speeded up from 25 Hz to 33 Hz and that in V2 slowed down from 50 Hz to the 35 Hz, so that the two subpopulations in V2 and V4 fired their electrical impulse at almost the same rate (more or less every 30 ms).[19] The actual occurrence of synchronization in the millisecond range was later confirmed, mainly in experiments on binocular rivalry in cats and monkeys.[20]

Even when the two subpopulations fire at the same *rate*, they might not fire at the same *time*. They might each fire every 30 ms, but in cycles that are 15 ms apart. However, there may also be a mechanism that brings two subpopulations to fire not only at the same rate, but also at the same time. The difference between synchronizing rate and synchronizing time may give the system the tools to represent a *hierarchy of binding*. For example, an audiovisual experience of a trumpet may involve representations of the trumpet's shape, color, and sound, so that the firings that represent the visual features of shape and color are time-synchronized with each other but only rate-synchronized with the firings that represent the auditory features pertaining to the trumpet's sound. In this case, the intra-modal unity of shape and color is stronger or tighter than the inter-modal unity of these visual features with sound, and the tighter unity is reflected in the tightness of synchrony.[21]

---

make sure that what is represented as going together are the redness and circularity, on the one hand, and the greenness and squareness, on the other, rather than some other combination.

[18] See Shadlen and Movshon 1999 for a powerful critique.

[19] The mechanism that brings about this alignment is the binding mechanism, and the alignment is the binding itself.

[20] See Singer 1994, Engel et al. 1999, Engel and Singer 2001, and Revonsuo 1999 for a more theoretical overview.

[21] This is, of course, a simple example, but much more can be said about the relationship between different levels of synchrony. Indeed, the relationship between rate coding and temporal coding via

Such a hierarchy of binding is called for by the existence of large-scale binding in the brain (Varela et al. 2001). Large-scale binding is defined roughly as binding of information across parts of the brain between which transmission of information would take at least 8 ms. It has even been speculated that a hierarchy of binding extends across the entire cognitive system, with a weak level of unity imposed at the highest level, that of our standing world model, which includes, as part, our self-model (Metzinger 1995).[22]

In essence, the rate of firing is the brain's medium for representation of individual features, but the brain may employ other media for representing certain central relationships *among* features, such as compresence ("togetherness"). Synchrony of rate and time are two such media, but there may well be others. The more media the brain can avail itself of for representing relationships among stimuli, the more complex the resulting representations will be, possibly including varying degrees of unity among the stimuli.

Cross-Order Integration

Synchronization takes place within the visual cortex, but also across brain areas. To effect cross-modal feature binding, there needs to be synchronization between brain areas dedicated to different kinds of perceptual information. There is even evidence of sensorimotor synchrony, which presumably effects binding of perceptual representations with motor representations (Roelfsema et al. 1997). There is no reason why there would not similarly be some kind of binding of perceptual representations with higher-order representations. This might involve synchronization of representations in, say, the visual cortex and the prefrontal cortex. And what it would subserve would effectively be cross-order integration.

An interesting fact regarding synchrony is that, although it connects what are at the sub-personal level separate representations, it results in what is at

synchrony is an issue that is continuously addressed in computational neuroscience. Our understanding of the issues involved is still very incomplete, but further research over the next decade or so should shed much more light on the possibilities raised in the main text.

[22] Given that binding mechanisms range from the quite local (e.g., binding of information represented in adjacent areas of visual cortex) to such large scale (including cross-hemispheric binding—see Bressler 1995), one would expect the brain to have the capacity to recognize different levels of unity and organize them hierarchically.

the personal level a unified single representation. When representations of a trumpet's color, shape, and sound in V4, V2, and A1 are synchronized, we do not experience ourselves to have three closely related representations. Rather, we experience ourselves to have a single representation of a colorful, shapely, melodious trumpet.[23] Presumably, however, this is so regardless of what sub-personal mechanism we postulate to explain personal-level feature binding. I have focused here on the synchronization model because of its elegance and familiarity. But it should be stressed that this is just one illustration of how cross-order integration might be subserved.

In any case, the COI hypothesis for the NCC is based on the idea that the same sort of synchronization we have focused on may unify a first-order representation with a representation of that very representation. If the brain harbored two synchronized representations, one in V4 representing redness and another in (say) the dlPFC representing increased firing rate in V4, at the personal level we would experience ourselves to have a single representation that folds within it both an awareness of red and an awareness of that awareness. That is the sort of cognitive character that, according to self-representationalism, distinguishes conscious states from non-conscious ones.

This, then, is the COI hypothesis about the neural correlate of color consciousness: it is constituted by synchronized representations in V4 and (say) the dlPFC.[24] As for other kinds of visual consciousness, their neural correlates are given by synchronized representations in the relevant parts of the visual cortex and (say) the dlPFC.[25] The neural correlates of *auditory* consciousness are given by synchronized representations in the relevant parts of the auditory cortex and the dlPFC. And so on and so forth. In each case, the neural correlate of consciousness *as such* is given by synchrony with representations in the dlPFC, or whatever area turns out to subserve higher-order representation, while the neural correlate of the *contents* of

---

[23] One of the fascinating questions in this area is *how* sub-personal synchronization underlies or realizes personal-level unity. This question ought to receive much more attention than it has to date. Here I do not offer any account of this phenomenon, but ultimately an account ought to be provided.

[24] Keep in mind, however, that the dlPFC is only one of the options the COI theorist may advert to—though perhaps the most appealing option at this point.

[25] For example, a visual experience of recognizing a friend's face would have as its neural correlate the synchronized activity of the fusiform gyrus and (say) the dlPFC.

consciousness is given by whatever representations are thus synchronized with the relevant higher-order representation.[26], [27]

In complicated cases involving multiple sub-personal first-order representations, a question arises as to what enters the subject's overall phenomenology at the time. There are two main views to consider here. One view is that what enters are all and only those first-order representations that are synchronized with the higher-order representation. The other view is that, in addition to those, also any other first-order representations that are independently synchronized with the first-order representation that is bound with the higher-order one enter the phenomenology. To appreciate the difference between these two views, consider a case where a dlPFC representation represents a V4 representation, the two are synchronized, and the V4 representation is also synchronized with a V2 representation, but the V2 representation is not synchronized with the dlPFC representation. On the first view, only the V4 representation enters the phenomenology; on the second view, the V2 representation enters as well. The rationale for the first view is that, since the dlPFC representation implements the for-me-ness of experience, only those first-order representations represented by it should be possessed of for-me-ness and thus enter the phenomenology. The rationale for the second view is that, once

---

[26] Presumably, there is some functional significance to such cross-order synchronization, and it ought to be of a piece with the functional significance of regular binding. This suggests that, when a mental state is conscious, its representation of the stimulus, and the representation of that representation, are treated "as one" by downstream consumer systems, such as those concerned with decision-making and verbal report. Just how this functional difference between bound cross-order states and unbound ones plays out is something worth investigating in future work.

[27] The hypothesis we end up with renders determinate verdicts on specific cases. Let us consider several scenarios involving five sub-personally distinct representations: in V4 of a trumpet's color, in V2 of its shape, in A1 of its sound, in somatosensory cortex of a tickle in one's left arm, and in the dlPFC of the increased firing rate in V4. The first scenario is one in which the dlPFC representation is synchronized with the representations in V4, V2, and A1, but not with that in the somatosensory cortex. The hypothesis predicts that the subject undergoes a conscious experience of the colored, shaped, heard trumpet, but that the tickle remains non-conscious. In a second scenario, the representation in dlPFC is synchronized with the representations in V2 and V4, but not with those in A1 and the somatosensory cortex. The hypothesis predicts that the subject undergoes an experience of a colored and shaped trumpet, but that the sound and the tickle are non-conscious. In a third scenario, the dlPFC representation is synchronized with the somatosensory representation, but not with the V2, V4, and A1 representations. Here the hypothesis predicts that the subject experiences neither the trumpet (visually or auditorily) nor the tickle: not the trumpet, because the dlPFC representation is not synchronized with the trumpet-directed audiovisual representations, and not the tickle, because the dlPFC representation does not represent the somatosensory representation with which it is synchronized.

the V4 and V2 representations are bound, at the personal level they form a single representation, and so, by representing V4, the dlPFC representation represents just one part of a larger state, and thus perhaps represents V2 indirectly (in the sense brought out in the previous chapter).

The question of which view to prefer is a complicated one, and cannot be fully considered here. There are some important points of contact here with matters discussed toward the end of Section 2 in Chapter 5, but nor can we explore all these connections here. At this early stage of inquiry into the NCC, there is no particular need to commit to one of these two views rather than another. In any event, in practice there may not be much difference in the predictions produced by the two views. Keep in mind that *exact* synchrony is transitive: if a V4 representation is exactly synchronized with a dlPFC representation and with a V2 representation, then the latter two must be synchronized as well. Neural synchrony is *inexact* synchrony, and inexact synchrony is intransitive, so there is the principled possibility of a V4 representation being neurally synchronized with a dlPFC representation and a V2 representation in such a way that the latter two are not synchronized. But these occurrences are bound to be relatively infrequent, and most of the time whenever a higher-order representation is synchronized with a first-order representation it will also be synchronized with other first-order representations synchronized with the latter. Ideally, we would ultimately obtain an experimental verdict on which of the two views makes the correct predictions regarding what shows up in the phenomenology.

Comparison to Similar Hypotheses

There is one NCC hypothesis that is quite similar to this COI hypothesis. It is the hypothesis that the correlate of visual consciousness (or at least a major component thereof) is synchronized activity in the visual cortex with projections to the prefrontal cortex. This hypothesis was put forward both by some proponents of Global Workspace theory (e.g., Dehaene et al. 2003) and, on occasion, by Crick and Koch (1995, 2003). It features all the same ingredients as the COI hypothesis for visual consciousness: visual cortex, prefrontal cortex, synchrony. There are nonetheless two important related differences between this hypothesis and the COI hypothesis. The first is that this hypothesis refers to our visual cortex, prefrontal cortex, and synchrony as only *part* of the story about the NCC. The second is that only the COI hypothesis explains *why* it is that these areas are implicated in the NCC—namely, that these areas are implicated in aspects of cross-order integration. The two differences are related: given that the COI hypothesis appeals to prefrontal cortex activity and synchronization in order to recover what it takes to be the ontological and phenomenological marks of consciousness, as identified in previous chapters, once these marks are recovered there is no need to postulate any *further* elements in the NCC.

There is one NCC hypothesis that shares the present conception of the nature of consciousness as involving a peculiar fusion of world-awareness and self-awareness, but it designates a different underlying neural substrate. This is Hans Flohr's hypothesis, which designates the binding of neural assemblies by NMDA as the NCC. The hypothesis is very unlike the COI one, but, interestingly, it is inspired by a very similar macro-level view of consciousness. Of a system deploying NMDA for the binding of neural assemblies, Flohr (1995: 160) writes: "The system can bind diverse first- and higher-order representations, embed first-order representations in a model of itself and thereby represent itself as an actually representing system." In other words, the reason *why* NMDA-bound neural assemblies should underlie consciousness, according to Flohr, is that such assemblies will recover the distinguishing mark of consciousness, which Flohr evidently takes to be the ability of a system to represent while representing itself to represent—precisely the COI-theoretical perspective on the matter.

Tests and Testability

The concrete hypothesis that, say, color consciousness involves synchronized V4 and dlPFC activity is straightforwardly testable. If an experimental condition could be created in which a subject reports on a color experience despite lack of either (i) V4 activity, (ii) dlPFC activity, or (iii) synchronization of the two, then the hypothesis will have been falsified.

In search of such falsification, a natural place to start is lesion studies. If color consciousness survives lesion in V4 or the dlPFC, that would be evidence against the hypothesis. In fact, such lesion evidence exists for the parallel hypothesis in which the ACC is hypothesized to subserve higher-order representation. For subjects who have undergone cingulatomy are still conscious.

There is a methodological danger in using lesion studies exclusively, however (Chalmers 2000). It is well known that some functions subserved by one brain area in normal subjects can be subserved by another after lesion. Thus a possible interpretation of post-cingulatomy consciousness may well be that, although the ACC performs monitoring functions in healthy subjects, the functions are recovered by another brain area if the ACC is incapacitated.

A safer method for testing the present hypothesis may be using Transcranial Magnetic Stimulation (TMS) to inhibit activity in the dlPFC. If consciousness is no longer reported when dlPFC activity is sufficiently inhibited, that would constitute evidence in favor of the concrete hypothesis.[28]

It is important to keep in mind, however, the distinction between the concrete hypothesis sketched here and the self-representational approach to the NCC in general. If it is shown that consciousness remains unaltered despite inhibition of dlPFC activity, this would falsify the concrete hypothesis, but not the self-representational approach just yet. One interpretation of that result open to the self-representationalist would be that she was simply wrong to designate the dlPFC as the seat of higher-order representation. Another interpretation open to the COI theorist would be that the dlPFC is not the *only* seat of higher-order representations, and, when it is incapacitated, another brain area can still produce such representations.

These considerations illustrate the way in which self-representationalism is more loosely connected to the empirical evidence than the concrete hypothesis offered in the previous subsection. Evidence that might falsify the concrete hypothesis would not automatically falsify self-representationalism, since the latter is compatible with a number of different concrete hypotheses. We have focused on the one that takes higher-order representation to be grounded in the dlPFC and functional integration to be effected by neural synchronization, but other views about the neural correlates of higher-order representation and cognitive unity would result in other self-representational NCC hypotheses.

Nonetheless, the self-representational approach to the NCC ought to be falsifiable. It is compatible with a number of different concrete hypotheses,

---

[28] This would probably not work for testing the hypothesis that adverts to the ACC rather than the dlPFC, because the ACC is too deep inside the skull to be reliably incapacitated by TMS.

yes, but only a comparatively limited number. If all these were falsified, self-representationalism about the NCC would be thereby falsified as well. To falsify all these hypotheses would be to show that consciousness survives lack of activity in any area plausibly construed as responsible for higher-order representation or that it survives lack of any processes plausibly construed as underlying cross-order integration.

Interestingly, the self-representational approach to the NCC may also be empirically distinguished from a higher-order approach. According to the latter, although conscious states are targeted by higher-order represent-ations, and may well be integrated therewith, it is not part of what makes them conscious that they are so integrated. If so, consciousness should be present even in the absence of any functional integration of first- and higher-order representations. Thus higher-order theories would predict that there is not always synchronization of the first- and higher-order representations involved in a conscious experience, whereas self-representationalism pre-dicts that there is.[29] A higher-order theorist could, of course, incorporate into her theory the extra claim that functional integration of first- and higher-order representations is a necessary condition for consciousness. Such a modified higher-order theory would *not* be empirically distin-guishable from self-representationalism—not with the tools explored here, at any rate. But it is interesting to note that the necessity of functional integration *falls out of* self-representationalism, whereas it is merely *added on* to this modified higher-order theory.[30]

In summary, I have attempted to use the ontological account of the structure of consciousness from Chapter 6, as well as the phenomenological account from Chapter 5, to illustrate a way of giving self-representationalism

[29] This would not actually be the case for a higher-order theorist according to whom neural synchronization is precisely what makes the higher-order representation *represent* the lower-order one. However, such a view of neural synchronization is no part of standard higher-order theories and is anyway implausible.

[30] It has been pressed on me by both Rocco Gennaro and Bill Lycan that this is not really an *addition* to higher-order theory, but something it is very natural for the higher-order theorist to hold. I take both to be excellent trackers of what is natural for a higher-order theorist to maintain, so I hesitate to insist on the point. Nonetheless, I find it difficult to see in what way it is more natural for a higher-order theorist to impose a functional integration condition than not to impose one. It is perhaps more natural to impose the condition that the first-order representation causes the higher-representation of it than not to impose it (though I note that Rosenthal (1990) curiously comes close to imposing the condition that the first-order representation *not* cause the higher-order one). But such a one-way causal relation falls short of functional integration or cognitive unity. Something much stronger seems needed for the latter.

empirical flesh. It is an important theoretical virtue of a philosophical account of consciousness, in my view, that it can generate a relatively precise hypothesis about the neural correlate of consciousness. In this section I have attempted to show that self-representationalism exhibits this virtue. In the next section I will argue that it also delivers a relatively precise account of the function of consciousness, thus addressing the other major scientific issue surrounding consciousness.

2. The Function of Consciousness

The functional role of a mental state depends on how the state is. The picture is this: a state M has various properties, $F_1, \ldots, F_n$, and each property F_i contributes *something* to (or modifies *somehow*) M's fund of causal powers. One of the properties that some mental states have and some do not is the property of being phenomenally conscious. We should expect this property to contribute something to the fund of causal powers of the mental states that instantiate it, epiphenomenalism notwithstanding. The specific contribution that consciousness makes to any conscious state's fund of causal powers is the functional role of consciousness.

The full functional role of consciousness covers everything consciousness does. But it is important to distinguish what consciousness *does* from what consciousness is *for*. Plausibly, some of what consciousness does is what it is for—that is, what it is *supposed* to do—but some of what it does goes beyond what it is for. We may think of this distinction in evolutionary terms: it is possible that some contributions that consciousness makes to a conscious state's fund of causal powers enhance the subject's reproductive prospects, whereas some do not. The latter would also be part of what consciousness does, but they would not be part of what consciousness is for. Let us call the subset of a conscious state's total functional role that has to do specifically with what it is for (its reproductively enhancing contributions to causal powers) the *teleo-functional role* of consciousness. The phrase "the function of consciousness" is often used to pick out the teleo-functional role of consciousness, and this is how I will use it here.[31]

---

[31] Some may deny that there is any meaningful distinction to draw between teleo-functional role and functional role that is not "teleo," perhaps on the general grounds that everything anything does

As I have stressed in a number of places in this book, it is implausible to suppose that consciousness is *nothing but* its function. In other words, a functionalist account of consciousness is implausible.[32] But to engage in a search for the function of consciousness is not to subscribe to a functionalist theory of consciousness. It is merely to *unsubscribe* to an epiphenomenalist theory.[33]

Understanding the function of consciousness requires two things. It requires, first, understanding how a subject's having a conscious state disposes her—beneficially, evolutionarily speaking—in ways that having an unconscious mental state does not. That is, it requires that the function of consciousness be correctly *identified*. And it requires, on top of that, understanding what it is about a mental state's being conscious that endows it with this particular function. That is, it requires that the function of consciousness be correctly *explained*, so that we see *why* consciousness has just the function it does. This latter requirement is of the first importance. Our conception of consciousness must make it possible for us to see what it is about consciousness that yields the kinds of dispositions associated with conscious states and not with unconscious states. It must allow us not only to *identify* the function of consciousness, but also to *explain* it.

If consciousness were nothing more than a bundle of dispositions, as per functionalism about consciousness, there would be no question as to why consciousness is associated with just those dispositions. Consciousness would just *be* those dispositions. But because consciousness is *more* than a bundle of dispositions—because it is the *categorical basis* of those dispositions—there

is part of what it is for. I do not wish to take a substantive position on this matter. If there is no such distinction to draw, then the functional role and teleo-functional role of consciousness coincide, and an account of one is *eo ipso* an account of the other.

[32] As I have noted in several places (including in Chapters 2, 4, and 6), a principled problem for functionalism is that functional role is a *dispositional* notion, whereas consciousness is *manifest*. There may be *some* mental properties or states that are plausibly construed as *nothing but* bundles of dispositions. A subject's tacit belief that there are birds in China is plausibly identified with a set of dispositions; there appears to be no need to posit a concrete item that *underlies* those dispositions. This is because nothing needs *actually to happen* with a subject who tacitly believes that there are birds in China. But many mental states are not like that. A subject's conscious experience of the blue sky is more than a set of dispositions. Here there *is* a concrete item that underlies the relevant dispositions. Something does *actually happen* with a subject when she has the experience. In virtue of having a conscious experience of the blue sky, the subject is disposed to do (or undergo) certain things. But there is more to the subject's having the conscious experience than her being so disposed. Indeed, it is precisely *because* the subject has her experience that she is disposed the way she is. The experience is the *reason* for the disposition; it is its *categorical basis*.

[33] The reasons to do so will be discussed toward the end of the next chapter.

are two separate questions that arise in relation to its function: What does consciousness do?, and Why is *that* what consciousness does? The latter arises because, when we claim that consciousness underlies certain dispositions, we assume that there is a reason why these are the dispositions it underlies. The matter can hardly be completely arbitrary, a fluke of nature. So, unless functionalism about consciousness is embraced, both questions must be answered. Conversely, functionalism about consciousness necessarily fails to explain *why* consciousness has the function it does, and is to that extent unsatisfactory.[34] A more satisfactory account of consciousness would meet both our theoretical requirements: it would both *identify* and *explain* the function of consciousness. Let us call the former the *identification requirement* and the latter the *explanation requirement*.

To these, let us add a third requirement. When discussing the teleo-functional role of consciousness, it is important to distinguish the role of conscious states from the role of consciousness proper. As noted, the causal powers of mental states are determined by these states' properties; each property a mental state instantiates contributes something to the state's fund of causal powers. Clearly, then, some of the causal powers of a conscious state are contributed to it not by its property of being conscious, but by its other properties. They are powers the state has, but not in virtue of being conscious. It would have them even if it were not conscious. It is important that we distinguish between the causal powers that a conscious state has and the causal powers it has precisely because it is conscious. Let us refer to the latter as the causal powers of consciousness *proper*. These are the powers contributed to a conscious state specifically by its property of being conscious.

Consider a subject's conscious perception of the words "terror alert" in the newspaper. Such a conscious experience is likely to raise the subject's level of anxiety. But it is unclear that the rise is due to the fact that the

---

[34] It may be thought surprising that a view that does not only ascribe a function to consciousness but also claims that this function is *constitutive* of consciousness would be explanatorily worse off (with respect to explaining the function of consciousness) than a view that does only the former. But functionalism about consciousness claims not only that the function of consciousness is constitutive of consciousness, but in addition that *nothing else is*, with the result that there is nothing more to consciousness than the function. The task of explaining why consciousness is associated with this function then becomes the task of explaining an identity, and arguably identities are brute and unexplainable. (When it seems as though we have an explanation of an identity before us, typically we only have an explanation of co-reference—of why two expressions pick out the same thing, but, obviously, not why that thing is identical to itself.)

subject's perception is conscious. Indeed, data on the effects of *subliminal* perception on emotion suggest that an unconscious perception of the same stimulus would also raise the subject's level of anxiety.[35] This suggests that, while the subject's perception of the words "terror alert" has the causal powers to increase anxiety, it is not in virtue of being conscious that it has those powers. The conscious perception's power to increase anxiety is not a function of consciousness *proper*.

An account of the functional role of consciousness must target the causal powers of consciousness proper. It must distill the singular contribution of consciousness itself to the fund of causal powers of conscious states. This constitutes a third requirement on an adequate account of the teleo-functional role of consciousness; call it the *singularity requirement*.

In the remainder of this section I lay out a self-representational treatment of the function of consciousness, and attempt to show that it meets all three requirements. The key to the self-representational treatment is this: the mark of consciousness is (normally) peripheral inner awareness. To understand the function of consciousness proper, then, we must understand the function of peripheral inner awareness. To that end, I proceed in two steps. First I sketch an account of the function of peripheral *outer* awareness, then I extend it to peripheral *inner* awareness in a suitably modified way.

The Function of Peripheral Outer Awareness

Let us start with a well-understood form of peripheral awareness: peripheral vision. The fact that our visual system employs peripheral awareness cannot be a brute, arbitrary fact. There must be reasons for it. What are they?[36]

Our cognitive system handles an inordinate amount of information. The flow of stimulation facing it is too torrential to take in indiscriminately. The system must thus develop strategies for managing the flux of incoming

---

[35] For very concrete effects of subliminal perception on anxiety, see Silverman et al. 1978. For more general discussion of subliminal perception and its functional significance, see Dixon 1971. Another well-known form of unconscious perception, which retains some of the causal powers of conscious perception, is blindsight (see Weiskrantz 1986). Unless the function of consciousness is implausibly duplicated, such that another mechanism has exactly the function consciousness has, any function a blindsighted subject can execute in response to her blindsighted perceptions must thereby not be part of the function of consciousness proper.

[36] The functional analysis of peripheral awareness that I will develop in this subsection owes much to the work of Bruce Mangan (1993, 2001).

information. The mechanism that mediates this management task is, in effect, what we refer to as *attention*.[37] There are many possible strategies the cognitive system could adopt—many ways the attention mechanism could be designed—and only some of them make place for peripheral visual awareness.

Suppose a subject faces a scene with five distinct visual stimuli: A, B, C, D, and E. The subject's attention must somehow be distributed among these stimuli. At the two extremes are the following two strategies. One would have the subject distribute her attention evenly among the five stimuli, so that each stimulus is (as it were) granted 20 percent of the subject's overall attention resources; let us call this the "20/20 strategy." The other would have the subject devote the entirety of her attention resources to a single stimulus to the exclusion of all others, in which case the relevant stimulus, say C, would be granted 100 percent of the subject's attention resources, while A, B, D, and E would be granted 0 percent; let us call this the "100/0 strategy." In between these two extremes are any number of more flexible strategies. Consider only the following three: (i) the "60/10 strategy," in which C is granted 60 percent of the resources and A, B, D, and E are granted 10 percent each; (ii) the "28/18 strategy," in which C is granted 28 percent of the resources and A, B, D, and E are granted 18 percent each; (iii) the "35/10 strategy," in which two different stimuli, say C and D, are granted 35 percent of the resources each, while A, B, and E are granted 10 percent each.

As a matter of contingent fact, the strategy our visual system actually employs seems to be something along the lines of the 60/10 strategy. This strategy has three key features: it allows for only one center of attention; the attention it grants to the elements *outside* that focal center is more or less equal; and it grants considerably more attention to the center than to the various elements in the periphery. When I look at the laptop before me, my visual experience has only one center of attention, namely the laptop; it grants more or less equal attention to the (say) two elements in the periphery, the coffee mug on the right and the bonsai on the left; and the attention it grants to the laptop is considerably greater than that it grants to the mug and the bonsai.

---

[37] At least this conception of attention has been widely accepted since Broadbent's seminal work (1958) on attention. See also Moray 1969.

Each of the other models misrepresents one feature or another of such an ordinary experience. The 20/20 strategy implies that my awareness of the mug and the bonsai is just as focused as my awareness of the laptop before me, which is patently false. The 100/0 strategy implies that I am completely unaware of the mug and bonsai, which is again false.[38] The 28/18 strategy misrepresents the contrast between my awareness of the laptop and my awareness of the mug and bonsai: the real contrast in awareness is much sharper than suggested. And the 35/10 strategy wrongly implies that my visual experience has two separate focal centers.[39, 40] (There may be highly abnormal experiences that one of the other strategies describes better, but normal experiences are clearly unlike that. Normal experiences are subject to the 60/10 strategy.[41])

The above treatment of the possible strategies for managing the information overload facing the visual system (and perforce the cognitive system) is, of course, oversimplifying. But it serves to highlight two important things. First, the existence of peripheral visual awareness is a *contingent* fact. In the 100/0 strategy, for instance, there is no such thing as peripheral awareness: the subject is either focally aware of a stimulus or completely unaware of it.[42] In a way, the 20/20 strategy likewise dispenses with

---

[38] I am assuming here that it is impossible to be aware of something when 0% of one's attention resources are dedicated to it. Awareness requires some minimal attention, though not focal attention.

[39] It may happen that two adjacent stimuli form part of a single center of focus for the subject, but this situation is not a case in which the experience has two independent focal centers. To make sure that the example in the text brings the point across, we may stipulate that A, B, C, D, and E are so distant from each other that no two of them could form part of a larger, compound stimulus that would be the focal center of attention.

[40] There are other possible strategies that would misrepresent other features of normal experience. Consider the strategy that grants 60% of attention to C, 2% of attention to A, 8% to B, 8% to D, and 22% to E. It violates the principle that all elements in the periphery are more or less granted equal attention, which is a feature of the 60/10 strategy. We need not—should not—require that the amount of attention granted to all peripheral elements would be exactly identical, of course, but the variations seem to be rather small—again, as a matter of contingent fact.

[41] For example, there might be a visual experience in which there are two independent centers of attention—say, one at 36 degrees on the right side of the subject's visual field and one at 15 degrees on the left side of the visual field.

[42] There are actually real-world conditions under which peripheral visual awareness is extinguished. When a subject comes close to passing out, for instance, more and more of her peripheral visual field goes dark, starting at the very edge and drawing nearer the center. The moment before passing out, the subject remains aware only of foveated stimuli (i.e. stimuli presented in foveal vision), while her entire peripheral visual field lies in darkness. It appears that the system, being under duress, cannot afford to expend any resources whatsoever on peripheral awareness. The presence of peripheral awareness is the norm, then, but hardly a necessity.

peripheral awareness, as it admits no distinction between focal center and periphery.[43]

Only the three other strategies we considered make place for peripheral awareness. Secondly, if the 60/10 strategy (or something like it) has won the day over the other possible candidates, there must be a reason for that. The 60/10 strategy has apparently been selected for, through evolution (and perhaps also learning), and this suggests that there must be some functional advantages to it.[44]

What are these advantages? It is impossible to answer this question without engaging in all-out speculation.[45] It does seem, however, that the distribution of attention resources in the 60/10 strategy accomplishes two things. First, with regard to the stimuli at the attentional periphery, it provides the subject with just enough information to know where to get more information. And, secondly, by keeping the amount of information about the periphery to the minimum needed for knowing where to get more information, it leaves enough resources for the center of attention to provide the subject with rich and detailed information about the salient stimulus.

My hypothesis is that the teleo-functional role of peripheral visual awareness is to give the subject "leads" as to how to obtain more detailed information about any of the peripheral stimuli, without encumbering the system overmuch (see Mangan 1993, 2001). By doing so, peripheral awareness enhances the *availability* of rich and detailed information about those stimuli. Peripheral visual awareness thus serves as a *gateway*, as it were, to *focal* visual awareness: it smoothes out—facilitates—the process of assuming focal awareness of a stimulus.

Consider the subject's position with regard to stimulus E, of which she is peripherally aware, and an object F, of which she is completely unaware. If the subject suddenly requires fuller information about E, she

[43] Although we might understand the notion of peripheral awareness in such a way that the 20/20 strategy entails that all (or at any rate most) awareness is peripheral. I think this would be a mistake, but let us not dwell on this issue. The possibility of the 100/0 strategy is sufficient to establish that there is no deep necessity in the existence of peripheral awareness.

[44] It does not matter for our purposes whether the 60/10 strategy is based in a mechanism that is cognitive in nature or biologically hardwired. It is probably a little bit of both, but in any event the mechanism—whether cognitive, biological, or mixed—has been selected for, because of its adaptational value.

[45] But then again, almost all psychological explanations in terms of evolutionary function are deeply speculative.

can readily obtain it simply by turning her attention onto it. That is, the subject already possesses enough information about E to be able quickly and (almost) effortlessly to obtain more information about it. By contrast, if she is in need of information about F, she has to engage in a "search" of some sort after the information needed. Her current visual experience offers her no leads as to where she might find the information she needs about F. (Such leads may be present in memory, or could be extracted by reasoning, but they are not to be found in the subject's visual awareness itself.) Peripheral awareness of a stimulus thus allows the subject to spend much less energy and time to become focally aware of the stimulus and obtain detailed information about it. It makes that information much more available to, and usable by, the subject, while at the same time leaving large attention resources to one central stimulus.

The Function of Peripheral Inner Awareness

The hypothesis delineated above, concerning the functional significance of peripheral visual awareness, suggests a simple extension to the case of peripheral *inner* awareness. The subject's peripheral awareness of her ongoing experience makes detailed information about the experience much more available to the subject than it would otherwise be. More specifically, it gives the subject just enough information about her current experience to know how to get more information quickly and effortlessly, should the need arise.

More accurately stated, the suggestion is that when, and only when, a subject S is peripherally aware of M, S possesses just enough information about M to put S in a position easily (that is, quickly and effortlessly) to obtain fuller information about M. Compare the subject's position with regard to some unconscious state of hers, a state of which she is completely unaware. If the subject should happen to need detailed information about that unconscious state, she would have to engage in much more energy- and time-consuming activities to obtain that information.[46]

---

[46] It is important to stress that the information provided by peripheral inner awareness concerns the experience itself, not the *objects* of the experience. Consider again my laptop experience. According to self-representationalism, in having my experience, I am focally aware of the laptop and peripherally aware of at least three things: the coffee mug, the bonsai, and my very experience of all this. My peripheral awareness of the mug provides me with just enough information about the mug to know how to get more information about it. My peripheral awareness of having the experience provides me

According to self-representationalism, peripheral inner awareness is a constant element in the fringe of ongoing, ordinary, non-introspective consciousness: we are at least minimally aware of our ongoing experience throughout our waking life. This continuous awareness we have of our experience multiplies the functional significance of the awareness. The fact that at every moment of our waking life we have just enough information about our current experience to get as much further information as we should need means that our ongoing experience is an "open source" of information for all other modules and local mechanisms in the cognitive system. This may be the basis for the notion that consciousness makes information globally available throughout the system. Baars (1988) puts it in what I think is a misleading way when he says that consciousness "broadcasts" information through the whole system; I would put it the other way around, saying that consciousness "invites" the whole system to grab that information.[47]

This account explains the function of peripheral inner awareness in terms of a gateway to focal inner awareness. Such an account illuminates the function of peripheral inner awareness only on the assumption that there is a function to *focal* inner awareness—that is, to introspection. But I think it is not hard to see that focal inner awareness, or introspection, is a good thing to have. Focal awareness provides one with rich and detailed information about the attended. Having rich and detailed information about one's ongoing mental life is beneficial in a variety of ways, such as detecting malfunction in the processes of information gathering, processing and integrating disparate bits of information into a coherent whole, and so on. What these various benefits have in common is that they involve an understanding of the difference between appearance and reality—that is, an understanding that there may always be a gap between how things are in themselves and how one represents them to be. A creature with this kind of understanding is bound to be more reflective and more careful. When certain situations consistently result in frustration of its needs or

---

with just enough information to know how to get more information not about the laptop or mug, but about the very *experiencing* of the laptop and mug.

[47] The contrast here is between consciousness making the relevant information globally available actively and its making it available passively, in some sense of these central terms. I endorse the passive model.

desires, it will be more likely to recognize that something has been going wrong in how it deals with those situations, to re-examine that way of dealing, and to seek alternatives to it. To the extent that consciousness is a gateway to such understanding and such capacities, it enhances the system's ability to engage in the activities that might solve problems of this sort.

I started this subsection by imposing three constraints on an adequate account of the function of consciousness: identification, explanation, and singularity. The account I have defended offers the following answer to the question of identification: the function of consciousness proper is to give the subject just enough information to know how quickly and effortlessly to obtain fuller information about her concurrent experience.

The answer to the question of explanation is a little more complicated, but should be clear by now. The reason consciousness has just this function is that an ordinary, non-introspective conscious state's being conscious is essentially a matter of the subject's peripheral inner awareness of it, and peripheral inner awareness involves just this function. The reason peripheral inner awareness involves just this function is that it is a form of peripheral awareness, and this is the kind of function peripheral awareness has in general. And the reason peripheral awareness has just this kind of function in general is that this is the cognitive system's best strategy for dealing with the information overload it faces.

Thus this model explains both why there is such a thing as peripheral inner awareness and why peripheral inner awareness plays the functional role of giving the subject just enough information about her ongoing experience to be able easily to obtain fuller information. The key point is that providing the subject with just this sort of information is not what consciousness *is*, but what consciousness *does*. What consciousness *is* (in the non-introspective case) is peripheral inner awareness—that is, peripheral awareness of one's concurrent experience. So in this account consciousness is not *identified* with the providing of the information, but is rather the *categorical basis* for it.

Finally, the account also appears to meet the singularity requirement. Since only conscious states involve normally peripheral inner awareness, and since their subjective character—which, I suggested in Chapter 1, constitutes the existence condition of phenomenality—*consists* in this normally peripheral inner awareness, this account singles out the function of consciousness proper.[48]

In summary, the account of the functional role of consciousness proposed here features three central tenets:

1. A mental state M is conscious normally when the subject is peripherally aware of M.
2. The function of consciousness is to give the subject just enough information to know how quickly and effortlessly to obtain rich and detailed information about her concurrent experience.
3. The reason this is the function of consciousness is that the cognitive system's strategy for dealing with information overload employs peripheral awareness, a variety of which is peripheral inner awareness (hence normal consciousness), and the function of peripheral awareness in general is to give the subject just enough information to know how easily to get fuller information about whatever the subject is thereby aware of.

The three tenets satisfy our three requirements on an account of the function of consciousness: (1) is intended to meet the singularity requirement; (2) is intended to meet the identification requirement; (3) is intended to meet the explanation requirement.

Libet's Findings Revisited

Let me close with discussion of one of the most interesting empirical findings about the function of consciousness. Libet (1985) instructed his subjects to flex their right hand muscle and pay attention when their intention to flex the muscle is formed, with the goal of finding out the temporal relationship between (i) muscle activation, (ii) onset of the neurological cause of muscle activation, and (iii) the conscious intention to flex one's muscle. Libet found that the neurological cause of muscle activation precedes conscious intention to flex the muscle by about 350 ms

---

[48] It might be objected that the sort of teleo-functional role attributed to consciousness in this chapter could in principle be performed by an unconscious mechanism, and that this would defy the singularity requirement. This objection would be misguided. The singularity requirement is intended to rule out functions that conscious states have, but not *in virtue* of being conscious. It is not intended to rule out functions that unconscious states could also have but do not in fact have.

and the muscle activation itself by 550 ms. That is, the conscious intention to flex one's muscle is formed when the causal process leading to the muscle activation is already well underway. This suggests that consciousness proper does not have the function of initiating the causal process leading to the muscle activation, and is therefore not the cause of the intended act. According to Libet, the only thing consciousness can do is undercut the causal process at its final stages. That is, the only role consciousness has is that of "vetoing" the production of the act or allowing it to go through.

Self-representationalism can be used to shed some light on this perplexing result, for it holds that conscious states are states we are aware of having. This means that a mental state must exist for some time before it becomes conscious, since the *awareness* of the state in question necessarily takes some time to form. Now, it is only to be expected that the state in question should be able to perform at least some of its functions before it becomes conscious. In many processes, the state can readily play a causal role independently of the subject's awareness of it. So it is unsurprising that consciousness proper should have a small role to play in such processes (see Rosenthal 2002c).

What would be surprising is for consciousness to play that limited role in *all* or *most* cognitive processes. But this cannot be established by Libet's experiment. One overlooked factor in Libet's experiment is the functional role of the subjects' conscious intention to follow the experimenter's instructions (Flanagan 1992). This introduces two limitations on Libet's findings. First, we do not know what the causal role of the conscious intention to follow the experimenter's instructions is in the production of muscle activation. Secondly, we do not know what causal role a conscious intention to flex one's muscle plays when it is *not* preceded by a conscious intention to follow certain instructions related to flexing one's muscle. Given that the majority of instances of muscle-flexing involve a single conscious intention (rather than a succession of two), we do not as yet know what the functional role of conscious intention to flex one's muscle is in the majority of instances.

In any case, observe that Libet's findings bear only on the role of consciousness vis-à-vis motor output. This is important, because internal states of the cognitive system can bring about not only motor output, but also further internal states.[49] On the account of the function of consciousness defended here, the latter is more central to the teleo-functional role of conscious states. The fact that a subject is peripherally aware of her mental states plays a role in bringing about states of focal inner awareness, and more generally a role in the operation of internal monitoring processes. These are not motor outputs but further internal states.

In conclusion, in this section I have sketched a self-representational treatment of the function of consciousness.[50] According to the account, when a mental state M is conscious, its subject has just enough information about M to be able easily to obtain fuller information about it. The account thus identifies a very specific function, which it claims characterizes the singular contribution of consciousness to the fund of causal powers of conscious states, and embeds this identification in a larger explanatory account of the purpose and operation of attention. What I would like to stress is this: the fact that a clear and precise account of the functional significance of consciousness follows rather straightforwardly from the tenets of self-representationalism is testimony to the theoretical force of the latter.

3. Conclusion

In this chapter, I have attempted to show that self-representationalism delivers relatively precise answers to the two big scientific questions surrounding consciousness, the question of the neural correlate of consciousness and the question of the function of consciousness. Take a visual experience of the blue sky. On the accounts I have offered, the neural correlate of this experience is given by synchronized brain activity in the visual cortex and (probably) the dorsolateral prefrontal cortex, and the function the experience has in virtue of being conscious is to give the subject just enough

---

[49] Thus, a thought that it is raining can play a causal role in taking an umbrella, which is a motor output, but it can also play a causal role in producing the thought that it has been raining for the past week, which is not a motor output but a further internal state.

[50] The treatment is grounded in empirical considerations but is quite speculative, in that it depends on a number of unargued-for assumptions. As such, it is a "risky" account, an account whose plausibility may be undermined at several junctures. At the same time, none of the assumptions made above is flagrantly implausible. So at the very least, the account of the functional role of consciousness here defended offers a viable alternative to the accounts currently on offer in the literature on consciousness. And, in any case, it shows that self-representationalism has something to say about the matter.

information about itself for the subject to know how quickly and easily to obtain much more information.

Once the neural correlate of consciousness is identified, the question arises whether it is *merely* a correlate, or also a *reducer*, of consciousness. The question is whether consciousness not only correlates, but in fact is *nothing but*, the neural structure or process identified as its correlate. The next chapter takes up this question.[51]

[51] For comments on a previous draft of this chapter I would like to thank Bill Lycan, Ken Williford, and an anonymous referee. For comments on or discussion of materials from this chapter, I thank Frances Balcomb, Marie Banich, Tim Bayne, David Chalmers, Ilya Farber, Rocco Gennaro, George Graham, J. Alan Hobson, Hakwan Lau, Jesse Prinz, Antti Revonsuo, Cybele Tom, and Logan Trujillo.

8

Self-Representationalism and the Reduction of Consciousness

In the previous chapter, I suggested, a little coyly, that the neural correlate of consciousness is neural synchronization with above-baseline activation of the dorsolateral prefrontal cortex. A physicalist theory of consciousness would want to argue that this physical property—synchronization with dlPFC activation—is not *merely* a neural correlate of consciousness, but also a neural *reducer* of consciousness. In this chapter I argue in favor of this further claim.

Many philosophers struggling with the problem of consciousness feel a tension between two pulls. On the one hand, they have a strong pull toward physicalism, which I will understand here as the thesis that (i) all particulars are physical and (ii) all properties are metaphysically supervenient upon physical properties. On the other hand, they also feel a strong pull to acknowledge that the case of consciousness is special and unrepeated in nature—and that consciousness genuinely presents a special problem for a thoroughgoing physicalism. Thus they wish to embrace a metaphysical picture of the world that both grants consciousness a special status and is thoroughly physicalist.

The general discomfort in the community of philosophers of consciousness seems to arise from the fact that treatments of the problem of consciousness have tended to yield to one of these two pulls at the expense of the other. On the one hand, there is discomfort with approaches that, while successful in securing a special status for consciousness, end up casting consciousness not only as *prima facie* mysterious but as *ultima facie* mysterious, and in the end render consciousness physically irreducible. On the other hand, there is also dissatisfaction with approaches that, while successful in securing the ultimate physicalization of consciousness, end up handling the case of consciousness as on a par with the case of (say) water, and in the end cast the philosophic anxiety surrounding consciousness as resting on some kind of confusion. Although there are certainly explicit defenses of these two extremes, I think the community as a whole is driven by a desire to avoid them: a desire to cast consciousness as ultimately a physical phenomenon, but one with unusual features that produce a genuine and well-founded conundrum.

The purpose of this chapter is to make the case that the self-representational theory has the resources to deliver this result. I open, in Section 1, by introducing the special challenges to the reduction of consciousness captured in the notions of the *explanatory gap* and the *hard problem*. In Section 2 I consider two leading accounts of reduction, and adopt the more demanding of the two. In Section 3 I consider the case for the irreducibility of consciousness based on that account of reduction. I then argue, in Section 4, that consciousness is reducible after all, even against the background of this demanding account of reduction, and that self-representationalism helps us see how this could be.

Before starting, a word on the term "reduction." This is by and large a theoretical term, and there could be many different notions of reduction. In what follows, I will be concerned only with the notion of reduction that is deemed necessary for a genuinely physicalist picture of the world. I point this out because there are also notions of reduction that are *not* deemed necessary for physicalism. Consider the well-known varieties of so-called non-reductive physicalism. Following Putnam's multiple realizability argument (1967), many philosophers have adopted the view that mental properties are not strictly *identical* to physical properties, but that this is entirely compatible with a genuinely physicalist picture of the world.[1] These philosophers called their view "non-reductive physicalism," implying that there is a kind of reduction lack of which does not undermine physicalism. More recently, other arguments (for example, the "zombie argument") have been discussed in the philosophy of mind, having to do not with mental properties in

---

[1] Putnam argued that mental properties are multiply realizable, in the sense that, while the property of (say) believing that p is realized in humans by neural substrate, it may well be realized by metaphysically possible Venutians in silicon substrate. This means that the property of believing that p cannot be identified with the relevant neural property in us and with the relevant silicon property in them, because that would entail (by transitivity of identity) that the neural property is identical to the silicon property, when *ex hypothesi* it is not. (The argument can also be run with *different* neural properties, but comes through more vividly when we consider neural and silicon properties.)

general but with phenomenal consciousness very specifically, that have attempted to show that consciousness is irreducible in a way *incompatible* with physicalism. The notion of reduction at play in these more recent arguments must therefore be different from the notion of reduction at play in the arguments that inspired non-reductive physicalism. The metaphysical difference between the two notions is this: the notion of reduction lack of which is deemed compatible with physicalism is that of reduction *as identification*; the notion of reduction lack of which is deemed incompatible with physicalism is that of reduction *as metaphysical supervenience*. There is daylight between the two, because there could be properties F and G, such that F ≠ G but F metaphysically supervenes upon G.[2] Thus the multiple realizability argument purports to undermine the identification of mental properties with physical properties, but does not threaten the metaphysical supervenience of the former upon the latter. The more recent arguments I have in mind do purport to undermine metaphysical supervenience as well. In this chapter I am concerned only with the notion of reduction as metaphysical supervenience. This is the notion of reduction that is necessary for physicalization (where "to physicalize" means "to make compatible with physicalism"). Any other, more demanding notions of reduction, which are not necessary for physicalization, will not concern me here.

1. The Explanatory Gap and the Hard Problem

In our world, water is H_2O and heat is mean molecular energy. For reasons we will not go into here, and that have to do with the way terms such as "water" and "heat" are thought to behave, it is thought to follow that *in every world* water is H_2O and heat is mean molecular energy.[3] And this seems to mean that water is *nothing but* H_2O and heat is *nothing but* mean molecular energy—that water *reduces* to H_2O and heat to mean molecular energy.

---

[2] For example, the properties of being scarlet and being red are like that: they are non-identical, but the former metaphysically supervenes upon the latter. These are sometimes thought of as determinate–determinable relations.

[3] This has to do with the fact that these terms, as well as the terms "H_2O" and "mean molecular energy," are natural kind terms, and therefore are rigid designators—they pick out the same kind property in every possible world.

In our world, I suggested in the previous chapter, consciousness is neural synchronization with above-baseline dlPFC activation, at least if we use the "is" of predication (or perhaps even constitution) rather than the "is" of identification. The term "consciousness" behaves as "water" and "heat" do, so it should follow that in every world consciousness is neural synchronization with dlPFC activation, and therefore that consciousness is *nothing but*—that is, *reduces to*—neural synchronization with dlPFC activation.

Many philosophers have felt that the cases are disanalogous, however. Nagel (1974) has already observed that, much less than being in a position to verify such a statement, we are not even in a position properly to understand it. Although we can *say* the words "consciousness is nothing but such-and-such neural property," we cannot really wrap our minds around what they might mean. Perhaps the idea is that, for us, the concepts of consciousness and of a neural feature are so different that we cannot genuinely contemplate the possibility that they might pick out the same property. Compare the statement "justice is nothing but cement mixed with wood fiber." Even if an experimentally robust and exceptionless correlation emerged between justice and cement mixed with wood fiber, such that the former was present where and only where the latter was, we could not really wrap our mind around the notion that justice might be *nothing but* cement mixed with wood fiber. The concept of justice just seems to be *too different* from the concept of cement mixed with wood fiber. Likewise, the concept of consciousness seems to be too different from the concept of a neural property to make it intelligible that the two might pick out the same property.

This profound difference is captured well by Levine's notion (1983) of the *explanatory gap*. Even if an oracle appeared and told us that, whenever neural property N is instantiated, so is consciousness, we would still not be able to see *why* that should be the case. The point was made, quite acutely, by the nineteenth-century British mathematician John Tyndall. In an address to the Mathematical and Physical Section of the British Association on 19 August 1868, he said this:

Were our minds and senses so expanded, strengthened, and illuminated as to enable us to see and feel the very molecules of the brain; were we capable of following all their motions, all their groupings, all their electric discharges, if such there be; and were we intimately acquainted with the corresponding states of thought and feeling, we should be as far as ever from the solution to the problem, "How are these physical processes connected with the facts of consciousness?" The chasm between the two classes of phenomena would still remain intellectually impassable.[4]

Tyndall's "explanatory chasm" highlights the fact that, no matter the amount of knowledge we have of the neural machinery underlying conscious experience, we seem incapable of using it to produce an *explanation* of the facts of consciousness. This is clearly disanalogous to the case of water/heat. The facts about the molecular behavior of H_2O, for example, are very useful in helping us explain the macroscopic behavior of water.

In discussing the explanatory gap, it is important to distinguish the gap between phenomenal properties, on the one hand, and two different types of property, on the other. The gap Levine focuses on most is between phenomenal properties and physical-neurophysiological properties. But, in the process of discussing this main gap, another gap arises—namely, between phenomenal properties and functional-cognitive properties. Levine (1983: 357) writes:

[W]e do feel that the causal role of pain is crucial to our concept of it, and that discovering the physical mechanism by which this causal role is effected explains an important facet of what there is to be explained about pain. However, there is more to our concept of pain than its causal role, there is its qualitative character, how it feels; and what is left unexplained by the discovery of c-fiber firing is *why pain should feel the way it does!* For there seems to be nothing about c-fiber firing that makes it "fit" the phenomenal properties of pain, any more than it would fit some other set of phenomenal properties.

From Levine's discussion, it is clear that, although the first gap is perhaps the more important in itself, this second gap is more basic, and underlies the first.

The explanatory gap between consciousness and functional role is targeted more exclusively by the so-called Hard Problem of consciousness (Chalmers 1995a, 1996). Chalmers (1995b: 64) writes:

The critical common trait among [the easy problems of consciousness] is that they all concern how a cognitive or behavioral function is performed...The

---

[4] This is quoted from Tennant, forthcoming. Everything I know about Tyndall I learned from that paper.

hard problem of consciousness, in contrast, goes beyond problems about how functions are performed. Even if every behavioral and cognitive function related to consciousness were explained, there would still remain a further mystery: Why is the performance of these functions accompanied by conscious experience? It is this additional conundrum that makes the hard problem hard.

Thus the easy problems of consciousness concern the way conscious states are involved in discrimination, deliberation, report, and a variety of other cognitive functions. The hard problem concerns why there should be anything it is like for a subject to perform such functions. Just as, with the explanatory gap between consciousness and its neural realizer/correlate, we cannot see *why* the instantiation of a certain neural property would implicate the instantiation of consciousness, so with the hard problem, or the explanatory gap between consciousness and functional/cognitive role, we cannot see *why* the instantiation of a certain functional-role property would implicate the instantiation of consciousness.

In Chapter 1 I suggested that we define "phenomenal consciousness," or at least fix its reference, by appeal to the sense of mystery surrounding consciousness.[5] Thus we might use the following rigidified definite description: "the property F, such that in the actual world, F generates the relevant sense of mystery." I also suggested that it is natural to unpack the sense of mystery in terms of the explanatory gap. But, given the distinction between two kinds of gap, we must note a corresponding distinction between two potential understandings of phenomenal consciousness. According to the first, phenomenal consciousness is something like this: the property F, such that, in the actual world, F appears to resist physical explanation (that is, appears to remain unexplained no matter how much knowledge of physical reality is brought to bear). According to the second, phenomenal consciousness is something like this: the property F, such that, in the actual world, F appears to resist functionalization (that is, appears to involve more than any collection of cognitive functions, however rich). For now, we do not have to worry about which concept of phenomenal consciousness we are using, and can use the term "phenomenal consciousness" to hover loosely over their disjunction. After all, the properties of appearing to resist

---

[5] It is important to stress here that this is not intended as a definition of (or reference-fixer for) the term "consciousness," but only the term "phenomenal consciousness." We could allow that there are several notions of consciousness, and that many are definable (or fixable upon) independently of any sense of mystery.

physical explanation and appearing to resist functionalization are certainly coextensive (in the actual world).

The hard problem (or explanatory gap between consciousness and functional role) is in some ways more surprising than the explanatory gap between consciousness and physical realizers. To see this, consider a certain resemblance between the two and the observation underlying G. E. Moore's (1903b) open-question argument against reductive theories of goodness. Moore observed that for, any property F, whenever we encounter an act *a* that is F, we can still coherently ask whether *a* is good. From this Moore inferred two things. In the first instance, he inferred that the concept of goodness must be simple and unanalyzable; that is, that for no F is it analytically true that F is goodness. In a second step, he inferred that there is no property goodness can be reduced to. The second inference is widely regarded as fallaciously conflating properties and concepts. But the first inference is often accepted as justified: an open question is indeed a good guide for (lack of) analyticity.

The explanatory gaps can also be seen through the prism of an open-question argument.[6] In connection with the first explanatory gap, we can make the following observation: for any neurophysiological property N, we can coherently ask, of a given state S that is N, whether S is conscious. From this we are entitled to infer that consciousness is not neurophysiologically analyzable; that is, that for no neurophysiological N is it analytically true that N is consciousness. This is unsurprising, however, inasmuch as, even for (say) water, we do not expect there to be a chemical property C, such that it is analytically true that C is water. In connection with the second explanatory gap (the hard problem), however, we can make a different and more dramatic observation: that for any functional-role property R, we can coherently ask, of a given state S that is R, whether S is conscious. From this we are entitled to infer that consciousness is not functionally analyzable; that is, that for no functional property R is it analytically true that R is consciousness. This is more surprising, inasmuch as in the case of water we *do* expect there to be some role property for which it is analytic that water is it—for example, the property of being the actual clear, drinkable liquid in the rivers, lakes, and so on. If we were assured that some quantity of matter played in the actual world the (perfectly specified) water role,

---

[6] Both Levine and Chalmers point out something like this.

it would be *incoherent* for us to ask, "But is it water?" By contrast, if we were assured that some mental episode played in the actual world the relevant consciousness role, it would still be coherent to ask "But is it conscious?"

This difference between the hard problem and the explanatory gap underwrites a difference in the intended dialectical force of the two. But, to appreciate this, we must take a closer look at the notions of reduction and reductive explanation.[7]

2. Reduction and Reductive Explanation

How does the scientific reduction of a property F to a property G proceed? There are two main models for this today. I will call them the *deductive model* and the *abductive model*.

According to the deductive model (Lewis 1972, Jackson 1994, 1998, Chalmers 1996, Kim 1998), there are three steps involved in reduction. They can be described very roughly as follows. First, the property up for reduction is "functionalized," meaning that a certain functional profile of it is produced, presumably through specification of its functional role. Second, scientific inquiry seeks a potential reducer property that exhibits just that functional profile. If such a property is found, the third step declares the reduction of the first property to the second.

Consider the case of water and H_2O. On this model, the first step functionalizes water, say by recasting it as the property that in the actual world is a clear drinkable liquid. In a second step, chemistry is fielded to establish that H_2O is the clear drinkable liquid in the actual world. The third step is to declare, on the strength of this, that water is nothing but H_2O.

I call this the deductive model, because it makes possible deduction of facts about the reduced property from facts about the reducer property

---

[7] As we will see later on, for Levine, the explanatory gap—or at least its unbridgeability—is supposed to rule out *reductive explanation* of consciousness, but not *reduction* of consciousness. Thus the explanatory gap does not exclude a *non-explanatory* reduction of consciousness, only an *explanatory* reduction. For Chalmers, however, the hard problem—or at least its insolubility—is supposed to undermine, against the background of certain assumptions, the very possibility of a non-explanatory reduction—with the result that ruling out reductive explanation implies ruling out reduction. These remarks may be somewhat opaque at this point, but will become clearer later on.

(Jackson 1994, 1998). For example, we can deduce water facts from H_2O facts, as follows:

(a) H_2O boils at 100 °C;
(b) H_2O = the actual (occupant of the) water role (scientific inquiry);
(c) the actual (occupant of the) water role = water (functionalization); therefore,
(d) water boils at 100 °C.

The general schema for such deduction of F-facts from G-facts is thus this:

(a) G has property P;
(b) G = the actual (occupant of the) F role (scientific inquiry);
(c) the actual (occupant of the) F role = F (functionalization); therefore,
(d) F has property P.

This deducibility of reduced-level facts from reducer-level facts makes reduction *epistemically transparent*: we can see *why it is* that water is nothing but H_2O. Water is nothing but H_2O because water is nothing but the actual (occupant of the) water role and H_2O is (the occupant of) that role.[8]

This epistemic transparency means that the facts about the reducer property *explain* the facts about the reduced property. Once we know that H_2O boils at 100 °C, and that H_2O plays the role that captures water, we understand *why* water boils at 100 °C. There does not seem to be left over a fact in need of explanation. Thus on this view reduction is incompatible with the persistence of any explanatory gap. Reduction *closes* any such gap, and, conversely, if an explanatory gap survives, reduction remains unattained.

Applied to consciousness, the deductive model would require the following procedure for reduction. First, the concept of consciousness is functionalized, so that consciousness is shown to be nothing but the actual (occupant of the) consciousness role—that is, the functional role distinctive of conscious states in the actual world. In a second step, scientific inquiry would attempt to identify a physical property—presumably the neural correlate of consciousness—which plays just the right functional role.[9] If such a property is found, consciousness would then be reduced

---

[8] I will explain the parenthetical reference to occupants momentarily.
[9] I am assuming here that it is unquestionable that neural properties are physicalizable—that they metaphysically supervene on physical properties.

to that physical property. Such reduction would enable an explanation of psychological facts about consciousness by neurophysiological facts about its neural correlate along the lines of the general schema presented above. Consider the fact that a mental state's being conscious makes its content better stored in short-term memory.[10] This fact might be deduced from the physical facts as follows:

(a) synchronization with dlPFC activation enhances short-term memory;

(b) synchronization with dlPFC activation = the actual (occupant of the) consciousness role (scientific inquiry);

(c) the actual (occupant of the) consciousness role = consciousness (functionalization); therefore,

(d) consciousness enhances short-term memory.

Here the psychological fact about consciousness is deduced from the combination of a functional recast of consciousness and the scientific facts about synchronization with dlPFC activation.

Before moving on, two points about functionalization. First, in all the formulations above, I make parenthetical reference to occupants. I do so in order not to prejudge a debate between two competing views of the relationship between (i) water, (ii) the water role, and (iii) the actual occupant of the water role—that is, H_2O. It is clear that the relation between (ii) and (iii) is not identity, but rather the relation between role and occupant, or (more or less equivalently) the relation between disposition and categorical basis.[11] One understanding of functionalization is that it casts (i) as identical to (ii); another is that it casts (i) as identical to (iii).[12] On the first view, water is identical to the water role, and their categorical basis is H_2O. On the second view, water is identical to H_2O, and they are the categorical basis of the water role. There is a way in

---

[10] Thus, the fact that a stimulus has been consciously perceived, as opposed to subliminally, makes it more probable that we could recall that stimulus in the future.

[11] It is natural to construe a role as a dispositional property: a token state's functional role is given by its bundle of disposition to cause and be caused by certain things. It is widely thought that dispositions can never be free-standing but always require a categorical basis. It is natural to think of a role's occupant as the categorical basis of the bundle of dispositions that constitutes the role.

[12] The majority view among post-Kripkean Anglo-American philosophers seems to be that water is identical to H_2O. But it is fully coherent to maintain that the relationship there is that of constitution: H_2O constitutes water rather than being identical with it. For a defense of this view, see Johnston 1997.

which the deductive model of reduction works more smoothly with the first view, but the model itself ought to be neutral between the two.

Secondly, there are two ways in which we might attempt to functionalize a property F. One is through conceptual analysis, the other is through scientific inquiry. Functionalization by conceptual analysis is most commonly thought of as proceeding through the collection of everyday platitudes about F (for example, "water is clear," "water is drinkable") and the construction of a Ramsey sentence from them.[13] Functionalization by scientific inquiry would proceed by collecting scientifically established theses about F and the construction of a Ramsey sentence from those.[14] In their model of reduction, Jackson (1994) and Chalmers (1996) require functionalization by conceptual analysis. But we can imagine a version of the model that allows the use of functionalization by scientific inquiry; it is natural to understand Kim's model of reduction (1998) as involving just this.[15]

According to the abductive model of reduction (Block and Stalnaker 1999), reduction does not require deducibility of reduced-level facts from reducer-level facts. On this model, reduction of F to G involves only two central steps. The first is the scientific demonstration of a perfect correlation between instantiations of F and instantiations of G.[16] The second is an inference to the best explanation to the effect that F metaphysically supervenes upon G. The F–G correlation is treated as an explanandum, and, when the metaphysical supervenience of F upon G is shown to be the best explanation of this, it is endorsed.

Thus, in the case of water and H_2O, a correlation is demonstrated between water and H_2O: wherever the former is present, so is the latter, and wherever the former is absent, so is the latter. This correlation calls

---

[13] The notion of a Ramsey sentence was discussed in Chapter 6, Section 2.

[14] The distinction here parallels a familiar distinction between two type of functionalist theory of mental states: *analytic functionalism* and *psycho-functionalism*. According to analytic functionalism, the very meaning of mental state terms is given by the armchair specification of their functional role, and therefore functionalism is true analytically and a priori. According to psycho-functionalism, by contrast, functionalism is true only synthetically or a posteriori: the scientific nature of mental state properties is given by their functional role.

[15] For a different version of an allegedly a posteriori functionalization, see Dowell, forthcoming.

[16] The notion of correlation is not entirely clear at a theoretical level, though it is fairly clear at an intuitive level. Presumably F correlates with G iff for any a, such that a is F, there is a b, such that (i) b is G and (ii) there is some specific relationship between a and b. One way to think about the relevant relationship is as two-way actual supervenience. That is, F and G correlate if F supervenes on G actually and G supervenes on F actually.

for explanation. One *prima facie* good explanation is that water is nothing but H_2O. Since this explanation is simple, conservative, and so on, we are justified in adopting it.

Note that the kind of reduction we get in the abductive model is *epistemically opaque*. Water's being nothing but H_2O is presented as a brute fact, one that is not itself in need—or possibility, for that matter—of explanation. To bring this out, consider again the scenario where a perfect correlation is found between justice and cement mixed with wood fiber. By the lights of the abductive model, the stark difference between the concept of justice and the concept of cement mixed with wood fiber presents no obstacle to the reduction of the former to the latter. Just how it could be that justice is nothing but cement mixed with wood fiber may remain completely opaque to us, but these are nonetheless one and the same property, the gap being purely epistemic and at the level of concepts.

According to the proponents of the abductive model, this is just as it should be, as identities are inexplicable: there is no explaining why I am identical to myself; I just am. That is, identities really are brute, and it is a virtue of an account of reduction that it leaves them brute. Accordingly, in one important sense reduction does not deliver, on this view, an explanation of the reduced-level facts. To the person asking why water boils at 100 °C, it does offer the answer that water is nothing but H_2O, and H_2O boils at 100 °C. But, since it does not shed light on water's being nothing but H_2O, it ultimately does not shed light on why water boils at 100 °C. In general, if our explanandum is the proposition that a is F, saying that a is F because b is F and $a = b$ qualifies as an explanation only if we already understand why the propositions that b is F and that $a = b$ are true. If we do not understand why (say) the proposition that $a = b$ is true any more than we understand why the proposition that a is F is true, then we do not have an explanation here. So, insofar as in the abductive model we are not given an explanation as to why the proposition that water $= H_2O$ is true, we have no explanation of why water boils at 100 °C.[17] Thus reduction is quite compatible, on this view, with the persistence of an explanatory gap between reduced and reducer.

---

[17] We may have an independent explanation of why it does, but the explanation is not delivered by the reduction itself.

Applied to consciousness, the abductive model calls for essentially nothing more than the scientific project of discovering the neural correlate of consciousness to be completed. Once such a correlate is discovered, the model allows us ampliatively to infer that it is not *merely* a correlate but also a reducer, on the grounds that consciousness being nothing but its neural correlate would be the best explanation for their correlation. The resulting reduction would not, on this model, explain the psychological facts about consciousness in terms of the neural facts about its correlate (as we saw in the previous paragraph). But it would still be valuable inasmuch as it would make for an economy in our ontological commitments.

A major difference, then, between the deductive and abductive models of reduction is that the former requires reduction to be epistemically transparent whereas the latter tolerates epistemically opaque reduction. Thus the former is incompatible, whereas the latter is compatible, with the persistence of an explanatory gap. In other words, the abductive model offers us reduction without reductive explanation, while the deductive model sees reductive explanation as a necessary component of reduction.

This epistemic difference corresponds to a modal one. Both models of reduction require the reduced property to supervene on the reducer property. But there is a difference in the modal strength of the supervenience each of them requires. Since, on the deductive model, when F reduces to G, F-propositions are logically deducible from the G-propositions, the model construes reduction as involving *logical* supervenience of the reduced on the reducer. By contrast, the abductive model requires only *metaphysical* supervenience: F can reduce to G even if there is a logical gap between G-propositions and F-propositions.[18]

In addition to the possibilities of logical and metaphysical supervenience, there is also the possibility of (mere) nomological supervenience—that is, supervenience in all worlds with the same laws of nature as the actual. Most parties to the dispute about the physical reducibility of consciousness would

---

[18] There are two different ways the necessity of logical supervenience could be upheld. One is to claim that, if there is a metaphysically impossible but logically possible world where all the G-facts are the same as in the actual world, but the F-facts are different, this bars reduction of F to G. Another is to claim that there could not be such a metaphysically impossible but logically possible world, because metaphysical supervenience entails logical supervenience and therefore failure of logical supervenience entails failure of metaphysical supervenience.

agree that mere nomological supervenience is insufficient for reduction.[19] If there is a nomologically impossible but metaphysically possible world in which F does not supervene on G, then it is not the case that F is *nothing but* G. Mere nomological supervenience could be the centerpiece of an account of F in terms of G, but it would have to be a *non-reductive* account.

These differences become extremely important when the models are applied to the case of consciousness, because even physicalistically inclined philosophers often appreciate that there is an unusual explanatory gap here. It is widely accepted that the conceivability of zombies—the fact that we can coherently conceive of creatures who are physically indistinguishable from us but lack consciousness—demonstrates that there is no physical property P, such that consciousness is conceptually or logically supervenient upon P. It is also widely accepted that, without substantive corollaries, such conceivability does *not* demonstrate that there is no physical property P such that consciousness is metaphysically supervenient on P. If so, the deductive model is likely to render a negative verdict on the reducibility of consciousness, whereas the abductive model is more likely to render a positive verdict. The question, therefore, is which of the two models is the more plausible.

One option is to take a conciliatory approach here. Since the abductive model promises only an epistemically opaque reduction based in mere metaphysical supervenience, whereas the deductive model delivers epistemically transparent reduction grounded in logical supervenience, we might suggest that there are simply two grades of reduction. We could distinguish *explanatory* reduction from *non-explanatory* reduction, and suggest that the deductive model is correct for explanatory reduction while the abductive model is correct for non-explanatory reduction.[20] Thus,

---

[19] There are two kinds of dissenter I can imagine. One is the philosopher who holds that nomological necessity entails metaphysical and perhaps even logical necessity—i.e., who holds that the actual laws of nature are necessary. This is sometimes associated with the idea that a property is nothing but a bundle of law-like causal dispositions (Shoemaker 1979). Another kind of dissenter is the philosopher who believes that reduction need not amount to more than realization or constitution. According to Johnston (1997), water is not identical to H_2O but only constituted by it. Some may take this to imply that water does not reduce to H_2O. Others, however, might take the relation between water and H_2O to be a paradigmatic case of reduction, and conclude that reduction requires constitution rather than identity. If constitution has no modal depth, as is quite plausible, the facts of actual constitution may suffice for reduction, on this line of thought.

[20] After all, as just noted, the deductive model offers us reductive explanations, whereas the abductive model does not.

corresponding to the three main grades of supervenience are three types of account of consciousness: a non-reductive account, a non-explanatorily reductive account, and an explanatorily reductive account. By way of illustration, consider the following three theses:

(LS) Consciousness logically supervenes upon synchronization with dlPFC activation.

(MS) Consciousness metaphysically supervenes upon synchronization with dlPFC activation.

(NS) Consciousness nomologically supervenes upon synchronization with dlPFC activation.

An explanatorily reductive version of the self-representational theory would be committed to LS, a non-explanatorily reductive version would be committed to MS & ~LS, and a non-reductive one to NS & ~MS. All three would be versions of self-representationalism, but of different metaphysical forces.

This approach is conciliatory, but not neutral. It is certainly favorable to the proponent of the reducibility of consciousness. For it does not require logical supervenience for reduction as such, only for a particularly satisfying variety. Accordingly, it allows us to adopt a reductive stance toward consciousness even in the face of a persisting explanatory gap. Ultimately, if we adopt this conciliatory approach, it is quite plausible that we would end up with a reductive account of consciousness, albeit a non-explanatory one. Some philosophers would therefore want to argue that reduction as such does require reductive explanation—that is, to argue against the abductive model of reduction.[21]

One argument is that correlation is not a sufficient basis for an abductive inference to metaphysical supervenience, because correlation can be equally accommodated by nomological supervenience (Chalmers and

---

[21] Alternatively, one might still think that (mere) metaphysical supervenience does not deserve the title of "reduction," or that, whatever the titles, genuine physicalism requires more than just metaphysical supervenience of all properties upon physical properties. It is reasonable to understand Horgan (1993) in this way. According to Horgan, supervenience relations weaker than logical supervenience cannot be legitimately accepted as *brute* by the physicalist. Genuine physicalism requires that such supervenience relations be themselves explained in physical terms. On this view, metaphysical supervenience is insufficient for physicalist reduction: physicalism requires, at the very least, metaphysical supervenience *plus* an explanation of it. The combination of metaphysical supervenience with explanation of the supervenience Horgan calls "superdupervenience." Metaphysical superdupervenience might suffice for physicalization, but it is not unlikely that metaphysical superdupervenience entails logical supervenience.

Jackson 2001). If our explanandum is a contingent correlation in the actual world between F and G, then (other things being equal) the nomological supervenience of F on G would be just as good an explanation of it as metaphysical supervenience. In one way, we might think it is the *better* explanation, or at least the less risky, inasmuch as it is modally less committal.

This argument strikes me as inconclusive. It calls for a complication of the abductive model, not its rejection. What the argument shows is that there is a lacuna in the abductive model, insofar as any inference to the best explanation would have to establish that metaphysical supervenience is superior to nomological supervenience as an explanation of actual correlation. But this seems to me eminently achievable.

Mere nomological supervenience of F on G means that instantiations of F are tied to instantiations of G by some sort of *natural law*. Such a law would probably be causal: instantiations of G would *lawfully cause* instantiations of F.[22] It is hard to see what kind of natural law could connect two properties in a non-causal way. This suggests a way in which the lacuna in the original inference to the best explanation could be filled: if it could be shown that, despite the correlation between F and G, there is no *causal* relationship between them, this would constitute a reason to prefer metaphysical supervenience over nomological supervenience as explanation of their correlation.[23] The modified abductive model of reduction would thus involve three steps: first, actual correlation between F and G would be established scientifically; second, lack of causal relationship between F and G would also be established scientifically; third, the metaphysical supervenience of F upon G would be abductively inferred. In this modified model there is no longer the lacuna pointed out above.

To my mind, however, there is something unclear about the whole notion that supervenience *explains* correlation. There are two parts to this. The only way I can think of analyzing correlation is as two-way supervenience: F correlates with G in the actual world iff (*a*) F supervenes on G in the actual world and (*b*) G supervenes on F in the actual world.

---

[22] This is, in effect, an emergentist view, according to which the higher-level property is caused by the lower-level property.

[23] In addition, it might be thought that the introduction of new causal laws makes the nomological-supervenience explanation less simple, and thus less theoretically virtuous, than the metaphysical-supervenience explanation. This by itself may give us some grounds for adopting the metaphysical-supervenience explanation.

Now, there are two problems with the idea that F's supervening on G *explains* F's correlating with G. First, regarding (*a*), it is a little generous to say that metaphysical supervenience explains actual supervenience. We do not usually think that we can explain the fact that *p* by citing the fact that necessarily *p*. Secondly, regarding (*b*), it is unclear in what way F's supervening on G metaphysically would explain G's supervening on F actually. If these challenges cannot be met, no sense can be made of the idea that metaphysical supervenience explains correlation. And, without that, the abductive model cannot get off the ground.

Another argument for preferring the deductive model is that functionalization of the reduced property is imperative if we are to make sure that what has actually been reduced is the property that we targeted for reduction—that we have not *changed the subject* is the process of constructing our reduction (Jackson 1994). The point is brought out nicely by Gertler (2002): to ensure that a putative piece of evidence E for the reduction of F to G is indeed evidence for reduction of F and not some other property F*, we must provide a characterization of F that excludes F*—that is, we must provide something that characterizes F but fails to characterize F*. The most natural way to do so—perhaps the only way to do so—is to construe F as the actual (occupant of the) F role, that is, to functionalize F.[24]

The most straightforward way to provide a characterization of F is by providing a conceptual analysis of "F." This may be thought to show that the present consideration supports not just the deductive model of reduction, but more specifically the version of the model that appeals to functionalization by conceptual analysis (as opposed to functionalization by scientific inquiry). However, it is quite likely that, whether or not

---

[24] Consider what this entails for the abductive model. To ensure that it is water that correlates with H_2O, and not some associated property schmwater, we must provide a characterization of water that does not characterize schmwater. The most natural way to do so is to characterize water as the (occupant of the) actual water role. This would split the initial step of the abductive model into two. In the case of water, first a contingent correlation is observed between H_2O and the (occupant of the) actual water role, then the (occupant of the) actual water role is identified with water, thus producing a correlation between H_2O and water. After a causal connection between water and H_2O is ruled out, the best explanation of that correlation becomes that water is nothing but H_2O. This newly modified abductive model can accommodate the need to ensure that we have not changed the subject in the process of performing the reduction, but it does so by incorporating the step of functionalization. Once functionalization is already introduced into one's model of reduction, however, there is no longer a motivation to settle for abductive inference and non-explanatory reduction. Since all the ingredients for explanatory reduction have already been admitted, we may as well embrace the deductive model.

properties can be *identified* with their full scientific functional profile, they can certainly be *individuated* by them. If so, for any properties F and F*, if F $\neq$ F*, then the full scientific functional role of F $\neq$ the full scientific functional role of F*. This suggests, in turn, that a posteriori functionalization could provide a characterization of F that would ensure that what is reduced is F, and not any associated but numerically distinct property. That is, it suggests that functionalization by scientific inquiry suffices for ensuring that we have not changed the subject in the process of performing the reduction.

I have offered two considerations against the viability of a non-explanatory reduction, a reduction based on abductive inference: the "no-genuine-explanation" consideration and the "no-changing-the-subject" consideration. In so doing, I have attempted to undermine the conciliatory approach that made logical space for two kinds of reduction. The upshot is that, if consciousness is to be reduced to synchronization with dlPFC activation, the explanatory gap must be closed and the consciousness facts must be shown to be deducible from the facts about synchronization with dlPFC activation in accordance with the schema presented above. The main hurdle for such deduction is the thought that consciousness is not functionalizable. In the next section we consider this possibility.

3. Functionalization and Consciousness

I opened this chapter with the claim that physicalist treatments of consciousness have tended to fail to explain in what way the case of consciousness is special and unlike the case of any other property. One way successfully to capture the special status of consciousness is to claim that consciousness is the only non-functionalizable property.

Water is *nothing but* the actual (occupant of the) water role: for something to be water *just is* for it to exhibit the actual functional profile of water. Minimally, if something exhibits the functional profile of water, then it must be water. The claim under consideration is that consciousness is an exception (the only exception, as it happens) to the rule that this is so with all properties. Consciousness is *not* nothing but the actual (occupant of the) consciousness role: for something to be conscious is *not* just for it to exhibit the actual functional profile of consciousness.

Because consciousness is more than just the actual (occupant of the) consciousness role, we can imagine something exhibiting the functional profile of consciousness—having all the actual causes and effects of consciousness—without being conscious. This is the basis for the zombie argument (Chalmers 1996, forthcoming). We can imagine this both for phenomenal creature consciousness and for phenomenal state consciousness.[25] We can imagine a zombie *creature*: a creature that interacts with the world in the same way a phenomenally conscious creature actually does but is unconscious—even if the two have the very same physical constitution. We can also imagine a zombie *state*: a mental state that has the same causal relations to input states, output states, and other internal states that a phenomenally conscious state actually has but is not itself phenomenally conscious. We can imagine these things because there is more to consciousness than its actual functional profile. And the fact that we can imagine these things, even in the most favorable circumstances, shows that consciousness does not logically supervene on any physical property.

It is worth highlighting that, on this way of thinking, the physical irreducibility of consciousness is ultimately grounded in its *functional irreducibility* (if you will). Using the deductive model, we know how to show, for any given functional property F, that F is nothing but some physical property G.[26] The question, for any given property H up for reduction, is whether there is a functional property F, such that we can show that H is nothing but F. The claim before us is that for all properties but one there is such a corresponding functional property, but for consciousness there is not.[27]

Recall that Chalmers and Jackson (2001) adopt the version of the deductive model in which the functionalization step is taken care of by a priori conceptual analysis. Chalmers goes on to argue for the irreducibility of consciousness. Against the background of the deductive model with a priori functionalization, the case for such irreducibility relies on the singular unavailability of a conceptual analysis for the term "consciousness." For "water," there is a sufficiently long (non-aqueous) description of the form "clear drinkable liquid that...," such that it does not make sense to ask,

---

[25] See Chapter 2 for the distinction between different types of consciousness properties.

[26] I am setting aside issues arising from the possibility of multiple realizability, given the notion of reduction I am interested in (as stated at the opening of the chapter).

[27] Note well: here and in the remainder I use the term "functional property" to cover both functional-role properties and functional-role-occupant properties, where the role-occupant properties are conceived *de dicto*.

of a given quantity of stuff, "it is clear drinkable liquid that... but is it water?" If the stuff is a clear drinkable liquid that has all the actual hallmarks of water, it is water. By contrast, for "consciousness," there is *no* (non-phenomenal) description, however long, that would make it incoherent to ask of something that satisfies that description whether it is conscious. If it walks like a duck and quacks like a duck, it is a duck, but if it walks like a conscious duck and quacks like a conscious duck, it is not necessarily a conscious duck—it could be a zombie duck.

Some philosophers have claimed that conceptual analyses are unavailable not only in the case of consciousness, but in a wide array of cases where physical reducibility is unquestionable—which suggests that conceptual analysis cannot be necessary for reduction (Block and Stalnaker 1999). Perhaps such terms as "bachelor" admit of (correct) a priori conceptual analyses, but many other terms do not: the term "life," for example, admits of no conceptual analysis, and arguably even "water" does not. Philosophers can appreciate this, it is claimed, simply by surveying the recent history of their own discipline: twentieth-century philosophy is replete with failed attempts to analyze a variety of concepts.

For reasons that I will not go into here, I do not share this view.[28] Nonetheless, I share these philosophers' more general suspicion of the notion that an ontological claim about the nature of consciousness should be derivable from facts about the linguistic behavior of the term "consciousness" and/or the structure of the concept of consciousness. On the face of it, it should be impossible to arrive at the thesis that the *property* of being conscious is physically irreducible from any thesis about how the *concept* of consciousness works. In order to undercut a reduction of consciousness, what seems to be needed is showing not only that the concept of consciousness is a supra-functional concept, but that the property of consciousness itself is a supra-functional property, that is, a property that is not nothing but some functional property. That is, what must be blocked is not only a priori functionalization, but also a posteriori functionalization.

---

[28] The traditional project of providing philosophical analysis called for exceptionless conjunctions of a small number of severally necessary and conjointly sufficient conditions, something that is much stronger than the kind of conceptual analysis needed to enable reduction (Chalmers and Jackson 2001). The kind of analysis that *is* needed—in the form of a relatively loose (i.e., containing many disjuncts) Ramsey sentence—may be much more easy to produce (in principle). None of this is to say that any *has* been produced, and an objector could legitimately insist that there are deep reasons why they *cannot* be produced. I do not share this view, but will not get into these matters here.

For someone like Chalmers, it is natural to think that consciousness is not functionalizable a posteriori either. For this seems to be the lesson of the distinction between the easy problems of consciousness and the hard problem. The easy problems are the problems about the psychological functions of consciousness—the kind of a posteriori functional role that can be assigned to consciousness through scientific inquiry. The fact that there survives a further problem that goes beyond the easy problems is an expression of the fact that there is more to consciousness than the bundle of functions associated with it. That is, it is an expression of the fact that there is a non-functionalizable residue in consciousness. Indeed, for Chalmers it is natural to use the term "phenomenal consciousness" to denote this non-functionalizable residue. On this usage, phenomenal consciousness is that property of conscious states that survives functionalizability.

It is interesting to note that, when we look at the dialectic from this angle, the explanatory gap between consciousness and functional-role properties clearly underlies the explanatory gap between consciousness and physical-realizer properties, and is thus the more basic of the two. The *reason* there is the gap between consciousness and its physical realization is that there is the gap between consciousness and its functional role. Conversely, the path to bridging the explanatory gap between consciousness and physical reality goes through solving the hard problem—that is, through bridging the explanatory gap between consciousness and its functional role. The hard problem, recall, is the problem of why there should be anything it is like for a creature (or associated with a state) to perform certain psychological functions (play a certain psychological role). If—and only if—we can answer this question, we will have the materials to bridge the explanatory gap between consciousness and physical reality. That explanatory gap concerns the alleged fact that no amount of physical knowledge can help us explain the facts of consciousness. But if we did have a functional characterization of consciousness, we could use the above schema for reductive explanation to do so. We could then say that the *reason* consciousness is so-and-so is that consciousness is nothing but the actual (occupant of the) consciousness role, such-and-such physical structure is the actual (occupant of the) consciousness role, and such-and-such physical structure is so-and-so. This is to use our physical knowledge of such-and-such to produce an explanation of the fact that consciousness is so-and-so.

Thus the main explanatory gap *can* be bridged—but only if the hard problem is solved.

In a way, this is just to repeat that, against the background of the deductive model, the physical reducibility of consciousness depends on the prior *functional* reducibility of consciousness: only if consciousness can be shown to be in the last count nothing but some functional property can it then be shown to be ultimately nothing but some physical property. The case against the physical reducibility of consciousness is essentially this: physical reducibility requires functional reducibility; consciousness is not functionally reducible; therefore, consciousness is not physically reducible.

In the next section I will claim that consciousness is (a posteriori) functionalizable after all, contrary to the second premise of the argument just sketched. But first I want to consider the thought that the second premise *must* be true, because a priori conceptual analysis reveals that the word "consciousness" denotes precisely that property which contains a non-functionalizable residue in consciousness. The term "phenomenal consciousness," it would then be natural to suggest, is precisely a technical term for that residue alone—for the aspect of consciousness that survives functionalization. If so, it is a priori that we cannot fully functionalize consciousness, and hence that we cannot reduce phenomenal consciousness to any physical property. This is to take the relationship between functionalizability and a prioricity one step further: not only is consciousness not a priori functionalizable; it is a priori non-functionalizable.

The problem with this thought is that, if it turns out that there is no non-functionalizable residue in consciousness, then by its lights this would entail eliminativism about phenomenal consciousness (see Rey 1988). And yet the putative fact that there is no non-functionalizable residue in consciousness nowise entails that there is no genuine distinction between two kinds of mental state, those that are distinctively experiential and those that are not, those that there is something it is like for a subject to be in and those there is nothing it is like. Those distinctions would still be very real, and they would carve out a real phenomenon, and moreover one that warrants the philosophic anxiety surrounding consciousness. This suggests that the analysis of "consciousness" according to which the very concept of consciousness is the concept of a property that contains a non-functionalizable residue is off the mark.

This consideration resembles one due to Braddon-Mitchell (2003). If an oracle appeared and informed us that mental states do not have a property that has an aspect that resists functionalization, we would not conclude that consciousness does not exist. This shows that it cannot be part of the very concept of consciousness that it contains such an aspect. At the same time, there is clearly a close conceptual connection between consciousness and the possibility of non-functionalizability. To preserve both these aspects of the concept of consciousness, Braddon-Mitchell offers a conditional analysis of the concept (see also Hawthorne 2002). According to this analysis, the following conditional is analytic and a priori: if some actual mental states have a property that contains a non-functionalizable residue, then consciousness is that property, but if no actual mental states have such a property, then consciousness is the actual (occupant of the) consciousness role. This analysis manages both to respect the oracle observation and to grant conceptual priority to any potential non-functionalizability.

As a piece of conceptual analysis, Braddon-Mitchell's account strikes me as much more plausible than the account that raises the specter of eliminativism.[29] Ultimately, what matters for our present purposes is that consciousness ought not to be understood as that property which *by definition* contains a non-functionalizable residue, but rather as that property which by definition *appears* to contain a non-functionalizable residue.[30] Recall that in Chapter 1 I suggested that we construe *phenomenal* consciousness as that property which produces the mystery of consciousness, that property which is the source of the philosophic anxiety surrounding consciousness. It is the appearance of non-functionalizability, I contend, that makes consciousness so *prima facie* problematic. If so, it is natural to construe phenomenal consciousness as

---

[29] Though see Alter 2006 and Chalmers forthcoming for responses—and Haukioja 2008 for a rejoinder.

[30] Correspondingly, whereas the eliminativism-threatening account construed *phenomenal* consciousness as that aspect of consciousness that survives functionalization, Braddon-Mitchell's account is consistent with its more liberal construal (which we have suggested in Section 1) as that property which *appears* to survive functionalization. In Section 1 I offered in fact two construals of "phenomenal consciousness": as resisting physical explanation and as resisting functionalization. Here I focus only on the second, and I use the word "survives" rather than "resists" because "resists" is ambiguous as between a success verb and a non-success verb. In the latter usage, it is possible for phenomenal consciousness to resist functionalization and still be functionalizable: it resists the functionalization in the sense that "gives up a good fight" (as in "resisting arrest"). With this usage in mind, we could say not only that phenomenal consciousness appears to resist functionalization but that it does. In the success usage, however, defining phenomenal consciousness in this way would collapse into defining it in the way suggested by the eliminativism-threatening account.

the property that appears to be non-functionalizable, and consciousness as the property that appears to contain a non-functionalizable residue.

I conclude that there is no a priori obstacle to the functionalizability of consciousness. It is not part of the concept of consciousness that consciousness contains a non-functionalizable residue. At the same time, it is clearly not a priori that consciousness *is* functionalizable. The challenge, at this point, is to offer an a posteriori functionalization of consciousness.

But it is not the only challenge. The other challenge is to explain the appearance of non-functionalizability. In the case of water, there is no temptation to posit a supra-functional residue, an aqueous essence that goes beyond any actual (occupant of) water role. The temptation exists only in the case of consciousness, and it can be accommodated in one of two ways: by conceding that consciousness is indeed not fully functionalizable, or by identifying something about consciousness that makes it appear so strongly to resist functionalization when in fact it is very much functionalizable.

This is related to the issue with which we opened this section and this chapter. A satisfactory approach to the problem of consciousness would manage to physicalize consciousness while accounting for the fact that the case of consciousness is special. The view that consciousness is the only non-functionalizable property manages the latter but (against the background of the deductive model) not the former. If we secure the physical reducibility of consciousness by simply adopting the view that consciousness is fully functionalizable, we run the risk of managing the former but not the latter. To manage both, we must tell a story that imputes on consciousness a feature present nowhere else in nature that explains why consciousness seems to resist functionalization—but maintain that the feature in question is itself physically reducible. In the next section I argue that this feature is the fact that consciousness can be known even if it does not make a causal impact on knowers. Consciousness has this feature, according to self-representationalism, because awareness of consciousness is already built into consciousness.

4. The Self-Representational Stopgap

My goal in this section is to explain why consciousness is bound to appear to be non-functionalizable, regardless of whether it is—and, moreover, that this is something self-representationalism predicts. The point of the exercise is this: the most natural explanation for the fact that consciousness appears non-functionalizable is that it *is* non-functionalizable. Showing that there is *another* explanation should relieve the pressure to adopt the more natural explanation.

The position I am attempting to defend is that what makes consciousness special, what sets it apart from all other properties, is not the fact that it alone is non-functionalizable, but rather the fact that it alone *appears* non-functionalizable in a robust way, or, more precisely, is *bound* to appear non-functionalizable. All other properties are functionalizable, yes, but in addition they ultimately also *appear* functionalizable.[31] The first question we should ask ourselves, therefore, is this: what is it about all other properties that makes them *appear* functionalizable? Once we have an answer to this question, we would be better positioned to see what sets consciousness apart.

Before continuing, let us pause to clarify the notion of "appearing non-functionalizable." For a property F to be functionalizable, recall, is for there to be some functional property G, such that F is ultimately nothing but G. But, if we try to construct a parallel criterion for a property's appearing non-functionalizable, a double ambiguity arises: concerning the scope of the negation and concerning the scope of the appearance operator. Thus there are four possible interpretations of "appears non-functionalizable":

1. F appears non-functionalizable iff for every functional property G, it appears that F is not nothing but G.
2. F appears non-functionalizable iff for every functional property G, it does not appear that F is nothing but G.
3. F appears non-functionalizable iff it appears that for every functional property G, F is not nothing but G.
4. F appears non-functionalizable iff it does not appear that for every functional property G, F is nothing but G.

---

[31] We tend to focus on the fact that something's appearing a certain way does not guarantee its being that way. But it is worth stressing what is otherwise quite obvious, that the converse is true as well: something's being a certain way does not guarantee its appearing that way. A house can be a three-storey house but appear from the outside to be a two-storey house, perhaps because of a strange design of its façade. Thus the house's being three storey is not a *full* explanation of its appearing three storey. Something else is needed, something about how it affects those to whom it appears three storey. Likewise, the fact that a property is functionalizable does not yet guarantee that it also appears to us to be functionalizable. That is a further fact, and therefore requires separate explanation.

The interpretation most relevant to our current purposes is the second, so in what follows I will work with it.[32] Accordingly, I will work with the complementary interpretation of "appearing functionalizable":

> 5. F appears functionalizable iff for some functional property G, it appears that F is nothing but G.

When I say that consciousness alone robustly appears non-functionalizable, I am making the following claim, then: for every property F other than consciousness, there is some functional property G, such that ultimately F appears to be nothing but G; but for consciousness there is no such functional property.

The question before us is why it is that every property other than consciousness appears functionalizable in this sense. There are two possible answers to this, depending on whether one has in mind *a priori or a posteriori functionalization.*

The first answer is that this simply follows from the meaning of the terms, or contents of the concepts, we use to pick out those properties. What makes the property of being water appear to us to be nothing but the actual (occupant of the) water role is that the word "water" just *means* "the actual (occupant of the) water role," or that the concept of water just *is* the concept of an actual (occupant of the) water role.[33] Following the remarks in the middle of the previous section, I want to focus here on the prospects for a posteriori functionalization, and so I will set aside this a priori-inspired explanation of functionalizability-appearance.

The a posteriori-inspired explanation is a little more complicated: the reason water appears to us to be nothing but the actual (occupant of the) water role is that, intuitively, water is the kind of property science should be able to tell us about, but science can tell us only about functionalizable

---

[32] The reason I take the second interpretation to be more pertinent than the first one is that there are some complicated questions concerning what it would take for consciousness to appear positively distinct from any functional property, rather than not to appear the same as any such, but, as we saw above, certainly the idea that it is analytic of consciousness that it is non-functionalizable is false, so at least by one standard consciousness' appearing non-functionalizable is not its matter of providing a positive appearance of being different from any functional property.

[33] This claim is of course very controversial. It is typically denied by philosophers who adopt a direct-reference account of natural kind terms and maintain that "water" is a natural kind term. I happen to reject both parts of this—I think "water" is a manifest kind term and that natural kind terms are not directly referential but instead refer via rigidified descriptions. But the prevalence of the opposing view is such that I do not wish my discussion to rely on these views of mine.

properties. More generally, any property that is up for reduction would have to be the kind of property science can tell us about—it makes little sense to worry about the reducibility of scientifically untouchable properties. So, if science tells us only about functionalizable properties, all properties up for reduction must be functionalizable.

The sense in which science can tell us only about functionalizable properties is this.[34] Let us say that two worlds W and W* are "functionally indistinguishable" just in case they are indistinguishable in terms of functional-role properties and role-occupant properties: for any role property R or occupant property O (where O is conceived of obliquely as the property of occupying a certain role), if R or O is instantiated in some location L in W, then it is also instantiated in L (or L's counterpart) in W*—and vice versa. So W and W* are role- and occupant-duplicates: the distribution of role and occupant properties in them is the same. With this notion of functional indistinguishability of worlds, we can state the sense in which science can tell us only about functionalizable properties as follows: the one true and complete scientific theory of functionally indistinguishable worlds must be the same. More precisely, for any two worlds W_1 and W_2, and any two scientific theories T_1 and T_2, such that T_1 is the one true complete scientific theory of W_1 and T_2 is the one true complete scientific theory of W_2, if W_1 and W_2 are functionally indistinguishable, then T_1 and T_2 are identical.[35] The idea, then, is that functionally indistinguishable worlds are *scientifically equivalent*: as far as science is concerned, they are indistinguishable *simpliciter*. Thus science is blind to any supra-functional features of a world.

This also provides us with a gloss on "it appears that F is nothing but G." Suppose that in W_1 and W_2 there are occupant properties O_1 and O_2 that are exactly the same except for one difference: O_1 contains a supra-functional component C but O_2 does not. The difference, then, is that O_2 really is nothing but the (occupant of the) O_2 role, whereas O_1 is

[34] This explication of the notion of what science can tell us about is adapted from Stoljar (2001), who focuses on the claim that science can tell us only about dispositional properties. As Stoljar notes, we can also understand "tells us about" as "incorporates terms that refer to," but in that sense it may be false that science can only tell us about dispositional (and we can probably add, functionalizable) properties.

[35] We must suppose, of course, that the theories are couched in the same vocabulary and more generally use the same system of representation. We may flag this by saying that the theories of functionally indistinguishable worlds are *substantively* identical, where this means that, if they are not identical, then it cannot be that they are using the same system of representation.

not nothing but the (occupant of the) O_1 role. Note that the properties of being the (occupant of the) O_1 role and being the (occupant of the) O_2 role are one and the same, since the only difference between O_1 and O_2 is supra-functional. So O_2 is nothing but, whereas O_1 is more than, the (occupant of the) O_1 role. However, since the ultimate scientific theories in W_1 and W_2 are identical, O_1 and O_2 appear identically in those theories and hence appear identical. In this situation, we can say that O_1 *appears* to be nothing but O_2, even though it is not.[36]

All this depends, of course, on it being the case that functionally indistinguishable worlds are scientifically equivalent. What is the reason to believe this? The thought one comes across is that the only way a property can be taken into account by science is if it has causal impact on scientists. The impact may not be direct or immediate, it may be extremely circuitous and indirect, but impact there must be. A property's causal impact, however, or at least its causal power to have the impact, is an aspect of its causal profile, and is thus within the purview of functionalization. As I will argue more explicitly below, to say that X is a non-functionalizable residue of property F is to say that X does *not* translate into any modification in F's overall fund of causal powers, wherefore it cannot be captured in F's functional profile.

We may put this in terms of a familiar problem regarding the connection between knowledge and causality, a problem that arose first in the philosophy of mathematics. The original problem was that mathematical knowledge seemed to be excluded by the combination of two claims: that we have no causal contact with mathematical entities and that knowledge of an entity requires causal contact with it.[37] The same reasoning could suggest that, while non-functionalizable properties may be knowable, their supra-functional component may not. If a property is non-functionalizable, then it has an aspect or component that goes beyond its causal profile; that aspect or component is thus epiphenomenal. But epiphenomenal features, including epiphenomenal property-aspects/components, are features we

---

[36] Note as well: since O_1 appears to be nothing but O_2, and O_2 is nothing but the (occupant of the) O_1 role, it follows that O_1 appears to be nothing but the (occupant of the) O_1 role—even though it is not.

[37] See Steiner 1973 and Benacerraf 1973. The reason it seems implausible that we have causal contact with mathematical entities (at least on one way of thinking of matters) is that such entities seem to be abstract, whereas we are concrete, and there does not seem to be causal interaction between the abstract and the concrete.

cannot come in causal contact with, and therefore cannot know. If we cannot know about them, then our best science cannot take account of them.

Is it so obvious that, if a property is non-functionalizable, then it has an epiphenomenal aspect or component? We may argue for this as follows. Suppose property F is non-functionalizable. Then F has an aspect or component C, such that C is something over and above the (occupation of the) functional role of F. Now, either C has no functional role whatsoever or it does. That is, either there is a functional role R, such that C plays R, or there is not. If there is not, then C is epiphenomenal. If there is, then either C is nothing but (the occupation of) R or it is not. If C is nothing but (the occupation of) R, then C is functionalizable, and therefore so is F—contrary to hypothesis. If C is more than (the occupation of) R, then C has an aspect or component C*, such that C* is something over and above (the occupation of) R—that is, over and above (the occupation of) the functional role of C. But now we reiterate for C* the dilemma applied above to C: either C* has no functional role whatsoever or it does. The only way to stop an infinite regress is to suppose that F has an aspect or component that has no functional role whatsoever, is epiphenomenal.[38] So, whenever we have a non-functionalizable property, it will involve an epiphenomenal residue.[39]

The purpose of this discussion is to explain what makes most properties appear functionalizable. My answer is that what makes them appear functionalizable is that they can be taken into account by science, but science can take into account only functionalizable properties. And science can take into account only functionalizable properties (or can take into account properties only insofar as they are functionalizable) because causal contact

---

[38] I am assuming here that an aspect of an aspect of a property is an aspect of that property (a component of a component of F is a component of F). This assumption is made only for the sake of presentation; it makes no difference to the argument. If we lift it, the conclusion would simply have to be stated as saying that, if a property F is non-functionalizable, then there is an aspect of an aspect of an aspect of... F that is epiphenomenal.

[39] This argument does not support the (stronger) view that all properties are dispositional, or are role properties, and there are no categorical or realizer properties (or that such properties must be epiphenomenal). For its construal of "functional property" is (as is the entire discussion in this chapter) neutral between a role interpretation and an occupant interpretation of what it means to be a functional property. It is thus neutral between a construal of functionalization as showing that a property is nothing but a disposition or a functional role and a construal showing that it is nothing but the categorical basis or realizer of a disposition or a functional role. Thus the argument allows there to be realizer properties that are not epiphenomenal.

with supra-functional residues is impossible and science cannot take into account what it cannot come in causal contact with.

With this explanation in place, we can see why consciousness can be an exception. It can be an exception because knowledge of consciousness, and of consciousness alone, does not require causal contact with the known.[40] The phenomenal character of a conscious state might contribute nothing to the state's causal powers and we would still know of this phenomenal character. The reason is that, while no other property is such that our awareness of it is built into the property itself, consciousness is: because of the subjective dimension of phenomenal consciousness, its for-me-ness, phenomenal consciousness cannot be instantiated in the absence of awareness of its instantiation.

The point can be put as follows. The relationship between knowledge and the known is either causal or constitutive: either the knowing is caused by the known, or it is a constituent of it. If knowledge of a property is not causally related to that property, it must be constitutively related to it. For most properties, it is obvious that there is no constitutive relation between them and knowledge of them. The property of being water is not constitutively related to awareness of water. Things are different with phenomenal consciousness, however. For phenomenal consciousness, there *is* a constitutive relation between it and knowledge of it: the instantiation of a phenomenal property entails the occurrence of an awareness of that instantiation. To repeat, this is due to the inherent for-me-ness of phenomenal consciousness.[41]

It should be stressed that not *all* knowledge of consciousness is constitutive of consciousness. By far most of it is not. But what matters is that *some* knowledge of consciousness *is* constitutively related to consciousness. Because the relation between phenomenal consciousness and (some) knowledge of it is constitutive, it need not be causal, and therefore does not require that phenomenal consciousness be causally efficacious. Phenomenal

[40] It may be objected that mathematical and logical properties would keep consciousness company. But in the case of such properties, we are more inclined to accept the verdict that either there is no genuine knowledge associated with them (though there may be justified belief) or they are somehow causally efficacious after all.

[41] This is not in tension with the claim made in Chapter 6 that there must be a broadly causal relation underlying self-representation. For the causal relation I urge holds between a *part* of a conscious state and the awareness of it. The relation between the *whole* conscious state and the awareness of it is constitutive, not causal.

consciousness can be causally inert, and knowledge of it would still be possible. Thus for phenomenal consciousness, and phenomenal consciousness alone, being epiphenomenal does not rule out knowability.[42]

Correspondingly, worlds that differ only in incorporating a supra-functional aspect of consciousness would not be scientifically equivalent.[43] Consider two worlds with two properties, Consc1 and Consc2, which are exactly the same except that Consc1 contains a non-functionalizable residue R whereas Consc2 does not. As above, Consc2 is nothing but the (occupant of the) Consc2 role, hence nothing but the (occupant of the) Consc1 role, but Consc1 is more than that. Unlike in the case of other properties, however, the ultimate scientific theories of these two worlds are *not* identical, because the scientist in the first world does know about R, for, whenever she instantiates R, she is aware of R. The one true complete scientific theory of the first world thus contains at least one more proposition than that of the second—namely, that there exists R. In this sense, Consc1 does *not* appear to be nothing but Consc2, and therefore does *not* appear to be nothing but the (occupant of the) Consc1 role.

So far I have focused on the fact that consciousness can be known even if it is non-functionalizable. But what is important for our present purposes is what this shows: that, even if consciousness is functionalizable, there is a sense in which it is not in its capacity as functionalizable that it is known. Every other property, if it is known at all, is known through its causal impact on the knower, and therefore precisely in virtue of its (having a) functional profile. By contrast, consciousness can be known in another way, not through its causal impact and therefore not in virtue of its (having a) functional profile.

This is why consciousness appears non-functionalizable. For consciousness to appear functionalizable, there would have to be some functional property that it appears to be nothing but. A property appears to be nothing

---

[42] Recall: phenomenal consciousness is the apparently supra-functional aspect of consciousness, its apparently non-functionalizable residue. So it is important to note that it has the special feature of not requiring causal contact with the knower in order to be known.

[43] Thus we can after all imagine functionally indistinguishable worlds whose true complete scientific theories are different—namely, if one scientific theory states that there is such a thing as phenomenal consciousness and the other does not. It is an open question whether the two theories can differ in that one of them attributes some properties to phenomenal consciousness that the other does not. I leave it an open question because it may well be that any particular property we might attribute to phenomenal consciousness does involve a functional profile, but that the existence of phenomenal consciousness does not.

but another property only if they can occur in two scientifically equivalent worlds; but this cannot happen with consciousness and any functional property. More slowly: for there to be some functional property F, such that it *appears* that consciousness is nothing but F, there would have to be a pair of worlds, W_1 and W_2, such that (i) consciousness occurs in W_1 and F occurs in W_2 and (ii) W_1 and W_2 are scientifically equivalent; but this is impossible: even if consciousness actually *is* nothing but F, the fact that F can be known only causally, whereas consciousness can also be known non-causally, guarantees that the two worlds are not scientifically equivalent.

The question I have been trying to answer is why it is that consciousness robustly appears non-functionalizable, in the sense that there is no functional property it appears to be nothing but. My answer is that, for any functional property, consciousness can be known—can appear to a knower—in a way that that functional property cannot. The reason for this is that consciousness can be known independently of any causal impact it makes on a knower, but functional properties cannot. And the reason consciousness can be known independently of any causal impact it may have is that it involves an inbuilt awareness of itself. That there is such an inbuilt awareness is, of course, not delivered by just *any* account of consciousness, but it is delivered by self-representationalism.[44]

We can now see why consciousness can be functionalizable and yet appear non-functionalizable. Suppose the aspect or component of consciousness that can be known non-causally does have a functional role—say, the functional role I identified in the previous chapter. Then that component would not resist functionalization, and thus would not make consciousness resist functionalization. Moreover, it would appear to knowers—make an appearance to them—in virtue of its functional profile. But, *in addition*, it would also appear to knowers—make another appearance to them—independently of its functional profile. In this situation, consciousness both is functionalizable and appears non-functionalizable.

We can bring this out by considering two worlds, W_1 and W_2, with two properties, F_1 and F_2, which are both fully functionalizable and are exactly the same except for this difference: there are components C_1 of F_1 and C_2

---

[44] The awareness is representational, according to self-representationalism, and it is inbuilt in the sense that it is built into every conscious state that there is an awareness of it, which means that the representation of that conscious state is part of (built into) that very state—as per Chapter 6.

of F_2, such that C_1 is knowable both causally and non-causally, but C_2 is knowable only causally. Thus, we may suppose that, in addition to their causal impact on knowers, instantiations of C_1 constitutively involve their subject's awareness of them, whereas instantiations of C_2 impact knowers but do not constitutively involve their subjects' awareness of them. In a situation such as this, it would seem that W_1 and W_2 are again not scientifically equivalent: there is extra knowledge in W_1 unobtainable in W_2. The upshot is that C_1 does not appear to be nothing but C_2 even though both have the same functional profile. This brings home clearly the way a property that can be known non-causally necessarily appears non-functionalizable, even if it actually is fully functionalizable.

In this section I have tried to show that it is not necessarily because consciousness is non-functionalizable that it appears non-functionalizable. Rather, it appears non-functionalizable because it can be known non-causally. And it can be known non-causally because it involves an inbuilt awareness of itself, which is grounded in its self-representational nature. That in itself does not show that consciousness is in reality functionalizable, but it does remove the major reason to think it is not. And, of course, my view is that there is a distinctive functional role of phenomenal consciousness—namely, the one identified in the second half of the previous chapter.

5. Conclusion: A Hard Solution to the Hard Problem

We can divide approaches to the hard problem of consciousness into three. One approach says that the problem is insoluble; a second approach says that the hard problem has an easy solution; the third insists that the hard problem requires a hard solution. According to the first approach, there is an unbridgeable gap between a conscious state's functional role and its phenomenal character, and therefore consciousness cannot be functionalized, which excludes the bridging of any explanatory gap. The second approach claims that in reality there is no principled difference between consciousness and all other properties, including with respect to functionalizability, which shows that the hard problem of consciousness rests on some kind of confusion or error. The third approach claims that there is something about consciousness that does set it apart from all other properties, but that nonetheless consciousness is fully functionalizable, and so the hard problem has a solution.[45]

I have adopted the third approach here. On the view I have defended, consciousness is set apart from all other properties in that the relation it bears to knowledge of it is not causal but constitutive (because of the self-representational nature of consciousness). This difference makes consciousness appear to evade functionalization in a way no other property does. It is significant, however, that the reason consciousness appears to evade functionalization does not have to do with the metaphysics of consciousness, but with its epistemology.[46] The reason is not that consciousness can *occur* independently of its functional profile, but that it can be *known* independently of its functional profile. Thus we can safely suppose that consciousness is functionalizable, despite being set apart from all other properties epistemologically.

In the first part of the chapter I argued that the alleged non-functionalizability of consciousness is the basis for its alleged irreducibility, because reduction seems to require functionalization. Once consciousness has been shown to be functionalizable, there is no reason to think it irreducible. The explanatory gap can be closed and the consciousness facts can be reductively explained in terms of facts about the neural correlate of consciousness.[47]

[45] It is an interesting question how to classify, within this scheme, the various views one finds in the literature on the explanatory gap and the hard problem. Some views, such as that of Loar (1990), certainly appear to belong in the third category of approach, as does the view I have defended here.

[46] It is also interesting to note, in connection with this, that all the most initially compelling arguments for the irreducibility of consciousness are epistemic. Although I will not undertake to do so here, one might conjecture that a diagnosis of these arguments may be offered that traces their apparent plausibility back to the fact that consciousness is non-causally knowable.

[47] For comments on a previous draft of this chapter I would like to thank Bill Lycan, Ken Williford, and an anonymous referee. In addition, I have benefited from conversations with Tim Bayne, Stephen Biggs, and David Chalmers.

Phenomenal Consciousness and Subjective Consciousness

This book has focused on what I called at the end of Chapter 2 *subjective consciousness*. Although I offered an account of qualitative consciousness as well, most of the effort went into subjective consciousness. This reflects my belief that subjective consciousness is more central to phenomenal consciousness than qualitative consciousness. Recall, however, that at the end of Chapter 2 we decided officially to remain neutral on this issue and treat the theory of phenomenal consciousness as a cluster of conditionals, of the form "if phenomenal consciousness is subjective consciousness, then p; if phenomenal consciousness is qualitative consciousness, then q; if phenomenal consciousness is combination C of subjective and qualitative consciousness, then r; if it is combination C*, then..." The reason I have chosen this approach is that it is incredibly hard to argue about how to construe the proper explanandum of the theory of phenomenal consciousness.

Nonetheless, in this appendix I want to offer a map of the case for taking subjective consciousness to be at least a necessary component of phenomenal consciousness. Since I construe subjective consciousness as a matter of the subject's suitable awareness of her conscious state (M is a subjectively conscious state iff S is suitably aware of M), I will focus on defending the following thesis:

(AT) Necessarily, for any mental state M of a subject S, M is phenomenally conscious (at a time t) only if S is aware of M (at t).

Call this the *awareness thesis*. This thesis differs from the thesis of the ubiquity of inner awareness (UIA) from Chapter 5 mainly in that it does not require that the subject's awareness be itself conscious. Although I believe it is, that is not a commitment definitive of taking subjective consciousness to be necessary to phenomenal consciousness.[1]

---

[1] Thus, higher-order theorists take subjective consciousness to be necessary to phenomenal consciousness, but do not think of subjective consciousness as necessarily involving conscious awareness of one's subjectively conscious state.

AT is not to be confused with other, neighboring theses, which it does not entail. Here are some:[2]

(T1) Necessarily, for any mental state M of a subject S, M is phenomenally conscious (at *t*) only if S is aware (at *t*) *that* she is in M.

(T2) Necessarily, for any mental state M of a subject S, M is phenomenally conscious (at *t*) only if S is aware (at *t*) *that* M is occurring.

(T3) Necessarily, for any mental state M of a subject S, M is phenomenally conscious (at *t*) only if S is aware (at *t*) of *her being in* M.

(T4) Necessarily, for any mental state M of a subject S, M is phenomenally conscious (at *t*) only if S is aware (at *t*) of M *qua conscious*.

(T5) Necessarily, for any mental state M of a subject S, M is phenomenally conscious (at *t*) only if S is aware (at *t*) of M *qua M*.

(T6) Necessarily, for any mental state M of a subject S, M is phenomenally conscious (at *t*) only if S is *attentively* aware (at *t*) of M.

(T7) Necessarily, for any mental state M of a subject S, M is phenomenally conscious (at *t*) *if and* only if S is aware (at *t*) of M.

AT does not require that the awareness of M be propositional—that is, awareness *that* (as T1 and T2 do). It does not require that S's awareness of M involve awareness of *herself* (as T1 and T3 do). It does not require that S be aware of M in any particular *way* (as T4, T5, and T6 do). Finally, AT is a necessity claim, not a sufficiency claim (as T7 is). Note well: AT is certainly *compatible* with each of T1–7; but, in arguing for AT, we remain silent on T1–7.

Some philosophers have found AT self-evident, others entirely fictional. The purpose of this appendix is to present the bare outlines of a number of arguments in favor of AT. None of the arguments will be sufficiently developed here to constitute a sustained, self-standing reason to adopt AT. The purpose is rather to offer as nearly comprehensive as possible a set of options for *pursuing* the case for AT. Many of the arguments will have substantive assumptions that make their starting point less than perfectly neutral. But different arguments will have

[2] Caveat: the enumeration herein, of certain theses not entailed by AT, shall not be construed to deny or disparage the existence of other theses also not entailed by AT.

different assumptions, and so hopefully many readers may find an argument whose assumptions are acceptable to them. In addition, the fact that the appeal to AT can account unifyingly for all of the phenomena appealed to in those arguments casts them as converging lines of evidence in favor of AT.[3]

A. The Sub-Personal Argument

The argument of this section relies on the conceptual interrelations between consciousness, awareness, and the personal/sub-personal distinction often employed in cognitive science. The argument proceeds as follows: For any mental state M of a subject S, (1) if S is completely unaware of M, then M is a sub-personal state of S; (2) if M is a sub-personal state of S, then M is not phenomenally conscious; therefore, (3) if S is completely unaware of M, then M is not phenomenally conscious; or, contrapositively, (4) M is phenomenally conscious only if S is aware of M. Call it the *sub-personal argument*.

Premise 2 appears unquestionable: conscious states are states of persons, not of some sub-personal modules or processes taking place in them—a module is never conscious, only persons are.[4] But Premise 1 may be thought to require some defense. In particular, dispositional beliefs and other standing states might be thought by some to constitute a counter-example to it.

My own view, however, is that there *are* no standing states. Consider the view that there are no dispositional beliefs, only dispositions to believe. Jane has the disposition to believe that there are more than four countries in the world, but it does not follow that there is a dispositional belief to that effect that she has. There is certainly no *need* to posit such dispositional beliefs, since arguably dispositions to believe would be sufficient to do any explanatory work we might want dispositional beliefs to do (Manfredi 1993). By extension, we might claim that persons do not have standing states, only dispositions to enter occurrent states. If there are no standing states, a fortiori there are no personal-level ones.[5]

---

[3] The resulting picture portrays AT as the explanatory center of gravity for a number of diverse phenomena. That itself should count as evidence for AT. This should be especially so for those of us who see with a kind eye Kitcher's unification model of explanation (1981). One might also take a disjunctive approach: each argument is reasonably plausible, so the likelihood that one of them is sound is relatively high.

[4] Block (2007) argues that deep sub-personal states may be phenomenally conscious, but for my part I cannot understand this claim. In any case, I note that Block holds that these sub-personal phenomenal states would still have a kind of for-me-ness. Another objector might cite the bundle theory of the self as a view in which conscious states are not of persons. But, first, the bundle theory is quite implausible, and, secondly, it nowise entails that conscious states are not of persons. Rather, it recasts what is involved in a conscious state's being a person's in terms of the membership of the state in a bundle.

[5] A similar point applies to Freudian deep-unconscious states. They are explanatorily pre-empted by deep dispositions (or clusters thereof). For example, when we say that a person has a suppressed

If this consideration is accepted, then standing states are not counter-examples to Premise 1. There may yet be a different counter-example to it, but I can think of none. I conclude that we have in the present consideration the basis for something that could be developed into an argument for AT.

B. The Memorability Argument

It is true that I remember Obama's inauguration. It is not true that I remember Bush's. It is also not true that I remember Jefferson's. But the last two are untrue in very different ways. There is a sense in which I *could* remember Bush's inauguration—for example, if I had better memory. There is no sense in which I *could* remember Jefferson's inauguration—and my memory has nothing to do with it. The reason I cannot be coherently said to remember Jefferson's inauguration is that I was not aware of it *when it took place*. To be coherently said to remember event *x*, one has to be aware of *x* when *x* takes place.

This applies not only to outer events, such as presidential inaugurations, but also inner events, such as thoughts and experiences. Thus, I remember having the experience of tasting orange juice when I had breakfast this morning. I *also* remember having the breakfast, which is an outer event. But in addition, I remember my gustatory experiences during the breakfast, which were inner events.[6] I even remember having the thought that the orange juice did not seem entirely freshly squeezed, as advertised; that, too, was an inner event.

Given that I remember having my experience of, and thought about, the orange juice, and that memory requires original awareness, it follows that, when I was originally *having* the experience and the thought, I was *aware* of their taking place.

Observe, more generally, that every conscious state is *memorable* in the sense that there is a time after its occurrence at which its subject can remember it. For the subject to be able to remember the conscious state *after* its occurrence, she would have to have been aware of it *at* its occurrence. Therefore, every conscious state is a state of which the subject is aware at the time of its occurrence.

Call this argument—which hails, interestingly, from the sixth-century Buddhist philosopher Dinnāga—the *memorability argument*.[7] We may present it, loosely, as follows: (1) every conscious state is memorable; (2) a conscious state would not be memorable if the subject was not aware of it at the time of its occurrence; therefore, (3) every conscious state is such that the subject is aware of it at the time

Oedipal desire, the truthmaker of our statement is the cluster of tendencies to behave in certain ways in certain circumstances, not the existence of a *state* a person is actually in.

[6] I remember the orange juice's *flavor*, but I *also* remember, on top of that, concentrating on my *experience* of the orange juice's *taste*.

[7] The main contemporary expositor of this argument is Jonardon Ganeri (1999). See also Perrett 2003, as well as Janzen 2005. Gennaro (1992) develops, independently, a parallel argument about creature consciousness. My present interest, however, is in state consciousness.

of its occurrence. A more precise formulation might be: for any conscious mental state M had by a subject S at a time t, (1) there is a time t^*, $t^* > t$, such that S can remember M at t^*;[8] (2) S can remember M at a time t^* only if S is aware of M at t; therefore, (3) S is aware of M at t. Note that the modal force of Premise 2 is conceptual. The claim is that it is part of the very concept of remembering that a subject can be said to remember an event only if she was aware of it at the time of its occurrence.

In evaluating the argument, it is important to keep in mind that the first premise states that all conscious experiences are memorable, but not that all conscious experiences are *always* memorable. That is, the claim is that, for every conscious experience, there is *some* future time at which the subject can remember it; not that the experience can be remembered at *every* future time. Thus, it would be misguided to object that Premise 1 denies conscious experiences to amnesiacs, who cannot later remember their experience. For, while amnesiacs lack long-term memory, they certainly have working memory and can remember an experience a second after it took place. Tulving's patient KC (1983), who had no autobiographical memories whatsoever and could not keep a question in his mind for longer than a minute, could nonetheless play a hand of cards competently. This is because KC's working memory was nonetheless functional.

An objection more to the point would be that it cannot be *metaphysically necessary* for conscious experiences that they be memorable. We can readily conceive of creatures who exist for a single instant, in which they have a conscious experience. However, the fact that a creature exists only one moment does not entail that its conscious experience at that moment is not memorable. The experience may well be memorable; it is just that the creature does not have the opportunity to capitalize on its memorability by actually remembering it. This is not because the experience itself is immemorable, but simply because the creature does not have future moments at which it might remember its experience. Thus the following counterfactual may still be true of the creature: if it did exist longer, it would be able to remember its initial experience. The counterfactual makes it true that the creature's experience is memorable.

A final objection, perhaps the hardest, would be that a person without any kind of memory—not even working memory—could still be conscious, and so her experiences would be conscious yet immemorable. More generally, the claim that consciousness is constitutively tied to memorability enjoys about as much antecedent plausibility as the claim that consciousness is constitutively tied to awareness, so no advantage could be gained by arguing for the latter through the former. This is indeed a difficult objection, and I have no strong reply to it. I want only to point out, first, that it is not all that obvious, upon reflection, that we can conceive of a conscious person without even minimal memory (from one second

---

[8] I am using the symbol > to mean "later than" (as is common in the relevant discussions).

to the next, say), and more generally, that prior credences vary, and so I can hope that some readers' prior credence regarding the constitutive tie to memorability is higher than that regarding the tie to awareness.

C. The Reportability Argument

Right now I have a conscious visual experience of the laptop before me. I am also in a position to report spontaneously having this experience. Interestingly, it appears that all and only conscious states are spontaneously reportable. More accurately, all and only conscious states of subjects capable of reporting (thus, who have linguistic abilities) are spontaneously reportable.[9] But forget the "only"; let us focus on the "all." All conscious states of reportage-capable subjects are states that can be spontaneously reported by their subject.

By saying that a conscious state is *spontaneously* reportable, I mean that it can be reported *at the time that it occurs*.

Note now that an event or state of affairs *x* can be reported only if the reporter is aware of *x at the time of the reporting*. I can, right now, report that my neighbor used to drive a convertible, because I am, right now, aware that my neighbor used to drive a convertible. If I were not aware (right now) of the fact that my neighbor used to drive a convertible, I would not be in a position to report so. This does not mean that my neighbor still does. That is, it does not mean that the reported fact holds in the present. It only means that the reported fact, whether present, past, or future, is one that I am aware of in the present. The reporting need not be contemporaneous with the reported fact, only with the awareness of the reported fact.

These considerations suggest another argument for AT. The argument is that all conscious states are reportable at the time that they occur (that is, are spontaneously reportable), reportability requires awareness at the time of the reporting, and therefore all conscious states are states we are aware of at the time that they occur. More formally: (1) for any conscious mental state M had by a subject S at a time *t*, S can report on M at *t*; (2) for any *x* and S, S can report on *x* at *t* only if S is aware of *x* at *t*; therefore, (3) for any conscious mental state M had by a subject S at a time *t*, S is aware of M at *t*. Call this the *reportability argument*.[10]

The modality of "can" in Premises 1 and 2 probably needs to be nomological or at least psychological. (Psychological modality may be understood as a lax nomological modality: whereas *p* is nomologically possible iff *p* is consistent with

---

[9] I am using the term "report" here in such a way that by definition all reporting is verbal. In the cognitive sciences, it is customary to use the term differently, so that some reporting is verbal and some is not. This is not how I use the term.

[10] The argument, and the label, can be found in Janzen 2005. A very similar argument has been propounded by David Rosenthal for years (see Rosenthal 1990, 1993, 2002a).

all the actual laws of nature, *p* is psychologically possible iff *p* is consistent with the *psychological* laws of nature—that is, the actual laws of psychology.) It appears to be a matter of the laws of psychology that one cannot report on what one is completely unaware of; and that one can always report one's ongoing conscious experiences and thoughts. There is no metaphysical necessity in this, but there does seem to be nomological necessity.

It may be objected that Premise 1 is false: the conscious experiences of animals and infants are not spontaneously reportable. I myself admitted above that only the conscious experiences of reportage-capable subjects, not those of *all* subjects, are spontaneously reportable. This objection is well placed, but it merely forces us to make the argument in two steps. The first step will establish (along the above lines) that, for any conscious mental state M had by a reportage-capable subject S at a time *t*, S is aware of M at *t*. The second step will be that, since the relation between reportage-capability and consciousness is entirely accidental, the fact that reportage-capable subjects are aware of their conscious states is strong evidence that reportage-incapable subjects are aware of theirs as well.

Another objection would erect an argument by counter-model centering on tacit beliefs. If asked whether you believe that there are more than four countries in Africa, you will doubtless respond with the utmost immediacy. We can thus spontaneously report our tacit beliefs. Yet tacit beliefs are unconscious. My response is twofold. First, as stated above, I reject the existence of tacit beliefs. Secondly, even if there were tacit beliefs, I would reject the claim that they were *spontaneously* reportable. The fact that, *when asked*, a subject could report immediately on her tacit belief does not entail that the belief was spontaneously reportable all along. After all, the subject would need to be *prompted* by the asking. There is no question that, once prompted, you were in a position to report spontaneously on your belief that there are indeed more than four countries in Africa. But were you in a position to do so before prompted? Not in any ordinary sense.

In this respect, let us dwell on the effect of the "prompting." By the time you confirm that you believe that there are more than four countries in Africa, you are aware that this is something you believe—indeed, you believe it consciously. So the prompting effected a transformation of your belief from tacit to conscious status: a tacit belief of which you were unaware had become a conscious belief of which you were aware. So by the time you report that you believe that there are more than four countries in Africa, the belief is no longer an unconscious state. The objector must argue that, even though the belief is always report*ed* when it is already conscious, it is nonetheless report*able* when it is still unconscious (where the "-able" indicates a psychological modality). There is no reason to suppose that this can be successfully argued.[11]

---

[11] Or at least it is the objector's burden to show what that reason might be.

D. The Argument from Surprise

The previous argument concentrated on the subject's ability to form a report at will. An analogous argument would concentrate on the subject's ability to form an introspective notice at will: the subject of a conscious state is always in a position spontaneously and introspectively to notice her concurrent conscious state.

More interestingly, when one does introspectively notice a conscious state, one is not *surprised* by what one has noticed. I am using the term "surprise" in a somewhat artificial way: for x to be "surprising" to S is for x to have been unexpected by S before S noticed x. That is, x "surprises" S at t if S notices x at t and S did not expect x just before t.[12] In this (artificial) sense, when I turn a corner and notice a pine tree at the end of the block, the pine tree is "surprising" to me. This simply means that I did not expect it to be there—not in the sense that I expected it not to be there, but in the sense that I did not form an expectation, however implicit, that it be there. It is in this sense that no conscious states appear to be surprising to notice upon introspection. If I turn my attention from the laptop to my visual experience of the laptop, I am unsurprised to find just the experience I do.[13]

How can we explain the fact that conscious experiences are unsurprising in this way? Most events and objects we encounter in our daily life *are* surprising: we do not expect them before noticing them. But conscious states are consistently unsurprising. Why is that?

The answer would be straightforward if AT obtained. If conscious states were states we were aware of, then they would not be surprising to notice when we turned our attention onto them. We would, in some sense, have expected them to "be there," since we would have been aware of them beforehand. This reasoning could be the basis for an *argument from surprise*. It is an argument from inference to the best explanation, not a demonstrative argument (an abductive, not deductive, argument).[14]

It may be objected that I have claimed that AT is the best explanation of spontaneous reportability, but I have not considered alternative explanations and

[12] This notion is artificial, or "technical," inasmuch as it does not involve the emotional reaction of (very) mild startle characteristic of surprise. Also, what counts as "just before" is a contingent psychological matter about when we normally form expectations regarding upcoming events in our cognitive life.

[13] Not every component of a conscious experience must be unsurprising to encounter—there may be peripheral components that are somewhat surprising, even in the present sense. But the overall global experience is never surprising to encounter.

[14] The argument, and the label, can be found in Williford 2003. Williford does not develop the argument as an inference to the best explanation, however. Rather, he develops it as a demonstrative argument. As a non-demonstrative argument, we might construe it as follows: (1) no conscious state is surprising to notice; (2) the best explanation of conscious states' being unsurprising to notice is that one is aware of one's conscious states whenever one has them; therefore, plausibly, (3) conscious states are states of which one is aware whenever one has them.

shown that they are worse. I concede that this makes the argument incomplete. A fuller development of the argument would have to go through all possible explanations and show that they are worse than AT's. As it happens, for my part, I cannot see any initially plausible alternative explanation. And in any case, an incomplete argument still puts pressure on the opposition.

E. The Argument from Volume Control

To introspect one's conscious state is to be aware of it in a focal, attentive manner. As expanded on earlier in this book, this is *not* the way one is *normally* aware of one's conscious state. Normally, one is aware of one's conscious state in a peripheral, inattentive manner. But there may be something to be learned about this normal, peripheral awareness from the more special, introspective variety.

A common misconception of introspective awareness construes it as merely *revealing* conscious experiences, experiences that are the way they are independently of being introspected. This misconception has been corrected by Chris Hill's "volume control" model of introspection (1988), which we encountered in Chapter 5. According to the volume-control model, introspection *affects* the intrinsic nature of the introspected experience, at least inasmuch as the *phenomenal intensity* of the experience changes when introspected: the more focused and attentive one's introspective awareness of one's experience, the more heightened and acute the experience's phenomenal intensity.[15] In this sense, introspective awareness functions as a volume-control device.

The volume-control model is very intuitive. Yet it has far-reaching consequences. For our purposes, it appears to imply an *internal connection* between the introspected experience and the introspective awareness of it.

We can take the argument a step further. A picture suggested—though not entailed—by the volume-control model is that the phenomenal intensity of an experience is *proportional* to one's degree of awareness of it. This is most certainly true of introspected experiences, and it would seem epistemically responsible to infer that it must be the case for unintrospected experiences as well: the degree of phenomenal intensity of a conscious experience varies concomitantly with the degree to which one is (introspectively or non-introspectively) aware of it.[16] This concomitant variation would be explained straightforwardly by the hypothesis that

[15] I do not mean this to be definitional, but substantive. I think we do have an independent conception of phenomenal intensity that is not derived from the notion of degree-of-awareness, and that, even when conceived in this independent way, phenomenal intensity correlates with degree of awareness.

[16] Given the discussions in Chapters 7 and 5, it is also clear how we would account for this notion of "degree of awareness"—namely, in terms of the amount of attention resources devoted to the awareness.

the degree to which one is aware of one's experience determines the experience's degree of intensity.[17]

This latter hypothesis in turn entails AT. It follows from it that, for an experience to have *any* phenomenal intensity, one must have *some* awareness of the experience. Zero awareness would result in zero phenomenal intensity (if you please)—that is, in the experience being phenomenally extinguished. The result is AT: in order to have minimal phenomenality, an experience must be something the subject is minimally aware of.

This *argument from volume control* proceeds in two phases. The first phase is an inference to the best explanation, where the explanandum is the truth of volume control and the explanans is the hypothesis of intensity-awareness covariation. The second phase is the derivation of AT from that hypothesis.

This argument is somewhat roundabout and as such may be attacked at a number of junctures. But both its phases strike me as fundamentally sound. If any part is particularly vulnerable, it would be the move from the straight volume-control model to the stronger claim that phenomenal intensity is proportional to degree of awareness. A full defense of this move cannot be pursued here. But note that the volume-control model already suggests, by itself, an internal connection between phenomenality and awareness.

F. The Sophisticated Argument from Blindsight

A more empirically based argument adverts to blindsight. Blindsighted subjects respond visually to stimuli in their environment, which they report not seeing. The scientist infers that the blindsighted perceives her environment but is unaware of doing so, with the result that her blindseeings are unconscious.

The attendant argument for AT is based, again, on an inference to the best explanation. Suppose that Blain the blindsighted and Norman the normally sighted are presented with the same visual stimulus, and that Blain and Norman perceive the stimulus the same way, but Blain's perception is unconscious while Norman's is conscious. The simplest explanation of this is (or involves the claim) that Blain and Norman are in the same visual state, but Blain is unaware of his state whereas Norman is aware of his. This explanation presupposes that awareness of a visual state is a condition of the state's being conscious. We may call this the *argument from blindsight*.[18]

---

[17] This hypothesis also accounts neatly for the fact that it appears possible for two conscious states to be the same in all other respects, including all qualitative respects, and yet one is experienced more vividly than the other. Our hypothesis accounts for this apparent possibility quite straightforwardly: the subjects of the two experiences are aware of them with different degrees of attentiveness.

[18] This sort of reasoning can be found in Rosenthal 1991 and Carruthers 2000: ch. 6.

The objection would be that there is a better explanation of the data—namely, that the visual states of Blain and Norman are different: Blain's is functionally and representationally impoverished relative to Norman's.

To accommodate this, let us envisage a similar condition in which the visual states of Blain and Norman are functionally and representationally indistinguishable; call it *hyper-blindsight*. The argument from hyper-blindsight is that the best explanation of the difference between Blain and Norman is that the former is not, but the latter is, aware of his visual state.

Again it might be objected that a better explanation is available—namely, that Blain's visual state does not have qualitative properties, whereas Norman's does.[19]

How should we decide between our two alternative explanations? Clearly, we cannot rely on Blain to report whether his blindseeings have qualitative properties, since he is unable to report that he has blindseeings at all. We must rely on third-person findings.

One finding of direct relevance is the phenomenon of "primesight" (Weiskrantz et al. 2002). It appears that D.B., a celebrity blindsight patient, experiences after-images after blindstaring at color stimuli. Thus, after staring at a bright red surface long enough, unconsciously perceiving it all the while, when the light is turned off, D.B. experiences a vivid green after-image. This after-image does have qualitative properties.[20]

This seems to suggest that the priming blindseeing had qualitative properties just as the primed after-image experience does. The supposition here is that a non-qualitative perception would not generate a qualitative after-image. It might relay information, playing its role in the information-processing system, but not generate a qualitative character. We may formulate this *argument from primesight* as follows: (1) some blindsight patients' perceptions prime qualitative after-image experiences; (2) it is unlikely that non-qualitative perceptions can prime qualitative experiences; therefore, (3) some blindsight patients' perceptions are probably qualitative.

To be sure, one could object to Premise 2 of this argument. But, on the face of it, the premise is quite plausible. Keep in mind that, this being part of an argument from inference to the best explanation, the premise states only likelihood. That is, the overall argument is not intended as demonstrative: it too is not deductive, but abductive. It does seem that an AT-involving explanation of blindsight, or at least primesight, would be more straightforward, at least, than its alternative(s).

I conclude that the weight of empirical evidence suggests that a key part of what is involved in blindsight is the subject's inability to become aware of the

---

[19] Note that this objection can work only if qualitative properties are understood as not involving inner awareness. So that is how we must think of qualitative properties in the discussion to follow—as what I called in Chapter 4 schmalitative properties.

[20] Observe that here we *can* rely on first-person reports that the after-image experience is qualitative. D.B.'s reports of experiencing the after-image have been confirmed by Weiskrantz and his collaborators with third-person experiments; but that the experience instantiates qualitative character we know simply by D.B.'s testimony.

relevant visual perceptions. At least an empirically based argument of this form is in the offing. This suggests, in turn, that normal conscious sight is sight of which the subject is aware. Call this the *sophisticated argument from blindsight*.

G. The Argument from Cognitive Phenomenology

Several philosophers have recently argued that purely cognitive states—propositional attitudes with no sensuous qualities whatsoever—can be phenomenally conscious; and I subscribed to this view in Chapter 5.[21] What could possibly account for such purely cognitive phenomenology? One answer is that it is my awareness of my thought that bestows on it its cognitive phenomenology. There are other answers, but, as I will argue shortly, none satisfactory. If so, we have to accept that conscious cognitive states are conscious in virtue of one's awareness of them. It would then be extremely odd to maintain that, although conscious cognitive states are conscious in virtue of the subject's awareness of them, conscious sensory experiences are not conscious—not even partially—in virtue of the subject's awareness of them.

This *argument from cognitive phenomenology* can be put as follows: (1) there are conscious mental states that are purely cognitive; (2) such states can be conscious only in virtue of the subject's awareness of them; therefore, (3) all conscious cognitive states are conscious in virtue of the subject's awareness of them; (4) it is implausible that what conscious cognitive states are conscious in virtue of is completely different from what conscious sensory experiences are conscious in virtue of; therefore, (5) it is plausible that conscious sensory experiences are conscious in virtue of the subject's awareness of them; therefore, plausibly, (6) all conscious states (cognitive and not) are such that their subject is aware of them. The premises in need of defense here are primarily 2 and 4.[22]

Premise 4 is plausible, because conscious states appear to be conscious *in the same sense* when cognitive and when not. An objector might suggest that in fact the senses are different: conscious experiences are such in the sense of phenomenal consciousness, whereas conscious cognitions are such in the sense of access consciousness. But our argument relies on the claim that there is a genuine cognitive *phenomenology*: a phenomenal way it is like for one to have a purely

---

[21] On this view, then, there is something it is like for me to think consciously that $2+2 = 4$. It is *not* part of this claim that what it is like for me to think that $2+2 = 4$ is different from what it is like for me to think that $234+112 = 346$. This claim is made independently, for instance, by Horgan and Tienson (2002). But it is not something our present argument is committed to (see Kriegel 2003c). As far as our argument is concerned, it may well be that *all* cognitive conscious states have one and the same phenomenal feel to them.

[22] Premise 1 is controversial as well, of course. But I will not argue for it here. I cannot hope to do justice to the issue here, and anyway have nothing (of non-esoteric nature) to add to the points already made in the literature. To my mind, the best case for it is made in Pitt 2004.

cognitive state. To be sure, this claim is not uncontroversial, and to that extent this argument is not for everybody. But the argument does not falter on a supposed ambiguity in the use of "conscious."

In defense of Premise 2, let us examine the alternatives to awareness of conscious cognitive states as what makes them conscious. In the first instance, one might suggest that the phenomenal character of cognitive states is bestowed on them by accompanying imagery. This suggestion is doubly implausible. First, it seems (metaphysically) *possible* to have conscious cognitive states unaccompanied by any imagery. Secondly, two cognitive states could share phenomenal properties without sharing imagistic properties. Next it might be thought that the phenomenal feel of conscious cognitive states is bestowed on them by their representational contents. This suggestion cannot account, however, for the difference between conscious and unconscious beliefs that *p*. Finally, it might be suggested that conscious cognitive states are conscious in virtue of playing a special cognitive or functional role, one that unconscious cognitive states do not play. However, as we have stressed a number of times in this book, functional role properties are dispositional, whereas phenomenal character is non-dispositional, so the latter cannot be constituted by the former.[23]

I conclude that the alternative accounts of cognitive phenomenology are unsatisfactory. The best account is that purely cognitive conscious states have their phenomenology in virtue of the subject's awareness of them.[24]

H. Conclusion

As I warned at the beginning of this appendix, none of the above arguments is satisfactorily developed. They are all better thought of as sketches of, or promises for, arguments. One could write a whole book that would make the case for subjective consciousness being a necessary component of phenomenal consciousness. I have chosen to write a different book, one developing a specific account of subjective consciousness (and remarking, more briefly, on qualitative

---

[23] In Chapter 8 I argued that phenomenal properties are functionalizable, but the notion of functionalizability used there was consistently neutral as between functionalization as reduction to a functional role property and functionalization as reduction to a role-occupant property. That is, one way to functionalize property F was to say that F is nothing but the occupant of a designated functional role.

[24] It might be objected that an absurd consequence of this account is that all cognitive conscious states have the same phenomenology. My response is twofold. First, this alleged consequence would not be all that implausible (see Kriegel 2003c). But, secondly, it is not a consequence. It is perfectly possible that all cognitive conscious states have *a* phenomenology in virtue of the subject's awareness of them, but, once they have a phenomenology, the particular phenomenology they have is determined by, say, their representational contents. In fact, I believe this to be the case. Different cognitive states could then have different phenomenologies in virtue of their representational content, even though they do not have a phenomenology in the first place in virtue of their representational content.

consciousness). This appendix was intended to suggest that it would be surprising if subjective consciousness were not a necessary component of phenomenal consciousness.[25]

---

[25] For comments on a previous draft of this appendix I would like to thank Miri Albahari, David Chalmers, Fred Dretske, Terry Horgan, Galen Strawson, Bob Van Gulick, Ken Williford, and an anonymous referee.

References

Adams, F. 1991. "Causal Contents." In D. McLaughlin (ed.), *Dretske and his Critics*. Oxford: Blackwell.

Alter, T. 2006. "On the Conditional Analysis of Phenomenal Concepts." *Philosophical Studies* 134: 235–53.

Amsterdam, B. 1972. "Mirror Self-Image Reactions before Age Two." *Developmental Psychobiology* 5: 297–305.

Armstrong, D. M. 1968. *A Materialist Theory of the Mind*. New York: Humanities Press.

—— 1977. "The Causal Theory of Mind." *Neue Hefte für Philosophie* 11: 82–95.

Baars, B. J. 1988. *A Cognitive Theory of Consciousness*. Cambridge: Cambridge University Press.

Baldwin, T. 1992. "The Projective Theory of Sensory Content." In T. Crane (ed.), *The Contents of Experience*. Cambridge: Cambridge University Press.

Bayne, T. and D. J. Chalmers 2003. "What Is the Unity of Consciousness?" In A. Cleeremans (ed.), *The Unity of Consciousness*. Oxford: Oxford University Press.

—— and N. Levy 2006. "The Feeling of Doing: Deconstructing the Phenomenology of Agency." In N. Sebanz and W. Prinz (eds.), *Disorders of Volition*. Cambridge, MA: MIT Press.

Bell, J. L. 2004. "Whole and Part in Mathematics." *Axiomathes* 14: 284–95.

Benacerraf, P. 1973. "Mathematical Truth." *Journal of Philosophy* 70: 661–79.

Block, N. J. 1986. "Advertisement for a Semantics for Psychology." *Midwest Studies in Philosophy* 10: 615–77.

—— 1990a. "Inverted Earth." *Philosophical Perspective* 4: 52–79.

—— 1990b. "Can the Mind Change the World?" In G. Boolos (ed.), *Essays in Honor of Hilary Putnam*. Cambridge: Cambridge University Press.

—— 1995. "On a Confusion about the Function of Consciousness." *Behavioral and Brain Sciences* 18: 227–47. Reprinted in Block et al. 1997.

—— 1996. "Mental Paint and Mental Latex." In *Philosophical Issues* 7: 19–50.

—— 1998. "Is Experiencing Just Representing?" *Philosophy and Phenomenological Research* 58: 663–70.

—— 1999. "Sexism, Racism, Ageism, and the Nature of Consciousness." *Philosophical Topics* 26.

—— 2007. "Consciousness, Accessibility, and the Mesh between Psychology and Neuroscience." *Behavioral and Brain Sciences* 30: 481–99.

Block, N. J., O. Flanagan, and G. Guzeldere (eds.) 1997. *The Nature of Consciousness: Philosophical Debates*. Cambridge, MA: MIT Press.

—— and R. Stalnaker 1999. "Conceptual Analysis, Dualism, and the Explanatory Gap." *Philosophical Review* 108: 1–46.

Boghossian, P. and J. Velleman 1989. "Colour as a Secondary Quality." *Mind* 98: 81–103.

Botvinik, M. M., T. S. Braver, C. S. Carter, D. M. Barch, and J. D. Cohen 2001. "Conflict Monitoring and Cognitive Control." *Psychological Review* 108: 624–52.

Braddon-Mitchell, D. 2003. "Qualia and Analytical Conditionals." *Journal of Philosophy* 100: 111–35.

Brentano, F. 1874. *Psychology from an Empirical Standpoint*, ed. O. Kraus; English edition, ed. L. L. McAlister, 1973; trans. A. C. Rancurello, D. B. Terrell, and L. L. McAlister. London: Routledge and Kegan Paul.

Bressler, S. L. 1995. "Large-Scale Cortical Networks and Cognition." *Brain Research* 20: 288–304.

Broadbent, D. E. 1958. *Perception and Communication*. London: Pergamon Press.

Burge, T. 1989. "Individuation and Causation in Psychology." *Pacific Philosophical Quarterly* 70: 303–22.

Byrne, D. 1997. "Some Like It HOT: Consciousness and Higher Order Thoughts." *Philosophical Studies* 86: 103–29.

Byrne, A. 2001. "Intentionalism Defended." *Philosophical Review* 110: 199–240.

—— 2006. "Color and the Mind–Body Problem." *Dialectica* 60: 223–44.

Carruthers, P. 1989. "Brute Experience." *Journal of Philosophy* 85: 258–69.

—— 1998. "Natural Theories of Consciousness." *European Journal of Philosophy* 6: 203–22.

—— 1999. "Sympathy and Subjectivity." *Australasian Journal of Philosophy* 77: 465–82.

—— 2000. *Phenomenal Consciousness*. Cambridge: Cambridge University Press.

Castañeda, H.-N. 1966. " 'He': A Study in the Logic of Self-Consciousness." *Ratio* 8: 130–57.

—— 1969. "On the Phenomeno-Logic of the I." *Proceedings of the 14th International Congress of Philosophy* iii. Reprinted in Q. Cassam (ed.), *Self-Knowledge*. Oxford: Oxford University Press, 1994.

Caston, V. 2002. "Aristotle on Consciousness." *Mind* 111: 751–815.

Chalmers, D. J. 1995a. "Facing up to the Problem of Consciousness." *Journal of Consciousness Studies* 2: 200–19.

—— 1995b. "The Puzzle of Conscious Experience." *Scientific American*, December: 62–8.

—— 1996. *The Conscious Mind*. Oxford and New York: Oxford University Press.

—— 1997. "Availability: The Cognitive Basis of Consciousness?" *Behavioral and Brain Sciences* 20: 148–9. Reprinted in Block et al. 1997.

—— 2000. "What Is a Neural Correlate of Consciousness?" In T. Metzinger (ed.), *Neural Correlates of Consciousness: Empirical and Conceptual Questions*. Cambridge, MA: MIT Press.

—— 2004. "The Representational Character of Experience." In B. Leiter (ed.), *The Future for Philosophy*. Oxford: Oxford University Press.

—— Forthcoming. "The Two-Dimensional Argument against Materialism." In B. P. McLaughlin and A. Beckermann (eds.), *The Oxford Handbook of the Philosophy of Mind*. Oxford: Oxford University Press.

—— and F. Jackson 2001. "Conceptual Analysis and Reductive Explanation." *Philosophical Review* 110: 315–61.

Churchland, P. M. 1984. *Matter and Consciousness*. Cambridge, MA: MIT Press.

Clark, A. 2000. "A Case Where Access Implies Qualia?" *Analysis* 60: 30–8.

Craik, F. I. M., T. M. Moroz, M. Moscovitch, D. T. Stuss, G. Winocur, E. Tulving, and S. Kapur 1999. "In Search of the Self: A Positron Emission Tomography Study." *Psychological Science* 10: 26–34.

Crick, F. and C. Koch 1995. "Are We Aware of Neural Activity in Primary Visual Cortex?" *Nature* 375: 121–3.

—— 2003. "A Framework for Consciousness." *Nature Neuroscience* 6: 119–26.

Cummins, R. 1989. *Mental Representation*. Cambridge, MA: MIT Press.

Davidson, D. 1987. "Knowing One's Own Mind." *Proceedings and Addresses of the American Philosophical Association* 61: 441–58.

DeBellis, M. 1991. "The Representational Content of Musical Experience." *Philosophy and Phenomenological Research* 51: 303–24.

Dehaene, S., C. Sergent, and J.-P. Changeux 2003. "A Neuronal Network Model Linking Subjective Reports and Objective Physiological Data during Conscious Perception." *Proceedings of the National Academy of Science USA* 100: 8520–5.

Dennett, D. C. 1988. "Quining Qualia." In A. Marcel and E. Bisiach (eds.), *Consciousness in Contemporary Science*. New York: Oxford University Press.

—— 1991. "Ways of Establishing Harmony." In B. McLaughlin (ed.), *Dretske and his Critics*. Oxford: Blackwell.

—— 1995. "The Path Not Taken." *Behavioral and Brain Sciences* 18: 252–3. Reprinted in Block et al. 1997.

Dixon, N. F. 1971. *Subliminal Perception: The Nature of a Controversy*. London: McGraw-Hill.

Dowell, J. Forthcoming. "Serious Metaphysics and the Vindication of Reductions." *Philosophical Studies*.

Dretske, F. I. 1981. *Knowledge and the Flow of Information*. Oxford: Clarendon Press.

Dretske, F. I. 1986. "Misrepresentation." In R. Bogdan (ed.), *Belief: Form, Content, and Function*. Oxford: Oxford University Press.

—— 1988. *Explaining Behavior*. Cambridge, MA: MIT Press.

—— 1993. "Conscious Experience." *Mind* 102: 263–83.

—— 1995. *Naturalizing the Mind*. Cambridge, MA: MIT Press.

—— 1996. "Phenomenal Externalism." *Philosophical Issues* 7: 143–59.

—— 2000. "Reply to Lopes." *Philosophy and Phenomenological Research* 60: 455–9.

Drummond, J. J. 2006. "The Case(s) of (Self-)Awareness." In Kriegel and Williford (eds.), *Self-Representational Approaches to Consciousness*. Cambridge, MA: MIT Press.

Engel, A. K., P. Fries, P. Konig, M. Brecht, and W. Singer 1999. "Temporal Binding, Binocular Rivalry, and Consciousness." *Consciousness and Cognition* 8: 128–51.

—— and W. Singer 2001. "Temporal Binding and the Neural Correlate of Sensory Awareness." *Trends in Cognitive Science* 5: 16–25.

Farrell, B. A. 1950. "Experience." *Mind* 59: 170–98.

Fernández, J. 2003. "Privileged Access Naturalized." *Philosophical Quarterly* 53: 352–72.

Field, H. 1977. "Logic, Meaning, and Conceptual Role." *Journal of Philosophy* 74: 379–409.

Flanagan, O. 1992. *Consciousness Reconsidered*. Cambridge, MA: MIT Press.

Flashman, L. A., T. W. McAlister, S. C. Johnson, J. H. Rick, R. L. Green, and A. J. Saykin 2001. "Specific Frontal Lobe Subregions Correlated with Unawareness of Schizophrenia: A Preliminary Study." *Journal of Neuropsychiatry Clinical Neurosciences* 13: 255–7.

Flavell, J. H. 1979. "Metacognition and Cognitive Monitoring: A New Area of Cognitive-Developmental Inquiry." *American Psychologist* 34: 906–11.

Flohr, H. 1995. "Sensations and Brain Processes." *Behavioral Brain Research* 71: 157–61.

Fodor, J. A. 1975. *The Language of Thought*. Cambridge, MA: Harvard University Press.

—— 1987. *Psychosemantics*. Cambridge, MA: MIT Press/Bradford Books.

—— 1990. *A Theory of Content and Other Essays*. Cambridge, MA: MIT Press.

—— 1994. *The Elm and the Expert*. Cambridge, MA: MIT Press.

Frith, C. D. and U. Frith 1999. "Interacting Minds—Biological Basis." *Science* 286: 1692–5.

Gallup, G. G. 1970. "Chimpanzees: Self-Recognition." *Science* 167: 86–7.

—— 1975. "Towards an Operational Definition of Self-Awareness." In R. H. Tuttle (ed.), *Socioecology and the Psychology of Primates*. Berlin: Mouton de Gruyter.

Ganeri, J. 1999. "Self-Intimation, Memory and Personal Identity." *Journal of Indian Philosophy* 27: 469–83.

Gehring, W. J. and R. T. Knight 2000. "Prefrontal–Cingulate Interactions in Action Monitoring." *Nature Neuroscience* 3: 516–20.

Gemes, K. 1998. "A New Theory of Content II: Model Theory and Some Alternatives." *Journal of Philosophical Logic* 26: 449–76.

Gennaro, R. J. 1992. "Consciousness, Self-Consciousness, and Episodic Memory." *Philosophical Psychology* 5: 333–47.

——1996. *Consciousness and Self-Consciousness*. Philadelphia and Amsterdam: John Benjamin Publishing Co.

——1999. "Leibniz on Consciousness and Self-consciousness." In R. J. Gennaro and C. Huenemann (eds.), *New Essays on the Rationalists*. New York and Oxford: Oxford University Press.

——2002. "Jean-Paul Sartre and the *HOT* Theory of Consciousness." *Canadian Journal of Philosophy* 32: 293–330.

——2004. "Higher-Order Thoughts, Animal Consciousness, and Misrepresentation." In R. Gennaro (ed.), *Higher-Order Theories of Consciousness*. Amsterdam and Philadelphia: John Benjamin Publishing Co.

——2006. "Between Pure Self-Referentialism and (Extrinsic) HOT Theory of Consciousness." In Kriegel and Williford 2006.

——2008. "Representationalism, Peripheral Awareness, and the Transparency of Experience." *Philosophical Studies* 139: 39–56.

Gertler, B. 2002. "Explanatory Reduction, Conceptual Analysis, and Conceivability Arguments about the Mind". *Noûs* 36: 22–49.

Goldman, A. 1967. "A Causal Theory of Knowing." *Journal of Philosophy* 64: 355–72.

——1970. *A Theory of Action*. Princeton: Princeton University Press.

——1993a. "Consciousness, Folk Psychology, and Cognitive Science." *Consciousness and Cognition* 2: 364–83.

——1993b. "The Psychology of Folk Psychology." *Behavioral and Brain Sciences* 16: 15–28.

Gopnik, A. and J. W. Astington 1988. "Children's Understanding of Representational Change and its Relation to the Understanding of False Belief and the Appearance–Reality Distinction." *Child Development* 59: 26–37.

Gurwitsch, A. 1950/1985. *Marginal Consciousness*. Athens, OH: Ohio University Press.

Gusnard, D. A., E. Akbudak, G. L. Shulman, and M. E. Raichle 2001. "Medial Prefrontal Cortex and Self-Referential Mental Activity: Relation to a Default Mode of Brain Function." *Proceedings of the National Academy of Science USA* 98: 4259–64.

Hardin, C. L. 1988. *Color for Philosophers: Unweaving the Rainbow*. Indianapolis: Hackett.

Harman, G. 1987. "(Non-Solipsistic) Conceptual Role Semantics." In E. Lepore (ed.), *New Directions in Semantics*. London: Academic Press.

——1990. "The Intrinsic Quality of Experience." *Philosophical Perspectives* 4: 31–52. Reprinted in Block et al. 1997.

Haukioja, J. 2008. "A Defence of the Conditional Analysis of Phenomenal Concepts." *Philosophical Studies* 139: 145–51.

Hawthorne, J. 2002. "Advice for Physicalists." *Philosophical Studies* 109: 17–52.

Hellie, B. 2007. "Higher-Order Intentionality and Higher-Order Acquaintance." *Philosophical Studies* 134: 289–324.

Henry, M. 1963/1973. *The Essence of Manifestation*, trans. G. Etzkorn. The Hague: Nijhoff.

Hilbert, D. R. 1987. *Color and Color Perception: A Study in Anthropocentric Realism*. Stanford, CA: CSLI.

Hill, C. 1988. "Introspective Awareness of Sensations." *Topoi* 7: 11–24.

Horgan, T. 1993. "From Supervenience to Superdupervenience: Meeting the Demands of a Material World." *Mind* 102: 555–86.

——2006. "Internal-World Skepticism and Self-Presentational Nature of Phenomenal Consciousness." In Kriegel and Williford 2006.

——and U. Kriegel 2007. "Phenomenal Epistemology: What is Consciousness that We may Know It so Well?" *Philosophical Issues* 17.

————2008. "Phenomenal Intentionality Meets the Extended Mind." *Monist* 91.

——and J. Tienson 2002. "The Intentionality of Phenomenology and the Phenomenology of Intentionality." In D. J. Chalmers (ed.), *Philosophy of Mind: Classical and Contemporary Readings*. Oxford and New York: Oxford University Press.

————and G. Graham 2003. "The Phenomenology of First-Person Agency." In S. Walter and H. D. Heckmann (eds.), *Physicalism and Mental Causation: The Metaphysics of Mind and Action*. Exeter: Imprint Academic.

Huntington's Disease Collaborative Research Group 1993. "A Novel Gene Containing a Trinucleotide Repeat that is Expanded and Unstable on Huntington's Disease Chromosomes." *Cell* 72: 971–83.

Hurley, S. 1998. *Consciousness in Action*. Cambridge, MA: Harvard University Press.

Husserl, E. 1928/1964. *Phenomenology of Internal Time-Consciousness*, ed. M. Heidegger, trans. J. S. Churchill. Bloomington, IN: Indiana University Press.

Jackson, F. C. 1977. *Perception: A Representative Theory*. Cambridge: Cambridge University Press.

—— 1994. "Finding the Mind in the Natural World." In R. Casati, B. Smith, and G. White (eds.), *Philosophy and the Cognitive Sciences*. Vienna: Verlag Hölder-Pichler-Tempsky.

—— 1998. "Reference and Description Revisited." *Philosophical Perspectives* 201–18.

James, W. 1890/1918. *The Principles of Psychology* (2 vols.). 2nd edn. London: McMillan.

—— 1961, *Psychology: The Briefer Course*, ed. G. Allport. New York: Harper and Row.

Janzen, G. 2005. "The Reflexive Nature of Consciousness." Ph.D. Dissertation, University of Calgary.

Johnson, S. C., L. Baxter, L. Wilder, J. Heiserman, J. Pipe, and G. Prigatano 2002. "Neural Correlates of Self-Reflection." *Brain* 125: 1808–14.

Johnston, M. 1989. "Dispositional Theories of Value." *Proceedings of Aristotelian Society* 63: 139–74.

—— 1997. "Manifest Kinds." *Journal of Philosophy* 94: 564–83.

Kanwisher, N. 2000. "Domain Specificity in Face Perception." *Nature Neuroscience* 3: 759–63.

Kapitan, T. 1999. "The Ubiquity of Self-Awareness." *Grazer Philosophische Studien* 57: 17–44.

Kelley, W. M., C. N. Macrae, C. L. Wyland, S. Calgar, S. Inati, and T. F. Heatherton 2002. "Finding the Self? An Event-Related fMRI Study." *Journal of Cognitive Neuroscience* 14: 785–94.

Kim, J. 1982. "Psychophysical Supervenience." *Philosophical Studies* 41: 51–70. Reprinted in his *Supervenience and Mind*. Oxford: Oxford University Press.

—— 1991. "Dretske on How Reasons Explain Behavior." In B. McLaughlin (ed.), *Dretske and his Critics*. Oxford: Blackwell.

—— 1998. *Mind in a Physical World*. Cambridge, MA: MIT Press/Bradford Books.

Kitcher, P. S. 1981. "Explanatory Unification." *Philosophy of Science* 48: 507–31.

Kobes, B. W. 1995. "Telic Higher-Order Thoughts and Moore's Paradox." *Philosophical Perspectives* 9: 291–312.

Kriegel, U. 2002a. "Phenomenal Content." *Erkenntnis* 57: 175–98.

—— 2002b. "PANIC Theory and the Prospects for a Representational Theory of Phenomenal Consciousness." *Philosophical Psychology* 15: 55–64.

—— 2002c. "Consciousness, Permanent Self-Awareness, and Higher-Order Monitoring." *Dialogue* 41: 517–40.

—— 2002d. "Emotional Content." *Consciousness and Emotion* 3: 213–30.

Kriegel, U. 2003a. "Consciousness as Intransitive Self-Consciousness: Two Views and an Argument." *Canadian Journal of Philosophy* 33: 103–32.

—— 2003b. "Consciousness, Higher-Order Content, and the Individuation of Vehicles." *Synthese* 134: 477–504.

—— 2003c. "Consciousness as Sensory Quality and as Implicit Self-Awareness." *Phenomenology and the Cognitive Sciences* 2: 1–26.

—— 2003d. "Is Intentionality Dependent upon Consciousness?" *Philosophical Studies* 116: 271–307.

—— 2004a. "Consciousness and Self-Consciousness." *Monist* 87: 185–209.

—— 2004b. "The Functional Role of Consciousness: A Phenomenological Approach." *Phenomenology and the Cognitive Sciences* 4: 171–93.

—— 2005. "Naturalizing Subjective Character." *Philosophy and Phenomenological Research* 71: 23–57.

—— 2006a. "The Same-Order Monitoring Theory of Consciousness." In Kriegel and Williford 2006.

—— 2006b. "Consciousness: Phenomenal Consciousness, Access Consciousness, and Scientific Practice." In P. Thagard (ed.), *Handbook of Philosophy of Psychology and Cognitive Science*. Amsterdam: Elsevier.

—— 2007a. "The Phenomenologically Manifest." *Phenomenology and the Cognitive Sciences* 6: 115–36.

—— 2007b. "Intentional Inexistence and Phenomenal Intentionality." *Philosophical Perspectives* 22: 307–40.

—— 2008. "The Dispensability of (Merely) Intentional Objects." *Philosophical Studies* 141: 79–95.

—— and K. W. Williford 2006. *Self-Representational Approaches to Consciousness*. Cambridge, MA: MIT Press.

Landini, G. MS. "Consciousness and Non-Wellfoundedness."

Lane, R. D., G. R. Fink, P. M. Chau, and R. J. Dolan 1997. "Neural Activation During Selective Attention to Subjective Emotional Responses." *NeuroReport* 8: 3969–72.

Lau, H. C. and R. E. Passingham 2006. "Relative Blindsight in Normal Observers and the Neural Correlate of Visual Consciousness." *Proceedings of the National Academy of Science USA* 103: 18763–8.

Levey, S. 1997. "Coincidence and Principles of Composition." *Analysis* 57: 1–10.

Levine, J. 1983. "Materialism and Qualia: The Explanatory Gap." *Pacific Philosophical Quarterly* 64: 354–61.

—— 2001. *Purple Haze: The Puzzle of Consciousness*. Oxford and New York: Oxford University Press.

—— 2003. "Experience and Representation." In Q. Smith and A. Jokic (eds.), *Consciousness: New Essays*. Oxford: Oxford University Press.

Levine, J. 2006. "Awareness and (Self-)Representation." In U. Kriegel and K. Williford (eds.), *Self-Representational Approaches to Consciousness*. Cambridge, MA: MIT Press.

Lewis, D. K. 1966. "An Argument for the Identity Theory." *Journal of Philosophy* 63: 17–25.

——1972. "Psychophysical and Theoretical Identifications." *Australasian Journal of Philosophy* 50: 249–58.

——1994. "Reduction of Mind." In S. D. Guttenplan (ed.), *Companion to the Philosophy of Mind*. Oxford: Blackwell.

——1991. *Parts of Classes*. Oxford: Blackwell.

Libet, B. 1985. "Unconscious Cerebral Initiative and the Role of Conscious Will in Voluntary Action." *Behavioral and Brain Sciences* 8: 529–66.

Loar, B. 1990. "Phenomenal States." *Philosophical Perspectives* 4: 81–108.

——2002. "Phenomenal Intentionality as the Basis for Mental Content." In D. J. Chalmers (ed.), *Philosophy of Mind: Classical and Contemporary Readings*. Oxford and New York: Oxford University Press.

——2003. "Transparent Experience and the Availability of Qualia." In Q. Smith and A. Jokic (eds.), *Consciousness: New Philosophical Perspectives*. Oxford: Oxford University Press.

Lopes, D. M. M. 2000. "What Is It Like to See with Your Ears? The Representational Theory of Mind." *Philosophical and Phenomenological Research* 60: 439–53.

Lurz, R. 1999. "Animal Consciousness." *Journal of Philosophical Research* 24: 149–68.

Lycan, W. G. 1996. *Consciousness and Experience*. Cambridge, MA: MIT Press.

——2001a. "A Simple Argument for a Higher-Order Representation Theory of Consciousness." *Analysis* 61: 3–4.

——2001b. "The Case for Phenomenal Externalism." *Philosophical Perspectives* 15: 17–35.

——2004. "The Superiority of HOP to HOT." In R. Gennaro (ed.), *Higher-Order Theories of Consciousness*. Amsterdam and Philadelphia: John Benjamin Publishing Co.

MacDonald, A. W., 3rd, J. D. Cohen, V. A. Stenger, and C. S. Carter 2000. "Dissociating the Role of the Dorsolateral Prefrontal and Anterior Cingulate Cortex in Cognitive Control." *Science* 288: 1835–8.

McGinn, C. 1988. "Consciousness and Content." In *Proceedings of the British Academy* 76: 219–239. Reprinted in N. J. Block, O. Flanagan, and G. Güzeldere (eds.), *The Nature of Consciousness: Philosophical Debates*. Cambridge, MA: MIT Press, 1997.

——1989a. "Can We Solve the Mind–Body Problem?" *Mind* 98: 349–66.

McGinn, C. 1989b. *Mental Content*. Oxford: Blackwell.

—— 1995. "Consciousness and Space." *Journal of Consciousness Studies* 2: 220–30.

—— 1999. *The Mysterious Flame*. Cambridge, MA: MIT Press.

—— 2004. *Consciousness and its Objects*. Oxford: Oxford University Press.

Manfredi, P. A. 1993. "Tacit Beliefs and Other Doxastic Attitudes." *Philosophia* 22: 95–117.

Mangan, B. 1993. "Taking Phenomenology Seriously: The 'Fringe' and its Implications for Cognitive Research." *Consciousness and Cognition* 2: 89–108.

—— 2001. "Sensation's Ghost: The Non-Sensory 'Fringe' of Consciousness." *Psyche* 7(18). http://psyche.cs.monash.edu.au/v7/psyche-7–18-mangan.html.

Masrour, F. 2008. "Phenomenology and Intentionality: A Neo-Kantian Reading." Ph.D. Dissertation, University of Arizona.

Maund, B. 1995. *Colors: Their Nature and Representation*. Cambridge: Cambridge University Press.

Merleau-Ponty, M. 1945. *Phénoménologie de la perception*. Paris: Gallimard.

Metzinger, T. 1995. "Faster than Thought: Holism, Homogeneity, and Temporal Coding." In T. Metzinger (ed.), *Conscious Experience*. Thorverton: Imprint Academic.

Milham, M. P., M. T. Banich, A. Webb, V. Barad, N. J. Cohen, T. Wszalek, and A. F. Kramer 2001. "The Relative Involvement of Anterior Cingulate and Prefrontal Cortex in Attentional Control Depends on Nature of Conflict." *Cognitive Brain Research* 12: 467–73.

———— E. D. Claus, and N. J. Cohen 2003. "Practice-Related Effects Demonstrate Complementary Roles of Anterior Cingulate and Prefrontal Cortices in Attentional Control." *NeuroImage* 18: 483–93.

Miller, G. A. 1956. "The Magical Number Seven, Plus or Minus Two: Some Limits on our Capacity for Processing Information." *Psychological Review* 63: 81–97.

Millikan, R. G. 1984. *Language, Thought, and Other Biological Categories*. Cambridge, MA: MIT Press.

—— 1989. "Biosemantics." *Journal of Philosophy* 86: 281–97.

—— 1990. "Seismograph Readings for *Explaining Behavior*." *Philosophy and Phenomenological Research* 50: 819–39.

—— 1993. *White Queen Psychology and Other Essays for Alice*. Cambridge, MA: MIT Press.

—— 1984. *Language, Thought, and Other Biological Categories*. Cambridge, MA: MIT Press.

Moore, G. E. 1903a. "The Refutation of Idealism." In his *Philosophical Papers*. London: Routledge and Kegan Paul.

—— 1903b. *Principia Ethica*. Cambridge: Cambridge University Press.

Moran, R. 2001. *Authority and Estrangement: An Essay on Self-Knowledge*. Princeton: Princeton University Press.

Moray, N. 1969. *Listening and Attention*. Harmondsworth: Penguin Books.

Mulligan, K. and B. Smith 1985. "Franz Brentano on the Ontology of Mind." *Philosophy and Phenomenological Research* 45: 627–44.

Mumford, S. 1998. *Dispositions*. Oxford: Clarendon Press.

Nagel, T. 1974. "What Is It Like to Be a Bat?" *Philosophical Review* 83: 435–50. Reprinted in Block et al. 1997.

Natsoulas, T. 1993. "What is Wrong with Appendage Theory of Consciousness?" *Philosophical Psychology* 6: 137–54.

—— 1996. "The Case for Intrinsic Theory: I. An Introduction." *Journal of Mind and Behavior* 17: 267–86.

—— 1999. "The Case for Intrinsic Theory: IV. An Argument from How Conscious Mental-Occurrence Instances Seem." *Journal of Mind and Behavior* 20 (1999): 257–76.

Neander, K. 1998. "The Division of Phenomenal Labor: A Problem for Representational Theories of Consciousness." *Philosophical Perspectives* 12: 411–34.

Papineau, D. 1993. *Philosophical Naturalism*. Oxford: Blackwell.

Paul, L. A. 2002. "Logical Parts." *Noûs* 36: 578–96.

Peacocke, C. 1983. *Sense and Content*. Oxford: Clarendon Press.

—— 1998. "Conscious Attitudes, Attention, and Self-Knowledge." In C. Wright, B. C. Smith, and C. Macdonald (eds.), *Knowing Our Own Minds*. Oxford: Oxford University Press.

Perner, J., S. R. Leekam, and H. Wimmer 1987. "Three-Year-Olds' Difficulty with False Belief: The Case for a Conceptual Deficit." *British Journal of Developmental Psychology* 5: 125–37.

Perrett, R. 2003. "Intentionality and Self-Awareness." *Ratio* 16: 222–35.

Perry, J. 1979. "The Problem of the Essential Indexical." *Noûs* 13: 3–21.

Pettit, P. 1991. "Realism and Response-Dependence." *Mind* 100: 597–626.

Pitt, D. 2004. "The Phenomenology of Cognition; or *What Is It Like to Think that P?*", *Philosophy and Phenomenological Research* 69: 1–36.

Plotnik, J. M., F. B. M. de Waal, and D. Reiss 2006. "Self-Recognition in an Asian Elephant." *Proceedings of the National Academy of Sciences* 103: 17053–7.

Povinelli, D. J., A. B. Rulf, and D. T. Bierschwale 1994. "Absence of Knowledge Attribution and Self-Recognition in Young Chimpanzees (*Pan troglodytes*)." *Journal of Comparative Psychology* 108: 74–80.

Priest, G. 2005. *Towards Non-Being: The Logic and Metaphysics of Intentionality*. Oxford: Oxford University Press.

Proust, J. 1997. *Comment l'esprit vient aux bêtes*. Paris: Gallimard.

Putnam, H. 1967. "The Nature of Mental States." Originally published as "Psychological Predicates," in W. H. Capitan and D. D. Merrill (eds.), *Art, Mind, and Religion*. Reprinted in D. M. Rosenthal (ed.), *The Nature of Mind*. Oxford: Oxford University Press, 1991.

—— 1975. "The Meaning of 'Meaning'." In his *Mind, Language, and Reality*, Cambridge: Cambridge University Press.

Reiss, D. and L. Marino 2001. "Mirror Self-Recognition in the Bottlenose Dolphin: A Case of Cognitive Convergence." *Proceedings of the National Academy of Sciences USA* 98: 5937–42.

Revonsuo, A. 1999. "Binding and the Phenomenal Unity of Consciousness." *Consciousness and Cognition* 8: 173–85.

Rey, G. 1988. "A Question about Consciousness." In H. Otto and J. Tueidio (eds.), *Perspectives on Mind*. Norwell: Kluwer Academic Publishers.

—— 1998. "A Narrow Representationalist Account of Qualitative Experience." *Philosophical Perspectives* 12: 435–57.

Roelfsema, P. R., A. K. Engel, P. Konig, and W. Singer 1997. "Visuomotor Integration is Associated with Zero Time-Lag Synchronization among Cortical Areas." *Nature* 385: 157–61.

Rosenthal, D. M. 1986. "Two Concepts of Consciousness." *Philosophical Studies* 94: 329–59.

—— 1990. "A Theory of Consciousness." ZiF Technical Report 40, Bielfield, Germany. Reprinted in Block et al. 1997.

—— 1991. "The Independence of Consciousness and Sensory Quality." *Philosophical Issues* 1: 15–36.

—— 1993. "Thinking that One Thinks." In M. Davies and G. W. Humphreys (eds.), *Consciousness: Psychological and Philosophical Essays*. Oxford: Blackwell.

—— 2000. "Consciousness and Metacognition." In D. Sperber (ed.), *Metarepresentation*. Oxford: Oxford University Press.

—— 2002a. "Explaining Consciousness." In D. J. Chalmers (ed.), *Philosophy of Mind*. Oxford and New York: Oxford University Press.

—— 2002b. "How Many Kinds of Consciousness?" *Consciousness and Cognition* 11: 653–65.

—— 2002c "The Timing of Consciousness." *Consciousness and Cognition* 11: 215–20.

—— 2005. *Consciousness and the Mind*. Oxford: Oxford University Press.

Ryle, G. 1949. *The Concept of Mind*. New York: Barnes and Noble.

Saharaie, A., L. Weiskrantz, J. L. Barbur, A. Simmons, S. C. R. Williams, and M. J. Brammer 1997. "Pattern of Neuronal Activity Associated with Conscious and

Unconscious Processing of Visual Signals." *Proceedings of the National Academy of Science USA* 94: 9406–11.

Sartre, J.-P. 1936. *La Transcendance de l'ego*. Paris: Vrin.

—— 1943. *L'Être et le néant*. Paris: Gallimard.

Schmitz, T. W., T. N. Kawahara-Baccus, and S. C. Johnson 2004. "Metacognition, Self-Reflection, and the Right Prefrontal Cortex." *Neuroimage* 22: 941–7.

—— H. A. Rowley, T. N. Kawahara, and S. C. Johnson 2006. "Neural Correlates of Self-Evaluative Accuracy after Traumatic Brain Injury." *Neuropsychologia* 44: 762–73.

Schurz, G. 1991. "Relevant Deduction." *Erkenntnis* 35: 391–437.

Seager, W. 1999. *Theories of Consciousness*. London: Routledge.

Searle, J. 1983. *Intentionality*. Cambridge: Cambridge University Press.

Shadlen, M. N. and J. A. Movshon 1999. "Synchrony Unbound: A Critical Evaluation of the Temporal Binding Hypothesis." *Neuron* 24: 67–77.

Shoemaker, S. 1979. "Identity, Properties, and Causality." *Midwest Studies in Philosophy* 4: 321–42.

—— 1994a. "Phenomenal Character." *Noûs* 28: 21–38.

—— 1994b. "Self-Knowledge and 'Inner Sense.' Lecture II: The Broad Perceptual Model." *Philosophy and Phenomenological Research* 54: 271–90.

—— 1994c. "Self-Knowledge and 'Inner Sense.' Lecture III: The Phenomenal Character of Experience." *Philosophy and Phenomenological Research* 54: 291–314.

—— 2002. "Introspection and Phenomenal Character." In D. J. Chalmers (ed.), *Philosophy of Mind*. Oxford and New York: Oxford University Press.

Siegel, S. 2005. "The Phenomenology of Efficacy." *Philosophical Topics* 33: 265–84.

Siewert, C. P. 1998. *The Significance of Consciousness*. Princeton: Princeton University Press.

Silverman, L. H., A. Martin, R. Ungaro, and E. Medelsohn 1978. "Effect of Subliminal Stimulation of Symbiotic Fantasies on Behavior Modification Treatment of Obesity." *Journal of Consultative Clinical Psychology* 46: 432–41.

Simons, P. 1987. *Parts: A Study in Ontology*. Oxford: Clarendon Press.

Singer, W. 1994. "The Organization of Sensory Motor Representations in the Neocortex: A Hypothesis Based on Temporal Coding." In C. Umlita and M. Moscovitch (eds.), *Attention and Performnace XV: Conscious and Nonconscious Information Processing*. Cambridge, MA: MIT Press.

Smith, B. 1994. *Austrian Philosophy: The Legacy of Franz Brentano*. Chicago and La Salle: Open Court.

—— and K. Mulligan 1983. "A Framework for Formal Ontology." *Topoi* 3: 73–85.

Smith, D. W. 1986. "The Structure of (Self-)Consciousness." *Topoi* 5: 149–56.

Smith, D. W. 1989. *The Circle of Acquaintance.* Dordrecht: Kluwer Academic Publishers.

Stampe D. 1977. "Towards a Causal Theory of Linguistic Representation." *Midwest Studies in Philosophy* 2: 42–63.

Steiner, M. 1973. "Platonism and the Causal Theory of Knowledge." *Journal of Philosophy* 70: 57–66.

Stich, S. 1979. "Autonomous Psychology and the Belief–Desire Thesis." *Monist* 61: 571–91.

Stoerig, P. and A. Cowey 1992. "Wavelength Sensitivity in Blindsight." *Brain* 115: 425–44.

Stoljar, D. 2001. "Two Conceptions of the Physical." *Philosophical and Phenomenological Research* 62: 253–81.

—— 2006. *Ignorance and Imagination.* New York: Oxford University Press.

Strawson, G. 1994. *Mental Reality.* Cambridge, MA: MIT Press.

Stroop, J. R. 1935. "Studies of Interference in Serial Verbal Reactions." *Journal of Experimental Psychology* 18: 643–62.

Suarez S. D. and G. G. Gallup 1981. "Self-Recognition in Chimpanzees and Orangutans, but not Gorillas." *Journal of Human Evolution* 10: 175–88.

Tennant, N. Forthcoming. "Mind, Mathematics and the *Ignorabimusstreit.*" *British Journal for the History of Philosophy.*

Thau, M. 2002. *Consciousness and Cognition.* Oxford: Oxford University Press.

Thomas, A. P. 2003. "An Adverbial Theory of Consciousness." *Phenomenology and the Cognitive Sciences* 2: 161–85.

Thomasson, A. L. 2000. "After Brentano: A One-Level Theory of Consciousness." *European Journal of Philosophy* 8: 190–209.

—— 2005. "First-Person Knowledge in Phenomenology." In D. W. Smith and A. L. Thomasson (eds.), *Phenomenology and Philosophy of Mind.* Oxford: Oxford University Press.

—— 2006. "Self-Awareness and Self-Knowledge." *Psyche* 12/2.

Tomasello, M. and J. Call. 2005. "Do Chimpanzees Know what Others See—or Only what They are Looking at?" In M. Nudds and S. Hurley (eds.), *Rational Animals.* Oxford: Oxford University Press.

Treisman, A. M. 1996. "The Binding Problem." *Current Opinions in Neurobiology* 6: 171–8.

—— and H. Schmidt 1982. "Illusory Conjunctions in the Perception of Objects." *Cognitive Psychology* 14: 107–41.

Tugendhat, E. 1979. *Self-Consciousness and Self-Determination,* trans. P. Stern. Cambridge, MA: MIT Press.

Tulving, E. 1983. *Elements of Episodic Memory.* Oxford: Oxford University Press.

Tye, M. 1990. "A Representational Theory of Pains and their Phenomenal Character." *Philosophical Perspectives* 9: 223–39.

—— 1992. "Visual Qualia and Visual Content." In T. Crane (ed.), *The Contents of Experience*. Cambridge: Cambridge University Press.

—— 1995. *Ten Problems of Consciousness*. Cambridge, MA: MIT Press.

—— 1996. "Perceptual Experience is a Many-Layered Thing." *Philosophical Issues* 7: 117–26.

—— 1997. "A Representational Theory of Pains and their Phenomenal Character." In Block et al. 1997.

—— 2000. *Consciousness, Color, and Content*. Cambridge, MA: MIT Press.

—— 2002. "Visual Qualia and Visual Content Revisited." In D. J. Chalmers (ed.), *Philosophy of Mind*. Oxford and New York: Oxford University Press.

—— 2003. *Consciousness and Persons*. Cambridge, MA: MIT Press.

Van Gulick, R. 2001. "Inward and Upward—Reflection, Introspection, and Self-Awareness." *Philosophical Topics* 28: 275–305.

—— 2004. "Higher-Order Global States (HOGS): An Alternative Higher-Order Model of Consciousness." In R. J. Gennaro (ed.), *Higher-Order Theories of Consciousness: An Anthology*. Amsterdam and Philadelphia: John Benjamins.

—— 2006. "Mirror Mirror—Is That All?" In Kriegel and Williford 2006.

Varela, F., J.-P. Lachaux, E. Rodriguez, and J. Martinerie 2001. "Phase-Synchronization and Large-Scale Integration." *Nature Reviews Neuroscience* 2: 229–39.

Velmans, M. 1992. "Is Human Information Processing Conscious?" *Behavioral and Brain Sciences* 14: 651–69.

von der Malsburg, C. 1981. "The Correlation Theory of Brain Function." Technical Report 81–2, Max-Planck-Institute for Biophysical Chemistry, Gottingen.

Weiskrantz, L. 1986. *Blindsight*. Oxford: Oxford University Press.

—— A. Cowey, and I. Hodinott-Hill 2002. "Prime-Sight in a Blindsight Subject." *Nature Neuroscience* 5: 101–2.

Williamson, T. 2000. *Knowledge and its Limits*. Oxford: Oxford University Press.

Williford, K. W. 2003. "The Structure of Self-Consciousness: A Phenomenological and Philosophical Investigation." Ph.D. Dissertation, University of Iowa.

—— 2006. "The Self-Representational Structure of Consciousness." In Kriegel and Williford 2006.

Wright, C. 1988. "Moral Values, Projection and Secondary Qualities." *Proceedings of Aristotelian Society* 62: 1–26.

Zahavi, D. 1999. *Self-Awareness and Alterity*. Evanston, IL: Northwestern University Press.

—— 2004. "Back to Brentano?" *Journal of Consciousness Studies* 11.

Zeki, S., J. D. G. Watson, C. J. Lueck, K. J. Friston, C. Kennard, and R. S. J. Frackowiak 1991. "A Direct Demonstration of Functional Specialization in Human Visual Cortex." *Journal of Neuroscience* 11: 641–9.

Zemach, E. M. 1985. "De Se and Descartes: A New Semantics for Indexicals." *Noûs* 19: 181–204.

Index